T0313282

Financial Management Strategies for Hospitals and Healthcare Organizations

Tools, Techniques, Checklists and Case Studies

Financial Management Strategies for Hospitals and Healthcare Organizations

Tools, Techniques, Checklists and Case Studies

Edited by
Dr. David Edward Marcinko, MBA, CMP™
Prof. Hope Rachel Hetico, RN, MHA, CMP™

Foreword by Neil H. Baum, MD
Foreword by David B. Nash, MD, MBA

CRC Press
Taylor & Francis Group
Boca Raton   London   New York

CRC Press is an imprint of the
Taylor & Francis Group, an **informa** business
A PRODUCTIVITY PRESS BOOK

CRC Press
Taylor & Francis Group
6000 Broken Sound Parkway NW, Suite 300
Boca Raton, FL 33487-2742

© 2014 by iMBA, Inc.
CRC Press is an imprint of Taylor & Francis Group, an Informa business

No claim to original U.S. Government works

ISBN-13: 9781466558731 (Hbk)

Library of Congress Cataloging-in-Publication Data

Financial management strategies for hospitals and healthcare organizations : tools, techniques, checklists, and case studies / edited by David Edward Marcinko, Hope Rachel Hetico.
    p. ; cm.
    Includes bibliographical references and index.
    ISBN 978-1-4665-5873-1 (hardcover : alk. paper)
    I. Marcinko, David E. (David Edward), editor of compilation. II. Hetico, Hope R., editor of compilation.
    [DNLM: 1. Financial Management, Hospital--economics--Case Reports. 2. Economics, Hospital--organization & administration--Case Reports. 3. Health Facilities--economics--Case Reports. 4. Health Services Research--Case Reports. 5. Hospital Administration--Case Reports. WX 157 AA1]

RA971.3
362.11068'1--dc23   2013027684

Visit the Taylor & Francis Web site at
http://www.taylorandfrancis.com

and the CRC Press Web site at
http://www.crcpress.com

Dedication

It is an incredible privilege to edit Financial Management Strategies for Hospitals and Healthcare Organizations: Tools, Techniques, Checklists and Case Studies.

One of the most rewarding aspects of this career has been the personal and professional growth acquired from interacting with protean professionals of all stripes. The mutual sharing and exchange of practice management ideas stimulates the mind and fosters advancement at many levels.

Creating this text was a significant effort that involved all members of our firm. Over the past year we interfaced with numerous outside private and public companies—as well as the Internet blogosphere—to discuss its contents. Although impossible to list every person or company that played a role in its production, there are several people we wish to thank for their support and encouragement: Kristine Mednansky, Senior Editor Business Improvement (Healthcare Management); Karen Sober, Editorial Assistant; and Richard O'Hanley, CRC Press (A Taylor & Francis Group). Any accolades are because of them. All other defects are my own.

Of course, this text would not have been possible without the support of our families, whose daily advocacy encouraged all of us to completion. It is also dedicated to our clients, and to the contributing authors, who crashed the development life cycle in order to produce time-sensitive material in an expedient manner. The satisfaction we enjoyed from working with them is immeasurable.

Dr. David Edward Marcinko, MBA, CMP™
Editor-in-Chief

Contents

SECTION I Costs and Revenues: Fundamental Principles

SECTION II Clinic and Technology: Contemporary Issues

SECTION III Institutional and Professional Benchmarking: Advanced Applications

Foreword

INSTITUTIONAL FOREWORD

It should come as no surprise to our readers that the nation faces a financial crisis in healthcare. Currently, the United States spends nearly 16 percent of the world's largest economy on providing healthcare services to its citizens. Another way of looking at this same information is to realize that we spend nearly $6,500 per man, woman, and child per year to deliver health services.

And, what do we get for the money we spend?

This is an important policy question, and the answer is disquieting. Although the man and woman on the street may believe we have the best health system in the world, on an international basis, using well-accepted epidemiologic outcome measures, our investment does not yield much! According to information from the World Health Organization and other international bodies, the United States ranks somewhere toward the bottom of the top fifteen developed nations in the world regarding outcomes in terms of improved health for the monies we spend on healthcare. From a financial and economic perspective then, it appears as though the 16–18 percent of the gross domestic product going to healthcare may not represent a solid investment with a good return.

It is then timely that our colleagues at the Institute of Medical Business Advisors, Inc. (iMBA), have brought us their newest work: *Financial Management Strategies for Hospital and Healthcare Organizations: Tools, Techniques, Checklists and Case Studies.*

Certainly, this textbook is not for everyone. It is intended only for those physicians, nurse-executives, and administrators who understand that clinics, hospitals, and healthcare organizations are complex businesses, where advances in science, technology, management principles, and patient/consumer awareness are often eclipsed by regulations, rights, and economic restrictions. Navigating a course where sound organizational management is intertwined with financial acumen requires a strategy designed by subject-matter experts. Fortunately, *Financial Management Strategies for Hospital and Healthcare Organizations: Tools, Techniques, Checklists and Case Studies* provides that blueprint. Allow me to outline its strengths and put it into context relative to other works around the nation.

For the last year, the research team at iMBA, Inc., has sought out the best minds in the healthcare industrial complex to organize the seemingly impossible-to-understand strategic financial backbone of the domestic healthcare system. The book, a follow-up companion to their *Hospitals & Health Care Organizations: Management Strategies, Operational Techniques, Tools, Templates, and Case Studies*, is organized into three sections, with twelve chapters, to appropriately cover many of the key topics at hand. It has a natural flow, starting with costs and revenues, progressing to clinic and technology, and finishing with institutional and professional benchmarking.

Section I, on Managerial Medical Cost Accounting, Structure, Modeling, and Behavior (Chapter 1), Understanding Medical Activity–Based Cost Management (Chapter 2), Lean Hospital Materials Processes and Throughput Costs in an Increasingly Tightened Economic Market (Chapter 3), and most especially Managing and Improving the Hospital Revenue Cycle Process (Chapter 4) has broad appeal and would be of interest to hospital chief executive officers, physician-executives and clinic administrators, and chief finance officers and comptrollers.

Section II, on the Financial and Clinical Features of Hospital Information Systems (Chapter 5), Community and County Mental Health Programs of the Future (Chapter 6), Internal Audit Control Measures for Medical Practices and Clinics (Chapter 7), has great appeal to chief executive officers, chief operations officers, psychiatrists, psychologists, health fraud and control auditors, and forensic accountants.

Section III continues in a well-organized theme, progressing through Interpreting and Negotiating Healthcare Contracts (Chapter 9), Investment Policy Statement Benchmark Construction for Hospital Endowment Fund Management (Chapter 10), Valuation of Hospitals in a Changing Reimbursement and Regulatory Environment (Chapter 11), and Research and Financial Benchmarking in the Healthcare Industry (Chapter 12). This section would be of greater interest to those in the financial services industry, health economists and analysts, financial advisors, certified financial analysts, certified medical planners™, wealth and portfolio managers, and business valuation experts.

Every day colleagues ask me to help explain the seemingly incomprehensible financial design of our healthcare system. This volume goes a long way toward answering their queries. I also believe it is appropriate as a textbook and reference tool in graduate level courses taught in schools of business, public health, health administration, and medicine. Judging from my travels around the nation, many faculty members would also benefit from the support of this volume as it is nearly impossible, even for experts in the field, to grasp all of the rapidly evolving details.

On a personal level, I was particularly taken with The Early Promise of Health 2.0 to Enable Wellness, Improve Care, and Reduce Costs in Support of Population Health Management (Chapter 8), in Section II, as it brought back enjoyable memories of my work nearly twenty-five years ago at the Wharton School, on the campus of the University of Pennsylvania. There, I was exposed to some of the best economic minds in the healthcare business, and it was a watershed event for me, forming some of my earliest opinions about the healthcare system. Congratulations to all authors, but this chapter in particular deserves specific mention. As a board member for a major national integrated delivery system, I am happy that there appears to be a greater interest in the intricacies of population health on the financial side of the ledger.

In summary, *Financial Management Strategies for Hospital and Healthcare Organizations: Tools, Techniques, Checklists and Case Studies* represents a unique marriage of iMBA, Inc., and its many contributors from across the nation. As its mission statement suggests, I believe that this interpretive text carries out its vision to connect healthcare financial advisors, hospital administrators, business consultants, and medical colleagues everywhere. It will help them learn more about organizational behavior, strategic planning, medical management trends, and the fluctuating healthcare environment, and consistently engage everyone in a relationship of trust and a mutually beneficial symbiotic learning environment.

Editor-in-Chief and healthcare economist Dr. David Edward Marcinko, MBA, CMP™ and his colleagues at iMBA, Inc., should be complimented for conceiving and completing this vitally important project. There is no question that *Financial Management Strategies for Hospital and Healthcare Organizations: Tools, Techniques, Checklists and Case Studies* will indeed enable us to leverage our cognitive assets and prepare a future generation of leaders capable of tackling the many challenges present in our healthcare economy.

My suggestion therefore, is to "read it, refer to it, recommend it, and reap."

David B. Nash, MD, MBA
*The Dr. Raymond C. and Doris N. Grandon Professor
and Chair of the Department of Health Policy
Jefferson Medical College
Thomas Jefferson University
Philadelphia, Pennsylvania*

PRACTITIONER FOREWORD

No one knows with any degree of certainty what healthcare will look like tomorrow or the days after that. Yet, there are a few predictions that I am sure will come to pass.

First, reimbursement for medical services will significantly decrease. This decrease in reimbursement will impact physicians, hospitals, and other allied healthcare providers. Next, there will be a decrease in reimbursements for pharmaceutical products and for medical devices. The medical pie that is $2.7 trillion dollars in 2013–2014 occupies 16–18 percent of the U.S. gross domestic product. It is expected to increase to 25 percent by 2025. This trajectory is unsustainable. Finally, and to compound this decrease in income or reimbursements for medical services, there will be an increase in medical overhead costs. You do not have to have an MBA to translate this as a formula for squeezing the profits out of healthcare.

It is fitting that Dr. David Edward Marcinko, MBA, CMP™ and his fellow experts have laid out a plan of action in *Financial Management Strategies for Hospital and Healthcare Organizations: Tools, Techniques, Checklists and Case Studies* that physicians, nurse-executives, administrators, and institutional chief executive officers, chief financial officers, MBAs, lawyers, and healthcare accountants can follow to help move healthcare financial fitness forward in these uncharted waters.

In 2001, the Institute of Medicine illuminated to the healthcare world and to the public in their report, *Crossing the Quality Chasm: A New Health System for the 21st Century*, that 98,000 Americans die each year from medical errors. This was the first time that our profession formally made public that the healthcare profession was fallible, imperfect, and fraught with preventable mistakes. This seminal report became a call to action as it gave those of us in the profession an opportunity to correct our errors and make improvements that would improve the care we provide our patients. Fortunately, more than a decade later, *Financial Management Strategies for Hospital and Healthcare Organizations: Tools, Techniques, Checklists and Case Studies* will show how something as simple as checklists can make healthcare administration less expensive.

It all began with Dr. Atul Gawande, a surgeon at Massachusetts General Hospital, who reviewed the airline industry and its use of checklists prior to an airplane's take-off. The history of aviation checklists began in 1934 when Boeing was in the final process of testing a U.S. Army fighter plane, with a potential contract of nearly 200 planes riding on the final test of the plane. The test aircraft made a normal taxi and take-off. It began a smooth climb but then suddenly stalled. The aircraft turned on one wing and fell, bursting into flames upon impact and killing two of the test pilots. The investigation found pilot error as the cause: One of the pilots was unfamiliar with the aircraft and had neglected to release the elevator lock prior to take-off. The contract with Boeing was in jeopardy. Thus, the pilots sat down and put their heads together. What was needed was some way of making sure that everything to prevent crashes was being done; that nothing was being overlooked. What resulted was a pilot's checklist for before take-off, during flight, before landing, and after landing. These checklists for the pilot and co-pilot made sure that nothing was forgotten and that the safety of the planes was insured.

So, what does airline safety have to with medical care? There are so many activities that take place in medicine, such as in the operating room, that are far too complicated to be left to the memory of doctors, nurses, anesthesiologists, and others involved in the surgical care of patients. Dr. Gawande identified the key components of a surgical procedure, which included the name of the patient, the procedure to be performed, the estimated length of the procedure, whether the right or left side is the surgical target, how much blood loss is anticipated, whether antibiotics have been given prior to making the incision, and the anesthetic risk of the patient. This use of a checklist, which takes approximately thirty seconds to complete, not only prevents wrong-side surgery but also instills a discipline of higher performance.

Dr. Gawande published an article in the *New England Journal of Medicine* in January 2009 about the use of a surgical safety checklist. This article reviewed a global study in eight hospitals from all over the world, including hospitals in developing countries, which compared a pre-study and post-study rate of surgical complications and mortality after the implementation of surgical safety checklists. This study clearly demonstrated that complications and mortality could be significantly reduced using a checklist prior to making a surgical incision. Dr. Gawande also wrote the book *The Checklist Manifesto: How to Get Things Right* (2011, Picador), which became a *New York Times* best seller.

I am certain that you will gain greater understanding of how to use checklists for the financial operations in your healthcare organization if you read *Financial Management Strategies for Hospital and Healthcare Organizations: Tools, Techniques, Checklists and Case Studies*. You can take the checklist concept from the airline industry to the operating room and then to the boardroom.

Senator Everett Dirkson (1896–1969) once said, "A billion here, a billion there, and pretty soon you're talking real money." This quote could not be more poignant today than it was then, only now we have traded the word trillion for billion! We have a challenge, and *Financial Management Strategies for Hospital and Healthcare Organizations: Tools, Techniques, Checklists and Case Studies* is a step in the direction of making all of the stakeholders in the healthcare arena sensitive to reducing and controlling costs, and at the same time preserving quality of care. This can be done. I suggest you start by reading, using, and referring to this excellent book.

And so, what is my final advice?

Some of you who read this book are chief executive officers, chief operations officers, chief medical officers, and maybe even chiefs of staff. But *all* of you should become CLOs (chief life officers)! Read this book and the initials CLO will appear after your name!

Neil H. Baum, MD
Clinical Associate Professor of Urology
Tulane Medical School
New Orleans, Louisiana
Author, Marketing Your Clinical Practice: Ethically, Effectively, and Economically, *4th Edition, Jones-Bartlett Publishers, 2010*

Preface

Financial Management Strategies for Hospitals and Healthcare Organizations: Tools, Techniques, Checklists and Case Studies will shape the financial management landscape, just as our companion text *Hospitals and Healthcare Organizations: Financial Management Strategies, Tools, Techniques, Checklists and Case Studies* did in the operational arena, by outlining four important principles.

First, we have assembled a world-class editorial advisory board and independent team of contributors and reviewers, and we have asked them to draw on their experience in operations, leadership, and lean managerial decision making in the healthcare industrial complex. Like many readers, each struggles mightily with the decreasing revenues, increasing costs, and high consumer expectations in today's competitive healthcare marketplace. Yet their practical experience and applied operating vision is a source of objective information, informed opinion, and crucial information to all working in this field.

Second, our writing style allows us to condense a great deal of information into *Financial Management Strategies for Hospitals and Healthcare Organizations: Tools, Techniques, Checklists and Case Studies*. We integrate prose, managerial applications, and regulatory policies and perspectives with real-world case studies, models, checklists, and reports, as well as charts, tables, and diagrams. The result is an integrated oeuvre of lean management and operation strategies, vital to all healthcare facility administrators, comptrollers, physician-executives, and consulting business advisors.

Third, as editors, we prefer engaged readers who demand compelling content. According to conventional wisdom, printed texts like this one should be a relic of the past, from an era before instant messaging and high-speed connectivity. Our experience shows just the opposite. Applied healthcare management and administration literature has grown exponentially in the past decade, and the plethora of Internet information makes updates that sort through the clutter and provide strategic analysis all the more valuable. Oh, and it should provide some personality and wit, too! Do not forget, beneath the management theory and case models are patients, colleagues, and investors who depend on you.

Finally, it is important to note that proper leadership and cultural expectations are implied in healthcare financial management, and we present case models and studies directly from that space; and not by indirect example from other industries. Healthcare financial management is our core, and only focus.

And so, rest assured that *Financial Management Strategies for Hospitals and Healthcare Organizations: Tools, Techniques, Checklists and Case Studies* will become an important book for the advancement of financial management and health economics principles in our field. In the years ahead, we trust that these principles will enhance utility and add value to this book. Most importantly, we hope to increase your return on investment.

If you have any comments, or if you would like to contribute material or suggest topics for future editions, please contact me.

Professor Hope Rachel Hetico
Managing Editor

TARGET MARKET AND IDEAL READER

Financial Management Strategies for Hospitals and Healthcare Organizations: Tools, Techniques, Checklists and Case Studies should be in the hands of all:

- Chief executive officers, chief financial officers, vice presidents, and other cheif-level executives from every type of hospital and healthcare organization, including: public, federal, state, Veteran's Administration, and Indian Health Services hospitals; district, rural, long-term care, and community hospitals; specialty, children's, and rehabilitation hospitals; diagnostic imaging centers and laboratories; and private, religious-sponsored, and psychiatric institutions.
- Accountable Care Organizations (ACOs), Physician Hospital Organizations (PHOs), Management Services Organizations (MSOs), Regional Extension Centers (RECs), Independent Practice Associations (IPAs), Regional Health Information Exchanges (RHIEs), Group Practices Without Walls (GPWWs), Integrated Delivery Systems (IDSs), Medical Homes (MHs), and their administrators; and all healthcare organization managers, health attorneys, executives, consultants, and their strategic advisors.
- Ambulatory care centers, hospices, and outpatient clinics; skilled nursing facilities, integrated networks, and group practices; academic medical centers, nurses, and physician executives; business schools and health administration students, and all economic decision makers and directors of allopathic, dental, podiatric, and osteopathic healthcare organizations.

Collectively known as emerging and mature healthcare 2.0 organizations (EMHOs) because of the merger, acquisition, and consolidation fervor in the industry, readers from these entities should use this textbook in the following way.

First, read the Table of Contents for an overview of the hospital, health economics, and healthcare financial R&D community, and then browse through the entire book. Next, slowly read chapters that are of specific interest to your professional efforts. Then, extrapolate portions that can be implemented as pertinent strategies helpful to your health institutional setting. Finally, read the epilogue and use it as an actionable reference for consulting personal; and return to the text time and again as needed. Learn and enjoy!

ABOUT THE INSTITUTE OF MEDICAL BUSINESS ADVISORS, INC.

The Institute of Medical Business Advisors (iMBA), Inc., is a leading practice management, economics, and medical valuation consulting firm, and focused provider of textbooks, CD-ROMs, handbooks, templates, tools, dictionaries, and on-site and distance education for the healthcare administration, financial management, and policy space. The firm also serves as a national resource center and referral alliance providing financial stability and managerial peace of mind to struggling physician clients. As competition increases, iMBA, Inc., is positioned to meet the collaborative needs of medical colleagues and institutional clients, today and well into the disruptive Health 2.0 participatory future.

Institute of Medical Business Advisors, Inc.
Peachtree Plantation—West
Wilbanks Drive, Suite 5901
Norcross, Georgia 30092-1141 USA
Telephone: 770-448-0769
MarcinkoAdvisors@msn.com
http://www.MedicalBusinessAdvisors.com

CORPORATE COMMUNICATION SUBSIDIARIES

Advisors: http://www.CertifiedMedicalPlanner.org
Blog: http://www.MedicalExecutivePost.com
Dictionaries: http://www.SpringerPub.com/Search/Marcinko
Management: http://www.BusinessofMedicalPractice.com
Physicians: http://www.MedicalBusinessAdvisors.com

Disclaimer

This publication is designed to provide information in regard to the subject matter covered. It is not intended to constitute business, insurance, financial, technology, legal, accounting, or managerial advice. It is sold with the understanding that the editors, authors, and publishers are not engaged in these or other professional services. Examples are generally descriptive and do not purport to be accurate in every regard. The health economics, organization, and strategic management space is evolving rapidly, and all information should be considered time sensitive. If advice or other assistance is required, the services of a competent professional person should be sought.

Modified from a *Declaration of Principles* jointly adopted by:

- Committee of the American Bar Association
- Committee of Publishers and Associations

FAIR USE NOTICE

Financial Management Strategies for Hospitals and Healthcare Organizations: Tools, Techniques, Checklists and Case Studies contains URLs, blog snippets, links, and brief excerpts of material obtained from the Internet or public domain, the use of which has not always been specifically authorized by the copyright owner. We are making such material available to advance the understanding of related issues and for the general purpose of reporting and educating. We believe this constitutes a "fair use" of any copyrighted material as provided by section 107 of U.S. Copyright Law. In accordance with Title 17 U.S.C. Section 107, the material is distributed to those who have expressed an interest in text purchase. Moreover, all register, trade, service, and copyright marks are the intangible intellectual property assets of their respective owners. Mention of any specific product, service, website domain, or company does not constitute endorsement. No compensation was obtained for including same.

ABOUT INTERNET CITATIONS

Financial Management Strategies for Hospitals and Healthcare Organizations: Tools, Techniques, Checklists and Case Studies makes use of Uniform Resource Locators (URLs) to direct subscribers to useful Internet sites with additional references. However, host entities frequently re-organize and update sites, so URLs can change rapidly. Citations for this text are therefore "live" when published, but we cannot guarantee how long they will remain so, despite our best efforts to keep them current.

The financial, economics, business, technology, accounting, and healthcare managerial information presented in *Financial Management Strategies for Hospitals and Healthcare Organizations: Tools, Techniques, Checklists and Case Studies* is presented for general informational and educational use only. Prior to engaging in the type of activities described, you should receive independent counsel from a qualified relevant professional. Care has been taken to confirm the accuracy of the information presented, but we offer no warranties, expressed or implied, regarding its currency and are not responsible for errors or omissions or for any consequences from the application of this information. Examples are generally descriptive and do not purport to be accurate in every regard. Case models have been blinded. Checklists are not all-inclusive. The healthcare industry is evolving rapidly, and all information should be considered time sensitive.

Although sponsored by the Institute of Medical Business Advisors (iMBA), Inc., we maintain an arm's-length relationship with the independent authors and firms who carried out research and prepared the book. The goal of iMBA, Inc., is to be unbiased to the extent possible and to promote protean professional perspectives and opinions.

Acknowledgments

Creating this interpretive text was a significant effort that involved all members of our firm. Over the past year we interfaced with various public resources such as state governments, the federal government, the Federal Register (FR), the Centers for Disease Control and Prevention (CDC), the Centers for Medicare and Medicaid (CMS), the Institute of Medicine (IOM), the National Research Council (NRC), and the U.S. Department of Health and Human Services (DHHS), as well as numerous private firms and professionals to discuss its contents.

Thank you all for believing in *Financial Management Strategies for Hospitals and Healthcare Organizations: Tools, Techniques, Checklists and Case Studies* and helping to make it a success.

David Edward Marcinko Hope Rachel Hetico Mackenzie Hope Marcinko	**Institute of Medical Business Advisors, Inc.** Peachtree Plantation—West Wilbanks Drive, Suite 5901 Norcross, Georgia 30092-1141 770-448-0769 MarcinkoAdvisors@msn.com http://www.BusinessofMedicalPractice.com http://www.MedicalBusinessAdvisors.com http://www.CertifiedMedicalPlanner.org http://www.MedicalExecutivePost.com http://www.SpringerPub.com/Search/Marcinko

Editors

EDITOR-IN-CHIEF

 **Dr. David Edward Marcinko** is a healthcare economist, managerial and technology futurist, and former board-certified surgeon from Temple University in Philadelphia. In the past, he edited seven practice-management books, three medical texts in two languages, five financial planning books, dozens of interactive CD-ROMs, and three comprehensive administrative dictionaries for physicians, accountants, attorneys, medical management consultants, and healthcare business advisors. Internationally recognized for his work, he provides litigation support and expert witness testimony in state and federal courts, and his clinical publications have been archived in the Library of Congress and the Library of Medicine at the National Institute of Health. His thought leadership essays have been cited in journals such as *Managed Care Executives, Healthcare Informatics, Medical Interface, Plastic Surgery Products, Teaching and Learning in Medicine, Orthodontics Today, Chiropractic Products, Journal of the American Medical Association, Podiatry Today, Investment Advisor Magazine, Registered Representative, Financial Advisor Magazine, CFP™ Biz (Journal of Financial Planning), Journal of the American Medical Association* (JAMA.ama-assn.org), *The Business Journal for Physicians, and Physician's Money Digest;* by companies and professional organizations like the Medical Group Management Association (MGMA), American College of Medical Practice Executives (ACMPE), American College of Physician Executives (ACPE), American College of Emergency Physicians (ACEP), Health Management Associates (HMA), and PhysiciansPractice.com; and by academic institutions like the UCLA School of Medicine, Northern University College of Business, Creighton University, Medical College of Wisconsin, University of North Texas Health Science Center, Washington University School of Medicine, Emory University School of Medicine, the Goizueta School of Business at Emory University, University of Pennsylvania Medical and Dental Libraries, Southern Illinois College of Medicine, University at Buffalo Health Sciences Library, University of Michigan Dental Library, and the University of Medicine and Dentistry of New Jersey, among many others. Dr. Marcinko also has numerous primary and secondary editorial and reviewing roles to his credit.

Dr. Marcinko received his undergraduate degree from Loyola University, Maryland, completed his internship and residency at Atlanta Hospital and Medical Center, earned his business degree from the Keller Graduate School of Management (Chicago), and his financial planning diploma from Oglethorpe University (Atlanta). He is a Fellow of the American College of Foot and Ankle Surgeons. Dr. Marcinko was a licensee of the CERTIFIED FINANCIAL PLANNER™ Board of Standards (Denver) for a decade, and he holds the Certified Medical Planner™ designation (CMP™). He earned Series #7 (general securities), Series #63 (uniform securities state law), and Series #65 (investment advisory) licenses from the National Association of Securities Dealers (NASD), as well as a life, health, disability, variable annuity, and property-casualty license from the State of Georgia. Dr. Marcinko was also co-founder of an ambulatory surgery center that was sold to a public company, and he has been a Certified Professional in Healthcare Quality (CPHQ), a certified American Board of Quality Assurance and Utilization Review Physician (ABQAURP), a medical-staff vice president of a general hospital, an assistant residency director, a founder of a computer-based testing firm for doctors, and president of a regional physician practice-management corporation in the Midwest. He was a member of the American Health Information Management Association (AHIMA) and the Healthcare Information and Management Systems Society (HIMSS); a member of the Microsoft Professional Accountant's Network (MPAN); website engineer and beta tester for Microsoft Office Live Essentials program, and a member of the Microsoft Health User's Group (MS-HUG); and a registered member of the United States Microsoft Partners Program (MPP). And, as president of a privately held physician practice-management corporation in 1998, he consolidated 95 solo medical practices with $50 million in revenues. Since 2011, he has been on the Physician Nexus Medical Advisory Board.

Currently, Dr. Marcinko is chief executive officer for the Institute of Medical Business Advisors, Inc. The firm is headquartered in Atlanta and works with a diverse list of individual and corporate clients. It sponsors the professional Certified Medical Planner™ (CMP™) charter designation program and counsels maverick physicians, health managers, and financial advisors making the transition to niche healthcare advisory careers. As a nationally recognized educational resource center and referral alliance, the Institute of Medical Business Advisors and its network of independent professionals provide solutions and managerial peace-of-mind to physicians, healthcare organizations, and their consulting business advisors. A favorite on the lecture circuit, Dr. Marcinko is often quoted in the media and frequently speaks on related topics throughout this country and Europe in an entertaining and witty fashion. He is also a social media pioneer and publisher of the *Medical Executive Post,* an influential syndicated Health 2.0 interactive blog forum. Dr. Marcinko is available to colleagues, clients, and the press at his corporate office in Atlanta, GA.

Institute of Medical Business Advisors, Inc.
Corporate Headquarters
Peachtree Plantation—West
Wilbanks Drive, Suite 5901
Norcross, GA 30092-1141
770-448-0769
MarcinkoAdvisors@msn.com
http://www.MedicalExecutivePost.com

MANAGING EDITOR

Hope Rachel Hetico received her nursing degree (RN) from Valparaiso University and her Master of Science in Healthcare Administration (MSHA) from the College of St. Francis, in Joliette, Illinois. She is the author or editor of a dozen major textbooks and is a nationally known expert in managed medical care, medical reimbursement, case management, health insurance, security and risk management, utilization review, National Association of Healthcare Quality (NAHQ), Health Education Data Information Set (HEDIS), and Joint Commission on Accreditation of Healthcare Organizations (JCAHO) rules and quality compliance regulations.

Prior to joining the Institute of Medical Business Advisors as Chief Operating Officer, Ms. Hetico was a hospital executive, financial advisor, insurance agent, Certified Professional in Healthcare Quality (CPHQ), and distinguished visiting assistant professor of healthcare administration for the University of Phoenix, Graduate School of Business and Management in Atlanta. She was also national corporate Director for Medical Quality Improvement at Abbey, and then Apria Healthcare, a public company in Costa Mesa, California.

A devotee of health information technology and heutagogy, Ms. Hetico was also responsible for leading the website www.CertifiedMedicalPlanner.org to the top of the exploding adult educational marketplace, expanding the online and on-ground CMP™ charter designation program and nurturing the company's rapidly growing list of medical colleagues and financial services industry clients.

Professor Hetico recently completed successful consulting engagements for Resurrection Health Care Preferred in Chicago, Illinois, and Saint Joseph's Hospital of Atlanta. She is currently on assignment for Emory University Hospital, Atlanta, Georgia.

PROJECT MANAGER

Mackenzie Hope Marcinko is an engineering, computer science, and healthcare informatics business management major at the University of Pittsburgh.

Contributors

Dr. Gary L. Bode was the chief financial officer (CFO) for a private mental healthcare facility, and previously the chief executive officer (CEO) of Comprehensive Practice Accounting, Inc., in Wilmington, NC. The firm specialized in providing tax solutions to medical professionals. Dr. Bode was a board-certified practitioner and managing partner of a multi-office medical group practice for a decade before earning his Master of Science degree in Accounting (MSA) from the University of North Carolina. He is a nationally known forensic health accountant, financial author, educator, and speaker. Areas of expertise include producing customized managerial accounting reports, practice appraisals and valuations, re-structurings, and innovative financial accounting, as well as proactive tax positioning and tax return preparation for healthcare facilities. Currently, Dr. Bode is chief accounting and valuation officer (CAVO) for the Institute of Medical Business Advisors, Inc., and CEO and founder of Gary Bode CPA, LLC.

Dr. Gary L. Bode, CPA, MSA, CMP™ [Hon]
CEO: Gary Bode CPA, LLC
CPA Wilmington NC
1006 Summerlin Falls Ct.
Wilmington, NC 28412
910-399-2705
http://garybodecpa.com
http://www.cpawilmingtonnc.org

Robert James Cimasi is President of Health Capital Consultants (HCC), a nationally recognized healthcare financial and economic consulting firm. With more than 25 years of experience in serving clients in 49 states, his professional focus is on the financial and economic aspects of healthcare service sector entities: valuation consulting; litigation support and expert testimony; business intermediary and capital formation services; certificate-of-need and other regulatory and policy planning consulting; and healthcare industry transactions including joint ventures, sales, mergers, acquisitions, and divestitures.

Mr. Cimasi holds a master's degree in Health Administration from the University of Maryland, the Accredited Senior Appraiser (ASA) designation in Business Valuation, and a fellowship in the Royal Institution of Chartered Surveyors (FRICS), as well as the Master Certified Business Appraiser (MCBA), Accredited Valuation Analyst (AVA), and the Certified Merger & Acquisition Advisor (CM&AA) designations. He is a nationally known speaker on healthcare industry topics, and he has served as conference faculty or presenter for such organizations as the American Society of Appraisers (ASA), the Institute of Business Appraisers (IBA), the American Institute of Certified Public Accountants (AICPA), the National Association of Certified Valuation Analysts (NACVA), the American College of Healthcare Executives (ACHE), the National Society of Certified Healthcare Business Consultants (NSCHBC), Academy Health, Alliance of Merger & Acquisition Advisors (AM&AA), the Healthcare Financial Management Association (HFMA), the American Association of Ambulatory Surgery Centers (AAASC), Physician Hospitals of America (PHA) [formerly known as the American Surgical Hospital Association (ASHA)], the National Litigation Support Services Association (NLSSA), as well as many other national and state healthcare industry associations and professional societies, trade groups, companies, and organizations. He has been certified and has served as an expert witness on cases in numerous states, and he has provided testimony before federal and state legislative committees. In 2006, Mr. Cimasi was honored with the prestigious Shannon Pratt Award in Business Valuation conferred by the Institute of Business Appraisers.

Mr. Cimasi has written articles that were published in peer review journals, has frequently presented research papers and case studies before national conferences, and is often quoted by healthcare industry professional publications and the general media. Mr. Cimasi's latest book, *The Adviser's Guide to Healthcare,* was published in 2010 by AICPA.

Robert James Cimasi, MHA, ASA, FRICS, MCBA, AVA, CM&AA
President: Health Capital Consultants, LLC
1143 Olivette Executive Parkway
St. Louis, MO 63132-3205
http://www.HealthCapital.com

Perry D'Alessio has more than 20 years' experience in public accounting. He specializes in the taxation of closely held businesses and their owners, as well as high-wealth individuals. He has a broad range of experience that includes individual, corporate, partnership, fiduciary, estate, and gift taxation. Business development has also been a focus. Particularly in the healthcare and fitness industry, he worked with successful entities whose emphasis was on growth through development of strategic relationships and unit building. Mr. D'Alessio received his Bachelor of Business Administration degree in Accounting from Baruch College. He is a certified public accountant in New York, and he is a member of the American Institute of Certified Public Accountants (AICPA) and the New York State Society of Certified Public Accountants (NYSSCPA). Mr. D'Alessio has served on several New York State Society tax committees, including the Public Company Accounting Oversight Board and HealthCare.

Perry D'Alessio, CPA
D'Alessio Tocci & Pell LLP
Certified Public Accountants and Business Advisors
20 West 36th St., 10th Floor
New York, New York 10018
http://www.dalecpa.com

Adam Higman is a Soyring Consultant with management and consulting experience related to cost reduction initiatives, market analysis, physicians/staff relations, and operational objectives. Mr. Higman has developed and implemented cost-reduction strategies in various healthcare settings, from operating rooms and cath labs to hospital-wide initiatives. He has negotiated with vendors, increased group purchasing organization compliance, analyzed staffing function, and coordinated implementation efforts with medical, clinical, and support staff members.

Adam Higman, BS, MS
Soyring Consulting
880 21st Avenue North
St. Petersburg, FL 33704

Carey Huntington is an Associate at CFAR, a member of the American College of Healthcare Executives, and an active member of CFAR's Healthcare and Change practices. She holds a Master of Business Administration with a concentration in International Business from Temple University.

Carey Huntington, MBA
Center for Applied Research (CFAR)
Four Penn Center
1600 John F. Kennedy Blvd., Suite 600
Philadelphia, PA 19103
http://www.CFAR.com

Jerzy Kaczor has been a consultant with Soyring Consulting for six years. His areas of expertise include data and financial analysis, materials flow, information system and productivity assessment and analysis, patient flow, data analysis, information systems, marketing, and financial analysis. His consulting experiences include a variety of process improvement projects, productivity standards development, throughput analysis, interviews, observations, data analysis, and staff work flow studies.

Jerzy Kaczor, BSBA, MBA
Soyring Consulting
880 21st Avenue North
St. Petersburg, FL 33704

Dr. Brent A. Metfessel is currently Senior Medical Informaticist in Clinical Analytics at UnitedHealthcare, where he designs physician measurement algorithms and statistical methods and leads the application of risk adjustment methodologies to various healthcare quality and cost-efficiency measurement initiatives. His prior corporate positions have included clinical research coordinator at Anthem Blue Cross/Blue Shield and senior medical informaticist for Crossroads Technology Solutions. Dr. Metfessel has created and enhanced evidence-based medical policy as well as client reporting and analytic technologies using episode-of-care methodologies. He has also designed custom-built primary care and specialist provider profiling systems and is a visionary in the application of the industry-leading clinical episode-of-care methodology to healthcare databases. Dr. Metfessel also has a decade of experience in general computer science, statistical analysis, artificial intelligence, and computational biology. Dr. Metfessel received his Master of Science degree in health informatics from the University of Minnesota and his Medical Doctorate degree from the University of California, San Diego. He also holds a professional certificate in management for physicians from the University of St. Thomas.

Dr. Brent A. Metfessel, MS
17704 Hackberry Court
Eden Prairie, MN 55347
BrentMet@aol.com

Carol S. Miller has an extensive healthcare background in operations, business development, and capture in both the public and private sectors. Since the early 2000s, she has provided management support to projects in the Department of Health and Human Services, Veterans Affairs, and Department of Defense medical programs. Ms. Miller has served as Vice President and Senior Account Executive for NCI Information Systems, Inc., Assistant Vice President at SAIC, and Program Manager at MITRE. She has led the successful capture of large IDIQ/GWAC (indefinite delivery indefinite quantity/government wide acquisition contract) programs, managed the operations of multiple government contracts, interacted with many key government executives, and increased the new account portfolios for each firm she supported. She earned her Master of Business Administration from Marymount University, her Bachelor of Science degree in Business from Saint Joseph's College; and her Bachelor of Science degree in Nursing from the University of Pittsburgh. She is a Certified Project Management Institute Project Management Professional (PMI PMP) and a Certified HIPAA Professional (CHP), with Top Secret Security clearance issued by the Department of Defense. Ms. Miller is also a Healthcare Information and Management Systems Society (HIMSS) Fellow.

Carol S. Miller, BSN, MBA, PMP
President: Miller Consulting Group
7344 Hooking Road
McLean, VA 22101
Telephone: 703-407-4704
Fax: 703-790-3257
millerconsultgroup@gmail.com

Brian Mullahey is a Soyring Consultant with a strong background in organizational design, premium labor management, staffing, scheduling, and process improvement. Brian is proficient in consolidation and streamlining of organizational structures, and in the development and implementation of cost-reduction strategies related to high-preference surgeon items. He has negotiated with vendors, increased group purchasing organization compliance, and coordinated implementation efforts with medical, clinical, and supply chain staff members. He is a current board member and an American Council for Technology/Industry Advisory Council Fellow.

Brian Mullahey, BA
Soyring Consulting
880 21st Avenue North
St. Petersburg, FL 33704

Fabian Poliak is an Analyst at the Center for Applied Research. He holds a Bachelor of Arts in Sociology with a secondary in Global Health and Health Policy from Harvard College.

Fabian Poliak
Center for Applied Research (CFAR)
Four Penn Center
1600 John F. Kennedy Blvd., Suite 600
Philadelphia, PA 19103
http://www.CFAR.com

Anne P. Sharamitaro focuses on the areas of Certificate of Need (CON), regulatory compliance, managed care, and antitrust consulting for Health Capital Consultants. Ms. Sharamitaro is a member of the Missouri Bar and holds a Juris Doctor and Health Law Certificate from St. Louis University School of Law, where she served as an editor for the *Journal of Health Law,* published by the American Health Lawyers Association, and she has been admitted to the Missouri Bar. She has presented healthcare industry–related research papers before the Physician Hospitals of America (formerly known as the American Surgical Hospital Association) and the National Association of Certified Valuation Analysts, and she co-authored chapters in *Healthcare Organizations: Financial Management Strategies* (2008, STP Financial Management).

Anne P. Sharamitaro, Esq.
Senior Vice President: Health Capital Consultants, LLC
1143 Olivette Executive Parkway
St. Louis, MO 63132-3205
http://www.HealthCapital.com

Kristin Spenik has a Bachelor of Science degree in Marketing from the University of South Florida St. Petersburg. Her experience includes research, writing press releases and media alerts, designing print media and creating newsletters, social media marketing, and budgeting, placement, and review of media schedules for print, television, and radio spots.

Kristin Spenik, BS
Soyring Consulting
880 21st Avenue North
St. Petersburg, FL 33704

Jennifer Tomasik is a Principal at CFAR, a boutique management consulting firm specializing in strategy, change, and collaboration. Ms. Tomasik has worked in the healthcare sector for nearly

20 years, with expertise in strategic planning, large-scale organizational and cultural change, public health, and clinical quality measurement. She leads CFAR's Health Care practice. Ms. Tomasik has a master's degree in Health Policy and Management from the Harvard School of Public Health. Her clients include some of the most prestigious hospitals, health systems, and academic medical centers in the country.

Jennifer Tomasik, MS
Center for Applied Research (CFAR)
Four Penn Center
1600 John F. Kennedy Blvd., Suite 600
Philadelphia, PA 19103
http://www.CFAR.com

Todd A. Zigrang focuses on valuation and financial analysis for hospitals and other healthcare enterprises for Health Capital Consultants. Mr. Zigrang has significant physician integration and financial analysis experience and has participated in the development of a physician-owned multi-specialty management services organization and of networks involving a wide range of specialties, and of physician-owned hospitals and several limited liability companies for the purpose of acquiring acute care and specialty hospitals, ambulatory surgery centers, and other ancillary facilities. Mr. Zigrang has participated in the evaluation and negotiation of managed care contracts, performed and assisted in the valuation of various healthcare entities and related litigation support engagements, created pro-forma financials, written business plans, conducted a range of industry research, completed due diligence practice analysis, overseen the selection process for vendors, contractors, and architects, and worked on the arrangement of financing.

Mr. Zigrang holds a Master of Science in Health Administration and a Master of Business Administration from the University of Missouri at Columbia. He is a member of the American College of Healthcare Executives and Healthcare Financial Management Association. He has co-authored chapters in *Healthcare Organizations: Financial Management Strategies* (2007, STP Financial Management, 2007) and *Financial Planning for Physicians and Healthcare Professionals 2002* (2002, Aspen Publishers). He has taught before the Institute of Business Appraisers and has presented healthcare industry valuation–related research papers before the Healthcare Financial Management Association, the St. Louis Business Valuation Roundtable, and the Physician Hospitals of America (formerly known as the American Surgical Hospital Association).

Todd A. Zigrang, MBA, MHA, ASA, FACHE
Senior Vice President: Health Capital Consultants, LLC
1143 Olivette Executive Parkway
St. Louis, MO 63132-3205
http://www.HealthCapital.com

Section I

Costs and Revenues
Fundamental Principles

1 Managerial Medical Cost Accounting, Structure, Modeling, and Behavior

David Edward Marcinko and Hope Rachel Hetico

CONTENTS

INTRODUCTION

Controlling hospital and healthcare organization costs is a function of internal controls and the decision-making process to purchase assets and incur expenditures. This includes operations, processes, human resources, healthcare information technology (HIT), and purchasing. Thus, while this was not, strictly speaking, a financial strategy in the past, cost accounting is now considered by most healthcare executives an important financial management function.

In today's competitive medical marketplace, managerial cost accounting is often used to set short- and long-term healthcare entity business policy. The information is used to increase profitability by decreasing costs, increasing revenues, or decreasing operating assets. More than ever, cost accounting can mean the difference between a successful healthcare entity and a moribund one. Managerial cost accounting consists of many goals, such as:

- Providing vital costing information for internal entity use
- Developing proactive future entity strategic plans information
- Accentuating the relevancy and flexibility of financial data
- Reviewing real-time medical service segments, rather than just total entity operations
- Acquiring nonfinancial healthcare business data

WHAT IS MEDICAL OR HEALTHCARE COST ACCOUNTING?

Definition: A method or means of accounting in which all incurred costs and expenses carrying out a medical activity or service, or accomplishing a patient care purpose, are collected, classified, and recorded. This data is then summarized and analyzed to arrive at a service, invoice, or selling price, or to determine where cost savings are possible.

Medical cost accounting is designed for healthcare managers and administrators. Because managers are making decisions only for their own unique entity, there is no need for the data to be comparable to similar data from other organizations. Instead, the important criterion is that the information must be relevant for decisions that healthcare administrators make in their particular environment. The accountants who handle the cost accounting information add value by providing good information to managers who are making decisions.

Cost accounting is regarded as the process of collecting, analyzing, summarizing, and evaluating various alternative courses of action involving costs, and then advising management on the most appropriate course of action based on the cost efficiency and capability of the management.

All health organizations are interested in costs. The control of past, present, and future costs is the job of all healthcare managers. In the entities that try to have profits, the control of costs affects them directly. Knowing the costs of medical services and products is essential for making decisions regarding price, payer mix of products, and services. As a result, there is a wide variety in the cost accounting systems for different hospitals and sometimes even in different parts of the same hospital or healthcare entity. Therefore, the following different healthcare cost accounting approaches are discussed in this textbook:

- Standard and lean accounting
- Activity-based cost (ABC) accounting
- Relative resource-based accounting
- Throughput cost accounting
- Cost-profit-volume analysis, and
- Revenue cycle accounting

In contrast to the financial accounting of a Certified Public Accountant (which considers money as the measure of economic performance), cost accounting considers money as the economic factor of production.

Managerial cost accounting is not governed by generally accepted accounting principles (GAAP) as promoted by the Financial Accounting Standards Board (FASB). Rather, a healthcare organization costing expert may be a Certified Cost Accountant (CCA) or Certified Managerial

Accountant (CMA), designated by the Cost Accounting Standards Board (CASB), an independent board within the Office of Management and Budget's (OMB) Office of Federal Procurement Policy (OFPP).

CASB consists of five members, including the OFPP Administrator, who serves as chairman, and four members with experience in government contract cost accounting (two from the federal government, one from the industry, and one from the accounting profession). The Board has the exclusive authority to make, promulgate, and amend cost accounting standards and interpretations designed to achieve uniformity and consistency in the cost accounting practices governing the measurement, assignment, and allocation of costs to contracts with the United States.

CASB's regulations are codified in 48 CFR, Chapter 99. The standards are mandatory for use by all executive agencies and by contractors and subcontractors in estimating, accumulating, and reporting costs in connection with pricing and administration of, and settlement of disputes concerning, all negotiated prime contract and subcontract procurement with the United States in excess of $500,000. The rules and regulations of the CASB appear in the federal acquisition regulation (see https://acquisition.gov).

North American Industry Classification System (NAICS) codes are used to categorize data for the federal government. In acquisition they are particularly critical for size standards. The NAICS codes are revised every five years by the Census Bureau. As of October 1, 2012, the federal acquisition community began using the 2012 version of the NAICS codes (available at http://www.census.gov/epcd/www/naics.html).

Healthcare organizations and consultants are obligated to comply with the following cost accounting standards (CAS) promulgated by federal agencies:

- CAS 501 requires consistency in estimating, accumulating, and reporting costs.
- CAS 502 requires consistency in allocating costs incurred for the same purpose.
- CAS 505 requires proper treatment of unallowable costs.
- CAS 506 requires consistency in the periods used for cost accounting.

The requirements of these standards are different from those of traditional financial accounting, which are concerned with providing static historical information to creditors, shareholders, and others outside the public or private healthcare organization.

Most healthcare organizations also contain **cost centers** that have no revenue budgets or mission to earn revenues for the organization. Examples include human resources, administration, housekeeping, nursing, and the like. These are known as responsibility centers with budgeting constraints but no earnings. Furthermore, **shadow cost centers** include certain non-cash or cash expenses, such as amortization, depreciation and utilities, and rent. These non-centralized shadow cost centers are cost-allocated for budgeting purposes and must be treated as costs.

COST BEHAVIOR, STRUCTURE, AND MODELING

Cost behavior is the study of how costs change in relation to variations in activity, service, or use. Kaizen costing, a Japanese method of cost reduction, is the pursuit of "continuous improvement" to reduce costs. Its prime purpose is to gather cost data for managerial control. Inherent in every Kaizen costing strategy are the following goals:

- Create waste-free systems with economic policy and procedures.
- Define clear leadership buy-in to financial initiatives.
- Sustain a culture of unrelenting continuous quality and economic improvement.

Installing a Kaizen costing culture is a top-down, bottom-up process. Like cost accounting itself, there is no single best way to implement it. Rather, mature and emerging healthcare organizations must find their own ways to effectively manage costs (see http://www.kaizen-institute.com).

Healthcare organizational costs may be divided into several categories, including fixed, variable, hybrid mixed, extraneous, differential, controllable, opportunity, sunk, relevant, carrying, future, and human resource costs. These costs are accounted for through some relevant range, which is an economic principle that can be defined as the range of medical service activity within which certain assumptions are neither too high nor too low, and relate to variable and fixed cost behavior with validity.

TYPES OF COSTS

Fixed Cost

A **fixed cost** can be viewed in the aggregate or on a per-unit basis, but it always remains constant. For example, clinic rent does not increase if hours are expanded into Saturday or Sunday.

Total fixed costs are not usually affected by changes in activity (i.e., clinic rent, taxes, insurance, depreciation, salaries of employees and key personnel). Rent is still due even if no patients are seen. A fixed cost remains constant, over the relevant range, even if the level of activity changes (i.e., busy summer or winter slow down). However, fixed costs decrease on a per-unit basis as the activity level rises and increase on a per-unit basis as the activity level falls.

Generally, decisions or changes do not alter fixed costs in the short term. They remain constant in total amount throughout a wide range of clinic activity, and they vary inversely with activity if expressed on a per-unit or per-patient basis.

Example

Assume that a physical therapy clinic dispenses durable medical equipment (DME) devices for various biomechanical conditions. The rent is fixed over the course of its lease at $9,000 per month. Therefore, the total and per-unit rent costs at various levels of device activity would be depicted as follows:

Fixed Rent: Cost per Month	Number of Uses	Fixed Rent Cost per Use
9,000	1	$9,000
9,000	10	900
9,000	100	90
9,000	200	45

The table shows the effect of volume (cost per month and number of uses) on the cost of rent per use. In other words, the more frequently the DME devices are used, the lower the fixed cost on a per-unit basis.

Variable Cost

Total **variable cost** increases and decreases in proportion to activity, while per-unit variable costs remain constant per unit. A variable cost changes in total in direct proportion to changes in the level of activity but is constant on a per-unit basis. Clinic costs that are normally variable with respect to volume include: DME, indirect labor, and indirect materials such as utilities, air conditioning, clerical costs, and other medical supplies. Generally, variable costs change as a direct result of making a decision or altering a course of action.

Example

The same physical therapy clinic dispenses a custom-made latex wrist splint for $30 per device. The per-unit and total costs of the splints at various levels of activity would be depicted as follows:

Number of Splints Dispensed	Cost per Splint	Total Variable Cost per Splint
1	$30	$30
10	30	300
100	30	3,000
200	30	6,000

Generally, the manufacturing community has embraced the trend toward fixed business costs. Conversely, the medical community is trending toward more variable costs for two primary reasons:

- Medicine is a personal service industry.
- Migration is toward *locum tenens* and hired physician employment (i.e., non-owner physicians).

The current trend of healthcare organizations moving toward variable cost accounting leads to the following cost calculations:

Simple Cost Calculations

Total Costs = Total Fixed Costs plus Total Variable Costs:

$$TC = TFC + TVC$$

Furthermore, total variable costs for a medical clinic can be further equated to:

$$\text{Total Variable Costs} = (\text{TVC per visit}) \times (\text{number of visits})$$

So that:

$$\text{Total Costs} = TFC + \{(VC/\text{visit}) \times (\text{number of visits})\}$$

And, if given as Total Profit = Revenue (Price × Volume) – Costs, then:

$$\text{Total Profit} = (P \times V) - (FC + VC)$$

Hybrid Cost

A **hybrid cost**[*] is one that contains both fixed and variable elements. Although the designation may change from clinic to clinic, internal consistency is important for cost behavioral purposes. For example, an X-ray unit is leased for $3,000 per year, plus $10 per film. In this case, the yearly lease is the fixed element while the per-unit film charge varies depending on use.

Extraneous Cost

An **extraneous cost** is not related to a specific healthcare product, department, procedure, intervention, drug, patient, or service, and includes step-down, direct, and indirect costs.

---

[*] Also known as mixed, semi-variable, or step-fixed costs.

- A **step-down cost** is at the top of a hierarchy, where a primary center provides resources to other cost centers, such as human resources or nursing. The costs from the primary center are allocated to the other centers. Then, the primary center is closed and no other costs are allocated to it.
- A **direct cost** can be traced from its destination and can be traced specifically to the performance of a procedure. The more procedures done, the higher the direct costs. In a medical clinic or hospital, radiographs, surgical supplies, blood panels, durable medical equipment, and other procedures can be traced to a specific patient, while labor is traced to the organization's staff.
- An **indirect cost** must be allocated to general clinic overhead rather than specifically assigned to the cost driver in question. Such expenses as the rent, leaseholds, mortgages, or the office manager's salary are constant. They have no relationship to frequency of use.

Differential Cost

Any cost that is present under one alternative but is absent in whole or part under another alternative is known as a **differential cost.**

Example

Dr. Lindsay is an internist with a solo practice. He has been offered a hospitalist position* in a small rural hospital. The differential revenue and costs between the two jobs are depicted below:

	Office	Hospital	Differential Cost
Weekly Salary	$900	$1,200	$300
Weekly Expenses			
Commuting	30	90	60
Lab Coat Rental	0	50	50
Food	10	0	(10)
Total Weekly Expenses	40	140	100
Net Weekly Income	$860	$1,060	$200

Controllable Cost

A **controllable cost** occurs at a particular level of the clinic or healthcare entity if the physician-executive has the power to authorize the expenses. There is a risk/benefit and time dimension to controllable costs. For example, costs that are controllable over the long run may not be controllable over the short time. In the very long term however, all costs are variable and controllable.

Opportunity Cost

An **opportunity cost** is the potential advantage or benefit that is either sacrificed or lost when selecting one course of action over another. It is also known as an either/or decision.

For example, if Dr. Young Ophthalmologist were invited to speak at a local Lion's Club meeting about a new eye surgical technique, will the publicity garnered help his reputation enough to compensate for the actual time and revenue lost during his absence from the office? Some intangible opportunity costs cannot be mathematically calculated.

Sunk Cost

A **sunk cost** is an expense that has already been incurred and cannot be changed by any decision, either now or in the future. It is committed and irreversible. For example, the fancy new treatment

---

* A **hospitalist** is a physician stationed primarily in a hospital to handle all admissions from a specific medical practice or group, or a doctor that is responsible for treatments or processes during a hospital stay.

chair purchased by podiatrist Dr. Foot Haley, for cash, is a sunk cost. Nothing can be changed since she owns the chair outright.

Of course, hospitals and healthcare organizations should experiment with costing methodologies that are consistent with real-world and CCA, CMA, and CASB accounting principles. This includes practices that allocate fixed and sunk costs to determine variable costs. However, when cost adaptive principles are used to adjust price, a **sunk cost bias** may be observed. Biased sunk cost methodologies that falsely increase profits may be reinforced, as the degree of bias changes with demand, product differentiation, or the number of competing entities, and so on.

Relevant Cost

A **relevant cost** is avoidable as a result of choosing one alternative over another. All costs are considered avoidable, except sunk costs and future costs that do not differ between the alternatives at hand. The healthcare entity administrator should follow the steps below to identify the costs (and revenues) that are relevant in any costing decision:

- Assemble all of the costs and revenues associated with the alternative.
- Eliminate sunk costs.
- Eliminate those costs and revenues that do not differ between alternatives.
- Decide based on the remaining costs and revenues. These are the costs and revenues that are differential or avoidable and are therefore relevant to the medical business decision to be made.

Example

Dr. Hartwell, an orthopedic surgeon, is considering replacing an old X-ray processing machine with a new, more efficient, automatic processing machine. Data on the machine are listed below:

New Machine:	
List Price New	$9,000
Annual Variable Expenses	8,000
Expected Life	5 years
Old Machine:	
Original Cost	$7,200
Remaining Book Value	6,000
Disposal Value Now	1,500
Annual Variable Expenses	10,000
Remaining Life	5 years

Dr. Hartwell's office revenues are $200,000 per year and fixed expenses (other than depreciation) are $70,000 per year. Should the new processing machine be purchased?

ERRONEOUS SOLUTION

Some administrators would not purchase the new machine since disposal of the old machine would apparently result in a loss:

Remaining Book Value	$6,000
Disposal Value Now	1,500
Loss from Disposal	4,500

CORRECT SOLUTION

The remaining book value of the old machine is a sunk cost that cannot be avoided by Dr. Hartwell. This can be demonstrated by looking at comparative cost and projected revenue data for the next five years.

	Five Years' Data		
	Keep Old Machine	Purchase New Machine	Differential
Sales	$100,000	$100,000	0
Less Variable Expenses	50,000 (5 × 10,000)	40,000 (5 × 8,000)	10,000
Less Other Fixed Expenses	35,000	35,000	0
Depreciation (New)	0	(9,000)	(9,000)
Depreciation (Old)/Book Value	(6,000)	(6,000)	0
Disposal Value (Old)	0	1,500	1,500
Total Net Income	**$9,000**	**$11,500**	**$2,500**

Using only *relevant costs,* the correct solution would be:

Savings in Variable Expenses Provided by New Machine ($2,000 × 5 years)	$10,000*
Cost of New Machine	9,000
Disposal Value of Old Machine	1,500
Net Advantage of New Machine	**$2,500**

* $10,000 − 8,000 = $2,000.

Carrying Cost

Carrying cost represents the cost of maintaining inventory in a clinic, office, or storage facility. This cost includes rent, utilities, insurance, taxes, employee costs (e.g., labor and human resource costs, salaries, fringe benefits, holidays, vacations, etc.), as well as the opportunity cost of having space or capital tied up.

Future Cost

A **future costs** represents decision making in a forward direction relevant to an alternate selection process. There are two types:

- **Avoidable future costs** can be eliminated or saved if the activity in question is saved, eliminated, or discontinued. For example, salary and administration costs might be reduced in a hospital if 35 percent of the beds were taken out of service.
- **Incremental future costs** represent a change from a specific management activity (e.g., starting or expanding a service, closing or opening a department, acquiring new equipment). For example, the incremental costs for signing a capitated managed care contract would generate 100 new patients next year.

Human Resource Costs

Labor or related human resources typically make up a large portion of the overhead costs of any healthcare entity or medical office. Several non-specific labor costs are reviewed below.

- **Idle time labor costs** represent the costs of an office employee (direct office labor) who is unable to perform his or her assignments due to power failures, slack time, and the like.

Example

Let's suppose that a full-time employee is idle for 4 hours during the week due to the doctor's unavailability while in surgery. If the employee is paid $20 per hour and works a normal 40-hour week, the labor cost would be allocated as depicted below between direct labor and office overhead.

Direct Labor Cost ($20 × 36 hours)	$720
Office Overhead ($20 × 4 hours)	+ 80
Total Costs for Week	$800

- **Overtime premium costs** are the overtime premiums paid to all healthcare office workers (direct and indirect labor) and are considered part of the general office overhead.

Example

Let's assume that an employee is paid time and a half for overtime. During a given week, this employee works 46 hours and has no idle time. Direct labor costs would be allocated as depicted below:

Direct Labor Cost ($20 × 46 hours)	$920
Office Overhead ($10 × 6 hours)	+ 60
Total Cost Week	$980

- **Fringe benefit costs** are typically made up of employment-related costs paid by the office. These costs may be handled in two different ways: as indirect labor added to general overhead costs or as fringe benefits added to direct labor costs.

Healthcare Sector Costs

Payments and revenue received by physicians and healthcare entities represent the cost of business for the government, insurance industry, or paying sector. Generally, the paying sector includes hospital inpatients and outpatients, medical providers, skilled nursing facilities, and home healthcare agencies, all of which are annually indexed for inflation (Centers for Medicare and Medicaid, Services 2012).

The Medicare Prospective Payment System

The Medicare Prospective Payment System (PPS) was introduced by the federal government on October, 1 1983, as a way to change hospital behavior through financial incentives that encourage more cost-efficient management of medical care. Under PPS, hospitals are paid a predetermined rate for each Medicare admission. Each patient is classified into a diagnosis-related group (DRG) on the basis of clinical information. Except for certain patients with exceptionally high costs ("outliers"), the hospital is paid a flat rate for the DRG, regardless of the actual services provided. Each Medicare patient is classified into a DRG according to information from the medical record that appears on the bill:

- Principal diagnosis (why the patient was admitted)
- Complications and co-morbidities (other secondary diagnoses)
- Surgical procedures
- Age and patient gender
- Discharge disposition (routine, transferred, or expired)

Diagnoses and procedures must be documented by the attending physician in the patient's medical record. They are then coded by hospital personnel using International Classification of Diseases, Tenth Edition (ICD-10-CM; CDC, 2012) electronic nomenclature. This is a numerical coding scheme of 13,000–25,000 diagnoses and more than 10,000 procedures. The coding process is extremely important because it essentially determines what DRG will be assigned for a patient. Coding an incorrect principal diagnosis or failing to code a significant secondary diagnosis can dramatically affect reimbursement.

Originally, there were more than 490 DRG categories defined by the Centers for Medicare and Medicaid Services (CMS, formerly known as the Health Care Financing Administration [HCFA]). Each category was designed to be "clinically coherent."

In other words, all patients assigned to a DRG are deemed to have a similar clinical condition. The PPS is based on paying the average cost for treating patients in the same DRG. Each year CMS makes technical adjustments to the DRG classification system that incorporates new technologies (e.g., laparoscopic procedures) and refines its use as a payment methodology. CMS also initiates changes to the ICD-10-CM coding scheme. The DRG assignment process is computerized in a program called the "grouper," which is used by hospitals and fiscal intermediaries. It was last significantly updated by CMS in 2006, 2010, 2012, and 2013.

Each year CMS also assigns a relative weight to each DRG. These weights indicate the relative costs for treating patients during the prior year. The national average charge for each DRG is compared to the overall average. This ratio is published annually in the *Federal Register* (2013) for each DRG. A DRG with a weight of 2.0000, for example, means that charges were historically twice the average; a DRG with a weight of 0.5000 was half the average; and so on.

Top 10 Diagnosis-Related Groups

The ten highest volume Medicare DRGs represent about 30 percent of total Medicare patients. Each of these higher-volume DRGs represents from about 2 percent to 6 percent of total Medicare volume (see Table 1.1).

The Medicare Inpatient Prospective Payment System

The final rule from CMS for the inpatient prospective payment system (IPPS) for fiscal year 2008 was published in the *Federal Register* (2007), and became effective on October 1, 2007. It applied

---

TABLE 1.1
Top 10 Diagnosis-Related Groups

	DRG	DRG Description	% Total	Relative Weight
1	127	Heart Failure and Shock	5.99	1.0234
2	089	Simple Pneumonia and Pleurisy Age > 17 with CC	3.85	1.1447
3	014	Specific Cerebrovascular Disorders Except Transient Ischemic Attack	3.18	1.2056
4	430	Psychoses	3.18	0.9153
5	088	Chronic Obstructive Pulmonary Disease	3.11	1.0067
6	209	Major Joint and Limb Reattachment Procedures, Lower Extremity	2.78	2.3491
7	140	Angina Pectoris	2.33	0.6241
8	182	Esophagitis, Gastroenterology, and Miscellaneous Digest Disorders Age > 17 with CC	2.09	0.7617
9	174	Gastrointestinal Hemorrhage with CC	2.07	0.9657
10	296	Nutritional & Misc Metabolic Disorders Age > 17 with CC	1.93	0.9313

CC: complications or comorbidities.
Source: Health Care Financing Administration (CMS), http://www.cms.gov, 2004.

to discharges occurring on or after that date as the August 16, 2010, update is still pending. Highlights of the most recent IPPS rules include:

- Payments to all hospitals increased by an estimated average of 3.5 percent or by more than $3.8 billion when all provisions of the rules were taken into account.
- CMS adopted the Medicare severity-adjusted DRG (MS-DRG) classification system that expands the current number of DRGs from 538 to 745. Weighting factors will be phased in over a two-year period.
- CMS will not pay for devices replaced at no cost or provide more than 50 percent credit to the hospital as part of a recall or warranty period servicing. Devices affected by the policy include pacemakers and defibrillators.
- CMS identified eight conditions that will not be paid at a higher rate unless they were present on admission, including three serious preventable events labeled "never events" that meet the statutory criteria. This change took effect in fiscal year (FY) 2009.
- CMS continues to use hospital costs rather than charges to set payment rates.
- CMS adopted a high-cost outlier threshold of $22,650, down from $24,485 in FY 2007.
- CMS measures 30-day mortality for Medicare patients with pneumonia and adopted two measures relating to surgical care improvement in the calendar year (CY) 2008 outpatient PPS final rule.
- CMS finalized two additional surgical care improvement measures by program notice after they receive National Quality Forum (NQF)* endorsement.
- The rules add new quality measures for a total of 32 measures that hospitals would need to report in CY 2008 to qualify for the full market basket update in FY 2009. Medicare payments for inpatient hospital services were reduced by 2.0 percent if hospitals fail to report this quality information.

Other features of the final IPPS rule are outlined below.

MS-DRG Classification System   CMS created 745 new MS-DRGs to replace the 538 existing DRGs from 2006 to better recognize severity of patient illness. The MS-DRGs are based on cost rather than charges and more accurately capture resource utilization by splitting the large number of former DRGs into three different categories based on the presence or absence of diagnoses classified as "major complications or comorbidities" (MCC), "complications or comorbidities" (CC), or "without MCC/CC" (non-CC).

CMS believed this scheme improved predictability and reliability of payments when combined with the reforms, more accurately reflected the costs of caring for a patient, and reduced incentives to "cherry pick" profitable patients.

The MS-DRGs were phased in over a two-year period, rather than at one time as originally proposed. For the first year of the transition (FY 2008–2009), half of the relative weight for each MS-DRG was based on the prior DRG relative weight, and half was based on the new MS-DRG relative weight. For the second year (FY 2009–2010), the relative weights were based entirely on the new MS-DRG relative weight.

CMS adopted its proposal to reduce the IPPS standardized amounts by 4.8 percent to maintain budget neutrality and account for expected changes in coding and documentation. Instead of applying a 2.4 percent adjustment over a two-year period as proposed, CMS applied an adjustment of −1.2 percent for FY 2008, and based on current projections CMS will apply adjustments of −1.8 percent each year to the IPPS standardized amounts for FYs 2009, 2010, and 2011.

---

* The National Quality Forum is a not-for-profit membership organization created to develop and implement a national strategy for healthcare quality measurement and reporting.

Hospital-Acquired Conditions   The final rule of Section 5001(c) of the Deficit Reduction Act of 2005 (DRA) required the secretary to select at least two conditions that (a) are high cost or high volume or both, (b) resulted in the assignment of a case to a DRG that had a higher payment when present as a secondary diagnosis, and (c) could reasonably have been prevented through the application of evidence-based guidelines.

Beginning in FY 2009 (October 1, 2008), hospitals did not receive additional payment for cases in which one of the selected six conditions was treated unless the condition was present on admission.

"Never-Events"   Below is the list of conditions that CMS first selected in the FY 2008 final rule.

- Serious preventable event: object left in surgery
- Serious preventable event: air embolism
- Serious preventable event: blood incompatibility
- Catheter-associated urinary tract infections
- Pressure ulcers (decubitus ulcers)
- Vascular catheter-associated infection
- Surgical site infection: mediastinitis after coronary artery bypass graft surgery
- Hospital-acquired injuries: fractures, dislocations, intracranial injury, crushing injury, burn, and other unspecified effects of external causes

Cost-Based Weights   CMS will continue to use hospital costs rather than charges to set payment rates. The change was introduced in FY 2007 to better align payment with the costs of care by using estimated hospital costs rather than list changes to establish relative weights for the DRGs.

In FY 2008, hospitals were paid based on a blend of one-third charge-based weights and two-thirds hospital cost-based weights for DRGs. For 2009–2012, hospitals were paid 100 percent based on cost-based DRG weights.

Outlier Thresholds   In addition to the base payment for the DRGs, the law requires Medicare to make a supplemental payment to a hospital if its costs for treating a particular case exceed the usual Medicare payment for that case by a set threshold. Medicare sets the threshold for high-cost cases at an amount that is projected to make total "outlier payments" equal to 5.1 percent of the total inpatient payments.

For FY 2008, CMS adopted a high cost outlier threshold of $22,650, down from $24,485 in FY 2007. By better recognizing severity of illness in the DRG reforms that are part of the final rule, fewer cases were paid as outliers than if CMS had not reduced the fixed-cost loss amount.

Example

Let us calculate payments on a UB-92 form for DRG 1 (craniotomy, in an urban hospital, age > 17 years, except for trauma), with a federal rate of $400 and a geographical adjustment factor of 1.194. Total payment to the hospital, or cost to Medicare, would be provided by the formula:

$$\text{Payment} = \text{DRG weight} \times (\text{federal capital cost rate} \times \text{urban adjustment} \times \text{geographical adjustment factor})$$

OR

$$3.2713 \times (\$400 \times 1.03 \times 1.194) = \$1{,}609.24$$

2008: Projected Financial Impact Analysis   Reimbursement levels for hospitals under the 2008 rules varied depending on analysis. According to the CMS, payments as a whole to hospitals increased by $3.3 billion, or an average of 3.3 percent, to more than 3,500 acute-care hospitals in FY 2008–2009, provided they reported quality data to the agency. Projected aggregate spending is not expected to change under the MS-DRGs, but the CMS estimates that payments will be more likely to increase for hospitals serving more severely ill patients.

Payments are more likely to decrease for hospitals that treat less sickly patients—such as rural and specialty hospitals. Urban hospitals, for example, which are expected to get a 3.5 percent to 3.6 percent increase, generally treat sicker patients. Rural hospitals, by comparison, may get just a 0.9 percent increase, compared with the 3.7 percent increase they received for FY 2007.

The net effect is a slim increase, although hospital groups claim acute-care hospitals will lose billions of dollars under the CMS proposal to introduce an expanded system for evaluating patient severity.

DRGs and Case-Mix Severity Rates   It is important to recall that the average DRG weight for a hospital's Medicare volume is called the case mix index (CMI). This index is very useful in analysis because it indicates the relative severity of a patient population and is directly proportional to DRG payments.

When making comparisons among various hospitals or patient groups, the CMI can be used to adjust indicators such as average charges. (Case mix–adjusted average charges are the actual charges divided by the CMI. Such adjustments are sometimes referred to as "average charges for a weight of 1.0000.")

The DRG classification system is a useful tool for managing inpatient quality measurements and operating costs. It groups patients by diagnostic category for analysis and provides several key measurements of resource utilization (e.g., average length of stay *versus* published national averages).

Outpatient Prospective Patient System

The Outpatient Prospective Patient System (OPPS) was introduced in 2000 to reimburse hospitals based on over 660 Ambulatory Payment Classifications (APCs), as described below.

Services for Hospital Outpatients   These are paid per APC, as of the Balanced Budget Act of 1997, and as amended in 2000.

Example

Let us calculate payments for APC 80 (left heart catheterization) with a relative rate of 30 and a national conversion rate of $50, for a total of $1,500. Now, assuming a co-insurance rate of $840, to adjust actual payment to a hospital with a wage index of 1.200 (i.e., .60 labor-related), we use the formula:

$$\text{Total Payment} = (0.60\ \text{index} \times \$1,500 \times 1.200) + (0.40 \times \$1,500) = \$1,680$$

$$\text{Co-insurance} = (0.60 \times \$840 \times 1.200) + (0.40 \times \$840) = \$940.80$$

Extra payment may be available for outliers and transitional corridors.

Home Healthcare Agencies   As of October 1, 2000, these were paid per home health resource group (HHRG) if composed of six features: (1) 60-day episode, (2) case-mix adjustment, (3) outlier payments, (4) infrequent visit adjustments, (5) significantly changed conditions, and (6) beneficiaries who switch agencies.

As of December 26, 2007, home health (HH) PPS coding and billing information from CMS includes guidance to home health agencies (HHAs) on two issues related to the implementation of the refined HH PPS effective January 1, 2008:

- Billing options for HHAs whose systems are not ready to bill, based on the refined HH PPS, were released on January 1, 2008.
- There are upcoming revisions to the HH PPS grouper, which may result in underpayments to HHAs and the option available to HHAs on how to handle those potential underpayments. CMS released the revised grouper system software HAVEN™ 4.0 and associated pseudo-code on March 29, 2012.

New information regarding HH PPS case-mix refinements includes the following:

- Answers regarding transition episodes and steps for HHAs in completing the Outcome and Assessment Information Set (OASIS) assessments at the transition to the refined HH PPS January 1, 2008, have been determined. These will assure HHAs can create the proper payment group code for their claims.
- HH health insurance PPS (HIPPS) code weight table with spreadsheet maps for each of the 1,836 new HIPPS codes relates the refined HH PPS to its associated case-mix weight and supply payment amount.
- HH PPS claims processing changes are explained, with an outline describing the principal changes to HHA coding and billing that result from the refined HH PPS.

Medical Providers

These are paid per resource-based relative value unit (RBRVU), as of 1992, according to the lesser of the actual billed charges or the fee schedule amount. There are, however, two types of providers. Providers who accept Medicare assignment only bill the patient for the co-payment, which is usually 20 percent. Providers who do not accept Medicare assignment are offered a lower fee schedule of 95 percent of the approved schedule, which is a 115 percent maximum fee limit of the approved schedule.

Example

A participating physician's approved fee schedule charge of $100 would yield $80 from Medicare and $20 from the patient. A non-participating (Non-Par) doctor with charges of $200, and with an approved fee schedule of $100, would yield: $(0.95 \times \$100) \times 1.15 = \$109.25$ entirely from the patient. If the Non-Par doctor selects payment type on a case-by-case basis, Medicare will pay its portion of the bill directly to the physician, but the doctor must accept the Non-Par fee schedule. Continuing our example yields: $(0.8 \times \$95)$ plus the patient's co-payment of $(0.2 \times \$95)$, or $76 + $19 = $95.00.

Currently, there are more than 10,000 physician services designated by the current procedural terminology (CPT) or healthcare common procedure coding system codes. Each reflects the three major cost drivers of a particular procedure:

- **Physician work or the relative value unit of medical providers' work efforts (RVUw), pre-service, intra-service, and post-service:** Patients may exhibit anxiety when examined or during procedures, resulting in the need for additional time and effort by the physician to respond to and prepare for the examination or procedure. This uniformly adds more time and stress to the pre-service and intra-service period as doctors respond to constantly changing behavior, questions, and level of cooperation in varying specialties. Follow-up communication with employers, family, friends, and concerned others requires increased post-service time.

- **Practice expenses (RVUpe), including non-physician costs but excluding medical malpractice coverage premiums:** The practice expense component of the RBRVU scale includes clinical staff time, medical supplies, and medical equipment. The costs of supplies and equipment often are not proportional to practice size. Major factors affecting practice expense are the volume of telephone, cell, or Internet management services and the case management and administrative work required. For example, high patient turnover requires more examination rooms to maintain physician efficiency. High volume requires more clerical staff to deal with larger patient-flow volume and resulting phone calls, difficulties dressing and undressing patients, and increased complexity and time in collecting laboratory specimens. These factors must be accounted for in any resource-based practice expense study and in the resulting practice expense calculations for medical services.
- **Malpractice (RVUm) representing the cost of liability insurance:** The RBRVU system assigns RVUs to cover the malpractice expenses incurred by physicians. These malpractice RVUs, originally calculated for office-based physicians, may systematically undervalue the practice liability costs for some specialties. The prolonged statutes of limitation on some legal actions may result in increased malpractice risk exposure for physicians providing such services (e.g., pediatricians). The differences in exposure may not be calculated in the RBRVU system and were not included in initial studies. Specialty specific survey data for malpractice expense should be used for this component when assigning final RVU valuations. Without specialty-specific CPT codes, however, there is no way to do this objectively.

Skilled Nursing Facilities

These have been paid per Resource Utilization Group-III (RUG-III), with seven categories, six determinants, and 45 distinct patient types, since July 1, 1998. On January 1, 2006, a Medicare Part A skilled nursing facility (SNF) PPS price and a HIPPS coding update added nine new RUG-III categories that were effective for dates of service on or after January 1, 2006. In addition to these new RUG-III groups, CR3962 includes nine new HIPPS codes that are listed in Table 1.2.

The new Rule CR3962 also includes the following instructions:

- The case-mix system was refined and wage indices effective October 1, 2005, continue to apply.
- Medicare systems shall:
  - Apply the FY 2006 SNF PPS payment rates that are effective for dates of service on or after January 1, 2006, through September 30, 2006.
  - Discontinue temporary add-on payments, except for the add-on payment for residents with AIDS, with the implementation of the 53-group RUG-III coding system.
  - Edit the following therapy HIPPS codes, billed under the 0022 revenue code with units greater than 10 on bill types 18X or 21X, to ensure that at least one therapy ancillary revenue code, either 042X, 043X, or 044X, is reported on the claim: RHLXX, RHXXX, RLXXX, RMLXX, RMXXX, RVLXX, and RVXXX.
  - Edit the following therapy HIPPS codes, billed under the 0022 revenue code with units greater than 10 on bill types 18X or 21X, to ensure at least two different therapy ancillary revenue codes, either 042X and/or 043X and/or 044X, are reported on the claim: RULXX, RUXXX.*

---

* CMS information: Acting Administrator: Kerry Weems Publication 100-4, Transmittal# 630, CR# 3962 Medlearn Matters Number: MM3962 Related CR Release Date: July 29, 2005, Effective Date: January 1, 2006, Implementation Date: January 3, 2006.

TABLE 1.2
HIPPS Codes

HIPPS Code	Description		Plus Extensive Services	ADL Index
1. RUX XX	Rehabilitation	**Ultra High**	High	16-18
2. RUL XX	Rehabilitation	**Ultra High**	Low	7-15
3. RVX XX	Rehabilitation	**Very High**	High	16-18
4. RVL XX	Rehabilitation	**Very High**	Low	7-15
5. RHX XX	Rehabilitation	**High**	High	13-18
6. RHL XX	Rehabilitation	**High**	Low	7-12
7. RMX XX	Rehabilitation	**Medium**	High	15-18
8. RML XX	Rehabilitation	**Medium**	Low	7-14
9. RLX XX	Rehabilitation	**Low**		7-18

Note: The HIPPS code has five digits that include the following two components: a three-digit classification code assigned to each RUG-III code and a two-digit assessment indicator that specifies the type of Medicare-required assessment used to support billing.

Example

For an ultra-high rehabilitation patient with 720 minutes per week, the components under RUG-III might look like this:

Category	Dollar Amount	Adjustments
Nursing care	$142.32	
OT, PT, and speech therapy	186.01	
Capital, general and administration	55.88	
Total allowed per diem	384.21	
Labor percent		X 0.75888
Labor per diem	291.57	
Wage index		X 0.9907
Adjust labor per diem	288.86	
Non-labor per diem	92.86	
Case-mix adjusted per diem	$381.51	

Note: OT, occupational therapy; PT, physical therapy.

HIPPS Grouper Software and Documentation Codes

- **Medicare home health diagnosis coding:** Revised operational ICD-9-CM guidelines for several aftercare V-codes, effective December 1, 2005. A few changes were made to the V-Code Table in the updated version of the ICD-9-CM Official Guidelines for Coding and Reporting.
- **HH PPS grouper software and documentation (effective October 1, 2006):** Contains version 1.06 of the home health PPS case mix grouper software codes, which accommodates changes in OASIS reporting requirements effective October 1, 2006; also includes the grouper coding logic (pseudo-code), test records, and demonstration programs.
- **HH Consolidated Billing Master Code List:** An Excel workbook file containing a complete lists of all codes ever subject to the consolidated billing provision of HH PPS. A master list worksheet shows the dates each code was included and excluded from consolidated billing editing on claims, with associated CMS transmittal references. The master list also

associates each code with any related predecessor and successor codes. Supplemental worksheets show the list of included codes for each CMS transmittal to date.[*]

Example

The national unadjusted (wage index) per-visit rate payments paid per code were: home health aide, $44.37; medical social service, $153.55; occupational therapy, $105.44; skilled nursing care, $95.79; and speech pathology, $113.81.

COST ALLOCATION METHODS

The important point in cost allocation is that it is not objective—flexibility remains paramount. Generally, there are six types of cost allocation methods:

- **Step-down method** is the most common and allocates direct costs, plus allocated costs, to some department based on its ratio of services provided to that department.
- **Double distribution method** is a refinement of the step-down method because the original department remains open after allocating its costs and receives the costs of other indirect departments. A *multiple cost* distribution method recognizes that resources flow in multiple directions, not just from top to bottom. In this modified double distribution cost method, cost centers are not closed on the first pass of responsibility but are reconsidered in an upward direction. The process terminates when all costs are appropriately allocated.
- **Simultaneous equation method** is used to more precisely determine the exact cost allocation amounts.
- **Reciprocal cost method** recognizes that resources flow in many directions and requires considerable spreadsheet analysis to solve matrix-like cost allocation problems. Like other costing methods, the goal is to allocate revenues to costs.
- **Rate setting analysis,** a concept related to marginal cost and marginal revenue (see Understanding Marginal Costs and Marginal Revenue below), is reimbursement contract rate setting analysis, defined by this equation:

$$\text{Set Rate Price} = \text{Average Cost} + \text{Profit Requirements} + \text{Loss incurred on fixed-price patients}$$

- **Equipment payback method** involves making capital budgeting decisions that do not involve discounting cash flows. The payback period, expressed in years, is the length of time that it takes for the investment to recoup its initial cost out of the cash receipts it generates. The basic premise is that the sooner the cost of an investment can be recovered, the better that investment is. This method is most often used when considering equipment whose useful life is short and unpredictable, such as with medical instrumentation. When the same cash flow occurs every year, the formula is as follows:

$$\text{Investment Required} / \text{Net Annual Cash Inflow} = \text{Payback Period (\$100,000 X-ray machine)} / (\$35,000 \text{ annual additional revenue}) = 2.85 \text{ years}$$

UNDERSTANDING MARGINAL COSTS AND MARGINAL REVENUE

Marginal cost (MC) is the expense incurred to treat one additional unit (patient), whereas **marginal revenue** (MR) is the revenue received for treating that additional patient (unit). These two concepts are among the most important in the entire business environment of healthcare today.

---

[*] See http://www.cms.hhs.gov. This link includes the user manual for the above programs, with PDF downloads and Excel workbook spreadsheet files.

In the "clinical pathway" or "flow process," we assume that time remains on the doctor's schedule to treat any additional patients, and that an existing financial base exists to cover all fixed costs. This means that a managed care contract might be considered if the MR received by treating the patient is greater than the MC (i.e., MR > MC) incurred to treat that patient. Profit (total) will continue to increase up to the point where MR = MC; and then it will decrease as additional costs (e.g., more office space, equipment, or assistants) are incurred to accommodate the increased volume.

Maximum office efficiency (MOE) occurs where MR = MC. Because marginal cost can be thought of as the change in total costs associated with any given change in output quantity (Q), MC can be calculated from the following formula:

$$MC = \text{Change Total Costs} / \text{Change in Output Quantity}$$

$$MC = \text{Change TC} / \text{Change Q}$$

$$MC = CTC / CQ$$

Note that marginal costs depend only on changes in variable costs (VC). Because fixed costs do not change as output quantity changes, fixed costs do not influence marginal costs. MC is only influenced by variable costs.

The goal of such marginal cost and marginal revenue analysis is to treat the appropriate (optimum) number (quantity) of patients, not necessarily the most (maximum) number of patients. This may be contrary to the norm established in the fee-for-service medical payment environment, but this mindset must be broken to be efficient.

As a new medical office grows, marginal costs decline (Hultman, 1995). Later, as volume- and capacity-related inefficiencies begin to occur, marginal costs again increase. As illustrated in Table 1.3, MC almost always equals MR at a patient volume of 12 units, and total profit is the

TABLE 1.3
Example Marginal Cost

Patient Volume (A)	(Price) Marginal Revenue (B)	(A × B) Total Revenue (C)	Marginal Cost (D)	Total Cost (E)	(C − E) Total Profit (F)
0	20.1	00.00	NA	50	−50.00
1	20.1	20.10	15	65	−44.90
2	20.1	40.20	10	75	−34.80
3	20.1	60.30	8	83	−22.70
4	20.1	80.40	7	90	−9.60
5	20.1	100.50	6	96	4.45
6	20.1	120.60	4	100	20.60
7	20.1	140.70	4	104	36.70
8	20.1	160.80	6	110	50.80
9	20.1	180.90	10	120	60.90
10	20.1	201.00	12	132	69.00
11	20.1	221.10	16	142	73.10
12	20.1	241.20	20	168	73.20
13	20.1	261.30	22	190	71.30
14	20.1	281.40	25	215	66.40
15	20.1	301.50	30	245	56.50

Note: Total Costs (column E) are cumulative, derived by adding the marginal cost (D) to the prior total cost figure. This keeps a running total, adding each additional marginal cost to the total cost number.

greatest at this point. When volume increases beyond 12 patients, however, total revenue increases while total profit declines.

If the practice were to add patients beyond 12 units, the price (fees) would have to be raised to make the addition of these patients profitable. This cost/volume relationship exists in any mature medical office and emphasizes the point that the goal of an efficient office should be profit *optimization*, rather than revenue or volume *maximization*.

Additionally, the point of MOE is where patient volume, per-patient fee, and cost per patient produce the most profit, not necessarily the most revenue. "It is a unique equilibrium efficiency point for each healthcare organization and/or individual medical provider" (Hultman, 1995, 188).

In terms of managed care contracting, understanding the dynamics behind these numbers may provide an insight into making informed volume, fee, and profit decisions. Fee pricing and profit are "made at the margins," and an office with 60 percent overhead, for example, does not produce a marginal profit of 40 percent. Rather, the *total profit margin* is 40 percent, but the *marginal profit* might be only 10 percent or 15 percent for each new patient visit, and expense reduction programs will be more effective in increasing profit than increasing patient volume. Furthermore, consider that, if marginal profit for new patient business is 10 percent, cutting marginal costs by 33 percent (one-third) will produce the same profit as would increasing patient volume by almost 300 percent.

BREAK-EVEN COST/VOLUME ANALYSIS AND PROFITS

Break-even analysis is the concept used to determine or illustrate how many units of a product (medical intervention) or service (patients) must be sold (seen or treated) to make a profit at each sales volume level. The average number of active patients varies by physician and by specialty. For example:

- Internists typically treat from 1,500 to 2,500 patients a year.
- Pediatricians typically treat from 2,500 to 3,500 patients per year.
- Family practice physicians typically treat from 2,500 to 4,000 patients per year.
- Podiatrists typically treat from 2,250 to 4,500 patients per year.
- Concierge physicians typically engage 600 enrolled patients for treatment per year.

To illustrate the concept of break-even analysis relative to profit maximization and the costing concepts just discussed, let's use three more modified examples, again given by Dr. Jon Hultman.

Example One

The three doctors of ABC practice own a clinic whose fixed costs (FC) are $200,000. The average variable cost per patient (VC/PP) is $22. The break-even point (BEP) is reached when revenue and total costs intersect at approximately 2,500 patients. The VC ($22 × 2,500 = $55,000) plus the FC ($200,000) equals the total costs of $255,000, which at the BEP are equal to the total revenues, resulting in an economically neutral (break-even) clinical operation, as seen in the spreadsheet below:

Break-Even Analysis						
FC	VC/PP	REV/PP	Volume	Total Costs	Total Revenue	Profit
200,000	$22	$102	2,500	$255,000	$255,000	0
200,000	22	102	3,000	266,000	306,000	40,000
200,000	22	102	6,000	332,000	612,000	280,000
200,000	22	102	9,000	398,000	918,000	520,000

To determine revenue per patient (REV/PP), first divide the total collections by the number of unique patient visits. From this average REV, deduct the average overhead costs per visit. However, because surgery brings in more revenue than other services, REV per surgical patient may be calculated separately.

Furthermore, it can be appreciated that, when volume increases, total profit increases at a faster rate than total costs. This is known as high or positive clinic operating leverage.

Example Two

Now, if the doctors of ABC clinic accept a discounted managed care contract where the average REV/PP declines from $102 to $75, the BEP in patient volume is now increased to 3,774 patients. At this volume, profit is at $22 and total revenue and total costs are about equal. At 6,000 patients, profit is $118,000 (77 percent decline) and at 9,000 patients, profit is at $277,000 (47 percent decline). To get an appreciation for the leveraging effect of this decline in price, recognize a price decrease of 26 percent (from $102 to $75), as seen in the spreadsheet below:

Leveraged Break-Even Analysis						
FC	VC/PP	REV/PP	Volume	Total Costs	Total Revenue	Profit
200,000	$22	$75	2,500	$255,000	$187,500	−$67,500
200,000	22	75	3,000	266,000	225,000	−41,000
200,000	22	75	3,774	283,000	283,050	22
200,000	22	75	6,000	332,000	450,000	118,000
200,000	22	75	9,000	398,000	675,000	277,000

Example Three

The final example for ABC clinic is a very likely scenario under many managed care contracts today. A decrease in fees (from $102 to $75), combined with an increase in the fixed costs ($250,000) involved in servicing the contract, is illustrated below:

Non-Leveraged Break-Even Analysis						
FC	VC/PP	REV/PP	Volume	Total Costs	Total Revenue	Profit
250,000	$22	$75	2,500	$305,000	$187,000	−$67,500
250,000	22	75	3,000	316,000	225,000	−41,000
250,000	22	75	4,717	353,774	353,775	1
250,000	22	75	6,000	382,000	450,000	68,000
250,000	22	75	9,000	448,000	675,000	227,000

At a patient volume of 9,000, profit declines by 56 percent, along with the salaries of each doctor. If volume dropped to 6,000 patients, profit would decline to 87 percent. In order to produce the original profit of $520,000, volume would have to increase by 61 percent (14,528 patients), an unlikely scenario. ABC clinic profit will be determined by its cost position and efficiency in managing a larger volume of patients, along with clinic overhead expenses.

As long as the revenue received from a medical service is above the variable cost of providing that service, it is said to be making a contribution to fixed costs.

Additionally, any managed care contract that is below a clinic's variable costs will lower its profit and should not be considered. Therefore, an aggressive cost reduction program, along with more modest patient volume increases, might be a prudent strategy for the doctors of ABC clinic to pursue.

AMBULATORY PAYMENT CLASSIFICATIONS AND PHYSICIAN FISCAL CREDENTIALING

All healthcare administrators, financial executives, and doctors should be aware of the set of Medicare payment regulations implemented in 1997. APCs, originally termed ambulatory payment groups (APGs), have replaced existing cost-based or cost-plus-reimbursement contracts for all outpatient services. Much like DRGs, which were enacted for hospitals in 1983 and divided disease management into 497 groups (based on ICD-9-CM* diagnoses, procedures, age, sex, and discharge disposition), APCs have changed the hospital and Independent Physician Association (IPA) landscape. The federal government and the HCFA† planned this shift to prospective payments through its OPPS for more than a decade, as a result of the Omnibus Budget Reconciliation Act of 1989. Unlike DRGs however, with their multi-year phase-in period, APCs had no similar grace period, and hospitals, IPAs, and other outpatient centers needed to be compliant immediately. Thus, decreases in reimbursement correlate to costing and cost modeling behavior.

AMBULATORY PAYMENT CLASSIFICATIONS

The APC system was designed to explain the amount and type of resources utilized in outpatient visits. Each APC consists of patients with similar characteristics and resource usage and includes only the facility portion of the visit, with no impact on providers who will continue to be paid from the traditional CPT fee schedule and modifier system. The APC system effectively eliminates separate payments for operating, recovery, treatment, and observation room costs and charges. Anesthesia, medical and surgical supplies, drugs (except those used in chemotherapy), blood, casts, splints, and donated tissue are also packaged into the APC. Unbundled, fragmented, or otherwise separated codes, which are common in the CPT fee schedule, have been eliminated from claims prior to payment.

APCs group most outpatient services into 346 classes according to ICD-9-CM diagnosis and CPT procedures. This includes 134 surgical APCs, 46 significant APCs, 122 medical APCs, and 44 ancillary APCs. Surgical, significant, and ancillary APCs are assigned using only the CPT procedure codes, while medical APCs are based on a combination of ICD-9-CM and evaluation and management CPT codes.

Example: APC payment calculations

APC payments are determined by multiplying an annually updated "relative weight" for a given service by an annually updated "conversion factor." CMS publishes the annual updates to relative weights and the conversion factor in the November *Federal Register* (2013). The APC conversion factor for 2007 was $61.468.

To calculate the APC payment for APC 006 (includes incision and drainage of simple abscess-CPT 10060):

Given:
Relative weight for APC 006 = 1.510
Conversion factor for 2007 = $61.468
1.510 × $61.468 = $92.82 payment for APC 006 for year 2007 (for the "average U.S. hospital").

There is further modification of the APC payment according to adjustments for local wage indices.

Medicare determined that 60 percent of the APC payment is due to employee wage costs. Because different areas of the country have widely divergent local wage scales, 60 percent of each APC payment is adjusted according to specific geographic locality.

---

* The International Classification of Diseases, Ninth Revision, Clinical Modification (ICD-9-CM) is the official system used to assign codes to diagnoses and procedures associated with healthcare in the United States.
† The HCFA was renamed the Centers for Medicare and Medicaid Services (CMS) in 2001.

The full impact of this regulation on hospitals, healthcare facilities, outpatient ambulatory centers, and IPAs is still emerging, but generally it has decreased reimbursement for more than half of all ambulatory healthcare facilities since its inception. This occurred because the initial variable used in reimbursement determinations is the principal procedure. Payments are then calculated for each APC by multiplying the facility rate by the APC weight, and multiplying this product by a discount factor (if multiple APCs are performed during the same visit). Total payment is the sum of the payments for all APCs. However, no adjustment provisions were made for outliers or teaching facilities, rural hospitals, disproportionate share, or specialty hospitals or facilities.

Facilities affected by Medicare's OPPS include those designated by the Secretary of Health and Human Services, such as:

- Hospital outpatient surgical centers
- Hospital outpatient departments not part of the consolidated billing for skilled nursing facility residents
- Certain preventative services and supplies, covered by Medicare Part B inpatient services if Part A coverage is exhausted
- Partial hospitalization services in community mental health centers

Exempted facilities include clinical laboratories, ambulance services, end-stage renal disease centers, occupational and speech therapy services, mammography centers, and durable medical equipment suppliers.

The remaining facilities may experience a slight payment increase if they convert their management information systems to APC-compliant hardware and software. Compliance measures include electronic interconnectivity, data storage, retrieval, and the security features mandated by the Health Insurance Portability and Accountability Act (HIPAA) of 1996. Although the Balanced Budget Act of 1997 required HCFA to implement an OPPS by January 1, 1999, Y2K concerns delayed implementation until after January 1, 2000. This delay led to a 2001 implementation date and functionally to an April 2005 date, and beyond in some cases. However, APCs were fully implemented in 2008–2009.

Some hospitals languished and collapsed under the DRG system, while others flourished. If hospitals are to be successful in the OPPS/APC era, transition planning, monitoring, and implementation must continue, and the concept of surgeon or "proceduralist" fiscal credentialing will gain momentum in the future.

PHYSICIAN FISCAL CREDENTIALING

In the competitive market, practitioners are placed under pressure to demonstrate the economic and clinical value of care. This is especially true for procedurally based physicians and surgeons who perform costly interventions in the outpatient setting (i.e., surgery and related invasive procedures). The management methodology of "fiscal outcomes review" is one tool being used to evaluate such care. Initially developed for internal corporate management as an executive decision support system (EDSS), the process is being used as an external cost control technique to economically credential providers of procedural care.

In fact, some suggest that APCs bring the possibility of physician financial profiling a step closer to reality. This occurs because poor or delayed physician documentation often delays the submission of hospital bills. Additionally, unlike other hospital services, late charges are usually disallowed once the appropriate APCs are determined and paid. Therefore, resource utilization by physicians will continue to come under increased scrutiny.

Higher expense medications, for example, often represent pure cost and provide little added revenue. Choices of medications and the cost of supplies used go directly to the hospital's bottom line, and there may be more economic impetus to develop practice guidelines. In addition, insurance coders and billers look to physicians to appropriately and comprehensively identify their own procedures in order to assign the most accurate codes.

Consequently, the economic outcomes analysis of one or more procedures represents an attempt to gather, allocate, analyze, and interpret meaningful information relative to the practitioner or venue of performance. When used to establish comparative norms or when compared to the appropriate benchmarks, cost and charge reductions are documented without compromising quality. The long-held heuristic beliefs are then corroborated or dismissed.

Managerial Accounting Methodology

Accepting the assumption that financial instability is the ultimate healthcare liability, practice survival can be equated to the basic economic equation of net income = revenue – expenses. In the usual retail marketplace, income can be augmented by increasing price and/or volume, because pre-existing cost reductions are a given in the business community.

In the fee-for-medical service generation, an increase in service charges is possible and limited only by individual provider competition, not by aggregate payer competition. In the new environment of cost containment and managed care, this strategy is unacceptable: Price increase is of limited value in that most reimbursement schedules have switched to a fixed dollar payment methodology, and cost shifting is no longer a reasonable strategy.

On the expense side of the accounting equation there are two components. First are the traditional cost reduction methods of corporate downsizing, restructuring, re-engineering, and other cost containment strategies designed to reduce both fixed and variable operational overhead. Fixed costs are costs that remain constant regardless of changes in the level of medical activity, and variable costs are those that vary in direct proportion to changes in the level of activity. Mixed costs contain both fixed and variable components. Unfortunately, addressing only this side of the equation without increasing revenues usually results in a one-time charge reduction because some baseline cost of business always remains in place.

The second component of the accounting equation focuses on the efficiency in the way procedurally based care is delivered. For example, Table 1.4 illustrates the economic implications of hospital outpatient surgical resources consumed by a prototypical procedure, based on payment category.

For those insured patients covered under a fee-for-service or a discounted fee-for-service arrangement, the incentive is to acquire, maintain, and consume every patient resource possible. Under a per-procedure case in which fixed dollar reimbursement is based only on the patient's diagnosis, an outpatient admission is still desirable, if medically justified. Therefore, it is economically advantageous to reduce length of stay to outpatient status, if possible, or to perform the procedure in a less costly venue but still consume as many resources as possible.

Under the per-treatment, per-diem payment model, an outpatient admission and a longer length of stay is desirable because it is during the later stage of hospitalization that the per-diem rate begins to cover its costs. However, hospital denial is possible if the patient remains hospitalized longer than clinically necessary. The commonality of these categories, using the basic accounting equation (net income = revenue – expenses), is the fact that no additional revenue is gained from additional resources (inputs) provided. When marginal costs (cost of producing one additional unit of service

TABLE 1.4
Outpatient Hospital Incentives by Payer Class

Payer Category	Outpatient Admission	Resource Consumption
Fee-for-service	Increased	Increased
Discounted fee-for-service	Increased	Increased
Per surgical case	Increased	Decreased
Per treatment day	Decreased	Decreased

or product) exceed marginal benefits (revenue gained by producing one additional unit of service or product), additional revenues should not be pursued. However, decreasing costs will indirectly increase profits through a greater contribution margin, which is defined as the amount remaining from service revenue after variable costs have been deducted. This approach first contributes to fixed expenses, and then toward profits for the relevant range.

Continuous Quality Improvement

It is not enough to simply share data and highlight variances in care. Accounting numbers and raw data, regardless of etiology, are not informative until gathered, collated, interpreted, and disseminated. Once this is done, information must be used to develop positive alternative structures for care. This is accomplished by empowering physician leaders, who in turn educate those staff members who will take responsibility for driving the process to improve outcomes of care. Areas for continuous quality improvement (CQI) include:

- Physician education and information sharing
- Benchmarking and process improvement
- Utilization review and case management
- Guidelines, criteria, policies, and procedures
- Critical pathway methods and algorithms
- Outcomes management and financial incentives

These CQI areas, used for refinement, are not mutually exclusive, although each practice or clinic must decide which tools will be most effective in meeting corporate objectives.

As part of the CQI process, information sharing and comparing performance outcomes, both internally and externally, present each physician with the opportunity to evaluate his or her activities compared to peers. Internal benchmarking and process improvement implies identification of the optimal performers for the selected procedure and uses them as a model for the best demonstrated practice patterns. External benchmarking implies comparing selected outcomes to other practices in an effort to identify optimal treatment goals for the selected procedure. Once identified, techniques can be learned, taught, and adopted by other offices using the step-by-step process traditionally performed as part of a CQI program. Obviously, the comparison of a homogeneous group of patients is needed to accurately interpret this type of comparative analysis, and one will need to apply some type of case-mix, severity index, or risk-adjustment modifiers to validate conclusions.

Comparative information for single procedure events has become more prevalent. Increasingly, care trails, algorithms, or the critical (clinical) path method (CPM) developed by physician consensus is used as a framework for reducing variation in patients moving through an office system in an uncomplicated fashion.

Example

Using the CPM for data recapture, a coordinated economic outcomes review analysis of a simple orthopedic surgical procedure was performed at the Podiatric Medical Ambulatory Surgery Center (PMASC) in Atlanta, Georgia.

The first step involved the development of critical pathways for the selected surgical procedure (CPT #28296: hallux valgus repair) performed at PMASC using standard methodologies. In this case, the engineering concept of the CPM is used to determine the cost, quality, and time aspects of the project, in particular cost, time, and quality trade-offs.

Using the CPM, activities can be performed at extra cost to speed up completion time (e.g., immediate laboratory values, bone fixation type, no second surgical opinion or pre-certification, etc.). CPM can identify a project's critical path, in other words, activities that cannot be delayed (e.g., surgeon, anesthesia, radiographs, central supply), as well as the slack time that can be somewhat delayed without lengthening the project completion time (e.g., antibiotics). Realistically, critical activities in the relevant range constitute a small minority of total activities.

After defining the project (CPT # 28296: hallux valgus repair), the next step is to make a standard template or *network* from which all critical pathways will be developed. A crucial component of the system is the ability to track pathway activities that can then be attributed to physician, patient, or system-specific variations. Finally, all project events are concluded when the patient is discharged from immediate surgical service. An example of the pathway for this simple orthopedic procedure appears in the table below.

PROCEDURE CRITICAL PATHWAY

Patient Code Name:_____

_____ASA 1 _____ASA 2 _____ASA 3 _____ASA 4 ____Diabetes

Activity	Pre-Surgical	Intra-Operative	Post-Surgical
Referral	Physician/Patient/Plan/etc.		
Prior Care	Physician//MD/DO/DPM/etc.		
History and Physical	PCP/Surgeon/etc.		
Laboratory	CBC/SMAC/Diff/etc.		
Antibiosis		IV/PO and Agent	
Surgery		Procedure (CPT #)	
Fixation		Wire(s) or Screw(s)	
Radiology		A-P/Lat/Oblique Views	
Infection		Yes or No	
Results		Satisfactory/ Unsatisfactory	
Orthoses (post-op)		Required or Not Required	

POSSIBLE PATHWAY SOLUTION

A possible path is to use the CPM to select those cost drivers most suitable for financial process improvement. Economic priorities may be based on volume, cost, risk, specialty, procedure, or any pertinent feature or institution, within its relevant range.

Finally, relevant cost drivers are gathered. This table lists the eight-tiered allocation process, in seven-dollar amounts and one-time allotment, as applied to the procedure.

Average Charges per Procedure									
(DR)	(#)	(Labs)	(Pharma)	(Anes)	(Fix)	[Time]	(Radio)	(Sup)	=Total
AB	2	150	197	545	33	[155]	142	2,724	= $3,790
CD	4	358	430	1,029	66	[480]	328	4,260	= 6,471
EF	5	231	592	1,293	83	[430]	340	5,190	= 7,729
GH	5	540	748	1,925	83	[555]	340	5,190	= 8,826
IJ	14	856	1,810	3,802	0	[1,045]	1,148	12,340	= 19,956
Total	30	2,135	3,770	8,594	265	[2,665]	2,298	29,704	= 46,772
Avg.	6	427	755	1,719	53	[533]	460	5,941	= 9,354
AVG.	1	71	126	286	9	88	77	990	= 1,559

As the current healthcare and business industrial complex merges, increasing emphasis will be placed on data analysis and economic outcomes as a method to identify ways to improve both the inputs (costs) and outputs (quality) of care. Third-party payers will use this information in an effort to identify and selectively contract with efficient ambulatory centers and purge the miscreants. Later, managed care organizations (MCOs) will use such data to evaluate physician performance profiles as a form of second tier "economic credentialing" to screen healthcare providers prior to center entry and to continually monitor performance as a barometer for continued participation in the plan. Although often counterintuitive, this credentialing will not be heuristic but may take the form of the business model presented in this review.

Nevertheless, we might consider if the PASC administrators were correct about the following parameters:

- Selection of the CPM mode
- Selection of the CPM cost driver
- Average charges per procedure
- Relevant service production range

Although raw data as captured above may not be statistically significant, various aggregate patterns and trend information may be ascertained when evaluating the eight cost drivers represented in this case model. Of course, the use of other drivers is encouraged as individual circumstances dictate. For example:

(1) The average laboratory charge was $71. Preoperative laboratory costs may be decreased in healthy patients and increased in non-ASA Class I patients. In those cases of true medical necessity, MC = MB or MB > MC.

(2) Preoperative antibiosis was a component of the $126 pharmacy charge that might be safely omitted because IV prophylaxis is not medically indicated for a virgin brief surgical procedure. Oral agents after surgery are also not recommended, as the potential for antibiotic resistance is likewise reduced. In this instance, the MC > MB.

(3) Average anesthesia charges of $286 may be reduced in the psychologically prepared patient, who can benefit from effective but less expensive anxiolytic methods of analgesia, such as nitrous oxide sedation and monitored anesthesia care. Relative to patient educational expenses, MB > MC in almost all cases.

(4) Fixation (screws or K-wires) is a $9 average charge that may be obviated, but marginal benefits likely supersede marginal costs if complications attributed to non-use result in excessive osseous motion (i.e., MB > MC). Fixation may therefore be considered cost-effective relative to the charge expense incurred through use.

(5) Slow surgeon (89-minute time driver) may not necessarily increase charges if equipment such as a tourniquet or electrocautery is not used to decrease time in the operating room. In other words, anatomical dissection and hand ligatures are less costly than these specific equipment expense drivers (i.e., MC > MB).

(6) The average radiology charge of $77 can be reduced by taking two views (anteroposterior and lateral) after surgery, rather than three views. Of course, in questionable cases, X-rays are an extraordinary value when comparable to potential dislocation complications (MB > MC).

(7) The total central supply charges of $990 include such items as sutures, suction tips, saw blades, blankets, drape sheets, catheters, irrigation fluids, and scrub materials, among others, which may be carefully evaluated to further reduce expenses. Many of these supplies can be considered incidental and may be omitted, reduced, or substituted without compromise (MC > MB). Of course, further charge allocations can be continued with increasing smaller drivers, as required.

THE PMASC ANSWER?

The aggregate charges for the procedure performed at PMASC were approximately $1,559. This might be compared to a $3,000–$3,500 relevant range from a local community hospital, or to a $2,500–$3,000 range for another competing ambulatory surgical center. Thus, hospital outpatient charges exceeded charges in this examined economic model (MC >> MB), all things being equal (*ceteris paribus*), and should be economically reconsidered.

CPM TERMINOLOGY

Project: Surgical procedure identification by means of CPT code number.

Activity: Task required by the project that consumes economic resources, such as radiographs, laboratory tests, fixation devices, or central supply items.

Event: Identifiable activity end state occurring at a particular point, such as anesthesia operating room time.

Network: Combined activities (arcs) and events (nodes) that define the surgical procedure.

Path: Series of connected activities between any two events in a network, or the entire process of examining, testing, scheduling, performing, and follow-up after the surgery.

Critical: Activity, event, or path that, if adverse or absent, will hinder completion of the procedure or surgical project (e.g., aberrant laboratory value).

It is important to keep in mind that the more paths, subsets, or decision points that exist for the CPM, the fewer the number of patients that will complete the actual pathway. Moreover, while there is no single standard definition of a successful procedural or surgical outcome, financial managers usually refer to some combination of patient satisfaction, cost, and quality (e.g., function, alignment, pain amelioration, radiographs, or infection control). Although several of these parameters are predisposed to patient (pain, function) and physician (alignment, scarification) subjectivity, others are more objectively quantified (infection, radiographs, range of motion), and all are overlapping. Regardless of definition, there is a growing demand for aggregate economic procedural outcomes that will hold physicians more accountable for the fiscal result of procedural care.

One of the most effective ways to change adverse behavior is to align financial incentives to a physician and his or her behavior. Although it is considered illegal to directly reimburse physicians for efficient behavior, much of this is changing as medicine moves into a more integrated healthcare delivery system.

COST OF HOSPITAL CAPITAL AND CREDIT

Finally, the subprime mortgage and commercial bank crisis of 2008 has caused lenders to tighten their practices, and this is having an impact on the revenue and cost management structure of hospitals and large healthcare organizations. Recent comments from Moody's Investors Service are cautiously pessimistic about the financial future of U.S. non-profit hospitals in the short term.

In comments on its preliminary FY 2007 median ratios for not-for-profit hospitals, Moody's implied that, while hospitals are surviving in 2008, the outlook remains grim in the industry. Noted key volume and revenue growth measures are not robust, and newly reported FY 2007 medians may not hold up. As hospitals are still losing liquidity, real concerns exist for both for-profit and not-for-profit facilities through at least 2014, pending political fiat.

For example, it is now more difficult to restructure longer-term corporate debt regardless of hospital bond credit ratings (Triple B rating or higher). In addition, despite the potential for funding from private investment firms, banks, and private equity funds—all of which are seeking quality, for-profit (bond/debt) issues—tax-exempt debt for non-profits still seems the most cost-effective source of funding, despite the costs of bond insurance.

CONCLUSION

Of course, the full impact of the hospital credit crunch and its impact on the cost of capital have not yet been discerned, as illustrated by the stunning collapse of the legendary investment bank Bear-Stearns on March 16, 2008, the "flash-crash" in 2008–2009, the presidential election of 2012, and implementation of the Affordable Care Act (ACA) of 2014.

CHECKLIST: Healthcare Entity Cost Accounting Concerns	YES	NO
Do I know and share medical cost and financial business data within my department?	o	o
Do I allocate fixed cost to:		
enterprise revenue centers?	o	o
department revenue centers?	o	o
Do I understand what costs are:		
fixed?	o	o
variable?	o	o
hybrid?	o	o
extraneous?	o	o
controllable?	o	o
opportunity?	o	o
sunk?	o	o
carrying?	o	o
future?	o	o
overtime premium?	o	o
health sector costs?	o	o
Do I know the direct cost of a patient visit?	o	o
Do I understand the variable costs of a patient visit?	o	o
Do I know the marginal cost of a patient visit?	o	o
Do I know the marginal revenue produced by a patient visit?	o	o
Do I know the margin profit of a patient visit?	o	o
Do I know the total costs of a patient visit?	o	o
Have I familiarized myself with FASB and CASB accounting?	o	o
Which is more appropriate for my circumstances?		
Do I distinguish between product and healthcare service costs?	o	o
Do I account for relevant costs?	o	o
Do I consider relevant costs in my budget?	o	o
Do I know what costs are avoidable in my budget?	o	o
Do I understand my differential costs?	o	o
Do I perform simple statistical cost analysis for my department or center?	o	o
Do I know my total human resource costs?	o	o
Do I know my idle time labor costs?	o	o
Do I know my fringe benefit costs?	o	o
Do I know the procedure for allocating costs using:		
the step-down method?	o	o
the double distribution method?	o	o
the simultaneous equation method?	o	o
Do I know why it may be proper to allocate costs from a cost center to other cost or responsibility centers or departments?	o	o
Does my healthcare organization perform physician fiscal credentialing?	o	o
If not, does it plan to in the future?	o	o
Does my healthcare organization maintain a posture of continuous financial quality improvement?	o	o
If not, does it plan to in the future?	o	o
Do I perform break-even analysis for my department?	o	o
Do I perform equipment pay-back analysis for my department?	o	o
Do I calculate rate-setting procedures for my department?	o	o

Do I seek to reduce avoidable costs?	o	o
Do I anticipate future costs?	o	o
Do I consider sunk costs properly considering CCA, CMA, or CASB standards?	o	o
Am I familiar with the following prospective payment schemes:		
diagnosis-related groups (DRGs)?	o	o
Medicare severity-adjusted diagnostic-related groups (MS-DRGs)?	o	o
ambulatory payment classifications (APCs)?	o	o
home health resource groups (HHRGs)?	o	o
resource utilization groups-III (RUGs-III)?	o	o
resource-based relative value units (RBRVUs)?	o	o
Do I understand the concept of case-severity mixes?	o	o
Do I understand the concept of outlier thresholds?	o	o
Do I understand the concept of cost-based weighted averages?	o	o
Does my hospital have a policy on "never-events"?	o	o
Am I familiar with it?	o	o

CASE MODEL 1

THE HOPE OUTREACH MEDICAL CLINIC

The Hope Outreach Medical Clinic (HOMC) is a private, for-profit, single-specialty medical clinic in a southeastern state. It submitted its bi-annual request for proposal (RFP) to continue its current managed care fixed-rate contract. Upon review of the RFP, however, Sunshine Indemnity Insurance Company, the managed care organization (MCO), denied the contract request for the upcoming year.

In shock, the clinic's CEO asked the clinic's administrator to work with its legal team to develop a defensible estimate of economic damages that would occur as a result of the lost contract. The clinic intended to bring suit against the MCO for breach of contract. However, the administrator is not an attorney and is loathe to enter the fray. After consideration, however, he decided to assist in filing the statement of claim (SOC) because he realized that changes in patient services (unit) volume would be a valid economic surrogate. He then requested the following information from his controller so that he could develop a change in economic profit [damages] estimate:

- Change in patient visits (unit) volume
- Fees (price) per patient (unit)
- Marginal (incremental) cost per patient (unit)
- Change in current fees (prices)
- Patient volume (units) affected

Key Issues

(1) Fee (price) per patient (units) may be obtained from the fee schedule used by the MCO to pay HOMC.
(2) Marginal (incremental) costs per patient (unit) are approximated using variable costs.
(3) Higher cost payers exist because lower patient volumes raise the average cost per patient (unit) due to existing fixed costs.

The administrator's financial work-product to estimate monetary damages and assist the legal team is explained as follows:

CHANGE IN PROFIT FRAMEWORK ESTIMATE

Change in profit = change in patient (unit) volume ×
[fee (price per patient unit) – incremental (marginal) cost per patient (unit)] –
[change in current price (fees) × patient (unit) volume affected]

CASE MODEL 2

DR. JOSEPH SPINE: OSTEOPATHIC PHYSICIAN

Dr. Joseph Spine, an osteopathic physician, wants to install a new large piece of equipment in place of several smaller ones in his clinic. He will need to hire a therapist to administer the larger equipment and estimates that incremental annual revenues and expenses associated with the equipment would be as follows:

Revenues	$10,000
Less variable expenses	3,000
Contribution margin	7,000
Less fixed expenses	
Insurance	900
Salaries	2,600
Depreciation	1,500
	5,000
Net Income	**$2,000**

Parts for the equipment would cost $15,000 and have a 10-year life. The old machines could now be sold for a $1,000 salvage value. Dr. Spine requires a payback of 5 years or less on all investments.

Solution

Net Income (above)	$2,000
Add: non-cash deduction depreciation	1,500
New annual cash flow	3,500
Investment in the new equipment	15,000
Deduct: salvage value of old machines	1,000
Investment required	$14,000

Payback Period = ($14,000 × 10 years) / ($3,500 × 10 years) = $140,000 / $35,000 = 4.0 years

Key Issues

Was Dr. Spine correct or not with regard to:

- Revenues?
- Fixed and variable expenses?
- Contribution margins?
- Insurance?
- Salaries?
- Depreciation?

Using the framework reflected in this chapter, also consider what changes the osteopathic clinic might implement to ensure that it regularly makes good decisions on such issues as medical equipment payback analysis.

CASE MODEL 3

THE FEDERAL VETERAN'S ADMINISTRATION HEALTHCARE SYSTEM

Because the Federal Veteran's Administration (VA) Healthcare System does not routinely prepare patient bills, VA researchers and analysts at the Health Economic Research Center (HERC) must rely on other sources to calculate the cost of patient encounters (http://www. herc.research.va.gov).

Three cost accounting alternatives are available: mixed (micro) cost methods (MCM), average cost methods (ACM), and decision support systems (DSS).

1. **Mixed (Micro) Cost Methods** include three approaches:
    a. **Direct Measurement** is used to determine the cost of new interventions and programs unique to VA. Inputs such as staff time and supply costs are directly measured to develop a precise cost estimate. The time of each type of staff is estimated, and its cost is determined from accounting data. The analyst may directly observe staff time, have staff keep diaries of their activities, or survey managers. The cost of supplies, equipment, and other expenses must also be determined. Program volume is determined from administrative records, and average cost is estimated. When units of service are not homogeneous, unit costs may be estimated by an accounting approach, by applying estimates of the relative cost of each service, or via an econometric approach.
    b. **Pseudo-bill** method combines VA utilization data with unit costs from non-VA sources to estimate the cost of patient care. This is commonly referred to as the pseudo-bill method because the itemized list of costs is analogous to a fee-for-service hospital bill. The unit cost of each item may be estimated by using Medicare reimbursement rates, the charge rates of an affiliated university medical center, or some other non-VA sector source.
    c. **Cost Function** method requires detailed cost and utilization data for a specific, non-VA service to simulate the cost of a comparable VA service. If suitable non-VA data are available, a function can be estimated using cost-adjusted charges as the dependent variable and information about the encounter as the independent variable. VA costs are simulated using VA utilization data and the function's parameters. Its chief advantage is that it requires less data than is needed to prepare a pseudo-bill, making it a more economical way of (micro) mixed costing.
2. **Average Cost Methods (ACM)** combine relative values derived from non-VA cost datasets, VA utilization data, and department costs obtained from the VA cost distribution report. Every encounter with the same characteristics is assumed to cost the same. Average cost estimates are needed because detailed mixed-costing is too time-consuming and laborious a method to apply it to all possible healthcare utilization. In many studies, and for some of the healthcare utilization in nearly every study, an average cost method can be used.
3. **Decision Support Systems,** a computerized cost-allocation system adopted by the VA, is beginning to be used by researchers. DSS staff is undertaking the difficult

task of allocating costs to VA healthcare products and patients' stays. If DSS is found to be accurate, it will be an extremely useful source of VA cost information. Validation is an important step in the use of DSS data. Work with DSS to date suggests that analysts should not rely exclusively on DSS cost estimates.

Key Issues

Was the VA healthcare system correct with regard to using its current cost accounting systems?

- Mixed (micro) cost methods?
- Health economic research center?
- Average cost methods (ACM)?
- Decision support systems (DSS)?

It became intuitively obvious that, even if a reliable DSS could be found, the financial manager should not rely exclusively on DSS cost estimates.

WEBSITES

http://www.MedicalExecutivePost.com (News, Trends and Career for Doctors and Their Advisors), iMBA, Inc., Norcross, GA, 2013.

http://www.hcfa.gov/pubforms/transmit/A002360.pdf (Hospital Outpatient Prospective Payment System (OPPS) Implementation Instructions).

http://www.hcfa.gov/medicare/hopsmain.htm (Overview of the Hospital Outpatient Prospective Payment System).

http://www.census.gov/epcd/www/naics.html (North American Industry Classification System).

https://acquisition.gov (Acquisition Central).

http://www.herc.research.va.gov (United States Department of Veterans Affairs, Health Economics Resource Center).

REFERENCES

APC Payment Manual. New York: St. Anthony Publishing, 2006.

APC Training and Implementation Manual. New York: St. Anthony Publishing, 2007.

Brunner, R. *Case Studies in Finance*. Boston, MA: McGraw-Hill Primis, 2000.

Centers for Disease Control. International Classification of Diseases, Tenth Revision, Clinical Modification (ICD-10-CM), 2013. http://www.cdc.gov/nchs/icd/icd10cm.htm

Centers for Medicare and Medicaid Services. Home. http://www.cms.gov. 2012.

Cleverly, W.O. and Cameron, A.E. *Essentials of Healthcare Finance*. Sudbury, MA: Jones and Bartlett, 2005.

Federal Register. Medicare Program; Changes to the Hospital Inpatient Prospective Payment Systems and Fiscal Year 2008 Rates. https://www.federalregister.gov/articles/2007/08/22/07-3820/medicare-program-changes-to-the-hospital-inpatient-prospective-payment-systems-and-fiscal-year-2008, 2007.

Federal Register. The Daily Journal of the United States Government. https://www.federalregister.gov/. 2013.

Financial Management of the Medical Practice. Chicago: AMA Press, 1996.

Finkler, S.A. *Issues in Cost Accounting for Healthcare Organizations*. Gaithersburg, MD: Aspen Publishers, 2005.

Gallagher, P.E., Klemp, T., and Smith, S.L., eds. *CPA Medicare RBRVS: The Physicians' Guide*. 5th ed. Chicago, IL: Coding and Medical Information Systems Group, American Medical Association, 2002.

Hsiao, W.C., Braun, P., Dunn, D., and Becker, E.R. Resource-based relative values: An overview. *JAMA* 260: 2347–2353, 1998.

Hultman, J. *Here's How, Doctor*. Los Angeles: MBA Publishing, 1995.

Lubell, J. DRG proposal part of payment overhaul. *Modern Healthcare* April, 2007.

Marcinko, D.E. *Financial Planning for Physicians and Healthcare Professionals*. New York: Aspen Publishers, 2003.

Marcinko, D.E. Medical activity based cost management. In *The Business of Medical Practice* (p. 407), ed. Marcinko, D.E. New York, NY: Springer Publishing, 2012.

Marcinko, D.E. and Bode, G.L. Medical office expense costing and modeling. In *The Business of Medical Practice* (p. 507), ed. Marcinko, D.E. New York, NY: Springer Publishing, 2012.

Marcinko, D.E. and Hetico, H.R. Economic outcomes analysis from an ambulatory surgical center. *Journal of Foot Surgery* 35(6): 544–548, 1996.

Marcinko, D.E. and Hetico, H.R. *Dictionary of Health Insurance and Managed Care*. New York, NY: Springer Publishing, 2006.

Marcinko, D.E. and Hetico, H.R. *Dictionary of Health Economics and Finance*. New York, NY: Springer Publishing, 2007.

Marcinko, D.E. and White, K. Understanding cash flow and medical accounts receivable. In *Hospitals and Healthcare Organizations* (p. 111), ed. Marcinko, D.E. Boca Raton, FL: Taylor and Francis Group and Productivity Press, 2013.

Meredith, J.R. and Mantel, S.J. *Project Management*. New York: John Wiley and Sons, 1996.

National Direct Coding Guide. New York: St. Anthony Publishing, 2006.

Pershing-Yoakley Associates. Inpatient prospective payment system (IPPS) final rule implements new MS-DRGs. *PYA Alert*, August 10, 2007. http://www.pyapc.com/alert_finalruleippsmsdrgs.htm.

Peterson, C. New payment system will have indirect affect on MCOs. *Managed Care*, October, 2000.

Rogosti, R. Credit crunch hits hospitals. *Healthcare Informatics,* Spring 2008.

Rosenstein, A.H. and Moore, K. Using data to improve clinical effectiveness: An orthopedic case study. *Healthcare Resource* 14 (January/February): 1, 1996.

Ross, A. and Richardson, M. Ambulatory healthcare case studies for the health services executive. *Medical Group Management Association* Item #4901, 2000.

Ross, A., William, S.J., and Pavlock, E.J. Ambulatory care management. *Medical Group Management Association* Item #5009, 2000.

Ross, S.A. *Corporate Finance*. Boston, MA: McGraw-Hill Primis, 2000.

Sinaiko, R. and Mote, S. Medicare's APC reimbursements mandate planning and preparation. *Managed Care* October, 2000.

Tinelsy, R. *Medical Practice Management Handbook*. New York: Aspen Publishers, 2003.

2 Understanding Medical Activity–Based Cost Management

David Edward Marcinko

CONTENTS

As a consequence of the Patient Protection and Affordable Care Act of 2010 (PP-ACA), Accountable Care Organizations (ACOs), and the Medical Home global payment concept, etc., astute physicians and healthcare executives are becoming aware of the need to demonstrate the cost-effectiveness of healthcare, as this can be an important competitive advantage over other providers. Whether this scenario occurs in the office, emergency department (ED), or hospital setting, hard numerical business information is required. Such information may be obtained by using the managerial accounting tools known as Activity-Based Cost Management (ABCM) and the Clinical (Critical) Path Method (CPM).

In the traditional financial accounting practice system, costs are assigned to different procedures or services on the basis of average volume (quantity). So, if a general surgical service is doing more "surgical procedures" (high volume) than primary care "medical services" (low volume), more indirect overhead costs will be allocated to the surgical services portion of the practice.

ABCM and CPM, on the other hand, determine the actual costs of resources that each service or procedure consumes. Therefore, because primary care actually requires more service resources than surgery, ABCM will assign more costs to the medical services (low volume) practice.

The idea is to get a handle on how much every task costs by factoring in the labor, technology, and office space to complete it. In this way, the next time a discounted managed care contract is offered, or your medical office or hospital department is over budget, you will know whether to accept or reject the contract or how to solve the variance problem.

THE MEDICAL CRITICAL (CLINICAL) PATH METHOD

An activity is any event or service that is a cost driver. To activity cost any critical or clinical medical pathway, five steps are used:

1. Identify key transactions.
2. Identify the time and resources required for each step.
3. Define non-economically valued activities.
4. Note office operational inefficiencies.
5. Determine the cost of each resource.

Examples of several specific medical office activities that are cost drivers include the following:

- Surgery setups
- Vital sign checks
- Cast changes
- X-ray processing
- Taking radiographs
- Blood test runs
- Records requests
- Insurance verifications
- Referral orders

ABCM improves managerial accounting systems and flow process re-engineering in three ways:

1. ABCM increases the number of cost pools (expenses) used to accumulate general overhead office costs. Rather than accumulate overhead costs in a single office-wide pool, costs are accumulated by activity, service, or procedure.
2. ABCM changes the base used to assign general overhead costs to services or patients. Rather than assigning costs on the basis of a measure of volume (employee or doctor hours), costs are assigned on the basis of medical services or activities that generated those costs.
3. ABCM changes the nature of many overhead costs in that those formerly considered indirect are now traced to specific activities or services. The office service mix of procedures (current procedural terminology (CPT) codes) may then be adjusted accordingly for additional profit.

In general, the most important end result of ABCM is the shift of general overhead costs from high volume services to low volume services.

ABCM/CPM IN THE EMERGENCY DEPARTMENT SETTING

Many experts opine on the nursing shortage in the United States. This shortage may in part be caused by the assignment of too many non-medical activities to nurses. As a result, administrators experiencing the shortage, with related profit losses, turned to ABCM and the CPM for a solution.

Case Study: St. Paul Emergency Department

Upon CPM evaluation, it was discovered that about half of all activities performed at the St. Paul emergency department by nurses and ED staff were previously done by materials management, maintenance, admissions, or housekeeping employees. This work, however, was not visible in traditional budget reports. On the other hand, ABCM analysis made both the work and the workers visible. ABCM helped the ED administrator eliminate non–value-added overhead activities, re-deploy non-medical activities from nurses to lower-cost employees, improve nurse morale, improve processes, and much more.

Intuitively, it was obvious that increased overtime or the importing of nurses from other countries did not address the root cause of impending nurse shortages. ED managers benefited by using ABCM as a diagnostic tool to fully understand departmental challenges.

ABCM/CPM IN THE PRIVATE OFFICE SETTING

Dr. Smith works in a large medical group consisting of twenty-five healthcare practitioners. In the aggregate, they render 4,000 office visits to the patients from XYZ managed care organization (MCO) and 20,000 visits to patients from the UVW-MCO each year. Each doctor averages forty hours per week and dispenses various pieces of durable medical equipment (DME) to their elderly patient population. The office currently uses doctor hours (DH) to assign general overhead costs to medical services rendered. The predetermined (given) overhead rate is:

Office Overhead Costs	$900,000 (given)
——————————— = ———— =	$18/DH
Doctor Labor Hours (DLH)	50,000*

*(25 doctors × 40 hours/week × 50 week/year)

XYZ-MCO requires 2.5 DLH, and UVW-MCO requires 2.0 DLH. According to a traditional general overhead cost system, the costs to treat one patient in each MCO are determined as follows:

	XYZ	UVW
Direct Materials	$36.00	$30.00
Direct Labor	17.50	14.00
General Office Overhead		
2.5 DLH × 18/DLH	45.00	
2.0 DLH × 18/DLH		36.00
Total Cost per Patient	$98.50	$80.00

Now, for simplicity, let's suppose that office overhead costs are actually composed of the five activities listed in Table 2.1.

Let us also assume that the transactional data in Table 2.2 were collected by the medical office manager.

These data can be used to develop general overhead rates for each of the five activities (Table 2.3).

The general office overhead rates can now be used to assign overhead costs to the respective services, in the following assigned overhead cost manner (Tables 2.4 and 2.5).

Medical service and product costs using the two different methods can now be contrasted (Tables 2.6 and 2.7).

Again, these tables demonstrate that the per-unit costs of the low-volume services increase and the per-unit costs of the high-volume services decrease. These effects are not symmetrical as there is a bigger dollar effect on the per-unit costs of the low-volume services.

TABLE 2.1
Actual Activity Costs

CPM Activity	Traceable Cost ($)
Cast changes	255,000
Radiographs	160,000
Blood panels	81,000
Dressings	314,000
DME	90,000
TOTAL	900,000

Note: CPM, critical (clinical) path method; DME, durable medical equipment.

TABLE 2.2
Transactional Activity Costs

Activity	Number of Events	XYZ	UVW
Cast changes	5,000	3,000	2,000
Radiographs	8,000	5,000	3,000
Blood panels	600	200	400
Dressings	40,000	12,000	28,000
DME	750	150	600

Note: DME, durable medical equipment.

TABLE 2.3
Overhead Rates

Activity	Costs ($)	Transactions (*n*)	Rate per Transaction ($)
Cast changes	255,000	5,000	51/change
Radiographs	160,000	8,000	20/X-ray plate
Blood panels	81,000	600	135/panel
Dressings	314,000	40,000	7.85/bandage
DME	90,000	750	120/DME

Note: DME, durable medical equipment.

TABLE 2.4
Assigned Overhead Costs: XYZ-MCO

Activity	Rate ($)	Transactions (*n*)	Amount ($)
Cast changes	51	3,000	153,000
Radiographs	20	5,000	100,000
Blood panels	135	200	27,000
Dressings	7.85	12,000	94,200
DME	120	150	18,000
Total overhead (a)			392,200
Number units (b)			4,000
Overhead per unit (a/b)			98.05

Note: DME, durable medical equipment; MCO, managed care organization.

About ABCM and CPM

ABCM is not a new concept; it was born in the 1880s as manufacturers tried to get a handle on unit costs of production. For example, if a company built wagons, they could divide their total costs by the number of wagons to figure out how much it cost to build each one; however, they could not use that formula if they built wagons of different sizes. So producers began to use direct labor, materials, and overhead to calculate activity-based costs, as described above. By the 1970s, medicine was heavily skewed toward labor and technology costs, and managers began to apply ABCM to economic service sectors like medicine.

The CPM, on the other hand, is a concept originally developed by the DuPont Corporation in the late 1950s as a system of project management. Today, CPM is embraced by the healthcare industry

TABLE 2.5
Assigned Overhead Costs: UVW-MCO

Activity	Rate ($)	Transactions (n)	Amount ($)
Cast changes	51	2,000	102,000
Radiographs	20	3,000	60,000
Blood panels	135	400	54,000
Dressings	7.85	28,000	219,800
DME	120	600	72,000
Total overhead (a)			507,800
Number units (b)			20,000
Overhead per unit (a/b)			25.39

Note: DME, durable medical equipment; MCO, managed care organization.

TABLE 2.6
Costs Using Activity-Based Costing (ABC) Methodology

	XYZ-MCO ($)	UVW-MCO ($)
DME	36.00	30.00
Doctor hours	17.50	14.00
Office overhead	98.05	69.39
Total cost per unit	151.55	69.39

Note: ABC, activity-based costing; DME, durable medical equipment; MCO, managed care organization.

TABLE 2.7
Costs Using Traditional Accounting Methodology

	XYZ-MCO ($)	UVW-MCO ($)
DME	36.00	30.00
Doctor hours	17.50	14.00
Office overhead	45.00	36.00
Total cost per unit	98.50	80.00

Note: DME, durable medical equipment; MCO, managed care organization.

as a way to use deterministic time estimates to control the costs of medical care. In the CPM, medical activities can be *crashed* (expedited) at extra cost, deemed *critical* if unable to be delayed, or *slacked* if a moderate delay would not adversely affect patient care. Because ABCM determines the actual costs of resources rendered for each medical activity, it is a *de facto* measure of profitability. To determine the activity cost of any medical office activity path:

- Identify the key steps and individuals involved.
- Interview staff and clinicians about the time or resources involved in each step.
- Define non-clinical activities associated with patient care.

- Define and assess possible efficiencies.
- Ask each caregiver to define the costs of each resource he or she applies to the pathways.

Then, crunch the numbers as presented above to determine how low-volume medical costs increase and high-volume costs decrease. In fact, medical practices still using traditional cost accounting systems are often clueless about the financial effectiveness of their care on a forward-looking basis.

THE PRACTICE EXPENSE EQUITY COALITION

The Practice Expense Equity Coalition (PEEC) regularly asks the Centers for Medicare and Medicaid Services (CMS) to validate or disprove Medicare practice expense reimbursement fees. Specialties, such as gastroenterology, neurosurgery, and thoracic and cardiac surgery, are traditionally interested. This occurs because physicians argue that the CMS uses inaccurate cost information to set practice expense rates. Surgeons and procedure-based practitioners are especially worried that greater emphasis on a resource-based relative value system (RBRVS) reduces their reimbursements. Some selected specialties have been affected by evolving resource-based practice expense rules. Meanwhile, the American Physical Therapy Association joined forces with eighteen other major medical and healthcare organizations in 2009 to launch a grassroots and advertising campaign to ensure that the CMS will implement up-to-date practice expense rates into Medicare physician payments without unnecessary intervention by the U.S. Congress. Most recently, the PEEC supports new practice expense rates issued by the CMS, which use data from a rigorous survey supported by more than seventy medical and healthcare professional groups and recognize that overhead costs differ among different physicians and healthcare specialties.

Meanwhile, other major organizations like the American Society of Cataract and Refractive Surgery (ASCRS), the American Academy of Orthopedic Surgeons (AAOS), the American Dental Association, and the American Podiatric Medical Association often use their own costing studies.

RISK ADJUSTERS IN ABCM

Physician payment risk adjusters traditionally focused on variables such as gender, age, and geography to predict an individual's healthcare cost variability at any given time. Such methods needed only to explain 15–20 percent of all variation successfully to adequately reflect selection, and needed to predict only 10 percent of healthcare claim variability on a prospective basis or 33 percent variability on a retrospective basis, to be considered successful 4 percent of the time. Hence, accounting research has focused on ways to segment these variations to enhance the use of ABCM in medical practice and augment profitability. These newer methods use retrospective International Classification of Diseases, Ninth Edition (ICD-9-CM) and futuristic ICD-10 code utilization rates to indicate prospective healthcare needs for an individual or cohort. Although methods differ as to whether a highest-cost or multiple-cost diagnosis should be used, as group size increases, costs trend toward the average regardless of the factors selected.

Thus, when considering diagnosis-based risk adjusters with any capitated managed care plan, the size of plan, its stop-loss arrangements, and sound medical management are the keys to financial success, because higher-cost patients typically require greater medical skills to manage successfully,

MEDICAL PRACTICE COST ANALYSIS WITH ABCM, CPM, RBRVs, AND RVUs

In actuality, using ABCM as described above is a difficult and cumbersome task at best. Still, you must know your office costs to treat patients and perform medical services and procedures.

An excellent way to do this is to perform a medical practice cost analysis (MPCA) for any medical specialty, which assigns the total costs of operating a practice to the various CPT codes and services provided. To measure such productivity, the Medicare RBRVS sets benchmarks for the various procedures that may be used. Last reviewed in January 2010, this system served as a starting point for RVUs (relative value units),* which included:

- Physician's work component (PWC) for time, intensity, and procedural effort (54 percent)
- Practice expense component (PEC) for equipment, rent, supplies, utilities, and general overhead (41 percent), with a geographic practice cost index component (GPCIC)
- Professional liability insurance component (PLIC) for malpractice expenses (5 percent)

Each component is assigned an RVU, which is adjusted for local cost differences and then multiplied by a conversion factor to translate it into dollars. The formula used to calculate payment rates is: (PW RVU + PE RVU + PLI RVU) × conversion factor.

Example

In 2003, CPT code 27130 (total hip replacement arthroplasty) had a PW RVU of 20.12,† a PE RVU of 13.58, and a PLIC RVU of 2.82 with a conversion factor of $36.78. By including practice expenses in the mix, the incentive to perform equipment-oriented procedures is reduced. Thus, the payment for a hip replacement was (20.12 + 13.58 + 2.82) × $36.78 = $1,343. In 2010 this payment was $1,082.21.

Additionally, as the system evolves, pay and performance become even more closely aligned, with about 10 percent of projected revenues at risk for so-called citizenship fees of administrative duties, cost efficiency, various quality measures, and newer pay-for-performance initiatives. This allows the doctor to determine if the reimbursement for each service is enough to cover the cost of providing it. In other words, it will allow you to decide whether to participate in a certain discounted managed care plan, or to determine whether incurring the costs of more labor is justified.

To conduct an MPCA, the following information is needed.

1. Procedure code (CPT) frequency data for your specialty or office for the prior 12–18 months (sample spreadsheet with projected utilization costs for 5,000 members)

CPT Code	Cost by Component	Projected Utilization	Projected Cost
Totals	(historical data)	(historical data)	$60,000.00
Per member/per month calculation			

Total costs divided by 5,000 members divided by 12 months = $1.00 per member/per month

2. Office financial statements for the prior 12–18 months
3. Medicare fee schedule for your medical specialty
4. Computer spreadsheet, such as Microsoft Excel
5. Categorization all office expenses as direct or indirect
6. Costs assigned to each work activity in the office (i.e., time, number of procedures or patients, or assigned RVUs); best standard of measurement to be determined by practice management (the RVU system works best for most doctors; data are available from the U.S. Federal Registry)

---

* Current RVU values by CPT code are available for the Medicare Physician Fee Schedule, from CMS, which also provides links to download the relative value files from 2003 to 2013.
† In 2013, CPT code 27130 had a PW RVU of 38.08.

7. The RVU of each CPT code separated into its component parts (PLC, PEC, and PLIC)
8. List of all CPT codes or the ones used most frequently, as demonstrated in Table 2.8

Now, according to ABCM methodology, divide total direct and indirect costs by the correct RVU component, as shown in Table 2.9, which will allow you to calculate the cost of one unit of the CPT activity.

Next, unit costs are multiplied by the appropriate work expense and liability component RVUs to arrive at a total unit cost per procedure, as seen in Table 2.10.

Finally, the results are added to the cost drivers, other than RVUs, such as the number of patient encounters, as seen in Table 2.11.

The results are then benchmarked to determine reasonableness and compared with the health maintenance organization's fee schedule. The contract is then accepted, rejected, or re-negotiated on the basis of its fiscal merits. Alternatively, spreadsheet parameters can be changed and various "what if" scenarios can be manipulated in mere seconds.

Another simple example would be the physician allocation of monthly payments using the cost per RVU methodology, as given in Table 2.12. Thus, the financial power of ABCM for the physician, and more specifically the MPCA, is demonstrated.

ABCM/CPM IN THE HOSPITAL SETTING

To be paid and maintain cash flow, hospitals set up levels of specialization. This approach, however, usually creates more handoffs, delays, eroding financial positions, and a frustrated set of patients

TABLE 2.8
Medical Practice Cost Analysis

A	B	C	D (B × C)	E	F (B × E)	G	H (B × G)
CPT Code	Frequency (*n*)	Work RVU[a]	Total Practice Work RVU	Practice Exp. RVU[a]	Total Practice Exp. RVU	Liability RVU[a]	Total Office Liability RVU
11111	115	0.91	105	0.40	46	0.04	5
22222	44	0.43	19	0.37	16	0.03	1
33333	59	0.32	19	0.32	19	0.03	2
44444	285	0.23	66	0.23	66	0.02	6
55555	528	1.13	597	0.45	238	0.04	21
66666	788	1.66	1,308	2.10	1,655	0.19	150
77777	445	4.39	1,954	4.11	1.829	0.37	165
88888	2,216	4.41	9,773	4.37	9.684	0.39	864
99999	1,103	6.24	6,883	7.05	7,776	0.74	816
12345	1,085	8.69	9,429	8.81	9,559	0.98	1,063
54321	2,764	0.51	1,410	0.30	829	0.03	83
73620	490	0.16	78	0.54	265	0.04	20
73630	373	0.17	63	0.59	220	0.04	15
99203	4,632	1.14	4,973	0.52	2,268	0.06	262
99212	3,753	0.38	1,426	0.28	1,051	0.02	75
99213	1,825	0.55	1,004	0.38	694	0.03	55
Others	**2,006**						
Totals	**32,241**		**39,104**		**36,213**		**3,602**

[a] Specific data available from current Federal Registry.

Note: CPT, current procedural terminology; RVU, relative value unit.

TABLE 2.9
Cost per CPT Procedure

A	B	C	D	E	F	G	H
	Account	Doctor		Staff			
Expense	Management	Labor	MPCA	Labor	Miscellaneous	Insurance	Other
Doctor salary		1,362,300					
Staff salary	257,635		111,378	42,600			55,000
Malpractice						58,100	
DME lease					2,388		
Dues/subscriptions							13,850
File fee	9,350						
Laboratory						1,428	
DME					201,366		
Other expenses	30,000				22,000		368,850
Total expenses[a]	296,985	1,362,300	111,378	42,600	227,182	59,528	436,850
Total units[b]	32,241	39,104	39,104	36,213	36,213	3,602	36,213
ABCM/unit	9.21	34.84	3.08	1.18	6.27	16.13	12.06

[a]Total expenses for each column divided by total units.
[b]Total units from Table 2.8.
Note: Direct costs = B, C, D, E, F. Indirect costs = G, H. ABCM, activity-based cost management; CPT, current procedural terminology; DME, durable medical equipment; MPCA, medical practice cost analysis.

and physicians. Much seems beyond the control of individuals, and, when you factor in the maze of new Health Insurance Portability and Accountability Act (HIPAA) technologies, it can become overwhelming.

At the hub of the patient hospital experience is Access Management, formerly known as Admitting or Registration. This department collects information for clinicians treating the patient, facilitates medical record documentation, patient flow, revenue capture, billing and collections, and ultimately begins to settle accounts. In other words, the Access Management area has numerous customers in addition to the doctor, patient, or family member sitting across from them.

Without the benefit of relevant information, managers attempt to staff Access Management departments based on past history (i.e., if patient and physician complaints are not too high, there is probably enough staff). However, staffing in Access Management has not kept up with the increased demands and complexity of the process, and other hospital areas often suffer as a result. Clinicians and medical records personnel deal with incomplete or incorrect information; claims information may be incomplete and left to a back office to sort through.

All of these deficits make for an unhappy set of customers (physicians and patients) as they continually deal with the repercussions of inaccurate and incomplete information. This does not go unnoticed by patients and physicians, as these situations erode confidence in the hospital's ability to deliver high-quality healthcare.

Access Management is the hospital's first chance to create an "emotional contract" with the customer. It is here that the tone is set for the patient with respect to their hospitalization. It is here that the provider has the chance to begin working on the patient's behalf so that clinical outcomes are appropriate. All of this must happen in spite of an environment that reduces the likelihood of a favorable occurrence and fails to adhere to the complex legal requirements established by state and federal officials.

So, why do we let unresolved issues pass beyond the Access Management area? In a manufacturing environment, if there are problems with the front-end design, huge problems ripple downstream

TABLE 2.10
Patient Encounter Cost Drivers

A	B[a]	C[b]	D (BC)	E[a,c]	F[d]	G (EF)	H[a]	I[e]	J (HI)	K[a]	L[d] (KL)	M	N (D+G+J+M)
	Unit Cost	RVU	Unit Total	Unit Total	RVU	Unit Total	Unit Cost	RVU	Unit Total	Unit Cost	RVU	Unit Total	TOTAL
CPT Code	Physicians/Doctors			RN Staff/Labor			Insurance/Liability			Other Miscellaneous			
11111	34.84	0.91	31.70	10.53	0.40	4.21	16.13	0.04	0.65	12.06	0.40	4.82	$ 41.39
22222	34.84	0.43	14.98	10.53	0.37	3.90	16.13	0.03	0.48	12.06	0.37	4.46	23.82
33333	34.84	0.32	11.15	10.53	0.32	3.37	16.13	0.03	0.48	12.06	0.32	3.86	18.86
44444	34.84	0.23	8.01	10.53	0.23	2.42	16.13	0.02	0.32	12.06	0.23	2.77	13.53
55555	34.84	1.13	39.37	10.53	0.45	4.74	16.13	0.04	0.65	12.06	0.45	5.43	50.18
66666	34.84	1.66	57.83	10.53	2.10	22.11	16.13	0.19	3.06	12.06	2.10	25.33	108.34
77777	34.84	4.39	152.95	10.53	4.11	43.28	16.13	0.37	5.97	12.06	4.11	49.57	251.76
88888	34.84	4.41	153.64	10.53	4.37	46.02	16.13	0.39	6.29	12.06	4.37	52.70	258.65
99999	34.84	6.24	217.40	10.53	7.05	74.24	16.13	0.74	11.94	12.06	7.05	85.02	388.60
12345	34.84	8.69	302.76	10.53	8.81	92.77	16.13	0.98	15.81	12.06	8.81	106.2	517.58
73620	34.84	0.16	5.57	10.53	0.54	5.69	16.13	0.04	0.65	12.06	0.54	6.51	18.42
73630	34.84	0.17	5.92	10.53	0.59	6.21	16.13	0.04	0.65	12.06	0.59	7.12	19.90
99203	34.84	1.14	39.72	10.53	0.52	5.48	16.13	0.06	0.97	12.06	0.52	6.27	52.43
99212	34.84	0.38	13.24	10.53	0.28	2.95	16.13	0.02	0.32	12.06	0.28	3.38	19.89
99213	34.84	0.55	19.16	10.53	0.38	4.00	16.13	0.03	0.48	12.06	0.38	4.58	28.23

a Activity cost/unit from Table 2.9.
b Same RVU from column C in Table 2.8.
c Sum of activity cost/unit from columns D, E, and F in Table 2.9.
d Same RVU from column E in Table 2.8.
e Same RVU from column G in Table 2.8.

Note: Direct costs = physicians/MDs, RN staff/labor. Indirect costs = liability insurance, other, miscellaneous. CPT, current procedural terminology; RN, registered nurse; RVU, relative value unit.

TABLE 2.11
Activity-Based Cost Management

A	Bª	CᵇD	(B+C)
CPT	Account Mgmt.	Patient Encounter	Total Procedure Cost
11111	9.21	41.39	50.60
22222	9.21	23.82	33.03
33333	9.21	18.86	28.07
44444	9.21	13.53	22.74
55555	9.21	50.18	59.39
66666	9.21	108.34	117.55
77777	9.21	251.76	260.97
88888	9.21	258.65	267.86
99999	9.21	388.60	397.81
12345	9.21	517.58	526.79
54321	9.21	25.03	34.24
73620	9.21	18.42	27.63
73630	9.21	19.90	29.11
99203	9.21	52.43	61.64
99212	9.21	19.89	29.10
99213	9.21	28.23	37.44

ª Activity cost/unit from column B, Table 2.9.
ᵇ From column N, Table 2.10.
Note: CPT, current procedural terminology.

TABLE 2.12
Cost per CPT Methodology

Services Produced	Physician A	Physician B	Physician C	Physician D	Grand Totals
CPT Total CPT Cost	CPT Revenue	CPT Revenue	CPT Revenue	CPT Revenue	CPT Revenue

Note: CPT, current procedural terminology.

in terms of recalls, warranty-related expenses, lawsuits, and customers that abandon the company's products. World-class manufacturers dealt with these issues with their ISO-9000, Total Quality Management, and Six Sigma programs during the 1980s and 1990s. Hospitals, however, have allowed issues in their Access Management process to fester and create huge and costly problems in the downstream process, beyond the near future. Enter the hospital enterprise-wide resource planning (ERP) concept.

Example

StatCom's Hospital Operating System™ solution for 2010–2011, a new ERP product from Jackson Healthcare, is a comprehensive patient-throughput software solution that enables all patients to flow at their best possible rate with respect to service times, quality, safety, and resource consumption. It facilitates prioritized patient flow across various hospital departments, providing real-time information on the status of patient throughput so leaders can manage what is measured. StatCom transforms access management and patient throughput, according to David Pritchard.

The company reported that small to mid-sized hospital customers reduced their average length of stay in 2009 by 14 percent and realized $8.6 million in savings on average, an 11.2 percent increase in volume with a total impact of $10.3 million (personal communication, Dr. David Edward Marcinko).

THE PHYSICIAN'S ROLE

So, every provider must take a proactive role in dealing with this emerging trend. The next few years will be pivotal in adapting to the new age of the empowered customers, Internet technologies, and more demanding payment plans. The first step in this journey is physician-executive assessment.

Rest assured, this assessment is not a set of management engineering time studies aimed at micro-costing every second of work. The CPM information needed for this plan is reasonable and can be collected in a few days by talking to the people performing the work. Estimates are made on the basis of workers' views about how they spend their time. This information is combined with available workload measures and general ledger cost information, and activity-based reports are produced.

Going forward, ABCM is an exercise in planning. Activity-based information is used to look at areas where work can be restructured so errors and rework can be eliminated. New technologies that target problematic activities are selected and implemented. Outside companies that can perform complex activities more economically can be used. So, be sure to change your mindset and plan to get started, now!

ASSESSMENT

ABCM and the CPM hold great promise as a commonsense solution to the faults and frustrations of healthcare process budgeting, human resource management, and aberrant cost allocation methods:

- Traditional budgets do not identify waste. ABCM/CPM exposes non-value costs.
- Traditional budgets focus on office employees. ABCM/CPM focuses on workload.
- Traditional budgets focus on office costs. ABCM/CPM also focuses on process costs.
- Traditional budgets focus on fixed versus variable costs. ABCM/CPM focuses on used versus unused capacity.
- Traditional budgets measure "effect." ABCM/CPM measures "cause."

CONCLUSION

Activity-based cost management (ABCM) and the Clinical (Critical) Path Method (CPM) will become the *de facto* managerial accounting method of choice for the modern medical office, clinic, or hospital. It is replacing the traditional financial accounting methodology of average costs, moving to the more specific methodology of tracing actual resources consumed. The idea is to appreciate how much every task costs by factoring in every resource used to complete it.

Thus, by assigning overhead expense costs to low-volume activities, a better idea of each activity's profit (or loss) can be ascertained and adjusted. In this way, when your next financial crisis occurs, you will know how to deal with the problem through ABCM/CPM and more effectively return to profitability.

CASE MODEL 1

NEW-CO MEDICAL CLINIC, INC.

The relevant production range for the two-physician New-Co Medical Clinic, Inc. represents gross annual receipts of $600,000–$800,000/year. Fixed costs are $435,000, and the service mix is:

Surgery	18%
Laboratory	12%
Hospital	10%
Exams, injections, and vaccinations	24%
Care and treatment	33%
Miscellaneous	3%

New-Co Medical Clinic has determined the variable costs associated with each service to arrive at a contribution margin ratio (CMR) for each. The CMRs for New-Co Medical Clinic are:

Surgery	72%
Laboratory	84%
Hospital	95%
Exams, injections, and vaccinations	92%
Care and treatment	81%
Miscellaneous	89%

Now, let us determine an aggregate CMR to identify the patient break-even-point.
  Solution:
The aggregate CMR is found in the following way:

Service	Sales Mix	CMR	Aggregate CMR
Surgery	18%	72%	0.123
Laboratory	12%	84%	0.101
Hospital	10%	95%	0.095
Exams, injections, and vaccinations	24%	92%	0.221
Care and treatment	33%	81%	0.267
Miscellaneous	3%	89%	0.027
Totals		100%	0.834

Therefore, the aggregate CMR for the practice is 83.4%. When we divide the fixed costs of $435,000/83.4%, we see that the break-even point is $521,583.

Key Issues

Why should the New-Co Medical Clinic, Inc. doctors determine the following parameters?

(1) Fixed and variable costs?
(2) Case mix?
(3) Relevant production range?
(4) Aggregate contribution margin ratio?

For every dollar of gross, $0.166 (16.6 cents) pays the variable costs associated with generating that dollar, and $0.834 goes toward paying fixed costs and generating profit. Therefore, for every dollar earned by New-Co Medical Clinic over $521,583, $0.843 is pure profit.

CASE MODEL 2

ST. PETER'S HOSPITAL EMERGENCY DEPARTMENT

After critical (clinical) path method evaluation, St. Peter's Hospital administrators discovered that about half of all activities performed at the emergency department (ED) by nurses and ED staff were previously done by materials management, maintenance, admissions, or housekeeping employees. As a result, the work was not visible in traditional budget reports.

Activity-based cost management (ABCM) analysis made both the work and the worker visible. ABCM helped the ED administrator eliminate non–value-added overhead activities, re-deployed non-medical activities from nurses to lower-cost employees, improved nurse morale, improved processes, and much more.

St. Peter's Hospital Emergency Department Solution:

Traditional Costing View	ABCM View
Salary and fringes	Patient treatments
Space	Problem resolution
Depreciation	Paperwork
Supplies/durable medical equipment	Procure supplies
Other	Expedite supplies
	Housekeeping
$2,500,000	**$2,500,000**

Source: ICMS, Inc., http://icms.net, 2006.

Key Issues

Was St. Peter's Hospital correct or not with regard to the:

- Treated patients?
- Resolved problems?
- Paperwork?
- Procurement and expedition of supplies?
- Housekeeping?

It is obvious that increased overtime or the importing of nurses from other countries does not address the root cause of impending nurse shortages. ED managers can benefit by using ABCM as a diagnostic tool to fully understand departmental concerns.

CHECKLIST 1: Information and Variables Used to Influence Hybrid Medical Practice and Office Costs	YES	NO
Can I define and explain mixed office or hybrid practice costs?	o	o
Do I understand the high–low methodology?	o	o
Do I use linear regression analysis for hybrid office costing?	o	o
Do I possess, or have I set up, a spreadsheet for hybrid costing endeavors?	o	o
Do I have data checks for hybrid costing activities?	o	o
Do I have data adjudication authority?	o	o
Am I in a position of cost risk assumption for my office, medical practice, or department?	o	o

CHECKLIST 2: Information Used for Critical Path Method (CPM) Identification Activities	YES	NO
Have I identified all critical actions, bottlenecks, or key office transactions?	o	o
Have I identified the timeliness and major resources required for each CPM step?	o	o
Can I define and use non-economically valued practice or medical office activities?	o	o
Have I observed any operational inefficiencies in the office practice?	o	o

CHECKLIST 3: Transactional Information Useful in Activity-Based Medical Costing for the Modern Office Practice	YES	NO
Have I determined the cost of each medical office input and important resource?	o	o
Have I identified the key office operation steps?	o	o
Have I identified key office individuals involved?	o	o
Have I identified office activities and practice activity pools?	o	o
Have I interviewed staff and clinicians about the time involved in each step?	o	o
Have I interviewed staff and clinicians about the resources involved in each step?	o	o
Have I defined the clinical activities associated with patient care?	o	o
Have I defined the non-clinical activities associated with office patient care?	o	o
Have I defined and assessed possible office efficiencies?	o	o
Have I asked each caregiver to define the costs of each resource he or she applies to the pathways?	o	o
Have I traced practice costs to the extent possible?	o	o
Have I calculated the following:		
• Activity rates?	o	o
• The physician's work component for my ABCM activities?	o	o
• The physician's time component for my ABCM activities?	o	o
• The physician's procedural effort component for my ABCM activities?	o	o
• Practice expense component and equipment component for my ABCM activities?	o	o
• Practice rent component for my ABCM activities?	o	o
• Practice supplies component for my ABCM activities?	o	o
• Practice utilities component for my ABCM activities?	o	o
• Practice general overhead component for my ABCM activities?	o	o
• Malpractice liability insurance component and malpractice expenses component for my ABCM activities?	o	o
Have I determined a geographic medical practice cost index component for my ABCM activities?	o	o
Do I have physician or executive staff support for my ABCM activities?	o	o
Have I prepared an ABCM management report?	o	o

CHECKLIST 4: Information Used in a Medical Practice Organization Cost Analysis	YES	NO
Do I have the following information?		
• Consolidated financial statements for the prior 12–18 months?	o	o
• Medicare fee schedule for each exact medical specialty?	o	o
• All office expenses categorized as direct costs?	o	o
• All office expenses categorized as indirect costs?	o	o
Have I determined the best standard of measurement to assign costs to each work activity in the doctor's office (i.e., time, number of procedures or patients, or assigned resource-based relative value units)?	o	o

	YES	NO
Have I determined the best standard of measurement to assign costs to each work activity in the hospital, if applicable?	o	o
Have I determined the best standard of measurement to assign costs to each work activity in the outpatient setting?	o	o
Have I determined the best standard of measurement to assign costs to each work activity in a skilled nursing facility?	o	o
Have I determined the best standard of measurement to assign costs to each work activity by the Home Healthcare Agency?	o	o
Have I separated the resource-based RVUs, DRGs, APCs, RUG-IIIs, and/or HHRGs of each code into its component parts (e.g., RBRVSs = physician labor component, practice expense component, and malpractice liability risk component)?	o	o
Have I listed all codes or the ones used most frequently?	o	o

Note: APC, ambulatory payment classification; DRG, diagnosis-related group; HHRG, home health resource group; RBRVS, resource-based relative value system; RUG-III, resource utilization group-III; RVU, relative value unit.

CHECKLIST 5: Activity-Based Cost Management Processes	YES	NO
Do I define the major business processes and key activities of the medical practice or healthcare organization?	o	o
Do I trace operating office costs and practice capital charges to key activities?	o	o
Do I use existing accounting and financial data, which includes labor and capital equipment expenses, and any other resource that can be changed or eliminated?	o	o
Do I issue reports to analyze ABCM activities, such as budget, general ledger, or supplier invoices?	o	o
Do I link medical activities to processes and identify the office cost drivers?	o	o
Do I actively engage healthcare personnel performing the medical processes in determining ABCM costs?	o	o
Do personnel identify where the costs come from, and then do I seek out data from each source?	o	o
Do I summarize the total costs for each process?	o	o
Once processes are re-engineered, are the "new" costs tabulated and reduced?	o	o

Note: ABCM, activity-based cost management.

REFERENCES

Beebe, M. *Current procedural terminology (CPT) 2013: Standard edition.* Chicago, IL: AMA Press, 2013.

Bowie, M.J., Schaffer, R.M. *Understanding procedural coding: A work-text.* Dover, DE: Delmar Publishing, 2008.

Marcinko, D.E. *Healthcare organizations.* Atlanta, GA: iMBA, Inc., 2010.

Marcinko, D.E., Hetico, H.R. *Business of medical practice.* New York: Springer Publishers, 2012.

Pryor, T. *Using ABCM for continuous improvement.* Arlington, TX: ICMS, 1995.

Pryor, T. *Activity-based management: A healthcare industry primer.* Chicago, IL: The American Hospital Association, 2002.

Redmond, M. *The basics of medical billing.* New York: Seagate Publishing, 2008.

3 Lean Hospital Materials Processes and Throughput Costs in an Increasingly Tightened Economic Market

Adam Higman, Brian Mullahey, Kristin Spenik, and Jerzy Kaczor

CONTENTS

As today's current healthcare providers face significant pricing demands, cutting costs while at the same time delivering quality care to patients remains a clear priority. Though many initiatives to reduce costs focus on operational efficiency, the area often disregarded is the hospital supply chain. This area represents "nearly one third of all hospital operating budgets," (Motorola 2010).

With the supply chain being one of the most complex and multifaceted processes of a hospital, it continues to be underdeveloped when it comes to its level of collaboration, the absence of data standards, and proper documentation methods. (Motorola 2010). Whether your facility is tightening its proverbial belt or simply looking to efficiently and effectively reduce overall costs in the long run, the most successful approach is to plan ahead wisely. Budgets and goals are only one piece of the metrics puzzle. Your process must address the root issues and opportunities for improvement; identifying and knowing how to respond to key processes that have a significant impact on supply-related cost reduction opportunities is the first step.

In 2006, it was estimated that the United States would spend more than $2 trillion on healthcare, just about $7,000 for every individual (Behzad et al. 2011). With an increasing focus on cost cutting at both the federal and local levels, healthcare payments—and subsequently expenditures—will decrease, making a strategically focused materials management cost analysis plan all the more crucial.

Establishing proactive materials management strategies is crucial in remaining competitive and sustaining long-term success. Because materials cost savings has proven to be a delicate proposition, the need to meet or exceed long-term goals must be balanced with the handling of short-term problems. As much as 40 percent of a hospital's budget goes to materials expenses, specifically the cost of medical and surgical supplies, and poorly managed materials can leave a significant negative impact on the budget.

MATERIALS COST SAVINGS FROM START TO FINISH

Supplies, a close second behind labor when it comes to costs, travel along the supply chain each day, from manufacturers and distributors to group purchasing organizations (GPOs) and healthcare providers, and then directly to patients. Even though medical personnel are not within the conventional supply chain, they are the eventual users of products and equipment and remain a major part of any materials cost-savings process (Motorola 2010).

To start maximizing your cost-savings efforts, follow these action items:

- **Determine annualized savings goals at the beginning of each fiscal year.** The materials your facility uses on a day-to-day basis have greater potential to reduce costs than many people give them credit for. An instrument vendor choice here, a properly inventoried storeroom there, and you are on your way to realizing dramatic cost savings. Similar to other initiatives, cost savings need to be part of your plan that encompasses an end goal, with actionable steps and time lines. By establishing a goal and fostering a sense of urgency through specified milestones, actionable time lines, and firm due dates, you are setting up your organization for long-term success.
  - **Classify areas of opportunity.** To have an early effect on your facility or department, identify the major areas of opportunity. The possibility for improved pricing presents itself in many forms, with some of the most common being GPO compliance, vendor consolidation, product standardization, and negotiations.

  Begin by looking at large expense categories and work your way down. This process inevitably leads to a closer look at key departments, including the operating room (OR), pharmacy, and catheterization lab. When looking for the biggest "spend" categories, it is usually going to be rather clear-cut. For example, implants are a huge spend area, and then there are commodity items bought in greater volumes on a regular basis, such as gowns and procedure trays. A close look at specific programs such as spine, oncology, cardiothoracic, as well as specific products, will yield the best results when focused on your facility's big spenders.
- **Form or refocus your Value Analysis Committee to create internal value and physician buy-in.** Creating internal value and fostering end user (i.e., physician) buy-in is crucial for any cost-savings initiative. To facilitate participation in implementation, it is important to engage all major stakeholders in the cost-savings process. This is most effectively accomplished through the creation of a multidisciplinary panel that determines which cost-savings initiatives to implement and how.

  The Value Analysis Committee comprises staff, management, and physicians from a variety of departments and should be your facility's deciding body when evaluating materials cost savings. You should also include the individual who handles materials management and the individual who handles vendor contracts and negotiations, though the two duties may be carried out by one individual. Usually, the committee should include personnel who are familiar with different products and the tactics needed to take on product standardization. Ideally, the goal is to identify and implement cost-savings initiatives while new products are being critically evaluated, thereby controlling new expenses.

  It is also important that the committee maintain a high level of communication. Keep physicians and staff members in the loop as they go through this process. For example, if the committee suggests using a new intraocular lens because it is going to reap huge savings, the committee needs to ensure that decision is being communicated to all affected surgeons. Otherwise you run into the common problem where the departments within the facility end up operating in a vacuum because all of the physicians return to using different products.

- **Estimate potential savings.** Use internal and/or external resources to verify current usage and spending by category, and begin discussions with and collect proposals from current and prospective vendors. Vendors are willing to work with hospitals and offer a better price because they may be able to increase their volume of sales. The key is maintaining compliance with the vendor's contract and having mechanisms in place within the materials management system to maintain obligations.

For instance, when it comes to supply usage for custom procedure packs, ask yourself:

1. Are there supplies in the packs that are not being used? Should we eliminate these supply items from the packs?
2. Are there packs that should be eliminated due to low volume? What is the difference between the cost of keeping the pack versus picking the items individually?

In terms of current pricing, consider:

1. Can we reduce the cost of some items without changing current item usage?
2. Can we consolidate vendors, and thus increase the usage by vendor?
3. Can we change to a lower cost vendor?

If you can reduce the number of vendors to one or two, you will get better pricing because pricing is largely about volume. New vendors are willing to reduce their prices as long as they obtain an increase in volume. They are interested in how much money you will spend with them and, correspondingly, how much business they can get.

Once offers are in hand, the next step is to identify potential scenarios, which is best accomplished by a small team during a brainstorming session and should include potential issues that may foil each scenario from implementation. Finally, quantify the potential financial impact of each scenario and present the information to decision makers.

- **Capture savings.** Once your administrative team has decided to go forward with a materials cost-savings initiative and has established internal buy-in, take advantage of the momentum and move forward with implementation as quickly as possible. The same can be said about decisions made by the overseeing panel. The longer you wait, the higher the chance that internal buy-in will diminish, allowing resistance to increase.

ORGANIZATION AND STANDARDIZATION

With supply costs substantially on the rise, it is safe to say that materials may surpass labor costs in the future. This overtaking by materials has healthcare leaders opting for better, more efficient inventory management practices (Rossetti et al. 2008).

Sourcing, as well as contracting and product identification, is one reason why materials standardization is so important. From the facility standpoint, organizing and managing the locations and contract arrangements for more than 60,000 different supplies and products, depending on the size of the hospital, is a big undertaking (Campbell and Methvin 2011).

In looking at medical professional preference, standardization does not necessarily mean the hospital must choose one vendor or one product. For instance, decreasing the number of vendors to two can still go a long way in lowering costs and improving supply chain efficiency. Did you know that just 20 percent of materials management personnel actually develop and adhere to a written strategic plan (Campbell and Methvin 2011)?

Global standards assist hospital materials management processes and procedures and have been proven to have positive benefits and effects for the safety of patients and supply chain operations, including:

- Reduced pharmaceutical errors through better identification automation (the right product, in the right dosage, to the right patient, by the right route, at the right time)
- Well-organized traceability
- Proficient product verification
- Reduced manual documentation time
- Lower costs due to operational efficiencies
  - Better order/invoice procedures
  - Enhanced receiving/distribution processes
  - Higher-quality product recall
  - Well-organized shelf management
- High productivity rates
- Reduced inventory
- Enhanced service levels/fill rates
- Better benchmarking and administration of materials charges
- Eliminated need for relabeling and proprietary codes
- Regulatory compliance (*Healthcare Provider Toolkit* 2012)

Being used by 90 percent of organizations and companies throughout the world, and with endorsement from the Association for Healthcare Resource and Materials Management (AHRMM), GS1 standards have been widely utilized throughout the healthcare industry as a way of standardizing and controlling all operations along the entire supply chain process (AHRMM 2012b).

GS1 Healthcare advocates "successful development and implementation of global standards by bringing together experts [hospitals, GPOs, pharmaceutical companies, logistic providers, and regulatory and government groups] in healthcare to enhance patient safety and supply chain efficiencies" (Campbell and Methvin 2011, p. 13) They are striving to attain automated identification, data organization, and traceability while at the same time decreasing medical errors, recovering potential lost revenue, and putting an end to counterfeiting. Whether GS1 standards are suitable for your facility or not, a strong position and stance on managing your supply chain can prove to be cost-effective and enhance patient care (Campbell and Methvin 2011).

GLOBAL LOCATION NUMBERS

Global location numbers (GLNs) are widely used throughout healthcare supply chain groups. This unique, thirteen-digit number links the name, industry, and address of a particular item that pinpoints the "legal, functional, or physical location within a business or organizational entity," in particular, hospitals and healthcare organizations.

- **Legal:** Hospitals, healthcare organizations, distributors, suppliers, freight carriers, etc.
- **Functional:** Specific departments within legal entities (e.g., purchasing departments, nursing stations, wards, etc.) in hospitals
- **Physical:** Hospital rooms, hospital wings, cabinets, shelving units, delivery points, loading docks, warehouses, etc. (AHRMM 2012a).

According to AHRMM, GLNs can recover your facility's revenue stream, enhance the accuracy of documenting GPO sales, and end the use "of single-purpose proprietary supplier numbers" (AHRMM 2012a).

The ultimate objective is to get everyone involved in the supply chain process to use identical numbers. For instance, if the GPO communicates to the manufacturer that your hospital utilizes a specific GLN, then it is more likely that the manufacturer will associate the hospital's materials and supplies with the correct GPO contract price. In addition, if distributors utilize GLNs along with manufacturers and producers to determine the manufacturer's given price, the hospital will likely secure the correct rate when purchasing supplies directly from distributors (AHRMM 2012a).

AHRMM STANCE ON COMPARATIVE EFFECTIVENESS RESEARCH

In today's hospital setting, data and healthcare information is the most accessible it has ever been, making it necessary for healthcare professionals to assess and evaluate its accuracy. Additionally, the healthcare supply chain is filled with "me too" products, which often boast dubious improvements in clinical efficacy over competitive and legacy products.

AHRMM's Issues and Legislative Committee has advocated the usage of comparative effectiveness research (CER) to offer substantial, evidence-based data to aid healthcare organizations in their purchasing decisions. CER data includes unbiased conclusions regarding healthcare products and supplies after the advantages, usefulness, and possible harm of numerous pharmaceuticals, medical devices, equipment, surgical procedures, and tests for specific disease states and treatments of care have been compared (AHRMM Statement on Comparative Effectiveness, 2012).

By utilizing the CER-provided data, healthcare materials management professionals can:

- Warrant top-performing value analysis committees.
- Verify the cost-effectiveness and ability of salvaging single-use items.
- Regulate medical/surgical products.
- Capitalize information technology efforts to decrease expenditures and inaccuracies.
- Change supplies, services, and technologies to lower, budget-friendly, clinically acceptable options that endure needed specifications.
- Convert to supplies, services, and technologies that produce better patient outcomes at a lower total cost that meets needed specifications.
- Prioritize capital expenditures.
- Use third-party benchmarking methods to get the most out of resources (AHRMM Statement on Comparative Effectiveness 2012).

DEPARTMENT SPOTLIGHT: THE OR DATA PROBLEM

Obtaining Credible Information for Materials Cost Savings in the OR

As much as 40 percent of a hospital's budget goes to OR expenses, specifically, the cost of medical and surgical supplies. When looking at the OR charge-capture process, no hospital wants to jeopardize its financial stability because of mistakes and inaccuracies that could have easily been avoided.

Constructing an accurate process for capturing charges is a constant undertaking, and the OR is a major focus of operations as well as being a high-cost area for the hospital. Healthcare facilities can strategically tackle OR charge capture by establishing a proficient system that reviews all documented items to be billed and identifies the errors/inconsistencies so charges can be rectified before billing the patient. When errors go unnoticed, hospitals endure costly penalties, delayed payments, increased time in accounts receivable, and decreased patient satisfaction, which not only hurts the OR but ultimately affects the hospital's bottom line.

One of the main difficulties with capturing charges in the OR is determining the methodology best suited for your institution. There are two typical ways to capture charges: inclusion and exclusion.

- **Inclusion** consists of documenting every item that was used to perform the procedure and charging accordingly.
- **Exclusion** involves listing all materials that could possibly be used during a procedure, crossing off all unused items, and billing for the remaining supplies.

POTENTIAL PROBLEMS

As with any process, there is a potential for problems to surface. When charging for procedures in the OR, some items may be left off the list of items used/unused, some may be repeated multiple times and go unnoticed, and some may be recorded under different names, causing inaccurate records.

CAPTURING SUCCESS

That said, there are steps that facilities can take to resolve charge-capture inaccuracies and ensure a successful process in the OR:

- **Maintain accuracy** of the OR case schedule. Verify that the scheduled number of cases coincides with the number of completed cases to avoid discrepancies, taking into account any cancellations.
- **Anticipate charges** by reviewing surgical cases each day, and efficiently capture expenses to process billing correctly and in a timely manner.
- **Keep item numbers linked with the current contracts** to maintain effective pricing controls.
- **Establish a system that ensures process controls for billing procedures.** For accurate charges, those responsible for reconciling OR expenses should not also be responsible for documenting costs to patients.
- **Catch charge-capture errors early in the process** so they can be corrected before bills are sent to patients. This is most effective when the staff is retrained regarding charge capture and compliance sooner rather than later to stop errors and inconsistencies.

As a result, it is essential to the success of the healthcare facility that its practices and processes operate at a high level of efficiency. By examining the facility's charge-capture policies and procedures, hospitals can effectively tackle the difficulties of materials cost savings in the OR and considerably increase revenue and productivity. Success in this regard is about setting up a culture and expectation that the process of savings is ongoing.

BEST PRACTICES: MANAGING MATERIALS, EXPENSES, AND RESOURCES

In 2003, six key factors of best hospital materials management practices were recognized at the AHRMM annual conference as ways to reduce expenses and improve quality of care.

1. **Control dollars, not just materials.** Do not limit yourself strictly to the materials side of the supply chain. Consider that materials must be available at the right time, in the right place, and that there must be an adequate, cost-controlled supply of these materials and sufficient equipment to attend to patient needs.
2. **Work together with physicians and nurses.** Strong collaboration and communication among purchasers, physicians, management, and staff must be present if any process is to have significant, lasting, positive effects.

3. **Take into account total expenses, not just the rate.** All individuals involved in the decision-making process of materials should be aware of the total expenses for supplies and equipment. Determine the true cost of inventory rather than just the dollar amount. One product may appear to have an affordable price point and be within your budget, but make sure to identify additional charges such as ordering costs, carrying costs, shipping, delivery, etc.
4. **Establish cohesive and organized policies and procedures.** With consistent and well-organized guidelines, you reduce the risk of overspending and guarantee constant stock quality.
5. **Have a unified and structured process instead of a department emphasis.** Similar to the previous item, your methodology should be uniform across the hospital, rather than department-specific. Inventory management practices in the ER should have the same management practices as those in the pharmacy, surgical services, radiology, and so on.
6. **Create processes with a team mentality in mind, not individually focused.** Even though it is necessary to employ specialists in materials management, goals should be team-oriented and should not reflect the preferences of an individual (Purchasing & Procurement Center, n.d.).

CONCLUSION

While it may seem overwhelming to improve inventory levels, cut costs, and still increase the quality of patient care and safety, it is possible. Hospitals should utilize technologies, exploit resources, and effectively connect with all members of the supply chain for an efficient materials management department. Implementing a well-organized and sustainable approach to effectively assess and control supply and equipment service costs can help hospitals quickly reduce waste while improving both short- and long-term bottom-line results.

CASE MODEL

SUPPLY CHAIN AND MATERIALS MANAGEMENT COST REDUCTION OPERATIONAL IMPROVEMENTS OF A 12-HOSPITAL HEALTHCARE SYSTEM IN THE UNITED STATES

Background

A healthcare system operates 10+ acute care hospitals throughout the United States, ranging in size from 30 to 100+ beds for a total of more than 700 licensed beds. The system has been recognized for superior clinical results and has extended its capability beyond specialty services to include a number of high acuity services.

The hospital system's Materials Management Departments were lacking in strategic direction, experience, and leadership. The structure and organization of the system's supply chain was not fully optimized to take advantage of inherent economies of scale. The system had a decentralized corporate materials management organization structure, which accounted for its lack of contract compliance, standardization, monitoring of inventory assets, vendor controls, system communication, and direction and focus to achieve system goals.

Key Issues

- Inconsistent department policies and procedures
- No formalized orientation, competency, or education plans

- Insufficient interdepartmental communications and low employee morale
- Lack of performance benchmarks and utilization of best practices
- No established freight expense management program; abnormally high freight costs
- Lack of tools to audit validity and accuracy of vendor rebates, contract applications, and contract terms
- Underdeveloped physician engagement strategies to successfully manage supply chain costs
- Lack of system coordination and sourcing of capital expenditures
- Weak price negotiation tactics
- Poor management of the group purchasing organization (GPO) and distribution platform
- Staff frustration due to inconsistent processes, directions, and changing course of action
- System materials viewed as unreliable due to a perceived inability to "get things done"
- No standardization or methodology at the hospital level to manage pricing or contracts
- Wasteful spending; hospitals are purchasing the same product with similar volumes at different prices
- Lack of measurable data to estimate savings potential
- Lack of formal contract administration
- Flawed tools to measure contract compliance and inventory turnover
- No formal job descriptions or organizational structure/chain of command in place

Solutions/Outcomes

In response to the lack of measurable data, implementation of a strong inventory management system, with freight management, contract and pricing management, vendor controls, value analysis, physician-preferred items controls, and centralized capital procurement, yielded an estimated supply spend of more than $200 million. Implementation of a successful pricing strategy for customer relationship management (CRM) purchases alone identified a potential savings of more than $4 million.

A supply chain strategic plan for the system was developed and implemented to direct and enforce a more centralized approach to supply chain management.

A comprehensive supply chain cost reduction program was set up with specific initiatives, with input from clinical resources, physicians, and key individuals from the system.

A supply chain collaborative value analysis operations plan was established as part of the supply chain strategic plan to optimize the performance of the system with cost-effective product utilization, services, and processes while continuing to improve the quality of patient care. The greatest opportunity for savings was standardization, which included purchasing new controls, value-based selection, and physician buy-in. The accuracy of a system-wide Item File Master was critical to identify supply chain savings opportunities.

Specific jobs and their corresponding functions were detailed in new positions and job descriptions. To address organizational structure challenges, the system adopted a better chain of command within the system. As a result, the following positions were established:

- The Vice President of Supply Chain was created and given a detailed job description to ensure the authority and responsibility of enforcing system compliance, policies, and the strategic plan. This person now reported to the Vice President of Operations.

- The Contract Director had responsibility for analyzing and implementing GPO and system-specific contracts and service agreements, and was to provide system-wide contract management support.
- The Purchasing Director was employed to train and educate staff on policies and procedures, work with Information Systems to ensure proper data input, monitor corporate compliance, and serve as a liaison to all field operations and clinical resource management.
- The role of the Capital Procurement Director was established to implement and maintain a centralized sourcing process for capital acquisitions to achieve significant cost savings with bundled discount opportunities and aggregate bidding, and to improve standardization of capital equipment throughout the system.
- A Clinical Resource Manager with strong clinical, analytical, interpersonal, and leadership skills to gain credibility among key stakeholders was recruited. This individual was responsible for identifying and driving supply chain cost initiatives and reported directly to the Chief Clinical Officer. This individual was required to establish a Corporate Value Analysis Committee and provide assistance when necessary, serve as a liaison with Corporate Supply Chain Leadership, identify physician-preferred conversion opportunities, and lead the conversion process from non-contract to contract for clinical supplies in coordination with the GPO representatives and Materials Management Corporate Leadership.

A formal manual for supply chain operations was created with new policies and procedures, including purchasing conflict of interest, supply expense review, cycle-count procedures, a credit and return policy, new product request, and a vendor relations policy. A new policy was also developed that required all contracts for goods and services to be reviewed and approved by Corporate Leadership to assure contract usage and appropriate standardization with other contracts and vendors throughout the system.

In response to high freight costs, a formal Freight Management Program was established to utilize contractual agreements with distributors to review distribution and consolidation opportunities. The system developed key performance metrics to monitor supply trends, track purchases, utilize contractual agreements with the existing GPO, and validate compliance.

With these solutions, the hospital system now had direct accountability and authority to harness the entire supply spend of the organization and to leverage that power to lower costs and improve service. In the end, the hospital system went from a financially unstable organization to a profitable, high-quality care system.

Results

The hospital system's charge-capture processes were reviewed and resulted in the following:

- More than $300,000 in adjustments were found through identified inventory issues
- To decrease over $150,000 of inventory, processes were established to identify overstock of leads in CRM bulk purchases
- Exchanged $40,000 of slow-moving products and excess inventory for actual needed products to further reduce bulk inventory
- Addressed consignment issues, which resulted in credits of more than $100,000

CHECKLIST 1: Inventory Management	YES	NO
Is there an effective process for inventorying supplies?	o	o
What is it?		
_____		
_____		
Is there an adequate supply of products and supplies?	o	o
Does the medical staff feel there is an adequate supply?	o	o
Is the equipment in good condition?	o	o
Why or why not?		
_____		
_____		
Is unused material returned to the warehouse?	o	o
Is it managed in order to be returned to the vendor?	o	o
Is there currently a shortage of instrumentation within departments?	o	o
If yes, which departments and why?		
_____		
_____		

CHECKLIST 2: Materials Management	YES	NO
Is Materials Management communicating effectively with other departments?	o	o
If not, which areas are suffering?		
_____		
_____		
_____		
Is there an established process for supply management?	o	o
Is a Material Quality Assurance Program in place?	o	o
Is there compliance with it?	o	o
Is priority ranking part of the Materials Management process?	o	o
Is there a minimum quantity (par level) of each inventory item?	o	o
Is there someone in charge of purchasing for the hospital?	o	o

CHECKLIST 3: Purchasing Ability	YES	NO
Is there a high percentage of supplies and equipment being purchased through the Materials Management Department?	o	o
What is the percentage?		
_____		
Is there an effective process for delivering and receiving supplies?	o	o
What is it?		
_____		
_____		
Is the Purchasing Department able to get items as needed?	o	o
Are the correct items being secured?	o	o
Are the lowest prices being negotiated?	o	o
Are special orders being handled accordingly?	o	o
Does the Materials Manager screen sales calls?	o	o

		o	o
Is the demand for inventory:		o	o
	fixed for each item?	o	o
	variable for each item?	o	o
	constant for each item?	o	o
Is inventory waste occurring due to repeated orders?		o	o
Are vendor prices checked on a regular basis?		o	o
	How often?	o	o
Is the inventory budget fixed?		o	o
Is the inventory budget variable?		o	o

REFERENCES

AHRMM Healthcare Standards. *AHRMM Advancing the Healthcare Supply Chain*. Association for Healthcare Resource & Materials Management, 2012a. http://www.ahrmm.org/ahrmm/ext/standards/faq.html.

AHRMM Healthcare Standards. *What Are Data Standards, and Why Are They Important in the Healthcare Supply Chain Industry?* Association for Healthcare Resource & Materials Management, 2012b. http://www.ahrmm.org/ahrmm/ext/standards/index.html.

AHRMM Statement on Comparative Effectiveness. *AHRMM Issues & Initiatives*. Association for Healthcare Resource & Materials Management, 2012. http://www.ahrmm.org/ahrmm/news_and_issues/issues_and_initiatives/ahrmm_comparative_effectiveness.jsp.

Behzad, B., Moraga, R.J., Chen, S. Modelling healthcare internal service supply chains for the analysis of medication delivery errors and amplification effects. *Journal of Industrial Engineering and Management* 4(4): 554–576, 2011. http://www.jiem.org.

Campbell, A., Methvin, T. *Defining Materials Management*. Trinity University, 2011. http://www.trinity.edu/eschumac/HCAD5320/Departmental%20Papers/Fall%202011/Materials%20Management%20Inst%20Mgmt.pdf.

Healthcare Provider Toolkit: Improving Patient Safety and Supply Chain Efficiency. Rep. GS1 Healthcare US, March 2012. http://www.oneandonlycampaign.org.

Motorola, Inc. *Reducing Healthcare Costs with Supply Chain Best Practices*. Motorola Leadership Series, 2010. http://www.motorola.com/web/Business/Products/_ChannelDetails/_Documents/_StaticFiles/Healthcare-Industry-Brief-0610.pdf.

Purchasing & Procurement Center. *Six Best Practices in Hospital Materials Management*, n.d. http://www.purchasing-procurement-center.com/hospital-materials-management.html.

Rossetti, M.D., Marek, D., Prabhu, S., Bhonsle, A., Sharp, S., Liu, Y. Inventory Management Issues in Health Care Supply Chains. University of Arkansas, 2008. http://www.uark.edu/~rossetti/reports/healthcare_supply_chain_rep.pdf.

4 Managing and Improving the Hospital Revenue Cycle Process

Carol S. Miller and David Edward Marcinko

CONTENTS

INTRODUCTION

> Collectively the healthcare industry spends over $350 billion to submit and process claims while still working with cumbersome workflows, inefficient processes, and a changing landscape marked by increasing out-of-pocket cost for patients as well as increasing operating costs.[1]

For many years, hospitals and healthcare organizations have struggled to maintain and improve their operating margins. They continue to face a widening gap between their operating costs and the revenues required to cover current costs as well as the costs to finance strategic growth initiatives and investments. Faced with increased operational costs and associated declines in rates of reimbursement, many healthcare hospital executives and leaders are concerned that they will not achieve margin targets. To stabilize the internal financial issue, some hospitals have focused on lowering expenses to save costs—an area they control and an area that will show an immediate impact; that is not, however, the best solution. Executives are concerned with the effect that these reductions may have on patient quality and service. Finding ways to maximize workflow to lower operating costs is vital. Every dollar not collected negatively impacts short- and long-term capital projects, lowers patient satisfaction scores, and possibly affects quality of patient care.

Small community or rural hospitals, large hospital systems, university-based hospitals, free-standing clinics, small or large provider practices, long-term care facilities, and others are faced with the steps and processes involved in the management of the revenue cycle, but each to a different degree. As an example, many large, hospital-based systems have integrated clinical management systems with electronic health records whereby information entered at the point of care immediately transmits to those individuals in the billing department, whereas private practice physicians may rely on a remote billing service that supports multiple providers. Rural or smaller facilities may only have part-time staff to support their needs. In addition, some facilities or providers still rely on paper transmission, providing another cumbersome step in the process of claims submission and collection as well as the risk of missing supportive documentation and charges.

Revenue cycle operations appear to be straightforward: Render a service, bill for the service, and collect reimbursement; upon deeper examination, however, there are many components that have to be included to establish a high-performing, integrated, coordinated, seamless revenue cycle operation. The effectiveness of a hospital's revenue cycle drives the entire hospital operation because the cycle is the source of the resources needed to maintain a successful facility. Success rests in how well the cycle is integrated. A successful revenue cycle is a complex process involving many inter-related components. This process not only relies on the technology and software that support the collection of data related to a billable event, but also on the processes established, the capabilities and motivation of staff, and the culture of the organization. Trained staff is crucial to each part of the revenue cycle to ensure that all processes and systems are working efficiently. Regardless of what is in place, every hospital, to maintain viability, needs to either improve or create a detailed process for improving revenue cycle performance. Poorly managed revenue can lead to a significantly lower profit margin, clerical errors, problems with insurance providers, and shortage of staff to fulfill requirements.

Hospitals and providers need to be prepared and need to ensure that their revenue cycle process is performing effectively and efficiently to handle these changes. Every hospital and provider has the fiduciary responsibility to ensure that the revenue cycle is capturing the appropriate reimbursement for all clinical services rendered.

A basic role of hospital revenue cycle management is to measure how well a hospital maximizes the amount of patient revenue billed and how quickly it collects that revenue. An effective way to analyze patient revenue billed is to consider trends in the percentage of gross revenue written off versus collectible or net revenue. The speed at which the hospital collects net revenue can be analyzed by looking at trends in the percentage of accounts receivable (A/R) reserved for write-off versus collectible as well as the ratio of net A/R days outstanding. As an example, the Healthcare Financial Management Association noted that the percentage of gross revenue written off by hospitals rose steadily from 63.2 percent in fiscal year 2006 (FY06) to an astounding level of 66.9 percent in FY10. These trends suggest that hospitals spend considerable effort to capture revenues that they will never be able to collect. The percentage of A/R reserved for write-off also rose steadily during this five-year period, from 46.1 percent in FY06 to 62.3 percent in FY10. Conversely, the percentage of collectible A/R declined from 53.9 percent in FY06 to 47.7 percent in FY10.[2] These trends suggest that the net revenues billed by hospitals are getting harder to collect.

The objectives related to successful revenue cycle management are as follows:

- Improve cash flow
- Increase revenue
- Lower bad debt expense
- Improve patient/customer satisfaction with financial services
- Reduce operating cost
- Increase productivity
- Reduce the possibility of extended patient stays
- Understand problem areas and implement improvements

This chapter will review the issues affecting revenue cycle, the impact of regulations and healthcare reform, positioning the right organizational structure, information technology needs, a summary of the operational elements in the revenue cycle, quality and process improvement, and a summary of recommended performance metrics and measurements.

ISSUES IMPACTING THE REVENUE CYCLE

As stated, hospitals and providers are under increasing pressure to collect revenue to remain solvent. The significant issues facing the revenue cycle staff include the following:

- **Impact of consumer-driven health:** This process has emerged as a new approach to the traditional managed care system, shifting payment flows and introducing new "nontraditional" parties into the claims processing workflow. As market adoption enters the mainstream, consumer-driven health stands to alter the healthcare landscape more dramatically than anything we have seen since the advent of managed care. This process places more financial responsibility on the consumer to encourage value-driven healthcare spending decisions.
- **Competing high-priority projects:** Hospitals are feeling pressured to maximize collections primarily because of impending changes due to healthcare reform, and they know they will need to juggle these major initiatives along with the day-to-day revenue cycle operations.
- **Lack of skilled resources in several areas:** Hospital have struggled to find the right personnel with sufficient knowledge of project management, clinical documentation improvement, coding, and other revenue cycle functions, resulting in inefficient operations.
- **Narrowing margins:** Declines in reimbursement are forcing hospitals to look at their organization to determine if they can increase efficiencies and automate to save

money. Hospitals are faced with the potential of increased cost to upgrade and adapt clinical software while not meeting budget projections. There are a number of factors contributing to the financial pressure, including inefficient administrative processes such as redundant data collection, manual processes, and repetitive rework of claims submissions. Also included are organizations using outdated processes and legacy technologies.

- **Significant market changes:** Regardless of what happens with the Patient Protection and Affordable Care Act, hospitals will have to deal with fluctuating amounts of insured and uninsured patients and variable payments.
- **Limited access to capital:** With the trend towards more complex and expensive systems, industry may not have the internal resources and funding to build and manage systems that keep pace with the trends.
- **Need to optimize revenue:** There are five core areas that hospitals must examine carefully:
  - **International Classification of Diseases–Tenth Edition (ICD-10):** This is an entirely new coding and health information technology issue, but it also represents a revenue issue.
  - **System integration:** Hospitals need to look at integrating software and hardware systems that can combine patient account billing, collections, and electronic health records.
  - **Clinical documentation:** Meaningful use will require detailed documentation for payment to be made; this is another revenue issue.
  - **Billing and claims management:** Reducing denials and rejecting claims, training staff, improving point-of-service collections, and decreasing delays in patient billing can improve the revenue cycle productivity.
  - **Contract analysis:** Hospitals need to focus more on negotiating rates with insurers to increase revenue.

IMPACT OF REGULATIONS, LAWS, AND HEALTHCARE REFORM

There is a fair amount of activity that will take place in response to the transition to ICD-10, healthcare reform, the Affordable Care Act (ACA), meaningful use compliance and its financial incentives, and other regulatory issues that will require system or software upgrades to support the new efforts. As an example, the ACA is expected to significantly alter reimbursement structures and delivery of care. Below are several areas that will be affected.[3]

- With the projected increase in patient volumes, an associated cost of about 62 percent will emanate from Medicare cuts: $162 billion through reducing fee-for-service Medicare payments; $136 billion from setting Medicare Advantage rates based on fee-for-service payments; and $36 billion from cutting hospital Medicare/Medicaid disproportionate share.
- Compliance reviews will be increased through recovery audit contractors, where Centers for Medicare and Medicaid Services (CMS) expect to obtain $2.9 billion in additional savings. With recovery audit contractors in place, hospitals and providers need to increase their focus and attention on improving documentation quality and validating medical necessity to substantiate their reviews.
- Reduced payments for re-admissions and Medicare penalties for poor outcomes can and will affect the bottom line for both hospitals and providers in the future.
- By 2015, more than 19 million uninsured will receive coverage, and in 2016, another 11 million uninsured will be insured. This will create more patients per hospital/provider and will require more full-time equivalents to support the revenue cycle process of registration, documentation, billing, and collection.

- The ICD-10 conversion will create more complex requirements for documenting diagnoses and will require software modifications for hospitals and providers as well as significant training.

ORGANIZATIONAL STRUCTURE

Organizational structures in the past have been very fragmented islands of expertise that were and continue to be managed by different individuals with different goals and objectives. From a design and operations viewpoint, this approach has become antiquated and lends itself to issues regarding revenue collection. In addition, this approach does not provide a clear picture to those individuals who are responsible for overseeing the financial viability of a hospital or provider practice, in that they can not fully see all the issues or problems that relate to lost revenue. In today's structure, the trend is to place individuals working on front-end functions, middle functions (e.g., documentation and coding), and back-end functions under a senior financial executive to ensure that all sides are integrated and well-coordinated.

First and foremost, since the organizational structure is designed to help an organization achieve its purpose, the purpose itself must first be clearly defined. The purpose overall is very simple: to convert patient, payer, and service information into cash—more simply, to convert net revenue to cash.

If a traditional organization structure is used, the structure needs to have leaders in such areas as patient access/registration, health information management (HIM), and billing and collection, with oversight and management by a chief revenue cycle officer or chief financial officer. This governance model assures the applicable information is documented, billed, and reimbursed; resolves process or people issues that may be negatively impacting the flow of information; and enables cross-functional learning and information exchange.

An even more innovative approach is to design specific high-performance work teams on the back end in which several fully self-contained mini business offices are responsible for a given set of patient accounts. Within these teams, all skill areas are represented, including coding, billing, validation, collections, denial management, follow-up, etc. These teams are physically co-located such that intra-team communication is fast and easy, allowing team members to resolve issues, even cross-functional ones, immediately. Each team is held accountable to a set of revenue cycle metrics, and the metrics between teams are identical to allow for direct comparisons. With this design, most problems associated with traditional organizational structures are eliminated, and a platform for cross-training and team competition, along with performance-based pay, is built into the structure. In this model, the managerial responsibilities shift to performance management and process improvement while the team focuses on its own operations. The intent is to streamline patient services, minimize rejected claims, and accelerate reimbursement while improving patient satisfaction and overall revenue cycle performance.

BENCHMARKING

From the standpoint of patient accounting, coding allows for a common language between providers and payers during the reimbursement process. Accurate coding procedures limit the number of denied claims due to inaccuracies, thereby optimizing cash flow and managing A/R. Examples of what coders utilize in the coding process are referenced in Figure 4.1.

The expanded levels of specificity created in ICD-10 are expected to have a significant impact in terms of more accurate reimbursements and fewer rejected claims, but they will require more work and time. As would be expected, this new system is several orders of magnitude more complex than its predecessor, ICD-9. Successful transition will require significant modifications to existing healthcare information technology systems, new tools for analytics, and a tremendous amount of training for these new requirements.

An industry-acknowledged professional recommends the following targets for different levels of coding expertise:[4]

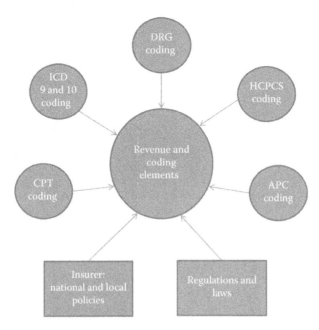

FIGURE 4.1   Revenue and coding element ecosystem.

The above table is for coding and light abstracting. The study assumes an 8-hour day and a 40-hour week.

Type	Coding Specialist I	Coding Specialist II	Coder I	Coder II
Inpatients	>45 records daily	>32 records daily	>15 records daily	>23 records daily
Outpatients and emergency department records	2 min/chart or 250/day	2 min/chart or 250/day	4 min/chart or 120/day	3 min/chart or 160/day
Ambulatory surgery	3.5 min/chart or 130/day	4 min/chart or 120/day	8 min/chart or 60/day	8 min/chart or 60/day

Coding averages referenced in the table above represent averages based on existing coding methodology, which have been in place for a period of time. Converting to ICD-10 will surely decrease the above averages per coder until they learn the nuances and structure of the new coding system.

Coding is one of the core HIM functions; due to the complex regulatory requirements affecting the health information coding process, coding professionals are frequently faced with ethical challenges, (e.g., does the level of care support a higher or lower coding structure, or which is the most appropriate diagnosis code to address multiple problems?). Even trained providers have difficulty selecting the most appropriate code. Therefore, the use of a common language or vocabulary is a fundamental component of performance measure and workflow. Re-engineering the work process and evaluation measures seeks to facilitate use of informatics tools to make the coding process more reliable and efficient.

TECHNOLOGY

Automation can lead to decreased paperwork, standardized processes, increased productivity, and cleaner claims. Automation also leads to a better control of expenses, higher productivity, and efficient utilization management.

Because the revenue cycle involves many different people and departments, one challenge to using technology is ensuring the systems are integrated. As stated in the Hospital Review articles, "Hospitals use 10–12 different technological systems throughout the entire revenue cycle. Sophisticated software may not benefit a hospital if there are different systems that are not integrated. Hospitals should assess their technology to identify deficiencies and areas of overlap. One of the biggest mistakes many providers make is purchasing too many pieces of software instead of looking for one robust solution."[5]

In addition, as stated in another article, "Only one in five hospitals expect to change their core revenue cycle management software within two years, but much of the change will be at large hospitals versus smaller facilities and/or provider hospitals," according to a recent survey by a health information technology research firm. "Only 18 percent of hospitals with less than 200 beds are looking to replace core systems; 21 percent of hospitals with 200–400 beds are considering; and 36 percent of hospitals above 400 beds are looking for a change."[6]

Technology plays an important role across the entire revenue cycle operation. Multiple systems in hospitals are not only inefficient for the staff but are cumbersome and repetitive for the patient. A more patient-friendly, integrated billing and registration system is needed. The large number of firms servicing the provider and hospital market is compounded by the complex diversity of business models that have emerged, even further fractionalizing the landscape.

The following lists provide a few critical areas in which technology has improved revenue management operations.

PATIENT ACCESS

- Call center capabilities with auto dialing, faxing, and Internet connectivity to quickly ensure and verify all insurance information
- Master Patient Index software to eliminate duplicate medical record numbers and assist with assigning a unique identifier for all patients
- Registration and admission software that scripts the admission process to assist staff in obtaining required elements and check that insurer-required referrals are documented

HEALTH INFORMATION MANAGEMENT

- Chart-tracking software to eliminate manual medical record out-guides and decrease the number of lost charts
- Encoding and grouper software to improve coding accuracy and speed and to improve reimbursement
- Auto-printing and faxing capabilities
- Internet connectivity for release of information and related document management tasks
- Electronic management of documents

PATIENT FINANCIAL SERVICES

- Automated biller queues to improve and track the productivity of each biller
- Claims scrubbing software to ensure that necessary data is included on the claim prior to submission
- Electronic claims and reimbursement processing to expedite the payment cycle

Each of these technologies, tools, software programs, and systems has the ability to connect to outside systems for bi-directional transmittals, reduces the gap time between a service being rendered and billed, generates a bill with correct coding, releases a clean bill to the appropriate insurer(s), and can achieve the ultimate desired result of reimbursement.

REVENUE CYCLE OPERATIONS

There are three functional areas in the revenue cycle: front end, middle, and back end, as depicted by Figure 4.2. The front end represents all the required functions and information associated with the patient's entry into the hospital system or provider's practice. The middle function represents the intersection between a patient entering the system, having clinical services, and the back-end function of billing. The back-end functions, more commonly referred to as the "back office," require information technology systems and processes to generate a timely bill and manage all the associated collections on accounts. Automated workflow management tools coupled with effective process governance can lead to meaningful streamlining of back-end processes.

Optimal performance in the revenue cycle is dependent on efficiency, speed, and accuracy. Elimination of manual tasks, automation edits and controls, and shared access are best achieved with a well-implemented and managed system from front to back end. The ideal of course is for a more comprehensive system that integrates the front-end functions, specific clinical documentation through an application process and the hospital and professional billing systems—one that can be used to generate accurate reports, identify duplication, and determine which accounts are outstanding. The traditional process of separate silo processes and systems does not enable efficiencies for operational management, control, and monitoring.

FRONT-END PROCESSES

PRE-REGISTRATION

The initial area identified to improve revenue cycle management rests with the pre-registration process and includes timely information capture and the quality of that data. All hospitals, clinics, and provider offices should pre-register and pre-schedule patients to better manage the entire intake process. If there is a rush during registration, there is the possibility of capturing inaccurate information, which may result in a denied claim. There is a significant opportunity during the pre-registration process to improve patient satisfaction and to either remind patients of deductibles, co-payments, or back payments owed, or to use this initial meeting as a means of collecting dollars prior to a hospitalization, visit, or procedure.

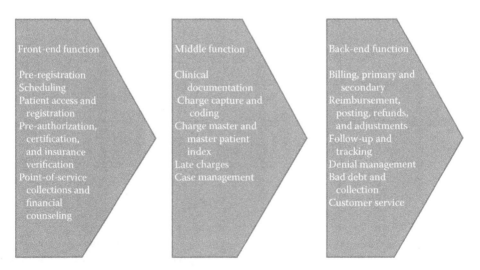

FIGURE 4.2   Revenue cycle operations.

SCHEDULING

Many individuals feel the revenue cycle begins at pre-registration, but scheduling and pre-registration could be combined to represent the starting point of the revenue cycle. Scheduling includes verifying a patient's demographic information and source of payment, either from insurance or as self-pay; validating the medical necessity requirements; accurately and efficiently scheduling the requested service; and assuring patient satisfaction throughout the process.

Most scheduling processes are automated to ensure efficient intake of information, incorporation of clinical rules or tests requiring pre-certification or pre-authorization, and the ability to schedule multiple services within a hospital setting at one given time. Performance metrics include multiple aspects of this process to include re-scheduled, cancelled, or no-show appointments that can occur either at the patient level or the provider level due to scheduling conflicts. Each of these measures needs to be evaluated on a monthly basis to determine how processes, procedures, and communications can be improved.

PATIENT ACCESS AND REGISTRATION

Most low performance rates for patient access teams are due to a lack of proper resources, inadequate training, and insufficient staffing levels. Fortunately, these can be resolved quickly and without huge expenses. Crucial to the revenue cycle is identifying the financial status prior to or directly upon admission. Patient access includes confirming the patient's identify, re-validating medical necessity, and ensuring all payer requirements are in place or being met prior to service, including notifications, pre-certifications, authorizations, and/or referrals.

Patient access is crucial to improving billing and collections efforts and increasing revenue cycle performance. Patient access can be improved significantly with several of the following information technology assets:

- Registration software that links with the hospital's or provider's electronic health record
- Master Patient Index software that assigns a unique patient identifier and eliminates duplicate medical record numbers
- Internet capability to quickly verify that all pertinent information, such as insurance, is correct
- Scheduling software that links with the electronic health record
- Technology upgrades to all hospital and provider systems as well as extensive training for staff

An important review includes monitoring the number of registration errors on a daily basis. Determining what caused the error can help the hospital or provider practice improve quality through retraining efforts, developing more detailed checklists during registration, or changing procedures. This process ensures that the team learns from its mistakes and reduces the number of mistakes in the future.

PRE-AUTHORIZATION, PRE-CERTIFICATION, AND INSURANCE VERIFICATION

Pre-authorization is a statement by a third-party payer indicating that proposed treatment will be covered under the terms of the benefits in the contract, whereas pre-certification authorization is obtaining the approval for a specific medical procedure before it is performed or for admission to an institution for care. The latter is required for payment by most managed care organizations in the United States.

Hospitals and providers need access to online/integrated insurance verification systems with real-time responses to verify, prior to admission or a service, that the patient-to-be has the stated coverage and insurance. This includes verifying coverage, approved length of stay, coverage terms, patient out-of-pocket obligations, requirements for pre-authorization or pre-certification, and any coverage limitations and maximum benefits.

As part of a routine process, all denials related to pre-authorization, pre-certification, and insurance verification should be tracked to determine if any continuous improvements could be included to eliminate future denials.

POINT-OF-SERVICE COLLECTIONS AND FINANCIAL COUNSELING

Today there are many patients who are struggling to pay for healthcare. Uninsured patients frequently utilize the emergency department or walk-in clinics for their "office visit" with no ability to pay. Likewise, charity cases based on federal, state, and local regulations are on the rise. Within the next three to four years, this problem is projected to decrease with the adoption and implementation of the ACA provisions, where all individuals will have insurance coverage. However, in today's marketplace, hospitals and providers still need to focus on identifying eligibility for third-party sponsorship and/or eligibility for charity care under state, local, or hospital programs. In addition, states and individuals can opt out of this new coverage, leaving uninsured or uncovered patients to be admitted to the hospital, emergency department, and office practices.

The discussion of patient access and registration includes the topic of financial obligations:

- Financial conversations with uninsured and underinsured patients
- Referrals to financial counseling
- Identifying any potential non-covered or patient residual amounts that will be due after services are rendered and payment is provided by insurers
- Identifying any patient prior balances past due for payment
- Screening patients for workmen's compensation, grants, or other third-party payments
- Requesting patient deposits for copayments, deductibles, and co-insurance

Hospitals and providers need to perform real-time editing to identify any missing or inaccurate information required by billing and to utilize tools for estimating patient out-of-pocket responsibility. Financial counseling is not only a pre-registration and registration function, but also one used prior to discharge.

MIDDLE PROCESSES

CLINICAL DOCUMENTATION/MEDICAL RECORDS

The hospital must evaluate the quality of the clinical documentation and justification of services rendered. At the same time, hospitals need to evaluate complications and/or co-morbidities that can extend a patient's stay and increase the cost of the admission.

Documentation requirements may vary depending on the whether the process is manual or automated, with the latter requiring providers to specifically document information in electronic health record fields. In addition, documentation may vary based on the different documentation requirements for specialty physicians or type of care. Increased standardization in documentation will help facilitate more accurate and timely information from the hospital staff and provider offices. Any element that is ambiguous in its interpretation will create a level of risk in completing the process correctly and in a reasonable time frame. Establishing standardized processes and procedures that providers understand will streamline the process, create efficiencies in the back-end process, and improve revenue flow. Accurate and detailed clinical documentation, including patient history, assessment, procedure notes, clinical plan, and progress notes, provides the basis for billing, reduces denials, and improves the revenue stream.

CHARGE CAPTURE AND CODING

Tracking the services a patient receives to ensure they are documented, accurate, and posted is crucial to assuring correct reimbursement. Coding is essential to the revenue cycle because it impacts the potential payment from payers.

There are two important questions regarding charge capture. Does the clinical staff document all aspects of the care accurately into the medical record not only in a timely manner? Are their services inadequately or not at all documented whereby the hospital or provider misses billing for these services? Accurate and complete documentation requires trained and skilled staff, knowledgeable of insurance benefits and exclusions, who can identify charges associated with supplies and services rendered and input these charges and codes accurately into the billing system.

Charge capture can be as simple and streamlined as the clinician entering the charge code for a service directly into the electronic medical record as part of his or her documentation, which in turn is integrated into the HIM system and billing application. However, many providers are still not documenting their care until the end of the day, are using manual records with handwritten notes, or are using the older concept of charge tickets that are then transferred to another department to decipher and code. This manual process creates significant delays in the revenue cycle due to such menial tasks as having a coder review a chart to interpret the provider's level of care from handwritten notes.

A diversity of processes and tools for charge capture and clinical documentation can add complexity to the revenue cycle process. Direct entry at the time of the service supports optimum revenue cycle performance, enables real-time edit checking, and eliminates delays or errors in processing. Regardless of the tools in place, standardization of clinical documentation and charge capture/coding should be utilized. In addition, continued education regarding missing or inadequate documentation needs to be reviewed with the providers within a short time frame to expedite the data being forwarded to billing as well as prevent re-occurrence.

Certified coders must be able to identify and access all clinical documentation for a given episode of care. Without proper education on tools and systems, there is always a risk that essential clinical information necessary to ensure coding accuracy is missing. There is a trend due to space, and supporting the concept of outsourcing, where coding functions are moving off-site to other complexes or to contracted firms. These processes require added security measures given the protected nature of patient data, and require that these outside professionals have access to appropriate systems and tools to assure clinical information is coded correctly. In addition, each insurer imposes specific coding regulations based on their coverage guidelines as well as local and national guidelines, which must be understood and readily accessible to each coder. In most hospitals and clinics, systems include built-in automated edits that are in place to identify discrepancies before submission.

As with all processes in the revenue cycle, operational controls that include checks and balances should be used for each task and each person.

CHARGE MASTER AND MASTER PATIENT INDEX

The Charge Description Master is an extremely complex file that is subject to continuous updates and requires continual maintenance. This file contains every single line item for which a charge may be made, including hospital services, all diagnostic and therapeutic procedures, equipment, supplies, drugs, and professional services. Each of these charges is correlated to a standard clinical code, such as ICD-9 or ICD-10, Current Physician Terminology (CPT-4), Healthcare Common Procedure Coding System (HCPCS), and others along with the appropriate modifiers that support these codes. Maintenance includes adding or deactivating charge codes, and pricing is related to the contracts and operating costs. The most important ingredients to the Charge Description Master are accuracy of information entered and the mapping of these line items to service codes.

To ensure proficiency in this process, a formal management process and annual review process should be developed and scheduled with clinical departments. A standardized pricing methodology should also be defined. Issues should be identified, discussed, communicated, and resolved by all accountable parties as they occur.

Consistent with the notion of consolidating functionality across the claims processing workflow is a broader class of opportunity: an electronic communications infrastructure that enables the sharing of information across disparate systems, databases, and stakeholders. This includes the creation and maintenance of common informational databases such as master patient indexes.

LATE CHARGE REDUCTIONS

Late charge services occur after discharge or are charges that were not charged or credited to a patient account from admission to discharge dates or through the last interim bill. This creates a re-submission of the claim with only the late charges. Each health facility has a preset minimum number of days that the information system will hold or suspend the account while awaiting additional charges that are necessary for proper billing. The most typical delay is around three days for outpatient accounts and five days for inpatient accounts. The rule of thumb to follow is to avoid late charges. Late charges should be a rare occurrence—an exception. Often the cost of rework in billing, information systems, accounting, and other areas far exceeds the value of the charges. If late charges are routine in a hospital system, then the system is likely experiencing other inaccurate charging as well, such as lost charges, misappropriated charges, overcharges, and undercharges. In addition, rebills to insurance firms can trigger audits, cause denials and delays, and require manual intervention and time. Hospitals need to review the causes of late charges and rectify the problems to prevent future occurrences.

CASE MANAGEMENT

Case management in healthcare is "a collaborative process of assessment, planning, facilitation, care coordination, evaluation, and advocacy for options and services to meet an individual's and family's comprehensive health needs through communication and available resources to promote quality cost-effective outcomes."[7] Case management is also a process to plan, seek, and monitor services from different social agencies and staff on behalf of a client. Usually one agency takes primary responsibility for the client and assigns a case manager, who coordinates services, advocates for the client, and sometimes controls resources and purchases services for the client. The case file must be accessible in a suitably controlled way to all who are involved in the case.

Case management focuses on delivering personalized services to patients to improve their care and to assist with discharges; the elements of case management include:

- Referral of new patients
- Planning and delivery of care
- Evaluation of results for each patient and adjustment of the care plan
- Evaluation of overall program effectiveness and adjustment of the program

In the context of a health insurer or health plan, case management is a method of managing the provision of healthcare to patients with high-cost medical conditions. The goal is to coordinate the care so as to improve continuity and quality of care and to lower costs. Case management requires an information system to manage the documentation and messages from multiple caregivers and to substantiate the level of effort in transitioning to an appropriate level of extended care.

Case management is assigned to providers and nurses who monitor admission progress with established clinical guidelines and provide the care planning and coordination for discharges. With the cost at hospitals on the rise, this professional team is integral to the process of controlling cost of care, assessing appropriate admissions based on admission and clinical parameters, and determining the validity of inpatient stay extensions beyond that which is medically necessary. This team sits at the crossroads representing the patients, providers, quality of care, and the chief financial officer and senior management to ensure that the care rendered is efficient without unnecessary costs, which sometimes is at cross purposes.

This area is very important during the registration and admission process to determine the medical necessity of a stay (i.e., will the insurer pay for the stay?). Secondarily, on the back end, the case management review assists the providers and hospitals in reviewing the length of stay and appropriate time for discharge (i.e., eliminating a lengthy stay that is not medically necessary).

Case management includes workload and performance measures such as:

- Number of admissions/case manager (with outcome measure of percent appropriate)
- Number of discharges/case manager (with outcome measure of percent delayed)
- Number of patient days managed and percent of total patient days

A consolidation of data either through systems integration or an integrated HIM system with an electronic medical record is crucial to the success of a case management process. Case managers heavily rely on admissions data as well as alerts such as observation cases with a length of stay approaching 24 hours, limit of days prescribed under pre-certification approval, and cases where discharges will require continued care under another service such as extended care or home health. Tracking and documentation by the case manager and team are extremely important to the hospital's fiscal outcomes.

BACK-END PROCESSES

BILLING: PRIMARY AND SECONDARY INSURANCE

Hospital or provider billing services, dependent on their internal operations and the quality and motivation of their staff, represent opportunities to increase efficiencies in the time frame between discharge and submission of the bill to the insurer. Many hospitals have been known to hold onto the bill longer than needed before submission, which in turn delays reimbursement.

Billing and claim submission can operate smoothly if strong processes and information technology solutions are in place that provide real-time, rules-based editing of accounts. The key to a successful billing process rests with a "clean claim" submission, where all patient insurance information, diagnosis and procedure coding, and pre-approvals are obtained. A "clean claim" should result in accurate payment. The entire billing process relies on biller-specific workloads, payer edits, automatic error identification, defined coordination of benefits denoting who is the primary, secondary, and/or tertiary insurer, and direct interface into the online insurer billing systems. Functions within the billing cycle need to be continually audited to determine the level of quality or the need for process improvement or training. Trained and cross-trained staff, sufficient staffing levels to minimize backlogs, access to clinical documentation, and guarantor backup is crucial to the success of billing.

REIMBURSEMENT, POSTING, REFUNDS, AND ADJUSTMENTS

Automation of billing, posting reimbursements and adjustments, and billing of secondary insurers will lead to the staff's ability to improve the back-office revenue cycle processes. Providers and hospitals need American National Standards Institute (ANSI) transaction capabilities that are integrated seamlessly with legacy systems to support full electronic data interchange claims, claim attachments, and payment processing, which will expedite the reimbursement/adjustment posting process.

The entire process of posting payments needs to be handled with a totally separate dedicated staff primarily for checks and balances. This includes cash payments, insurer manual or electronic fund transfers, refunds by check or money order, credit card payments and adjustments, third-party payments on behalf of a patient, guarantor payments, pre- and post-contractual adjustments, and all other write-offs.

Follow-Up/Tracking

Important in the revenue cycle is not only the documentation of services that a patient receives but also the back-end tracking that a submitted claim has been reimbursed. Tracking is crucial throughout the entire life cycle until final resolution of the claim. Many times the follow-up process in the back end is more cumbersome than it needs to be, because the staff must spend additional time cleaning up errors from registration or documentation that have occurred in the front-end and middle processes. This process is very time-consuming. The staff not only has to generate and review extensive reports, but also has to contact insurers, patients, patient families, and providers, address and further substantiate payment discrepancies, and many times follow-up with a re-billing process. These follow-up teams are key to obtaining the correct revenue for the hospital or provider. Without this team, revenue would be unclaimed or unpaid.

Follow-up functions can either occur with an in-house team dedicated to this process or be out-sourced to a firm that specializes in follow-up. The important element is to make sure that staffing levels are sufficient to minimize A/R backlog volumes and that staff is cross-trained on more than one payer type. In addition, system "tickler" reminders for each stage of follow-up and summary documentation for non-payment and underpayment are needed in this stage of the revenue cycle. Risk, age of claim, value, and other key elements need to be prioritized for pursuit. Wasting time on a $10 co-payment does not offset the benefit of receiving a large balance payment. Accounts that are of significant value and have aged past expected time frames need to be tracked, monitored, and documented on a weekly basis through resolution. Management needs to be informed of the working results of these follow-up teams, with tools such as core dashboard reports, trend reports, and drill-down reports.

Denial Management

Claims for services rendered can be submitted and denied for a number of reasons, such as failure to meet a deadline for submission; services not covered by the patient's insurer, such as cosmetic surgery; insufficient documentation to substantiate the service rendered; insurance billed is not the primary insurance; insurance was cancelled; and a multitude of other reasons. The hospital or provider needs to assess each denial and determine how it can resubmit information for reconsideration and/or what could be done on a future billing to prevent a similar denial from occurring.

Denials for non-covered services, inappropriate or non-justified coding, fragmented billing, coordination of benefits rejections, and deferrals of payments that request further substantiated documentation must be handled and managed until resolution. According to the Medical Group Management Association (MGMA), the cost to resubmit claims averages $25–$30. In addition, a United States Government Accountability Office report issued March 29, 2013 found that a significant percentage of denied claims went unpaid because of billing mistakes.[8] Many denied claims are paid on appeal, but resubmissions add to the expense of the process.[9] To improve revenue, the easiest established goal is to improve denied claims and submit cleaner claims from the start.

A claims denial management program is any system set up by a hospital or provider practice to determine why insurers are turning down claims. It allows the hospital or provider to address denials, whether they are caused by the insurer or the billing staff.

The process begins with a list of denied claims along with the reasons the claim was denied, the name of the insurer, the type of plan, and other relevant information. The next step is to identify the most common problems and devise ways to address them. These problems could be as simple as a transposed numbers, duplicate submission (original already paid but not posted), missing information, coverage ineligibility of patients, or just an error in payment by the insurer.

BAD DEBT AND COLLECTIONS

Collections include not only primary and secondary insurer payments, but also patient payments and third-party payments such as from workmen's compensation. It is even conceivable that a patient may have more than two insurance providers. Collection of these payments may rest with multiple individuals and different systems depending on the complexity and size of the medical provider or hospital. To improve the efficiency of collection operations and to increase the revenue, an efficient tracking and follow-up system is needed, one that will remind staff that payments are still owed.

Providers and hospitals are being affected by new reporting pressures from the Internal Revenue Service and the Sarbanes-Oxley Act on how bad debt and charitable care are reported. Each entity needs to determine when a collection process must be implemented in the revenue cycle or when accounts are determined to be bad debt accounts and must be forwarded to collection agencies. This is a delicate and sensitive process, but one that needs attention.

The use of integrated information technology and automated processes can significantly support high-performing collections and outsourcing for healthcare providers. Collections and outsourcing firms should possess direct experience in the healthcare industry due to the complex nature of patient accounting, as well as a track record demonstrating quantifiable results. These firms should be selected not only based on the level of fees proposed or charged but also on historical results, the capability to connect electronically with the hospital or provider's information systems, and the ability to produce meaningful reporting results and to demonstrate a strong customer-service orientation.

CUSTOMER SERVICE: FRONT, MIDDLE, AND END PROCESSES

To achieve best practices for revenue cycle management, one final element needs to be added. Hospitals or providers need to incorporate customer service and satisfaction into the pre- and post-service processes. Customer service includes addressing patient inquiries and issues regarding accounts and claims, as well as close coordination with other revenue cycle functions to resolve problems in a timely manner. Aside from experience, knowledge, and skills, efficient and effective customer service heavily depends on the information system infrastructure. Today's customer service information systems capabilities include integration with the main information systems to track and report key quantitative and qualitative aspects to measure their responsiveness and effectiveness. These individuals touch many facets of the revenue cycle and must be experienced in addressing a variety of patient inquiries. Their role is integral in the overall revenue cycle process.

MANAGEMENT EXPECTATIONS

Throughout the entire revenue management process, communications between all three functional areas must be improved and must occur on a regular basis. This will help ensure timely responses and compliance across all department boundaries. Along with communications, a weekly revenue cycle meeting should take place that includes key representatives from each area of the revenue cycle, such as patient access, registration, financial counseling, verification, case management, health information systems, billing, posting, follow-up, and others depending on the organizational structure. These individuals should be the ones accountable for status updates, identifying key issues and problems, recognizing accomplishments, and forecasting.

Finally, as each process and procedure is defined, the expectations from management should be determined, and quantifiable performance improvement goals should be established for each department. Managers need to focus on productivity, quality, operational efficiency, and excellence.

PERFORMANCE MEASUREMENTS

The revenue cycle for hospitals and provider offices is being impacted by changing dynamics and trends in the industry: real-time processing, consumer-driven healthcare, and changes in regulations and reimbursement structures. To achieve successful outcomes, a balanced combination of people, process, technologies used to support the processes, and the environment in which processes are carried out must be used. For the performance to be measured and used effectively, the level of metrics needs to be made at the specific operational levels that involve areas that can be quantified. Metrics for each of the categories—front end, middle, and back end—are based on existing best practice standards, executive reference, and organizational priorities.

REVENUE CYCLE IMPROVEMENT PROCESSES AND QUALITY MEASURES

An integrated approach is essential to the review of the revenue cycle to determine its inherent weaknesses and strengths. First of all, a detailed assessment of the current state of your revenue cycle must be performed. Once that is documented, a more tailored definition of the future state must be derived, taking into account resources and capabilities that are or will be available. The third step is a gap analysis, comparing the baseline revenue cycle processes, procedures, policies, and forms to the "to be" state envisioned. This assessment will enable the development of a transition plan and approach that will bridge the current practice to the future state and begin the development of process improvements and quality performance metrics that can evaluate the changes to the revenue cycle process and revenue income. Regardless of the tools and systems in place, a period of intensive follow-up is required to support the permanent improvement changes.

Quality measurements and metrics are important elements in the evaluation cycle, especially related to process improvement, for several reasons:

- Metrics support the analysis, recommendations, and conclusions—you cannot argue with quantifiable data.
- Metrics establish the tone where both negative and positive outcomes are measured.
- Metrics provid a mechanism for understanding outcomes and a way to obtain employee buy-in to change.
- Metrics establish accountability, especially for those employees not performing to par.
- Metrics provide data to leadership, enabling them to focus of issues, problems, and resolutions.
- Metrics are also used as a means to celebrate improvement once attained.

CONCLUSION

Revenue cycle management is a means to improve hospital revenue and reimbursement by streamlining workflow, processes, and education. The overall objectives are to provide financial stability and sustainability, increase cash flow, and improve operating margins. This process changes the traditional revenue cycle approach, which is more oriented toward labor, technology, and silo organizations, and does not address root-cause process breakdowns across the entire revenue cycle, to a different model. The new model looks at a whole new integrated approach that improves processes, capabilities, and technology across the life cycle. In challenging economic times, there is a unique opportunity to increase cash flow, reduce underpayments, improve quality, decrease denials, and evaluate staff performance. The goal is not to overwhelm a current system but to segmentally restructure the revenue cycle to achieve desired outcomes by way of the assessment of current processes (as is) and the identification of needed processes (to be).

Future reimbursement may change, operating costs are sure to increase, and rules and regulations impacting reimbursement will continue to evolve. Hospitals and providers need to pay attention to improving revenue cycle processes and systems to maintain viability for the future.

ACKNOWLEDGMENTS

To Karen White, PhD, of ACS-Xerox Healthcare Services, and Hope Rachel Hetico, RN, MHA, CMP™, of the Institute of Medical Business Advisors Inc., Atlanta, GA.

APPENDIX 1

The following tables provide the Key Performance Indicators and Best Practices Standards for select areas during the registration process, documentation/coding area, and billing/collection areas in the revenue cycle.[10]

Scheduling	
Pre-registration rate for schedule patients	>98 percent
Percent of tests scheduled in system	100 percent
Medical necessity checking at time of scheduling	100 percent
Legible order with all required elements at time of scheduling	>95 percent
Reminder calls for scheduled services	100 percent
Number of calls per test scheduled	Individual
Average speed of answer	<30 seconds
Percent of inbound call abandonment rate	<2 percent
Percent of patients rescheduled, cancelled, no show	Individual
Percent of patients postponed for lack of pre-certification	Individual
Next available appointment for diagnostic tests	<24 hours
Call abandonment rate	<2 percent

Patient Access	
Percentage of claims on hold for registration errors	<1/16 day of revenue
Number of statements in returned mail weekly	<5 percent
Percentage of patients waiting greater than 10 minutes for a registrar	<10 percent
Average face-to-face registration duration	10 minutes
Average registration throughput	35 inpatients (IP); 40 outpatients (OP)
Advanced beneficiary notices/Medicare secondary payer questionnaires obtained	100 percent
Data entry quality compared to established department standards	98 percent
Master Patient Index (MPI) duplication rate as percent of total registrations	<1 percent

Insurance Verification	
Eligibility is verified with the payer for scheduled services	98 percent
Denial rate of lack of pre-certification	Individual
Number of appeals, including those overturned and lost	Individual
Data quality as compared to pre-established standards	98 percent
Verification rate of IP within one business day	98 percent
Verification rate of high-dollar OP in one business day	98 percent

---

Financial Counseling

Medicaid eligibility screening for all uninsured patients	100 percent
Medicaid eligibility screening for all Medicare-only patients	100 percent
Percent of uninsured IPs screened for financial assistance	95 percent
Percent of uninsured OPs screened for financial assistance	Individual
Percent of uninsured emergency department patients screened for financial assistance	80 percent
Collects deposits for elective services prior to service	100 percent
Collects IP patient-pay balances prior to discharge	65 percent
Discusses options for account resolution with IPs	100 percent
Financial assistance approved within 10 days	100 percent
Medicaid approvals obtained within 30 days	100 percent

Case Management

Observation cases: two per length of stay (LOS) >24 hours (or other limit depending on case type)	0 percent
Cases denied reimbursement due to "inappropriate admission"	0 percent
Cases: two per discharge delays (by reason for delay)	0 percent
Ratio of the length of stay actual average over expected average	1:1
Current admission population on skilled nursing facility (SNF) wait list	0 percent

---

Charge Capture and Clinical Documentation

Professional/ambulatory charges entered <1 business day (2 days with exception for diagnostics charged on results posting; if expected results turnaround >1 day)	100 percent
Late charge hold period ("suspense days") (2–4 days)	2 days
Charges entered for admission encounters > 7 days (with exception for diagnostics charge on results posting; if expected results turnaround >7 day)	0 percent
Late charges as a percent of total charges	2 percent
Lost charges as a percent of total charges	1 percent
Clinical procedure/visit documentation entered <1 business day	100 percent
Final clinical procedure/visit documentation signed <3 business days	100 percent
Accounts/claims with charge coding errors (per subscriber)	1 percent
Accounts/claims with missing charges (per scrubber, coder review)	1 percent

---

Charge Description Master (CDM) from a Statistical Assessment of Records in the CDM

CDM duplicate items	0
CDM item price is $0 (other than 'no-charge' provider visit)	0
CDM item price less than HOPPS APC rate	0
CDM item description is "miscellaneous"	0
CDM item has missing modifier, if applicable	0
CDM item is missing the standard code (PHCPS, CPT-4, NDC, etc.) (type of code is dependent on type of charge the CDM item represents)	0

Note: APC, ambulatory payment classification; CPT, current procedural terminology; HOPPS, hospital outpatient prospective payment system; NDC, national drug code.

CDM—Includes Assessment and Analysis and Periodic Review (at least annually)	
Item is assigned an incorrect/invalid code (HCPCS, CPT-4, ICD-9/10)	0
CDM item is assigned an incorrect/invalid revenue code	0
CDM item has invalid/incorrect modifier	0
Surgery, lab, and radiology charges properly unbundled?	Yes
CDM items have consumer interpretable descriptions?	Yes

CDM—Track Activities of CDM Maintenance	
Number of CDM items updated in reporting period	100 percent
Aging report on update requests (timing from update request to update implemented)	Yes
Annual HCPCS, CPT-4 changes in place by January of each year?	Yes
Receive/review CPT-4 manual/addendum B annually?	Yes

Health Information Management (HIM)	
Discharged not final billed (DNFB) HIM work in process <X% of revenue or days A/R	5 percent
Average days age in pending queue <X days from entry into queue	3 days
Average days age in pending queue <X days from date of service or discharge	3 days
Coding status incomplete >5 days (DNFB) <X% of total cases	5 percent
Coding denials <X% of (number of accounts) ($ total charges)	1 percent
Coding write-offs <X% of (number of accounts) ($ total charges)	1 percent

HIM: Workload and Productivity	
IP charts codes per coder/per day (20–23)	23
Observation (OBSV) charts coded per coder/per day (30–34)	34
Ambulatory surgery (AMB SURG) charts coded per coder/per day (30–34)	34
OP charts coded per coder/per day (150–210)	210
Emergency department charts coded per coder/per day (150–210)	210

HIM: Manual Charts	
MPI duplicates as a percentage of total MPI entries (<0.05 percent)	0.5 percent
Chart delinquencies	5 percent
Missing charts	0 percent

Billing and Claim Submission	
HIPAA-compliant electronic claim submission rate	100 percent
Final-billed/claim not submitted backlog (one A/R)	1
Medicare supplemental insurance billing following adjudication (2 business days)	2
Non-Medicare COB-2 insurance billing following COB-1 payment (2 business days)	2
Medicare RTP (return to provider) denials rate	3 percent
Outsourced guarantor statement cost to produce/mail (20–25 cents)	$0.20
Clean claim submission rate	>85 percent

Cashiering, Refunds, and Adjustment Posting

HIPAA-compliant electronic payment posting percent	100 percent
Transaction posting backlog (during the month) (1 business day)	1
Transaction posting backlog (end of the month) (0 business days)	0
Credit-balance A/R days (gross) (1 A/R day)	1
Medicare credit-balance report submission timeliness (due date)	0

Third Party and Guarantor Follow-Up

Insurance A/R aged >90 days from service/discharge (15%–20%)	15 percent
Insurance A/R aged >180 days from service/discharge	5 percent
Insurance A/R aged >365 days from service/discharge	2 percent
Bad debt write-offs as a percent of gross revenue	3 percent
Charity write-offs as a percent of gross revenue	2 percent
Cost-to-collect ([PA+PFS+agency expenses]/cash)	3 percent
Patient cash as a percent of net revenue	100 percent
In-house inpatient A/R days (average LOS)	5
DNFB A/R days (4–6 A/R days)	4
Net A/R days (55 A/R days)	55
Cash as a percent of cash goal	100 percent
Total point-of-service cash as a percent of net revenue (2%–3%)	3 percent

Customer Service

Correspondence backlog (internal and external) (one business day from receipt)	1 day or less
Walk-in patient wait time (minutes)	5 or less
Automated call distribution (ACD) system average hold time (minutes)	0.5 or less
ACD system abandoned call percentage (percent of calls on hold more than 30 seconds)	2 percent or less
ACD system percentage of calls resolved in less than five minutes	85 percent or more
Calls resolved in customer service without complaint or referral to	5 percent or less
Administration/customer recovery office/related staff function	99 percent or more

Collections and Outsourcing

Bad debt net-back collection percentage (defined as: [collections minus fees] divided by placements)	11 percent or more (minimum of 7 percent)
Third-party extended business office (EBO) fee as a percentage of collections	15 percent (maximum of 18 percent)
Self-pay EBO fee as a percentage of collections	6 percent to 12 percent
Legal collections fee as a percentage of collections	25 percent or less (maximum of 30 percent)
Medicaid eligibility assistance fee as a percentage of collections	15 percent (maximum of 18 percent)
Routine auditing of collection agency minimum work standards	Every 60 days

Registration
Template   Name of Facility: Date:

Account Number	User Name	Patient Information	Guarantor	Emergency Contact	Primary Insurance	Secondary Insurance	Tertiary Insurance	Monthly Error Rate
XXX	Reg 1							
XXX	Reg 2							
XXX	Reg 3							
XXX	Reg 4							
								Total By Category

Monthly Registration Number by Area and User   Error % by User   Accuracy % per User

User Name	Total Accounts	Total Errors		Percent	Percent
XXX					
XXX					
XXX					

		Accuracy Requirement per Policy		Percent
		Efficient/Deficient Accuracy		Percent

Registration Error by Category

Patient Demo	Primary Insurance	Secondary Insurance	Tertiary Insurance	Other Insurance	Address	DOB	Etc.
XXX	XXX	XXX	XXX	XXX	XXX	XXX	

Sample Dashboard

Facility Name: Year:

Monthly Target	Location	POS Collections	Overall Collections	Registration Accuracy	Denials	Initial Denials %	Net Pt. Revenue per Pt. Encounter	Net Pt. Revenue % of Gross Pt. Revenue	Cash Collected as % of Net Pt. Revenue	Bad Debt Expense of Gross Pt. Revenue	Gross A/R Days	% A/R >90 Days
January	Admitting	Dollars		Percent								
	ED		Dollars		Dollars	Percent						
	Etc.											
February	Admitting	Dollars		Percent								
	ED		Dollars		Dollars	Percent						
	Etc.											
March												

Note: For registration accuracy, the stoplight colors need to be applied based on the percentage of accuracy established by the hospital.

Abbreviations: A/R, accounts receivable; ED, emergency department; POS, point of service; Pt., patient.

CASE MODEL 1

MEGA FEDERAL HOSPITAL CORPORATION

The MEGA Federal Hospital Corporation specializes in a certain type of high-risk heart coronary artery bypass graft (CABG) surgery, with revenue as seen below; revenues are recorded on the basis of generally accepted accounting principles (GAAP):

Description	GAAP	Taxable Income
Capitation revenue received	$60,000,000	$60,000,000
Administrative costs (15 percent)	$9,000,000	$9,000,000
Net available to pay medical costs	$51,000,000	$51,000,000
Paid and reported claims at year end	$43,500,000	$43,500,000
Incurred but not reported (IBNR) claims	$7,500,000	$0
Profit/Income	**$0**	**$7,500,000**
Tax rate	35 percent	
Federal income tax due on IBNR	$2,625,000	

Key Issues

Which of the following factors should have the greatest influence for MEGA Hospital in deciding whether to accept the contract?

- GAAP analysis
- IBNR deductions
- Pro-forma estimates
- Reserve amounts
- Profit or loss
- Taxes refunded or due

Solution

For a $60 million capitated contract, the MEGA Hospital did not profit and is responsible for a taxable income of $7,500,000. The $2,625,000 of taxes is payable to the IRS and is a direct reduction of the cash flow to the MEGA Federal Hospital Corporation.

CASE MODEL 2

THE MUNICIPAL HOSPITAL CLINIC, INC.

The Municipal Hospital Clinic, Inc. uses the historical cost analysis method of similar established organizations to estimate incurred but not reported (IBNR) accounts receivable calculations. It is based on the actual number of past claims on a per member/per month basis.

If the Municipal Hospital Clinic treated 5,000 and 6,000 HMO members, respectively, in two months, the total member year-to-date months would be 11,000, or 5,500 per month.

Therefore, if submitted medical costs were $3, and there were 11,000 members for the period, the total IBNR estimated reserve fund would be $33,000.

Key Issues

(1) What should be the Municipal Hospital Clinic's preferred method of analysis?
- Actuarial data analysis
- Historical cost analysis
- Open referral analysis
- Estimated comparable reserve fund analysis
- Pro-forma estimates

(2) Can you explain why it might be suggested that two to three times the average historical cost analysis claims history should be retained in the IBNR reserve fund for the Municipal Hospital Clinic, Inc.?

CHECKLIST 1: Revenue Cycle Organizational Structure	Yes	No
Determine the advantages of a centralized system.		
Is there more than one executive in charge of the areas of revenue cycle operations (defined as patient access, case management, health information management (HIM), and patient financial services (PFS)) at your hospital or healthcare facility?	o	o
If yes, what are their names and titles?		
_____		
_____		
_____		
Have you ever considered having the chief financial officer as the executive in overall charge?	o	o
If yes, do you think this organizational structure would provide better results?	o	o
Are any other executives in overall charge, and/or do you report to them?	o	o
• Chief information officer?		
• Director of revenue cycle management?		
• Director/manager(s) of PFS?		
• Director/manager(s) of patient access?		
• Director/manager(s) of HIM?		
• Director of case management?		
• Director of managed care?		
• CDM coordinator?		

CHECKLIST 2: Industry Benchmarking	Yes	No
Determine the benchmarks against which you will measure the performance of your hospital.		
Would application of industry standards improve processes?	o	o
Would processes improve through setting a baseline of current status performance levels?	o	o
Would performance be improved by re-engineering front-end processes?	o	o
Would performance be improved by re-engineering middle processes?	o	o
Would performance be improved by re-engineering back-end processes?	o	o

CHECKLIST 3: Information Technology Adoption	Yes	No
Assess the level of technology adopted by your hospital.		
Would re-training in systems improve the perception of system quality by staff?	o	o
Do you have a call center environment?	o	o

	Yes	No
Do you use the following software:		
Master Person Index?	o	o
Admission Process Scripting?	o	o
Chart Tracking?	o	o
Encoder?	o	o
Claims Editing?	o	o
Do you have automated biller queues for follow-up?	o	o
Do you utilize any imaging software in registration/admissions areas?	o	o
Do you issue claims to third-party payers and receive reimbursements electronically?	o	o

CHECKLIST 4: Revenue Cycle Performance Evaluation	Yes	No
Perform a Revenue Cycle Performance Evaluation with summaries.		
Are current state themes regarding people, process, and technology included in your evaluation?	o	o
• A review of known opportunities and threats?	o	o
• A gap analysis scorecard based on current versus optimal processes?	o	o
• A benchmark analysis?	o	o
• A benefits forecast?	o	o
• A prioritized list of appropriate solutions to consider for improvement of the financial position of the organization?	o	o
Are next-step recommendations for revenue cycle services implementations included?	o	o

APPENDIX 2

DIRECTOR OF REVENUE CYCLE MANAGEMENT JOB DESCRIPTION*

POSITION: Revenue Cycle Director
REPORTS TO: Chief Financial Officer
SUPERVISES: Revenue Cycle Managers

The revenue cycle is defined as all administrative and clinical functions that contribute to the capture, management, and collection of patient service revenue. The Revenue Cycle Director is responsible for enhancing and maintaining a properly functioning revenue cycle process through a cross-department organizational structure. These functional areas act interdependently during a patient visit, contributing critical information required for clinical service and procuring payment. Thus, the Revenue Cycle Director concentrates resources on improving core clinical care delivery and protecting the assets of the organization.

Critical responsibilities include achievement of annual and periodic goals for significant statistical indicators of revenue cycle performance and for the organization's overall financial performance.

The Revenue Cycle Director is expected to demonstrate, through plans and actions, that there is a consistent standard of excellence to which all departmental work is expected to conform. Such a standard should be based on establishing and maintaining a constancy of purpose, focusing on continuous improvement within the Director's area of influence, and delivering the highest degree of quality service possible.

The expertise of the Revenue Cycle Director should include:

---

* This Director of Revenue Cycle Management job description was compiled from actual job descriptions from several hospital and health systems, along with insights from the Healthcare Financial Management Association (HFMA) Patient Financial Services Task Force, HFMA's PFS Forum, and other advisors. Posted on the GE Healthcare website: http://www3.gehealthcare.com/en/Global_Gateway.

- Working knowledge in the areas of patient registration, billing, accounts receivable (A/R) and cash management requirements, managed care contractual terms and requirements, health insurance practices, industry regulatory requirements, business office operations, A/R and financial reporting technology, wage and hour regulations, basic accounting, and industry standards for healthcare revenue resolution management practices.
- Ability to analyze and resolve problems that affect the claim submission process, regardless of whether the problem originates in an area under direct or indirect control.
- Financial management skills, including the ability to financially analyze data for operations, budgeting, auditing, forecasting; basic accounting knowledge; AR and reserve analysis, market analysis; staffing; and financial reporting skills.
- Leadership skills to motivate cross-departmental teams' performance towards excellence and develop team concepts and consensus-building management styles.
- The ability to make a significant contribution to the organization's overall effectiveness.

Experience Required

Education
Bachelor's degree required, preferably in business, health or public administration, management, or a related field. Master's in hospital or business administration, accounting, finance, or related field and closely related clinical discipline preferred.

Work Experience
A minimum of seven years' management experience in the healthcare receivables field required, with a work record that demonstrates:

- In-depth knowledge of hospital and physician billing and reimbursement.
- Leadership in the core values of the organization.
- Clear, effective communication skills.
- A mature approach to problem solving for all types of issues.
- Skills in using mainframe and PC computers.
- Knowledge of medical terminology.
- Negotiating skills.
- Detail orientation.
- Experience with total quality management concepts and tools.
- Knowledge of healthcare industry financial statistical indicators.

Primary Responsibilities*
- Incorporate the facility's values into all business staff development practices and all departmentally directed activities.
- Complete (or contribute to the completion of) various financial forecasts, including cost center salary and direct expenses, month-end financial reporting, receivables levels (days in AR and aging), cost center productivity, and any long-range strategic plans for the department.
- Plan, coordinate, and prepare year-end audits with public accounting firms and third-party auditors as they relate to A/R operations. Mediate and resolve conflicts regarding public accounting firms, third-party auditors, and investigative parties.
- Directly manage all service programs, including external vendor programs and systems.

---

* The following functions are compiled from the essential duties listed for a variety of positions in this job classification. Individuals in this role may not perform all of these duties, or may perform additional, related duties not listed here.

- Monitor and support daily staff functions in all areas related to the scope of the manager's responsibility. Participate in revenue cycle, denial management, and access management work teams.
- Maintain appropriate internal control safeguards over A/R records and collection of cash.
- Maintain compliance standards for providing accurate information on all facility or health system billings.
- Assess and respond to organizational and customer needs with innovative programs to ensure customer satisfaction. Implement patient-friendly billing guidelines.
- Ensure compliance with relevant regulations, standards, and directives from regulatory agencies and third-party payers.
- Oversee the financial interface between and performance analysis of the patient financial service functions and fiscal service functions.
- Oversee the integrity of financial and clinical interfaces while facilitating the development of strategic system planning.
- Direct ongoing programs for staff development, which include:
  - Hiring and training for leadership positions and directing the hiring and training of all staff in the department;
  - Completing (or directing the completion of) all necessary human resources documentation and adhering to all human resources expectations for subordinates;
  - Communicating regularly and effectively with subordinates and superiors regarding the status and condition of the business operations under control of the Director; and
  - Developing multi-disciplinary patient financial services teams to enhance quality and efficiency.
- Carry out other assignments or special projects as assigned.

Denials Management by Adjustment Code

Name of Facility: Date:

Month Year	Incorrect Payment	Need Records	Wrong ID	Need EOB	Wrong Primary Insurance	Duplicate Claim	Timely Filing	Not Covered	No Authorization	Medical Necessity	Etc.
January 2014											
February 2014											
March 2014											
Etc.											
Total											
Percent of whole											

Note: Graphic bar charts can be created to assess changes in denials by month.

Abbreviations: EOB, explanation of benefits.

REFERENCES

1. Tenent Subsidiary Conifer Health Solutions Acquire Dell's Revenue Management System. *Dallas News Business*, 2012. http://bizbeatblog.dallasnews.com/2012/11/tenet-subsidiary-conifer-health-solutions-acquire-dells-revenue-management-system.html.
2. *Trends in Hospital Revenue Cycle Management*, Healthcare Financial Management Association, 2011. http://www.hfma.org.
3. *Health Reform's Impact on the Revenue Cycle*, McKesson, 2012. http://sites.mckesson.com/achievehit/revcycle.asp
4. *Best Practices for HIM Directors*, 3rd ed., Rose T. Dunn, 2012. Danvers, MA: HC Pro Inc.
5. *Comprehensive Revenue Cycle Services for Community Hospitals*, HealthTech Solutions Group. http://www.ht-llc.com/revenue-cycle-services.html.
6. *Survey: Hospital Looking at Revenue Cycle Changes*, Health Data Management, 2012. http://www.healthdatamanagement.com/news/hospital-survey.
7. *Dictionary of Health Insurance and Managed Care*, D.E. Marcinko and H.R. Hetico, 2006. New York, NY: Springer.
8. *Enhancements Needed for Improper Payments Reporting and Related Action Monitoring*, Government Accountability Office, GAO-13-229, 2013. http://www.gao.gov/products/GAO-13-229
9. *Denial Management: How to Improve the Process*, Shawn McKee, 2012. http://www.poweryourpractice.com/denial-management.
10. *Revenue Cycle Management: A Life Cycle Approach for Performance Measurement and System Justification*, HIMSS Financial systems, Revenue Cycle Task Force, May 2010.

Section II

Clinic and Technology

Contemporary Issues

5 Financial and Clinical Features of Hospital Information Systems

Brent A. Metfessel

CONTENTS

INTRODUCTION

Since the early 1980s, hospital information systems (HISs) have steadily grown in popularity. At present, nearly every acute-care hospital in the United States has at least some form of HIS, which at a minimum performs administrative tasks such as patient billing, accounting, and employee payroll tracking. Depending on the size of the hospital, an information system may initially cost from several hundred thousand dollars to tens of millions of dollars. Although hospitals face a wide array of budget challenges and potential cutbacks, hospitals are still expected to increase spending on information technology (IT). According to Healthcare Information and Management Systems Society (HIMSS) Analytics™ (2009), hospitals are estimated to spend 43 percent to 48 percent of their capital budgets on IT, growing at a rate of approximately 7.5 percent per year, due in large part to federal incentives and conversion to the International Classification of Diseases–Tenth Edition Clinical Module (ICD-10-CM) diagnostic coding system. Consequently, it is critical that such a system produce a positive return on investment (ROI) through patient care quality improvements, increases in organizational efficiency, or enhanced negotiating power with third-party payers and other stakeholders. For some facilities, past HIS projects, especially more complex undertakings, have been clear failures to the extent that the organization had to abandon the new HIS in favor of the previous manual system, although with experience the percent of implementations that become successful has increased. The goal of this chapter is to illustrate how hospitals can maximize the chances of successful implementations of HIS while at the same time providing a positive ROI.

OVERVIEW OF SYSTEM ARCHITECTURES

Hospitals can use a variety of configurations for HIS implementation depending on business needs and budgetary constraints. Staffing needed for these systems can range from a few full-time equivalents (FTEs) per 100 beds for very basic off-site processing systems to fifteen or more FTEs per 100 beds for sophisticated systems that attempt to combine several architectures into one system. Although off-site processing and mainframe systems were popular in the past, the vast majority of HISs are now based on a client–server architecture.

In this configuration, one or more "repository" computers exist, known as servers, that store large amounts of data and perform limited processing. Communicating with the servers are client workstations that perform much of the data processing and often have graphical user interfaces (GUIs) for ease of use. Both customizability and resource use are required, depending on the desired sophistication. For instance, the Veterans Health Administration, which has implemented what is likely the largest integrated HIS in the United States, uses client–server architecture. Known as the Veterans Health Information Systems and Technology Architecture (VistA), this system provides technology infrastructure to approximately 1,300 care facilities, including hospitals and medical centers, outpatient facilities, and long-term care centers. VistA utilizes a client–server architecture that links workstations and personal computers using software that is accessed via the GUI. Client–server architectures are preferred due in large part to their local adaptability and flexibility to meet changing hospital and medical center needs, despite the resource-intensive needs for implementation and maintenance. Client–server systems are also well-suited for web browsing and the use of wireless and mobile technologies, which can take place at the patient bedside.

Still, quite a bit of variation exists in the sophistication of hospital applications of client–server technology. In considering the optimal architecture for a hospital, management needs to take into account factors such as size of the institution, desired sophistication of the application, IT budget, and anticipated level of user community involvement.

Another important aspect of HIS is the need for integration. In less sophisticated technology environments, different hospital departments have their own stand-alone systems, such as a laboratory information system (LIS) or a pharmacy system, which do not communicate with each other or may even be from independent businesses. Duplicate data may be kept in separate systems, creating additional work to enter the data multiple times. In an integrated system, each departmental system communicates with other systems through either a centralized or decentralized network (Figure 5.1). A computerized provider order entry (CPOE) system, for example, would be much less effective if it did not communicate electronically with the pharmacy system that would process the medication orders.

FUNCTIONAL OVERVIEW OF HOSPITAL INFORMATION SYSTEMS

Administrative Systems

Nearly all hospitals have at least some functions computerized in an administrative system. Typical functions of an administrative HIS include the following:

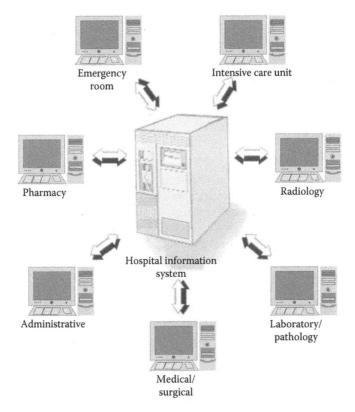

Emergency
room

Intensive care unit

Pharmacy

Radiology

Hospital information
system

Administrative

Laboratory/
pathology

Medical/
surgical

FIGURE 5.1 Schematic of an integrated system. All departmental systems can communicate with each other through the HIS.

- Admission scheduling
- Accounts payable and receivable
- Patient and payer billing
- Patient demographic information such as name, unique identifier, age, gender, reason for admission, and other data items
- Staffing and staff scheduling
- Pharmacy inventory
- Internal finance, budgeting, and accounting
- Patient census
- Facility maintenance

Billing functions are an area where a hospital can obtain more immediate ROI. Often, newly implemented billing systems can provide a hospital with a positive ROI within the first year of active system use. Automating the billing functions, such as the Centers for Medicare and Medicaid Services (CMS) UB-92 claim submission form, can save several FTEs per 100 beds.

Administrative functions are one of the areas where computerized systems can lead to significant revenue increases, as a faster turnaround time and computerized entry of patient information can lead to improved coding quality and efficiency. One hospital in the southern United States enhanced its surgery department billing system, reducing the billing turnaround from a three- to four-day cycle to a 24-hour process, leading to a significant increase in revenue. More accurate and complete coding also leads to an increase in the revenue stream as more secondary diagnoses are entered and overly general primary diagnoses are given more specific ICD-9 codes, as long as safeguards are in place to prevent inappropriate coding ("upcoding") to receive overly high payments for services provided.

Hospitals are now gearing up their IT systems for the introduction of the ICD-10-CM coding system, which provides a more sophisticated, granular coding of medical conditions and diseases. The CMS requires that healthcare institutions begin using the new coding system on October 1, 2014. This will be a major undertaking and will drive a significant proportion of information technology spend in the near future.

Clinical Systems

In contrast to administrative systems, clinical systems deal directly with patient care processes and outcomes. Clinical system sophistication varies widely from hospital to hospital and has the strongest presence in tertiary care centers and teaching hospitals. Some hospitals have become nearly paperless due to the installation of leading edge clinical information systems. Clinical information systems encompass a wide range of features and functions, and modules may include the following:

- Pharmacy information systems, which may include barcoding and drug interaction checking
- CPOE systems that allow clinicians to directly order tests and treatments online; these systems can also check for selected appropriateness of care parameters
- Other departmental systems such as LISs, radiology systems, and intensive care clinical computing
- Electronic medical record (EMR) systems, which allow physician orders, free text clinical notes, decision support, radiology images, and other areas to be almost entirely computerized, allowing a paperless medical institution

Both budget outlays and implementation strategies for these systems are highly variable and require much deliberation and foresight. The start-up costs of these systems can vary from several hundred thousand dollars for a departmental system in a community hospital to tens of millions of dollars for EMR systems in large centers. In addition, ROI calculations become more subjective, as ROI is more dependent on cost avoidance (e.g., from fewer medical errors, more efficient work processes) rather than revenue generation. However, improvements in quality of care from well thought-out system development and implementation can still provide significant financial returns.

Integration of Mobile Computing in HISs

With the advent of smart phones and tablet computing, a new dimension is available that could increase the quality and convenience of care while reducing cost. Physicians can use the technology to enter patient orders, take notes on patient progress, examine lab results, and access decision support applications that can integrate evidence-based medicine and "expert system" technology to aid in developing care plans, suggesting follow-up tests, and optimizing patient–treatment matching.

Based on a study by the Economist Intelligence Unit (2012),[1] 52 percent of consumers expect that mobile health will improve their healthcare from 2012 to 2015. However, physicians appear to be slower to embrace the technology. They are concerned about their ability to meet privacy and security legal obligations with the lack of proven models for healthcare applications. Interfaces may also be poorly designed and may not integrate well into existing physician workflows and other parts of HISs. Furthermore, the security of patient data is critical, and physicians may fear that patient data sent over wireless networks may be subject to interception. However, although the security of patient data is a legitimate concern with mobile systems, recently there have been significant improvements, including robust encryption technology for medical apps and, although data can be sent from the mobile device to the general HIS, the data are not actually stored on the mobile device.

As interfaces improve, the capability for the physician to enter data at the bedside rather than at a computer station in another location on the ward decreases workflow disruptions, as doctors no longer have to step away from patient rounds to enter data. Some of the most advanced apps can provide speech recognition technology, where a physician can verbally deliver patient history data to the app, within earshot of the patient so that the patient can then confirm that the physician has heard the patient correctly. This reduces distractions from having to take time to write notes manually or dictate and transcribe.

HOSPITAL INFORMATION SYSTEMS AND REGULATORY REQUIREMENTS

A critical feature of any healthcare computer system is that it complies with regulatory requirements. One of the most important requirements is compliance with the Health Insurance Portability and Accountability Act of 1996 (HIPAA). The key is to have computer systems, terminals, workstations, servers, and hand-held systems fully in communication with each other—including the ability to send data outside the walls of the institution as needed—while ensuring the confidentiality of protected health information (PHI), which is health information where the person to whom it belongs is identifiable. The federal government required compliance with HIPAA security regulations starting April 2005. Briefly, the following features of HIPAA concern HISs:

- HIPAA presents a unique opportunity for automation of information because it is easier to protect secure information electronically as compared to having a paper chart, which can be lost or open in front of patients and visitors.
- Secure password protection must be in place at multiple levels to ensure that access to PHI is restricted to those who need the information at that time.
- Appropriate encryption of data is essential for transmission between systems to prevent the interception of data.

Clinical information systems may offer a competitive advantage for hospitals as patients may feel more secure knowing that much of their medical information is stored electronically (with protection using passwords and encryption) rather than on paper, where visibility of information is much less controlled. As consumerism increases in healthcare, with the resulting competition for patients between facilities, this feature may increase the desirability of the hospital and result in revenue growth for the institution. Although HIPAA established standardized transaction code sets for administrative information between providers (facilities and physicians) and payers in 1997, there are relatively few technical standards for clinical information systems. The move toward such technical standards is accelerating with the enactment of the Health Information Technology for Economic and Clinical Health (HITECH) Act, which is covered in greater detail below. Standardized communications reduce errors and increase efficiency in interactions. Secure Internet connections will allow providers to remotely view patient and clinical information, greatly enhancing ease of use and provider buy-in.

The Joint Commission and CMS also require the reporting of various quality metrics. Such reporting allows external stakeholder evaluation of hospital performance and provides feedback directly to the hospital in terms of its standing in the quality arena, facilitating performance improvement plans if necessary.

The Joint Commission requires the reporting of "core measures" with respect to hospital quality of care performance as part of its ORYX® measurement and improvement initiative, which began in 1997 and since then has greatly expanded its measure set. Clinical conditions covered in these measures include:

- Acute myocardial infarction (AMI)
- Heart failure (HF)

- Perinatal care (PC)
- Pneumonia (PN)
- Hospital-based inpatient psychiatric services (HBIPS)
- Children's asthma care (CAC)
- Surgical care improvement project (SCIP)
- Hospital outpatient measures (HOP)
- Venous thromboembolism (VTE)
- Stroke (STK)
- Tobacco treatment (TOB; new in 2012)
- Immunizations (IMM; new in 2012)
- Substance use (SUB)

Hospitals are required to report on at least four core measures of their choosing to the Joint Commission. More specialized hospitals that do not have the requisite patient populations that enable reporting of at least four core measures can select a combination of core and non-core measures.

Other Joint Commission reporting measures include adverse "Sentinel Events" and "ORYX" perception measure sets such as data collection processes involving questionnaires or telephone interviews. CMS shares with the Joint Commission many of the measures to make reporting of measures easier and less costly because the same set can be used to satisfy the requirements of both agencies. Critical to the process are information systems that can store the measured results and provide electronic reports. Outside vendors also perform computerized reporting on behalf of client hospitals.

THE BUILD OR BUY DECISION

Another important consideration when looking at the development of new technological functionality is whether to obtain the system from an outside vendor or to build the system primarily using internal resources. The build or buy decision depends on the following aspects:

- The availability of internal resources to hire and manage the highly skilled staff needed to create a new system
- The availability of vendors with proven expertise in the area of technology relevant to the new project
- The importance of the use of interoperable and certified products, as opposed to systems that are built around an organization's unique needs
- The flexibility of vendors to customize their products for hospitals with unique needs

The temptation to use consultants rather than FTEs to develop and implement a new system should be explored. On the positive side, finding consultants that have highly specialized expertise relevant to the project is often less difficult than finding such expertise in people willing to come on board as FTEs. Such expertise in health information systems may be critical to the success of the project. Furthermore, given present economic uncertainties, consultants offer an attractive alternative to full-time employees because there is less "commitment" on the part of the employer, given that medical insurance and other benefits typically are not included in a consultant compensation package. On the negative side, the cash outlay for multiple consultants can be staggering, especially if multiple consultants come on board with long-term contracts and retainers. The hourly rates for specialized consultants may be significant. Organizations should evaluate their available resources relative to the complexity of their needs and the speed with which they want to move, and make decisions about staffing and consultants accordingly.

Overall, buying an application off the shelf may be favored for more sophisticated applications. For example, computerized order entry and EMR systems have a number of dedicated vendors that are vying to achieve market share. For major projects, distributing request for information (RFI) packages to selected vendors enables senior management to critically evaluate the different vendors in parallel and, in the end, select finalists and ultimately the vendor of choice. A critical requirement when evaluating vendors is a strong client reference base. The best predictor of future success is past success, and thus multiple existing satisfied clients are essential for the chosen vendor. Larger academic or tertiary care systems, however, tend to have more access to expertise and more significant customization requirements. Consequently, building a homegrown system rather than outsourcing the work to a vendor may be the best strategy for such institutions.

When working with vendors, one should be strategic in price negotiations. One suggestion is to link part of the vendor compensation to the success of the implementation. This puts the vendor partially "at risk" for project success and thus provides additional incentive for vendor cooperation. Additionally, one should not purchase a system or services from the initial bid. It is critical that more than one vendor bids for the project to provide a pricing and negotiation advantage.

There is nothing that states only one vendor can be chosen for a project. Although obtaining everything from one vendor can lead to a more seamless integration and prevent the juggling of multiple vendor relationships, using more than one vendor may in some cases lead to a higher quality end product. This is known as the "best of breed" approach, and it is a viable option especially for complex projects where a single vendor does not adequately meet user needs.

A hospital may also engage in a combined build and buy strategy. For example, the basic system could be built on-site, with vendors being subsequently chosen to create smaller, specialized systems. For example, some vendors may specialize in LISs, while others implement pharmacy systems. However, hospital IT staff are still needed to ensure that the vendor systems are fully integrated into the main HIS and its other subsystems, and that the systems are fully compatible and able to communicate with one another.

For more basic administrative systems, there are also off-the-shelf products from vendors that may be applicable. Where there is less need for customization, a single vendor may work out well. Where there are significant unique needs that require customization, once again it may be best to develop the system internally or outsource the work to multiple vendors. Given the increasing level of sophistication of HISs and the increasing hospital budget outlays for clinical information systems, hospitals that limit information system development to administrative systems may be less competitive and may lose market share as compared to hospitals with more sophisticated clinical systems, CPOE, and EMRs. Thus, hospitals with only administrative systems must seriously consider developing more complex systems and find a way to commit more financial resources to system development, especially given relevant government and public–private initiatives that promote implementation of sophisticated CPOE and EMR systems.

There is also the issue of small or rural hospitals that have limited resources. For such institutions, investments in more complex information systems may be difficult. Consequently, many vendors offer stripped-down versions of their systems at a more affordable price, specifically tailored to the small hospital. The ability to customize the system for unique needs, however, is significantly limited.

THE FINANCIAL EFFECTS OF IMPROVED QUALITY OF CARE

When today's practicing physicians went through medical school, the vast majority of them were tied to paper charts. When a provider wanted to enter data or text into a patient's chart, the provider needed to find or order the chart and in some cases had to physically go to another department to retrieve the document. On occasion, the document would be temporarily lost or reside in a place other than the hospital. Paper charts could actually delay the care process when such incidents happened. Although checks and balances to prevent these occurrences are more refined now, the potential for significant delays due to paper charts still exists in the care process, which also has ramifications for care quality and timeliness in service delivery. An EMR is designed to mitigate these problems, among others, through the creation of permanently stored documentation that can be accessed by appropriate parties via workstations or mobile devices essentially anywhere in the hospital, in affiliated outside clinics, or even in a physician's home. As older physicians retire and the Millennial generation of physicians begin their practice, these physicians will undoubtedly demand a computing environment like that in which they grew up. However, an institution does not need to implement a complete EMR system initially. Various stand-alone components exist, including CPOE systems, barcoding, departmental information systems, and clinical guideline implementation.

BARCODING SYSTEMS

It is now a requirement of the United States Food and Drug Administration (FDA) for barcodes to be installed on all medications used in hospitals and dispensed based on a physician's order. The barcode must contain at least the National Drug Code (NDC) number, which specifically identifies the drug. Although hospitals are not required at this time to have a barcode-reading system on the ward—in fact, it was estimated only about 10 percent of hospitals used bedside barcoding systems in 2006—this ruling has heightened the priority of implementing hospital-wide systems for patient/drug matching using barcodes, and implementation is expected to grow rapidly, although at this time hospitals that have fully implemented such a system are in the minority.

Conceptually, the procedure for barcoding is as follows:

- The drug is given to the nurse or other provider for administration to the patient.
- Once in the patient's room, the provider scans the barcode on the patient's identification badge, which positively identifies the patient.
- The medication container is then passed through the scanner, which identifies the drug.
- The computer matches the patient to the drug order. If there is not a match, including drug, dosage, and time of administration, an alert is displayed immediately, enabling correction of the error prior to drug administration.

The FDA estimates that more than 500,000 fewer adverse events will occur between 2013 and 2033, the result of an expected 50 percent decrease in errors in drug dispensing and administration. A recent study (2010) of the effect of barcoding at the Brigham and Women's hospital in Boston found that transcription errors were completely eliminated, medication administration error rates were cut almost in half (from 11.5 percent to 6.8 percent), and potential adverse drug events were also cut nearly in half (from 3.1 percent without barcoding technology to 1.6 percent with barcoding[2]). The decrease in pain, suffering, and length of stay due to drug errors is estimated to result in $93 billion in savings between 2013 and 2033. Avoidance of litigation, decreased malpractice premiums, reduced inventory carrying costs, and increased revenue from more accurate billing result from the improvement in quality and efficiency of care. This makes implementation of barcoding technology relatively low-risk, although there needs to be sufficient informatics capability to capture and store drug orders.

For a barcoding system, a 300-bed hospital may expect up-front costs of $700,000 to $1.5 million to establish the system, with about $150,000 or more in annual maintenance fees. The returns, however, in terms of improved patient safety and reduced cost of care make an investment in barcoding technology one of the more cost-effective information systems investments. In addition, given the increasing consumerism in healthcare, prospective patients will be more assured of care quality from a hospital investing in state-of-the-art technology in this area, giving the medical center a competitive advantage.

COMPUTERIZED PROVIDER ORDER ENTRY (CPOE) SYSTEMS

Since the late 1990s, there has been increasing pressure for hospitals to develop processes to ensure high quality of care. In a well-known publication, the Institute of Medicine estimated the number of annual deaths from medical error to be 44,000 to 98,000.[3] Although some improvements have been made since the report, the Institute of Medicine states that much more still needs to be done in this regard. Manual entry of orders, use of non-standard abbreviations, and poor legibility of orders and chart notes contribute to medical errors. They also concluded that most errors are the result of system failures, not people failures. Other studies suggest that between 6.5 percent and 20 percent of hospitalized patients will experience an adverse drug event during their stay. Both quality and cost of care suffer. The cost for each adverse drug event is estimated to be about $2,000 to $3,000, mainly resulting from longer lengths of stay. Of all causes of preventable deaths from medical error, medication errors appear to be the largest contributor.

In addition, the Joint Commission and the Leapfrog Group, a consortium of large employers, have pushed patient safety as a high priority, and hospitals are following suit. The Leapfrog Group in particular has highlighted CPOE systems as one of the changes that would most improve patient safety. These patient safety initiatives have further advanced CPOE systems, as one of the primary functions of these systems is the reduction of medical errors. State and federal legislatures have also stepped up activity in this regard, providing incentive payments to hospitals that adapt new electronic technologies, especially since the enactment of HITECH, as discussed below.

Many hospitals have data retrieval systems where a care provider on the ward can obtain lab results and other information. A CPOE system, however, allows entry of data from the ward and is usually coupled with a decision support module that does just that—supports the provider in making decisions that maximize care quality or cost effectiveness.

In this application of HIS, physicians and possibly other providers enter hospital orders directly into the computer. Many vendors of such systems make special efforts to create an intuitive and user-friendly interface, with a variable range of customization possibilities. The physicians can enter orders either on a workstation on the ward or in some cases at the bedside.

Features of CPOE include the following:

- **Medication analysis system:** A medication analysis program usually accompanies the order entry system. Either after order entry or interactively in real time, the system checks for potential problems such as drug–drug interactions, duplicate orders, drug allergies and hypersensitivities, and dosage miscalculations. More sophisticated systems may also check for drug interactions with co-morbidities (e.g., psychiatric drugs that may increase blood pressure in a depressed patient with hypertension), drug–lab interactions (e.g., labs pointing to renal impairment that may adversely affect drug levels), and suggestions to use drugs with the same therapeutic effect but lower cost. Naturally, physicians have the option to decline the alerts and continue with the order.
- **Order clarity:** Reading the handwriting of providers is a legendary problem. Although many providers do perfectly well with legibility, other providers have difficulty due to being rushed, stressed, or having inherently poor handwriting. Because the orders are accessible directly on the workstation screen or from the printer, time is saved on callbacks to decipher illegible orders and possible errors in order translation are avoided. A 1986 study by Georgetown University Hospital (Washington, D.C.) noted that 16 percent of all manual medical records are illegible.[4] Clarifying these orders takes professional time, and resources are spent duplicating the data; thus, real cost savings can be realized through the elimination of these processes.
- **Increased work efficiency:** Instantaneous electronic transmittal of orders to radiology, laboratory, pharmacy, consulting services, or other departments replaces corresponding manual tasks. This increase in efficiency from a CPOE system has significant returns. In one hospital in the southeast, the time taken between drug order submission and receipt by the pharmacy was shortened from 96 minutes (using paper) to 3 minutes. Such an increase in efficiency can save labor costs and lead to earlier discharge of patients. The same hospital noted a 72 percent reduction in medication error rates during a three-month period

after the system was implemented. Alerting providers to duplicate lab orders further saves costs as a result of more efficient work processes. In another instance, the time from writing admission orders to execution of the orders decreased from about six hours to 30 minutes. This further underscores the CPOE system utility in making work processes more efficient and thus positively affecting the bottom line.

Table 5.1 provides a summary of potential benefits of a CPOE system in terms of quality of care, error reduction, process improvements, and long-term costs.

A significant initial cost outlay for an organization-wide CPOE system is necessary, which for a large hospital may run into the tens of millions of dollars. The up-front cost outlay may be prohibitive for smaller or rural hospitals unless there is an increase in outside revenue or third-party subsidies. However, although it may take a few years before a positive ROI becomes manifest, there can be a significant financial return from such systems.

The potential benefits of a CPOE system extend beyond quality. Significant decreases in resource utilization can occur. In one study, inpatient costs were 12 percent lower and average length of stay (LOS) was 0.89 day shorter for patients residing on general medicine wards that used a CPOE system with decision support. Rather simple decision support tools can reap cost benefits as well. When a computerized antibiotic advisor was integrated with the ordering process, one institution realized a reduction in cost per patient ($26,325 versus $35,283) and average LOS (10.0 days versus 12.9 days), with all differences statistically significant.

Studies have shown that CPOE systems can significantly reduce medication error rates, including rates of serious errors. One large east coast hospital saw a 55 percent reduction in serious adverse medication errors after the system was installed. However, on occasion errors can actually be introduced due to the computing process; for example, errors can be introduced if the provider accidentally selects the wrong medication from the list or drop-down menu. Thus, a CPOE system should not be viewed as a replacement for the pharmacist in terms of checking for medication errors. In addition, proper user interface design, such as highlighting every other line on the medication screen for better visibility and having the provider perform a final check of the orders before sending, are some ways of reducing this kind of error. Overall, error rates from incorrect order entry on the computer are much lower than other medication errors prior to introduction of the system.

TABLE 5.1

Summary of Potential Benefits of Computerized Physician Order Entry

Quality Improvements and Error Reductions	Process Improvements and Cost Reductions
• Elimination of lost orders	• Expedited ordering process and reduced time from ordering to execution
• Improved documentation consistency and thoroughness	• Automated documentation standardized process
• Reduced variation in care from standard order sets	• Remote access to system
• Automated outcomes analysis and reporting	• Elimination of duplicate orders
• Reduction in dosing errors	• Reduction in order verification and processing time
• Drug–drug, drug–disease, drug–lab, and drug allergy checking and alerts prevent medication errors	• Improved charge capture
• Elimination of illegible orders	• Reduction in length of stay and cost per admission
• Verification of medication administration	• Reduced data entry needs
• Immediate access to online knowledge bases and libraries	• Decreased malpractice exposure
	• Alternative medication suggestions, including alternative cost-saving tests and formulary medications

Source: Modified from Gray and Felkey, *Am J Health-Syst Pharm* 2004; 61(2): 190–197.

Appropriate use of a CPOE system helps prevent errors and quality of care deficiencies due to problems with the initiation of orders. However, errors can also occur in the execution of orders, particularly with the administration of medications to patients. Barcoding of medications, discussed previously, is a simple way to close the loop in medication error prevention as well as further increase the efficiency of workflow.

Despite its advantages, implementing a CPOE system is not an easy task, and there is a significant risk of failure. Most hospitals utilize vendors for implementation rather than attempt to develop the system in-house, given the difficulty of hiring full-time IT talent that specializes in CPOE systems.

One critical step in the development of any CPOE system is to obtain physician buy-in to the technology because they will be doing most of the ordering. Unless the system is of the highest sophistication, physicians may claim it takes more time to write orders using a CPOE system than using the paper chart, as there may be a number of drop-down menus to negotiate prior to arriving at the appropriate drug. Real-time retrieval of information and electronic documentation, provision of online alerts, and the ability to use standard order sets (prepackaged sets of orders pertaining to a particular clinical condition or time period in an episode of care, often in the format of a checklist), when relevant, can make the net time spent on writing orders similar to or faster than using paper charts.

Furthermore, the use of secure mobile devices can allow order generation at the patient bedside, allowing live discussion of orders with the patient, nurses, and other personnel on hand, increasing communication and understanding of the patient's care for all stakeholders. Studies have shown that remote access to order entry and order status, such as the results of laboratory tests, are appreciated by clinical personnel and generate positive regard for the system.

It is also important, for physician acceptance, to not overwhelm them with online alerts. The system must point out serious errors, but if the physician's process is frequently interrupted by alerts, the physicians may increasingly resist the system. For example, medication allergy alerts may warn physicians not only of potential problems with medications that have an exact match to the allergen, but also, as a defensive maneuver ("better safe than sorry"), to other medications that have a related molecular structure, even though the patient may already be taking such a medication and tolerating it well. Furthermore, allergies to medications that may result in life-threatening anaphylactic shock may not be distinguished from sensitivities that consist of side effects that are not true allergies and are usually much less serious. Thus, the potential exists for frequent alert generation that would interrupt the work flow and require time spent to override the alerts, making the system difficult to use and leading to user resistance. A related problem, known as alert fatigue, may result in physicians overriding alerts that have actual clinical importance due to desensitization from frequent alerts. Past experience with CPOE systems shows that low-priority alerts were generated at a much higher rate than high-priority ones, with the potential to habituate to alerts in general. One solution is to have a hierarchy of importance, with alerts for potentially life-threatening situations being allowed to interrupt the work flow and requiring specific override or acknowledgment, and alerts for less serious problems being noninterruptive, allowing easy visibility of the alert without requiring stoppage of the work flow.

Other pitfalls with respect to CPOE systems include the following:

- Crowded menus, which increase the likelihood of selecting the wrong patient or wrong drug with the mouse
- Fragmented information, which requires navigation through numerous screens to find the relevant information
- Computer downtime (scheduled or unscheduled)
- Location of terminals in busy places, which can lead to distractions and incomplete or incorrect entries

Intelligent, well-planned system designs can serve to mitigate many of these problems. It is important that such difficulties are shared with system designers early in the process and are explicitly considered in the implementation of the system.

As for pharmacists, a CPOE system will not take them out of the process. Although a CPOE system has the capability to capture many drug errors and remove the need for manual order entry, there will always be a need for pharmacists, not only to give a second look at possible errors but to take a more active role in patient care, including going on ward rounds for complex cases, defining optimal treatment, and giving consultative advice.

A CPOE system has the potential to give physicians ready access to patient data anywhere in the hospital as well as at home or on the road, especially with Internet-based connections. This is significant given the difficulty in obtaining patient charts for mobile providers.

In today's environment of high expectations for care quality and pay-for-performance initiatives, enhanced quality of care can translate into financial gain. Although there is a significant up-front allocation of funds for CPOE systems, given present trends the time may come where there is no longer a choice but to fully implement such a system.

A CPOE system alone will reap significant benefits if intelligently implemented; to realize the greatest benefit, however, a CPOE system should be rolled up into a fully functioning EMR system where feasible.

CLINICAL GUIDELINE IMPLEMENTATION SYSTEMS

For medicine to continue to advance, a steady supply of scientific research is needed to determine the most effective diagnostic and therapeutic options for particular illnesses and subgroups of patients (patient–treatment matching). However, the length of time for the translation of scientific findings into actual patient care has been estimated to take an average of 17 years, by which time the scientific findings may already be outdated. To reduce the diffusion time from scientific study to bedside application, extensive efforts to develop evidence-based clinical guidelines and care pathways have taken place since the 1990s. Typically, such guidelines are updated every one to three years to take into account the latest scientific evidence.

Clinical guidelines are useful for guiding decision making using algorithms and rules. For example, values from a diagnostic test may guide the clinician to the most appropriate action or treatment option on the basis of guideline rules. One of the barriers to implementation of clinical guidelines has been that they are not accessible at the point of care. Paper guidelines often require reading on the physician's own time, or the provider may use them on the wards only for highly complex cases, if at all. Electronic strategies may contribute to an increased use of guidelines through the following features:

- **Point of care utilization:** Guidelines that are accessible through mobile devices or bedside terminals offer the advantage of decision support during the patient encounter. For some guidelines, software exists that allows a provider to interactively access guidelines through the selection of appropriate pathways on the online decision tree. An example of a guideline with an algorithmic decision tree is noted in Figure 5.2.[5]
- **Benchmarking and performance tracking:** The comparison of input data to evidence-based clinical guidelines allows the possibility of performance analysis compared to norms or benchmarks. One must be careful, though, not to apply the guidelines too rigidly because in specific instances it may be appropriate to vary from guideline algorithms.
- **Online alerts:** In similar fashion to medication alerts from a CPOE system, guideline-based alerts show a provider where a clinical decision may conflict with evidence-based guidelines. Once again, the provider should be allowed to override the alert if he or she feels the clinical situation warrants a special exception.

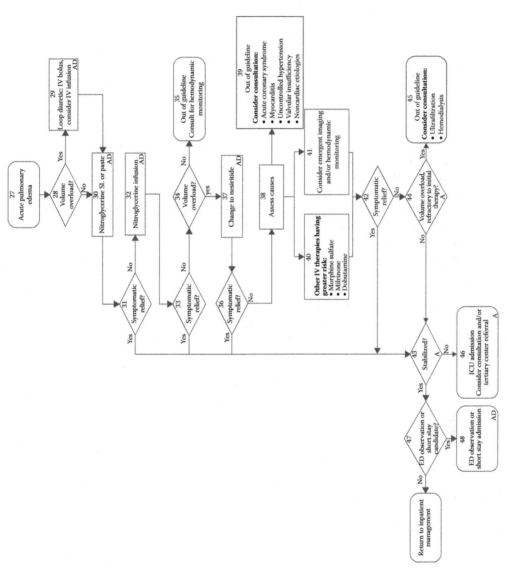

FIGURE 5.2 Example of a flowchart from an acute pulmonary edema algorithmic guideline (simplified).

- **Regulatory reporting:** An increase in guideline adherence can support improvements in regulatory reporting, such as the reporting of quality measures to the Joint Commission and CMS.

The National Guideline Clearinghouse (NGC; http://www.guidelines.gov/), an initiative of the Agency for Healthcare Research and Quality (AHRQ), contains a repository of evidence-based clinical guidelines from multiple sources for public access.

Representing a guideline in a computer may be a difficult task, depending on the type of guideline used. Guidelines that can be represented as if-then-else rules, such as with algorithmic guidelines discussed above and with clear, concise rules for decision points, are most amenable to implementation. Guidelines that have vague values for decision point (e.g., "severe heart failure" rather than "New York Heart Association Class III or IV failure") are more difficult to implement electronically. Narrative text and other formats that work well for human comprehension may not work well for representation on a computer screen or mobile device. Thus, choosing guidelines that are most amenable to specific algorithm development is essential. Specialized, focused guidelines may be the most amenable to implementation. In one anecdotal study that took place between 1988 and 1994, an antibiotic-use guideline implemented as part of a decision support system in an Intermountain West hospital noted a significant reduction in acquisition cost for antibiotics as a percentage of total pharmacy expenditures (12.9 percent versus 24.8 percent) during the study period. Antibiotic costs per treated patient decreased from $122.66 to $51.90, and total antibiotic use went down 22.8 percent. As for pre-operative antibiotic use, there was an increase in use from 40 percent to 99.1 percent, showing an improvement in the use of these medications. In addition, antibiotic-associated adverse drug events underwent a 30 percent reduction. Another study showed that inclusion of guideline-based decision support in two emergency departments decreased the percentage of radiology orders that did not conform to evidence-based guidelines from 33.2 percent to 26.9 percent, a statistically significant difference. As a result, well-designed systems using clinical guidelines can be associated with tangible improvements in cost and quality of care.

As a cautionary note, a large number of variables affect patient outcomes, including patient severity of illness, hospital environment, variations over time, and level of staffing. Consequently, attributing patient outcomes to a single intervention, such as electronic systems, can be tricky. For example, the evidence has been less clear as to whether electronic systems decrease hospital LOS, mortality, and hospital readmission rates. Further research in these areas is ongoing.

ELECTRONIC MEDICAL RECORDS

EMRs involve accessibility at the bedside through bedside terminals, portable workstations, laptops, wireless tablets, and other mobile devices. Information entered onto these devices can either be uploaded into the main computer system after rounds or transmitted immediately to the system with wireless technology. Bedside technology obviates the need to re-enter data from notes after rounds are complete. This improves recall and avoids redundancy in the work process, saving time that can instead be devoted to patient care. Common features of an EMR include the following:

- History and physical exam documentation, progress notes, and patient demographics
- Medication and medication allergy information
- Laboratory results
- Graphical displays of medical imaging studies including X-rays, computed tomography images, and magnetic resonance images
- Ordering of drugs, diagnostic tests, and treatments, including automated drug interaction alerts
- Alerts that can be sent to patients to remind them of appointments and necessary preventive care

- Scheduling of appointments
- Processing of claims for payment
- A GUI, which may include secure web-based and wireless technologies, that allows providers or other authorized healthcare personnel access to health information from remote sites, including outside offices and home
- Advanced decision support systems, including aids for interpretation of diagnostic tests and alerts pertaining to adherence of treatments and test ordering to evidence-based clinical guidelines

For example, instead of calculating fluid balance off-line, the computer can perform calculations immediately, once again saving time and ensuring accurate values. Medication orders can also be entered in real time, giving the provider the option to react to alerts at the bedside rather than waiting to load the orders into the system as a batch download.

EMRs are not without drawbacks. Some of the more notable negatives include the following:

- **Operator dependence:** The phrase "garbage in, garbage out" applies to EMRs as well. The computer only works as well as the data it receives. If one user of the system is resistant to computing and works begrudgingly, is not well-trained, or is rushed for time, the potential exists for incomplete or error-prone documentation.
- **Variable flexibility for unique needs:** When one sees a single hospital, one sees just that— a single hospital, with unique needs unlike any other facility. A one size fits all approach misses the target. Even within a hospital, needs may change rapidly over time, given dynamic external initiatives and measurement demands. Systems vary in flexibility and the ease with which they can customize options. More flexible systems exist but cost much more.
- **Data entry errors:** Although data items normally only have to be entered once, data entry errors may still occur and be propagated throughout the system. Most notably, patient data can more easily be entered into the wrong chart when there is an error in chart selection. In general, simple double-checking and "sanity checks" in the system usually catch these errors, but if the error goes through the system, the impact can be significant.
- **Lack of system integration:** Interconnectivity of systems and interoperability of the information contained in each system become more important with EMRs than with any other system. Personnel use the data in many different areas. If there are isolated departmental systems without connectivity, redundant data entry may occur and can lead to confusion and inconsistency.

Appropriate and intelligent clinical decision support systems can make the job of the physician easier through education, real-time feedback, and the presentation of choices that allow for clinical judgment.

Intelligently applied EMR implementations can also be reduce costs. One large east coast hospital found that EMRs saved $9,000–$19,000 annually per physician FTE. This savings was achieved through decreased costs for record retrieval, transcription, and non-formulary drug ordering, as well as improvements in billing accuracy. In radiology, storage of digital pictures and the use of a picture archival and communication system significantly decreased the turnaround time for radiology image interpretation from 72 hours to 1 hour.

However, there is significant front-loading of costs prior to achieving such savings. At the October 2006 American Health Information Management Association conference, panelists suggested that developing, purchasing, and implementing an EMR would cost over $32,000 per physician, with an outlay of $1,200 per physician per month for maintenance. While HITECH did not impose a required standard of interoperability and compatibility, it did create financial incentives for hospitals to adopt systems that met federally established standards for certification and interoperability. Over time, these standards may help improve interconnectivity and reduce frustration with proprietary systems. One example of success in this area is the use of Health Level 7 (HL7) data format and data interchange standards, which have been widely adapted by EMR systems for transferring documents and data between computer systems in hospitals and between hospitals, other medical facilities, and physician offices.

TRANSITION ORGANIZATION

The development and implementation of HISs, especially more sophisticated systems, can be a daunting task. Interestingly, however, the main obstacles are more likely to be organizational and cultural rather than technological.

When implementing an HIS, especially the more sophisticated type of system with clinical rules, a variety of stakeholders need to participate in the development and implementation of the system, especially because any HIS implementation needs to support clinical workflows and a team-based approach to patient care. These stakeholders include senior management, IT staff, vendor staff, and the user community such as physicians, nurses, and other ward personnel. In particular, the users need to feel a "pride of ownership," which helps ensure buy-in from the various stakeholders. Some health centers have used a two-committee approach. The first committee is an advisory/ steering committee composed of senior executives and other strategic thinkers who would plan the overall process of development and implementation. The second group is a stakeholder group made up of prospective users of the system, and they would have significant input into the development and implementation process, including drop-down menu content and features, GUIs, integration with other departments, relationship of workflow to system implementation, testing parameters, and other aspects. Communicating the intended benefits of the system to users, ensuring that the system is well-designed with user input in mind, and developing a plan for sufficient user training are important functions of the management steering committee and will facilitate a successful transition to the new system. Of critical importance are periodic evaluations of system functionality and user satisfaction with the system to support continuous improvements in system technology and usability. A static, unchanging system—even one that functions well in the present—may quickly become outdated as medical care and information technology continue to advance. Keeping up with needed system upgrades, along with new training programs, may require dedicated personnel, which can add to the cost of upkeep and maintenance.

Physician buy-in to the system is critical. If clinicians perceive the HIS as primarily targeted toward the needs of hospital management or believe that physician status is not appropriately acknowledged during the development process, they may resist participating in user groups and using the system once it is up and running. Physicians view long response times and too many steps to complete a process or order quite negatively, and this will synergize with physicians' (or anyone's) natural resistance to change to create serious obstacles to the system's success. On the other hand, if physicians believe that the system will help patient care processes or outcomes and make their work more streamlined (e.g., through more efficient medical record keeping), there is an excellent chance that physicians will feel positively about the new system. Physicians also view remote access to medical records from outside offices or homes, along with intuitive, easy-to-use interfaces, as pluses. Without physician advocacy, or at least acceptance, of the system, however, a successful implementation is nearly impossible.

To maximize the potential for success, the user community needs liaisons between the basic IT community and the users. These liaisons, called super users, often have considerable previous computing background and can navigate the system easily. Super users may be nurses on the wards, laboratory personnel for an LIS, pharmacists, physicians, and others. These users can help guide and train others during the implementation process. Having peers involved in leading the training and implementation increases buy-in of key stakeholders. Each hospital department should have at least one super user, and preferably several.

Although an HIS is intended to support rather than dictate work processes, one question to ask is whether the addition of the system leads to an opportunity to improve work processes. Through different departments working together on system issues, interdepartmental communication may improve.

Data can be captured for improved quality monitoring for regulatory requirements. Redundant data entry, for example, can be greatly reduced using an integrated system. Increased efficiency may leave more time for pharmacists, nurses, and physicians to spend on patient care. Furthermore, increases in efficiency may lead to a decreased need for manual or clerical operations. Consequently, work processes need to change to accommodate system impacts, including taking advantage of the automation of previously manual processes and the resulting increase in communication speed.

Still, adoption of information technology in medical care has been occurring at a slow pace relative to other industries. As of 2009, only about 16 percent of hospitals had a fully functional CPOE system. Recent government incentives, however, may change this. The HITECH, which became law in 2009 as part of the American Recovery and Reinvestment Act, will lead to the provision of incentive payments by CMS to encourage hospitals, medical centers, and physician offices to install and use certified EMR systems as long as meaningful use criteria are met. The report *CPOE 2011: The ARRA Effect*[6] states that 233 hospitals have gone live with CPOE in 2010, up from a previous rate of 87 hospitals per year. Meaningful use is a staged process that requires the following:

Stage 1 (implementation years 2011–2012): The electronic system should be able to capture health information in a standardized format, use the information to track important clinical conditions, enhance care coordination, engage patients and families in their care, report quality measures and public health data, and ensure information security and privacy. In this stage, one of the core objectives for hospitals is to have at least a basic CPOE system that can also detect drug–drug and drug–allergy interactions.

Stage 2 (implementation year 2014): The next stage, for which proposed rules have been issued, will involve more rigorous health information exchange, which enables hospitals, medical centers, and physician offices to move or transmit electronic clinical information across disparate medical information systems with full interoperability. Stage 2 will also require more complete and rigorous e-prescribing, incorporation of lab results, increased patient-controlled data, and the creation and transmission of patient care summaries across multiple settings.

Stage 3 (implementation year 2016): This stage goes beyond information system functionality to link EMRs with improved patient outcomes. The focus will be on the use of EMRs to improve care quality, safety, efficiency, and population health, advanced decision support for caring for patients with high-priority medical conditions, and patient-centered health information exchange, which includes patient access to comprehensive self-management tools.

As of February 2012, CMS has already made $3.12 billion in incentive payments to 41,000 physicians, 2,000 hospitals, and other health providers for the meaningful use of certified EMRs. The Congressional Budget Office estimates that the incentives will increase the adoption rates of EMRs to about 70 percent for hospitals and potentially 90 percent of physician practices by 2019.[7]

In preparation for Stage 2 implementation, the Certification Commission for Health Information Technology (CCHIT®) will lead a public–private partnership to certify EMR systems (i.e., to verify that the systems are fully able to transmit electronic data between systems and organizations and across state lines. The goal is to support a single set of standardized, easily implemented interoperability protocols and connections so that full communication between systems is supported. Given the wide variety of EMR systems available and the number of vendors selling systems at this time, interoperability between types of systems (such as LISs, pharmacy systems, and systems used on the hospital wards) and systems from different vendors has been a significant challenge.

Given the development of interoperability standards and the certification of EMR systems that meet those standards, improved transmissibility of medical information can increase quality of care and decrease waste and duplication of services for patients seeking care from multiple physician offices and medical centers, and for patients moving to new geographical locations. Furthermore, with the anticipated increase in the proportion of the U.S. population with medical insurance from the passage of the Patient Protection and Affordable Care Act in 2010, improvements in interoperability stand to have a significant positive impact on medical care processes and population health as the need for automated, secure, and fully interoperable transmission of medical information increases.

However, potentially problematic issues remain with incentive payments for meaningful use of EMRs. The Office of Inspector General (OIG) of the Department of Health and Human Services (HHS) launched a thorough review of government incentive payments to physicians and hospitals pertaining to the meaningful use of EMRs in 2012. The office cited troubling indications that some providers are using EMRs to facilitate "upcoding" of Medicare charges to receive payments to which they are not entitled. At the time of this writing, the investigation is ongoing.[8]

PATIENT PROTECTION AND AFFORDABLE CARE ACT: THE EXTENSION OF HOSPITAL INFORMATION SYSTEMS BEYOND THE HOSPITAL

The Patient Protection and Affordable Care Act, affirmed after the 2012 presidential election, includes a number of policies and potential projects that aim to improve quality of care while reducing costs—or at least greatly slowing increases in healthcare costs from year to year. Included in this effort are CMS payment incentives for providers that can show care patterns that meet the goals of high-quality, cost-efficient care.

On March 31, 2011, the Department of Health and Human Services (HHS) released a set of proposed new rules to aid clinicians, hospitals, and other health facilities and providers to improve coordination of care for Medicare patients using a model known as accountable care organizations (ACOs). ACOs that are shown to lower healthcare cost growth while meeting CMS quality benchmarks, including measures of patient/caregiver experience of care, care coordination, patient safety, preventive health, and health of high-risk populations, will receive incentive payments as part of the Medicare Shared Savings Program. In some proposed models, ACOs may also be held accountable for shared losses.

Coordination of care means that hospitals, physician offices, and other providers have a complete record of patients' episodes of care, including diagnostic tests, procedures, and medication information. This has the potential to decrease extra costs from unnecessary duplication of services as well as reduce medical errors from incomplete understanding of the patients' illness histories and medical care provided. It is also believed that better coordination of care may prevent 30-day hospital re-admissions (which occur for nearly one in five Medicare discharges), because necessary post-discharge care would be more readily obtainable with more aggressive care coordination. Medicare patients in ACOs, however, would still be allowed to see providers outside of the ACO, and proposals exist to prevent physicians in ACOs from being penalized for patients with a greater illness severity or complexity. According to a CMS analysis, ACOs may result in Medicare savings of up to $960 million over three years. Although the Affordable Care Act's ACO provisions primarily target Medicare beneficiaries, private insurers are also beginning to create care models based on the accountable care paradigm. Insurers could offer similar incentives to the ACO model described above, which might include features such as performance-based contracting or tiered benefit models that favor physicians who score highly on care quality and cost-efficiency measures.

ACOs and other implementations of the accountable care paradigm, however, are in their beginning stages, with a number of pilots around the country currently being conducted to more fully evaluate the concept, and there still is some controversy over the best way to achieve these goals. The critical point here is that, in all likelihood, with the advent of the Affordable Care Act and other initiatives, stemming the upward tide of medical cost increases will become an even higher priority; no matter what the final models will look like, the success of any of the models requires a high level of care coordination, requiring information systems that are fully compatible and allow seamless and errorless transmission of information between sites of service and the various providers that can be involved in patient care. Thus, wherever a patient goes for care, all the information needed to provide high-quality and cost-efficient care is immediately available.

THE EFFECT ON THE COST OF MEDICAL CARE

To justify the cost of an HIS, management should calculate the following:

- **Reductions in labor costs:** Factors that contribute to cost reductions include a decrease in manual or clerical tasks and streamlining the work processes of clinicians. Productivity gains can be in the neighborhood of 10 percent.
- **Reductions in the need for equipment and supplies:** Standardization and better inventory management through computerization is beneficial in this area.
- **Increased revenue generation:** Improved charge capture and elimination of lost charges occur through use of a CPOE system, along with a decrease in outstanding days of receivables, which can improve revenue generation. Elimination of written charge slips and the passing of charges from used services directly to the accounting system through a computer interface also can result in revenue generation. Expected charge revenue increases can amount to 10 percent to 30 percent over a previous manual system.
- **Improved employee satisfaction:** As users progress along the learning curve, increased employee satisfaction (e.g., through streamlining processes and eliminating redundant tasks) contributes to employee retention and decreases turnover costs.
- **Improvements in LOS and healthcare charges per admission:** As payment models evolve to reduce the overall trend in healthcare costs, improvements in LOS may become an attractive component of an accountable care program.
- **Enhancements in quality of care:** Although difficult to quantify financially, quality of care improvements, especially if publicized outside the hospital, may lead to the referral of more patients to the institution. In addition, given the new consumerism in healthcare, the importance of patient confidence in the quality of care in an institution may further enhance revenue if patients say, "I choose this hospital because its quality is higher" in a particular clinical area. The professionalism of the providers themselves also indicates their desire to supply high-quality care.
- **Legal and regulatory:** An increase in care quality, including a reduction in errors, due to the implementation of an information system may lead to lower malpractice insurance premiums. Reporting of quality of care measures to regulatory institutions such as the Joint Commission and CMS may be streamlined, saving the cost of preparing the reports manually.
- **Data privacy and security:** HITECH expanded liability for privacy and security breaches for PHI to individuals in the healthcare system and to the vendors of those directly involved in supplying and paying for healthcare. It also extended enforcement powers to state attorneys general, whereas before there had been only federal enforcement of HIPAA Privacy and Security rules. An effective and secure HIS that prevents loading (as opposed to viewing or reading only) of PHI onto mobile devices or laptops greatly mitigates the risks associated with the expanded liability and enforcement found in HITECH.

There are several ways that HIS can show a positive ROI. One means is through an increase in workflow efficiency. Although this increase in efficiency may be hard to quantify in terms of a reduction in FTEs, the improvements are real and money can be saved. For example, in an integrated system, tests performed and services rendered can be automatically invoiced to payers or to patients, thus eliminating the need for clerical personnel to perform such tasks. Savings may occur in a number of areas, such as those presented in Table 5.2.

However, some technologies may require millions of dollars initially for capital purchases, development, implementation, and training on the system. The costs of implementing a fairly sophisticated CPOE system for a 500-bed hospital have been estimated to be around $8 million. Subsequent

TABLE 5.2

Financial Data Supports the Value of Information Systems

Attribute	Technologically Advanced Hospitals	Other Hospitals
Highest AA credit rating	35%	15%
Average LOS (days)	3.24	3.73
FTEs per occupied bed	3.3	3.8
Expenses per adjusted facility discharge	$3,995	$4,511
Annual increase in hospital expenses	0.6%	2.8%

FTE, full-time equivalent; LOS, length of stay.

Source: Hospitals & Health Networks, third annual survey, http://www.hhnmag.com/hhnmag/index.jsp, 2001.

annual maintenance may cost as much as $1,350,000. These costs include allocations for hardware, software, workstations, network upgrades, IT personnel, and non-IT personnel such as user leadership. There also may be some temporary productivity losses during implementation of the system.

However, once implemented, savings from the system can be significant. One 1,100-bed academic health system saved approximately $6 million annually with the use of a CPOE system and a medication administration record. This figure combines the time savings realized for nurses, pharmacists, and unit secretaries. According to a report by Cerner Corporation,[9] another regional medical center saved about $3 million annually and avoided 36 deaths through the implementation of a computer-based data repository that contained medication rules. The majority of financial benefits from CPOE systems and EMRs are long term. One large nationwide managed care organization projected that it will take about nine to ten years to realize a positive net cash flow from its HIS. Once realized, it is projected that there will be a reduction of approximately 2.3 percent in long-term hospital cost structure trends and an increase of 0.6 percent in revenue. About 35 percent of the financial benefits from the system are attributed to improved LOS efficiency, and about 40 percent of financial benefits are attributable to greater efficiency in operating costs and staff work flow, given that many manual processes will be automated.

Although a system can save money almost immediately with the implementation of these systems, it may take several years to see a net positive ROI. In addition, calculating ROI for HIS is not as straightforward as in many other financial areas. Benefits from an integrated hospital IT system such as patient satisfaction, provider convenience, and improved communication are not easily quantifiable in terms of revenue and expense. The ROI for each institution is unique and depends on factors such as the extent of pre-existing information systems capability, acceptance of the new system, size of the institution, percent of at-risk versus fee-for-service billing, distribution of FTEs, level of dependence on outside vendors, ability to hire specialized personnel, and other factors. One way to increase the chances of a positive ROI is to tie variable income, such as bonuses, to the amount of cost savings from the systems. In other words, managers on the project may put part of their bonus at risk based on the financial performance of the system. This will enhance their commitment to the project as well as communication with users to garner acceptance and hopefully embrace the new system. The basic calculation for ROI is as follows[10]:

Definitions:
Annual revenue increase or savings = R
Expenses from operations = O
Expenses from maintenance = M
Interest on borrowed funds (if any) = I
Depreciation of capital = D

Calculation:

Obtain net or incremental profit (E): $E = R - (O + M + I + D)$

Obtain capital expenditure $= C$

Calculate the Annual Rate of Return or Required Investment (before taxes) (A)

$$A = (E / C)\ 100$$

A word of warning: Purchase of a pilot or "beta" system can lead to trouble. Although they are significantly less expensive, these systems are technically still under development and often have bugs and immature features. Remember the dictum: "You can always add but you cannot always take away." It is much better to start with a simpler system and add features later ("walk before you run") instead of obtaining a brand new system that has not been tried before and having to dismantle it later. Once a system is extinguished, it is much harder to obtain buy-in to a replacement system by users who have lost confidence.

Overall, although the ROI of an HIS and its enhancements may be difficult to quantify, its far-reaching impacts and relatively high cost make careful scrutiny critical. Analysis of HIS does not easily lend itself to a single number, and it may be several years post-implementation before the full benefits of the technologies are realized. Given the market and regulatory demands for sophisticated HIS, however, consideration of options for such an undertaking is essential.

CONCLUSION

The deployment of technology is becoming more and more critical to the success of an organization. There are many options one can choose, from a basic information system to more complex applications such as CPOE systems and EMRs. In addition, although precise quantitative ROIs are difficult to calculate for HIS, the association of clinical outcomes to financial outcomes is becoming more clear. Given the current governmental direction as well as the new consumerism movement in healthcare, systems that improve quality of care and go beyond just administrative functions are becoming more critical to hospital and medical center success. With careful implementation and a little luck, an HIS can turn quality improvement into financial gain.

CHECKLIST 1: Evaluating Hospital Performance Improvement Functions

Department/Team: Completed by:

	YES	NO
1. Have improvements been made over the past year as a result of your hospital's performance improvement activities?	o	o
a. If so, can more improvements be made using technology and HIS?	o	o
b. Did the hospital's improvement/s involve improving a process?	o	o
c. Did the hospital's improvement/s improve a patient outcome?	o	o
d. Was the improvement directly related to the performance improvement measures you chose?	o	o
2. Can you document how you choose performance improvement measurements?	o	o
3. Have any hospital performance improvement activities involved other departments or teams?	o	o
a. If so, were the other departments or teams involved in the measurement process or informed of the findings?	o	o
b. Were the other departments or teams involved in development of the performance measures or collection of data?	o	o
4. Have you used any statistical tools, such as charts or graphs, in analyzing your data?	o	o

5. Has the scope of your department or team changed over the last year?   o   o
   a. Has anything been added? If so, what?
   b. Has anything been eliminated? If so, what?
   c. Has performance been measured for new services provided?   o   o
6. Over the past year, has it been necessary for you to prioritize any of your hospital   o   o
   performance improvement activities due to multiple areas for improvement being identified?
   a. If so, how did you determine which area was the priority?
7. Were the performance measures reviewed with the staff in your department or team   o   o
   members before data collection was initiated?
8. Were findings of your performance improvement efforts reviewed with the staff in your   o   o
   department or with team members each month?
9. When problems or opportunities for improvement were identified, was input from those   o   o
   performing the functions requested and integrated into changes for improvement?
10. *Hospital Departments Only:* Are the results obtained from performance improvement   o   o
    activities used for employee evaluations in your department?
11. *Hospital Departments Only:* Has your department/service been involved in any team   o   o
    performance measurement activities?
    a. If so, have data directly relating to your department been collected?   o   o
    b. What team/s is your department involved in?
12. What suggestions do you have for improving the current hospital performance improvement
    reporting system?

CHECKLIST 2: Hospital Quality Improvement Program Assessment

Dear Members of the _____ Hospital/Organization/Agency: **Your input is critical in assessing our *current* quality improvement plan**. As you know, quality improvement—the ongoing measurement of key hospital processes and outcomes, in conjunction with strategic planning and other sources to improve clinical and administrative performance—is only as effective as we make it.

Please place an X in the Yes/No columns with explanations or suggestions of **who, what, where, how**, and/or **when** in the Comments column.

Does our hospital's culture:	YES	No	Comments
1. Demonstrate commitment from leaders that foster our vision?	o	o	
2. Exhibit transformational leadership by using systems thinking and processes and shared governance behaviors throughout the hospital organization?	o	o	
3. Promote total quality management in our patient/customer-driven strategic planning?	o	o	
4. Emphasize continuous quality improvement (CQI) as a key value in our philosophy/mission, goals, and hospital objectives?	o	o	
5. Create a constancy of purpose in aligning hospital philosophy/ mission statement, goals, and objectives with services and programs?	o	o	
6. Link all quality initiatives with the strategic plan, budget, policies, and procedures? (Are quality efforts integral or parallel to the daily workings of the hospital organization?)	o	o	
7. Value the uniqueness and contributions of all individuals in the organization; are all treated equally?	o	o	
8. Support an integrated network with a cross-functional team approach? Go beyond the traditional boundaries in learning to build patient-centered integrated models of hospital care versus professional-centered models of care?	o	o	

9. Provide a human resources program that supports interdependent teamwork and a patient/customer focus on the basis of the performance evaluation and compensation system?   o   o

10. Value learning and risk taking with adequate hospital resources?   o   o

11. Provide adequate human and technical resources to define, capture, statistically analyze, and report useful, understandable data?   o   o

12. Communicate how hospital best practice strategies and benchmarking significantly impact our competitive strategies?   o   o

13. Encourage replicating successful internal and external practices across the organization to accelerate the rate of improvement?   o   o

14. Understand the culture of our competitors? our suppliers?   o   o

Does our CQI plan:

15. Use an understandable framework?   o   o

16. State the facility's quality vision?   o   o

17. Clearly define our goals that stretch us, with achievable objectives?   o   o

18. Outline our program's scope of care and services?   o   o

19. Identify person(s) or position(s) responsible for coordinating/ facilitating the program?   o   o

20. Describe our CQI council's purpose, functions, membership, and roles?   o   o

21. Address the issues of responsibility and authority?   o   o

22. Delineate lines of communication, including reporting mechanisms?   o   o

23. Address confidentiality?   o   o

24. Delineate the approach to measuring dimensions of performance related to functions, processes, and outcomes?   o   o

25. Include a plan for periodic evaluation?   o   o

As a result of *our* CQI efforts, do *you* think: o   o

26. All employees support and can articulate our organization's core values and culture?   o   o

27. All employees can describe the CQI process and how it is working?   o   o

28. We use CQI language appropriately (no meaningless jargon/ buzzwords)?   o   o

29. We appropriately use standards established by:

    – Professional organizations?   o   o

    – Joint Commission, National Committee for Quality Assurance, National League for Nursing Community Health Accreditation Program, and other voluntary accrediting bodies?   o   o

    – State and/or federal government (e.g., Medicare, Medicaid, Agency for Health Care Policy and Research, etc.)?   o   o

30. Care plans, clinical guidelines, and care maps are written and used well across the continuum of services?   o   o

31. Critical processes are known and continuously improved?   o   o

32. You have assumed greater ownership of the work structures and the CQI processes (more self-motivated, self-managed, patient-focused versus professionally self-focused; do you feel empowered)?   o   o

33. Your practice has improved, including patient outcomes?   o   o

34. Ways to document patient care, including patient/family involvement, have improved?   o   o

Does our CQI plan: o   o

35. Eliminate professional and service organizational barriers/boundaries   o   o
    to achieve the necessary integrated work processes?

36. Link staff performance appraisals to job descriptions, expected   o   o
    competencies, and realistic performance outcomes?

37. Competently ensure patient and staff safety, including reducing the   o   o
    risk of infection?

38. Enhance patient and family education, fostering relevant and   o   o
    improved outcomes?

39. Increase internal and external customer satisfaction; meet needs and   o   o
    expectations?

40. Improve clinical and administrative performance and minimize costs   o   o
    and other resource consumption?

41. Decrease risks of litigation for our organization?   o   o

42. Value learning and self-development: orientation, continuing   o   o
    education, and competency systems?

43. Use CQI data as a marketing strategy?   o   o

44. Involve state, federal, and voluntary surveyors/accreditors to help our   o   o
    CQI efforts?

45. Evaluate performance improvement requirements, successes, and   o   o
    lessons learned on (at least) an annual basis?

Additional Comments:

_____

Name and Service (Optional)

_____

REFERENCES

1. The Economist Intelligence Unit. Country, Industry, and Risk Analysis from the Economist Intelligence Unit. 2012. http://www.eiu.com/default.aspx.
2. Poon, E. G., Keohane, C. A., Yoon, C. S., Ditmore, M., Bane, A., Levitzion-Korach, O., et al. Effect of Bar-Code Technology on the Safety of Medication Administration. 2010. *New England Journal of Medicine* 2010(362): 1698–1707.
3. Institute of Medicine, *To Err Is Human: Building a Safer Health System.* 1999. http://www.iom.edu/Reports/1999/To-Err-is-Human-Building-A-Safer-Health-System.aspx.
4. Bruner, A., and Kasdan, M. Handwriting Errors: Harmful, Wasteful and Preventable. 1986. Kentucky Medical Association, White paper.
5. Institute for Clinical Systems Improvement. 2013. Home. https://www.icsi.org/.
6. Klas. *CPOE 2011. The ARRA Effect.* 2011. https://www.klasresearch.com/store/ReportDetail.aspx?ProductID=640
7. Health Care Delivery System Reform and the Patient Protection & Affordable Care Act: A Report from Senator Sheldon Whitehouse for the U.S. Senate Committee on Health Education, Labor & Pensions. March 2012. http://www.whitehouse.senate.gov/imo/media/doc/Health%20Care%20Delivery%20System%20Reform%20and%20The%20Affordable%20Care%20Act%20FINAL2.pdf
8. *InformationWeek Healthcare*, Feds Take Critical Look at Meaningful Use Payments. October 24, 2012. http://www.informationweek.com/healthcare/policy/feds-take-critical-look-at-meaningful-us/240009661. Accessed on November 2, 2012.
9. Cerner, Physician Practice, 2013. http://www.cerner.com/solutions/Physician_Practice/.
10. Fleming, J. Medical Diagnostic Support Systems: Past, Present, and Future. *Healthcare Informatics.* 1994: 18–22.

6 Community and County Mental Health Programs of the Future

Carol S. Miller

CONTENTS

INTRODUCTION

Community Mental Health Centers, also referred to as County Mental Health Centers, treat patients usually with no or limited insurance in a domiciliary setting versus an inpatient state or community facility. Both children and adults are eligible to receive such assistance. These programs provide a wide range of psychiatric and counseling services to the residents in their community as well as other types of assistance, such as:

- Treatment services related to substance abuse
- Housing, including halfway hours
- Full or partial supervision day centers
- Employment services
- Information and education services
- Referrals
- Consultative services to schools, courts, and other agencies
- Self-help groups
- After-care services
- Other related activities

The community facilities generally include outpatient clinics, community/county mental health programs, short-term psychiatric facilities, day-care centers, de-toxification centers, residential rehabilitation centers for substance abuse, vocational training, residential care, long-term care psychiatric facilities, and Veterans Affairs (VA) psychiatric centers. The community centers may be co-located with other county services such as social services, occupational rehabilitation services, information technology services, human resources, maintenance services, and others or may be independently located.

DESCRIPTION OF A COMMUNITY MENTAL HEALTH CENTER

STAFFING

Staffing levels at community mental health facilities depend on the size and funding of each clinic and can vary in number, qualifications, and mix. Many personnel hold or are working on master's degrees and various professional certifications. Typical staffing models include:

- **Administrative or mental health director:** This individual, working under general policy directives, is responsible for planning, organizing, coordinating, and directing delivery of a community's comprehensive mental health programs and services. This would include the development and implementation of goals, objectives, policies, procedures, budget, standard compliance, and work standards for mental health services. The Director is responsible not only for the services offered under the program but also for extensive coordination with other county departments, public and private organizations, citizen groups, and the Board of Supervisors.
- **Case management staff:** These personnel are responsible for compiling all the services related to the treatment program.
- **Psychiatrists:** These individuals may work for a mental health center full or part time, and are Board-eligible or Board-certified in psychiatry.
- **Psychologists:** These individuals hold Ph.D., Psy.D., or Ed.D. qualifications and are licensed as clinical psychologists in the state.
- **Licensed independent social workers:** These individuals will have expertise in such services as family counseling, child psychology, geriatric dementia, psychological testing, and so on.

- **Licensed marriage and family therapists:** These individuals specialize in various fields and provide an array of counseling services to patients, depending on the nature of their problem.
- **Clinical nurse specialists:** These personnel are certified in psychiatric nursing by a national nursing organization such as the American Nurses Association to practice within the scope of these services; they are licensed to practice in the state.
- **Support staff:** These staff members include an administrative assistant to the Director, medical billers, transcriptionists, and possibly a receptionist.
- **Substance abuse counselor or licensed professional clinical mental health counselor:** These individuals take a holistic approach where they examine a person's external environmental and societal influences while monitoring inner emotional, physical, and behavioral health. A licensed mental health counselor has met or exceeded the following professional qualifications (USDHHS 2009):
  - Earned a master's degree in counseling or a closely related mental health discipline
  - Completed a minimum of two years post-master's clinical work under the supervision of a licensed or certified mental health professional
  - Passed a state-developed or national licensure or certification examination

TYPES OF COVERED SERVICES

A variety of services is offered by each state and many times by different counties within the state. Because there are no federal standards, nor even statewide standards within any state, there is little uniformity in services offered. Each center can add, delete, or customize services they wish to include or exclude from their program on the basis of funding allocation, resources, available space, etc. Mental health services typically include treatments for some combination of the following disorders, among others:

- Alcohol/drug abuse
- Anxiety/panic disorders
- Attention deficit hyperactivity disorder (ADHD, ADD)
- Autism spectrum disorders (pervasive developmental disorders)
- Bipolar disorder (manic-depressive illness)
- Borderline personality disorder
- Crisis/stress disorders
- Depression
- Eating disorders
- Generalized anxiety disorder
- Obsessive-compulsive disorder (OCD)
- Panic disorder
- Post-traumatic stress disorder (PTSD)
- Schizophrenia
- Social phobia (social anxiety disorder)
- Suicide and suicide prevention

Some states, like South Carolina, may provide grants to any county, city, town, or political subdivision, on the basis of population size and with the consent of the South Carolina Department of Mental Health, to establish a community mental health service program for its specific area. Examples of traditional services provided in a typical community mental health program include the following:

- Intake evaluations or assessments, which are usually performed by a staff psychiatrist
- Testing, which is performed by a staff social worker or psychologist

- Therapy, such as individual or group detoxification or narcotics treatment programs, which is performed by staff social workers and substance abuse counselors
- Case management, which may involve a combination of internal staff assessment and treatment as well as outsourced, community-based services. The treatment plan is a joint plan that is developed between the internal staff at the center and the external staff in the community. This combination of care is usually monitored through medical records to ensure that specific goals are addressed, that treatment providers are complying with the state and federal regulations in general terms, and that the level of care is appropriate. Once the treatment plan and care are approved and provided, a community mental health center will bill collectively for all staff services—both internal and external—and often will submit the billing to the insurer. Once reimbursement is received, the center will usually deduct a case management fee based on a percentage of the billing and pay the remainder as fees to the outsourced providers
- Medication clinics or checks, which are performed by a staff psychiatrist
- Acute stabilization, crisis intervention, or emergency services
- Referrals, which are made by the staff; clients are directed to traditional medical services, rehabilitation, occupational therapy, housing, vocational, homeless services, and life skills services within the community
- Various support services, which are offered to clients by such organizations as national foundations for specific diseases, support groups, etc.
- Support and advocacy services in which a team of volunteers and employees staff a 24-hour hotline offering peer counseling, hospital accompaniment, court advocacy, referrals for victims, sexual assault counseling, and school-based prevention and education
- Integration of clients into non-medical support services, which includes arranging for clients to attend various 12-step support groups
- Advocating for or against clients in family and criminal court

The aggregate service feedback continuum for these mental health services is depicted in Figure 6.1.

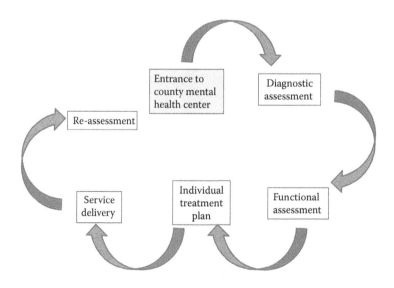

FIGURE 6.1   Mental health services feedback continuum.

Sources of Clients

Community mental health centers receive referrals from a variety of sources, including the following:

- The medical community; these referrals are traditionally for patients without insurance, or who have limited income, rely on Medicaid, or come from private medical practitioners, psychiatrists, internists, family practitioners, gynecologists, emergency departments, or urgent care centers
- The psychiatric medical community, which includes psychiatrists, psychologists, counselors, therapists, and a variety of social workers from private behavioral managed outpatient clinics
- The non-medical community, such as physical therapy, which refers individuals facing life-changing problems (e.g., amputation); osteopaths, chiropractors, and local private therapists all refer occasionally
- Acute private psychiatric centers
- Health departments at major local employers
- Local schools (e.g., when teachers report suspected developmental problems, suspected abuse, and behavioral problems to the school's counselor)
- Social Services, which refer clients of all ages
- Non-profit agencies that help mental health patients and homeless individuals
- Family members and family support friends
- Some self-referrals or self-help clubs
- Courts, which send defendants for evaluations
- Police, who sometimes bring referrals as an option against arrest and who monitor the homeless
- Staff from a sheriff's department jail, which houses offenders, some of whom are assumed to have mental health problems
- Homeless shelters and missions
- Probation officers, who refer probationers for evaluation and monitoring
- National foundations of specific diseases, which refer patients for care, like the American Diabetes Association
- Detox centers, which refer clients for evaluation and placement
- Domestic violence groups and protective services groups
- Twelve-step recovery groups like Alcoholics Anonymous (http://www.alcoholics-anonymous.org), Narcotics Anonymous (http://www.na.org), Cocaine Anonymous (http://www.ca.org), Emotions Anonymous (http://www.emotionsanonymous.org), Overeaters Anonymous (http://www.oa.org), and Sexaholics Anonymous (http://www.sa.org)
- Substance abuse rehabilitation centers, which refer Medicaid clients for evaluation of suspected co-morbidity and after-care
- Clergy members, who provide marriage and grief counseling
- Pharmaceutical companies that promote treatment, albeit indirectly, for depression, attention deficit disorder, etc.
- Bookstores (through their self-help manuals)
- Websites, such as the Substance Abuse and Mental Health Services Administration (SAMHSA) referral site
- Bartenders
- Industrial and company medical departments, which may refer clients who have conditions that are less expensive to treat at a county center
- Well-meaning individuals

In addition, public awareness programs often result in increased referrals from various sources.

REGULATORY ENVIRONMENT

Regulations from federal, state, and county governments have an impact on the day-to-day operations, procedures, and processes of a community mental health center.

- **Federal regulations:** The United States healthcare system is guided by programs such as those established under the Centers for Medicare and Medicaid (in the case of community mental health programs, Medicaid is especially important), SAMHSA for community health block grants, Americans with Disabilities Act (ADA), Occupational Safety and Health Administration (OSHA), Health Insurance Portability and Accountability Act (HIPAA), and others. In addition, various federal regulations have had or will have an impact on community mental health centers, such as the Paul Wellstone and Pete Domenici Mental Health Parity and Addiction Equity Act, the Patient Protection and Affordable Care Act (PPACA), and others.
- **State regulations:** These include general legislative guidelines and laws from 50 states and the District of Columbia, state management of benefits and reimbursement of the Medicaid program, and state allocations of budgets, which impact the centers' operations (NCSL 2011).
- **County regulations:** Each county defines its own community mental health program and decides which services will be provided or excluded.

TYPES OF REVENUE

Community mental health services are usually paid for with a mix of state, local, and federal funds. In addition, many of those receiving services (approximately 38 percent) are uninsured and another 35 percent are covered by Medicaid. Revenue is received from a variety of sources, including the following:

- Direct payment from patients
- Co-pays, sliding scale payments, etc.
- Health insurance payments, primarily Medicaid and some Medicare, which do not cover all mental health services
- Direct state funding (available in many states, but not all)
- Indirect state funding via the county (available in some states)
- General tax and fee revenues
- Federal stimulus dollars
- County or local levy funding (available in some states), funded largely by state appropriations
- Direct and indirect grants from various national foundations

As part of a prior transfer of mental health program responsibilities from the state to counties, in most states some state revenues are automatically set aside for the support of community mental health programs and thus may not be provided through the annual state budget act. Other state support for community mental health programs is provided through the annual state budget act and thus is subject to change by actions of the legislature and governor of that state.

The primary source of revenue, however, is Medicaid, with the secondary source being state general funds. Medicaid is a combined state and federal health insurance program administered by the states. Medicaid often provides broader mental health benefits than those provided by private insurance, including employment-related services as well as therapy and medications.

Medicaid operates as a vendor-payment program, with payments made directly to the providers. Providers participating in Medicaid must accept the Medicaid reimbursement level as payment in full. Each state has relatively broad discretion in determining (within federally imposed upper limits and specific restrictions) the reimbursement methodology and resulting rate for services, with three exceptions:

- For institutional services (payment may not exceed amounts that would be paid under Medicare payment rates)
- For disproportionate share hospitals (different limits apply)
- For hospice care

States may impose nominal deductibles, co-insurance, or co-payments on some Medicaid recipients for certain services. Emergency services and family planning services must be exempt from such co-payments. Certain Medicaid recipients must be excluded from this cost-sharing: pregnant women, children under age 18, hospital or nursing home patients who are expected to contribute most of their income to institutional care, and categorically needy health maintenance organization (HMO) enrollees. For the latter, an example would be those individuals who enroll in a Medicaid managed care program with the state and whose income is below a state- or federal-designated poverty level.

The amount of total federal outlays for Medicaid has no set limit (cap); rather, the federal government must match whatever the individual state decides to provide, within the law, for its eligible recipients. However, reimbursement rates must be sufficient to enlist enough providers so that Medicaid care and services are available under the plan at least to the extent that such care and services are available to the general population in that geographic area.

The portion of the Medicaid program that is paid by the federal government, known as the Federal Medical Assistance Percentage (FMAP) and the Enhanced Federal Medical Assistance Percentage (eFMAP), is determined annually for each state by a formula that compares the state's average per capita income level with the national average. By law, the FMAP cannot be lower than 50 percent nor greater than 83 percent. Wealthier states have a smaller share of their costs reimbursed. More information on FMAP rates by state is available from the U.S. Department of Health and Human Services (http://aspe.hhs.gov/health/fmap12.shtn).

The federal government also shares in the state's expenditures for administration of the Medicaid program. Most administrative costs are matched at 50 percent for all states. However, higher matching rates (75, 90, and 100 percent) are authorized by law for certain functions and activities.

Most Medicaid plans provide a broad range of professional mental health and substance abuse services, including evaluations, therapy, tests, and reports. Typical covered services under Medicaid for mental health include the following:

- Inpatient treatment and psychiatric evaluations
- Outpatient or clinic therapy services, including evaluations, testing, medication management, psychological testing, rehabilitative services, and individual, group, or family therapy
- Therapy in partial hospital settings for patients under 21 years of age
- Injections that are primarily used to treat a mental health condition
- Counseling and recovery programs aimed at treating substance abuse

In summary, external factors, such as government regulations, insurance reimbursement methodology, insurer's limitation of benefits for mental health, the ever-increasing cost of medications or limitations of certain medications, and internal factors, such as staffing issues, a shortage of qualified mental health providers (especially in rural areas), increased patient volumes, and managing the day-to-day operations of the center, all negatively affect the future viability of community mental health centers. These situations are causing community mental health centers to consider alternatives to their existing operational structure to survive.

OTHER MENTAL HEALTH RESOURCES

National Mental Health Information
Center
P.O. Box 2345
Rockville, MD 20847
Telephone: 800-789-2647
(TDD): 866-889-2647
E-mail: nmhic-info@samhsa.hhs.gov
Web: http://mentalhealth.samhsa.gov

National Alliance for the Mentally Ill
Colonial Place Three
3803 N. Fairfax Drive, Suite 100
Arlington, VA 22203
Telephone: 800-950-6264
Fax: 703-524-9094
Web: http://www.nami.org

National Council for Community
Behavioral Health Care
1701 K Street, N.W., Suite 400
Washington, DC 20006
Telephone: 301-984-6200
Fax: 301-881-7159
Web: http://www.nccbh.org

American Association of Pastoral
Counselors
9504-A Lee Highway
Fairfax, VA 22031-2303
Telephone: 703-385-6967
Fax: 703-352-7725
E-mail: info@aapc.org
Web: http://www.aapc.org

National Empowerment Center
599 Canal Street
Lawrence, MA 01840
Telephone: 800-769-3728
Fax: 978-681-6426
Web: http://www.power2u.org

American Self-Help Clearinghouse
Saint Clare's Hospital
100 E. Hanover Avenue
Cedar Knolls, NJ 07927
Telephone: 973-401-2121
Fax: 973-989-1159
E-mail: wrodenbaugh@saintclares.com
Web: http://www.mentalhelp.net/selfhelp

National Mental Health Consumer's
Self-Help Clearinghouse
1211 Chestnut Street, Suite 1100
Philadelphia, PA 19107
Telephone: 800-553-4539
Fax: 215-636-6312
E-mail: info@mhselfhelp.org
Web: http://www.mhselfhelp.org

ISSUES AFFECTING COMMUNITY MENTAL HEALTH PROGRAMS

Maintaining the goals of community mental health programs is difficult due to changing social priorities, funding deficits, and the increasing need for treatment. Since the turn of the twenty-first century, there has been nearly a four-fold increase in the number of patients seeking care at a community mental health center; this increase is not mirrored by a rise in physicians. These issues create incorrect allocation of resources to meet the needs of the patient population, poor coordination and communication both internally with the staff and externally with the medical community, staff attitude problems, access to care in a timely manner, and a host of other inequities, which cause organizational and operational discord. However, most importantly, these issues have an impact on the financial viability of the centers.

The following provides an overview of several of the major issues affecting community mental health programs and includes the impact of the PPACA, which was signed into law on March 23, 2010 (HealthCare.gov 2013). These issues are not prevalent in every mental health program, but they represent a sampling of typical issues. In addition, these issues may vary in intensity from one location to another, or may be totally different.

FRAGMENTED ENTRY PROCESS INTO THE MENTAL HEALTH SYSTEM

In a community program, no single gatekeeper refers patients to the center. Referrals come from a multitude of providers and services in the county without any type of coordination. The typical referral patterns were referenced earlier, under Sources of Clients.

SHORTAGE OF QUALIFIED MENTAL HEALTH PROVIDERS

Due to the increase in patient volumes in many rural and urban mental health centers, there is a shortage of qualified behavioral or mental health providers to serve the populations on hand, especially in rural areas. Without a local presence of specialized behavioral health providers, primary care providers play a large role in behavioral healthcare, even though many have not been specifically trained in this specialty. The PPACA is expected to ameliorate the provider shortage by establishing grant programs to train and educate new providers, especially those that would be co-located in rural areas, special needs populations, and schools and colleges.

Clinical social workers, who provide a higher volume of mental health services, also influence the roles and responsibilities of the provider community. Their scope of services is quite broad and many times overlaps the fields of psychiatry, professional psychology, psychiatric nursing, and marriage and family therapy. Several state laws have enabled these individuals to diagnose mental disorders, testify in court as expert witnesses, and admit crisis patients to mental facilities. Because of this broadening scope of duties, many higher paid psychiatrists are finding their duties and responsibilities limited or are seeking other positions outside the boundaries of community mental health centers.

ADMINISTRATIVE CHALLENGES

Community mental health programs may be staffed by personnel supplied by the state, personnel hired independently, and contractors (for services that have been outsourced). This patchwork arrangement creates management issues, including diminished authority, lack of compliance, discipline and attitude problems, potential salary discrepancies among similar staff functions, bureaucracy that hinders the transition to emerging mental healthcare treatment trends or new services, denial of services and the resulting labor-intensive appeal processes, and many more.

At the executive level, a Director may hold the title, may have a master's degree in healthcare administration, and may function as a chief operating officer, but may have little experience in working in a government-run facility and managing an archaic governmental accounting system. Also, a Director may work in parallel with a Medical Director, who is usually a psychiatrist but may only be interested in clinical services and not regulatory or administrative matters, which can create managerial or staff conflicts.

Recruitment—hiring and retention of qualified and culturally competent staff—is a significant problem, especially for small community mental health centers or areas that are sparsely populated. These centers usually are unable to compete with larger counties in terms pay, benefits, professional growth opportunities, and working conditions. As a result, smaller centers often have unfilled positions and limited patient care.

Community mental health programs yield no profitability, and many times the Director must arbitrarily reallocate funds to finance various internal projects or services. This incremental budgeting (i.e., "use it or lose it" funding) does not promote cost savings but instead is merely a money-shuffling exercise that keeps a center functioning on a day-to-day basis.

Another challenge for most mental health centers is the cultural diversity of the patients. Many speak multiple languages and may not be proficient in English, resulting in poor communications and difficulty in providing follow-up care. Additionally, because of the cultural stigma or the difficulty in communicating, these individuals may never return for additional care and instead will seek assistance from clergy or a general health provider who may not have the training or education needed to treat the behavioral issue.

Many of the typical funding models will not work for small counties, and use of a traditional funding model may in fact penalize the county or the mental health center. The amount of available funds is often so small that the administrative cost of applying for, tracking, and justifying the use of the funds is greater than the allocation itself. Consequently, many smaller counties do not obtain the funding set aside for them, which, in turn, can be collected and used by larger county programs. The result is a widening gap between resources and program availability between smaller and larger counties.

Increasingly, the cost of upgrades is a challenge. Many centers cannot afford the investment required to purchase modern computer equipment and software, nor to provide the necessary continued maintenance and technical support. Thus, as technology becomes increasingly sophisticated, the community mental health centers fall further behind. In addition, the cost of renovation of physical facilities to meet evolving program needs has become prohibitive.

MEDICAL AND MENTAL HEALTH PARITY

There has been a difference between the benefits covered under medical insurance for providers and facility charges compared to the benefits covered under mental health benefits. In addition, there have been caps on the annual number of visits allowed, higher co-pays, higher deductibles, restrictions of medications on the preferred drug list, and reduction of covered benefits, such as partial hospitalization and number-of-treatment limits for mental health. Managed care systems, like Medicaid Managed Care, focus on limiting costs either by keeping the total number of patients using services low or by reducing the cost of the service itself.

Congress touched on this issue in 1996 with the Mental Health Parity Act. This federal law prevented group health plans from placing annual or lifetime dollar limits on mental health benefits that are lower (i.e., less favorable) than annual or lifetime dollar limits for medical and surgical benefits. However, the law did not require group health plans and their health insurance issuers to include mental health coverage in their benefits package—it only applied to group health plan insurance that already included mental health benefits in its benefit package.

In 2003, Senators Peter Domenici and Edward Kennedy, with Representatives Patrick Kennedy and Jim Ramstad, introduced S. 486 and H.R. 953, called the Mental Health Equitable Treatment Act. The passage of the Mental Health Equitable Treatment Act in March 2005 closed a loophole so that insurers may no longer arbitrarily limit the number of hospital days or outpatient treatment sessions for people in need of mental healthcare. The law also eliminated separate and unequal deductibles and out-of-pocket costs for mental health and substance abuse services. It required a single deductible and the same out-of-pocket co-payments or co-insurance for mental health, substance abuse, and all other covered health services. It also removed separate yearly and lifetime visit limits and dollar maximums. Although the law required insurers to provide coverage for mental health and substance abuse services at the same level as other health services covered under the plan, insurers are allowed to offer benefit options with different out-of-pocket costs as long as one of the options provides the same coverage for mental health and substance abuse as other covered health services.

On October 3, 2008, the Emergency Economic Stabilization Act (H.R. 1424) passed Congress and was signed into law. Entitled the Paul Wellstone and Pete Domenici Mental Health Parity and Addiction Equity Act, this act included a major mental health provision and was attached to the economic bill and became law. This federal mental health law required health insurance plans that offer mental health coverage to provide the same financial and treatment coverage offered for other physical illnesses but again does not mandate that group plans must provide mental health coverage. This law is extremely protective of state law—only a state law that "prevents the application" of this act will be pre-empted; this means that stronger state parity and other consumer protection laws remain in place. Many states still have not enforced the law, and insurers still continue to limit mental health benefits.

None of the aforementioned laws mandates the coverage of any specific mental health condition; rather, where an insurer chooses to cover both mental health and medical and surgical benefits, they are required to do so in compliance with these parity requirements.

The PPACA (P.L. 111-148, as modified by P.L. 111-152 of the Health Care and Education Reconciliation Act of 2010 and approved by the Supreme Court on June 28, 2012, in National Federation of Independent Business v. Sebelius) contains a number of provisions that in general combine to extend the reach of existing federal mental health parity requirements. The PPACA contains a number of provisions that achieve two key goals with respect to mental health parity: They expand the reach of the applicability of the federal mental health parity requirements; and they create a mandated benefit for the coverage of certain mental health and substance abuse disorder services (to be determined through rule making) in a number of specific financing arrangements. The PPACA expands the reach of federal mental health parity requirements to three types of health plans: qualified health plans as established by the PPACA, Medicaid non-managed care benchmark and benchmark-equivalent plans, and plans offered through the individual market. The PPACA also:

- Bars insurance companies from considering pre-existing conditions or gender in coverage decisions
- Expands coverage to include 30 million uninsured individuals
- Requires insurers to offer the same premium to all applicants of the same age and geographical location
- Commences the operation of a Health Insurance Exchange to offer individuals and small business policies and premiums; low-income individuals and families 100 percent above and up to 400 percent above the federal poverty level, respectively, will receive federal subsidies on a sliding scale if they choose to purchase insurance via an exchange
- Extends Medicaid eligibility to those earning up to 133 percent of the poverty line; in states that choose to reject the Medicaid expansion, however, individuals and families at or below 133 percent of the poverty line, but above their state's existing Medicaid threshold, will not be eligible for coverage
- States that have annual and lifetime coverage caps will be banned
- Eliminates co-payments, co-insurance, and deductibles for select healthcare insurance benefits considered to be part of an essential benefits package for Level A or Level B preventive care or medical screening

The PPACA went into effect June 21, 2010, but will be put in place through 2018, with various provisions enacted each year. The issues affecting the immediate future of the community mental health centers are defining approved mental health benefits, handling the significant increase of potential new Medicaid patients who are now seeking mental health benefits, addressing the ratio of qualified mental health providers to the number of patients, and planning for the impact of continued cost to the mental health center. Until 2014, Medicaid health premiums will be paid by the federal government from a variety of taxes and offsets, but this cost will then revert to the states. Likewise, states may opt out of the expanded Medicaid eligibility requirements without losing pre-existing Medicaid funding from the federal government. To date, five states have opted out: Texas, Florida, Mississippi, Louisiana, and South Carolina.

More information for health plans subject only to federal law may be obtained from the U.S. Department of Labor by toll-free telephone at 866-275-7922 or by mail from:

U.S. Department of Labor
Employee Benefits Security Administration
ERISA/COBRA Office
JFK Federal Building, Room 575
Boston, MA 02203

CODING CLASSIFICATION

The classification and coding systems used by mental health insurers (i.e., diagnosis-related groups (DRGs) through revenue codes for facility and program services and current procedural terminology (CPT) for in- and outpatient professional services and consultations) are still being defined through historical methodologies and are vague compared to the medical classification coding structure. As an example, mental health insurers classify Tourette Syndrome (TS) as a mental disorder. In fact,

TS is an inherited, neurobiological disorder, and both neurologists and psychiatrists treat TS with the same medications. If TS were reclassified under the medical coding structure, TS would receive a potentially better reimbursement, and public perception of TS as a "mental disorder" would be changed.

The Diagnostic and Statistical Manual of Mental Disorders (fourth edition, text revision, also known as the DSM-IV-TR) is published by the American Psychiatric Association (APA 2000) and includes all currently recognized mental health disorders. The coding system utilized by the DSM-IV is designed to correspond with codes from the International Classification of Diseases (ICD). Because early versions of the DSM did not correspond with ICD codes, and updates of the publications for the ICD and the DSM are not simultaneous, some differences in the coding systems may still be present. For this reason, it is recommended that users of these manuals consult the appropriate reference when accessing diagnostic codes. In addition, the fifth edition of the DSM was published in May 2013 (APA 2013).

Besides the above coding manual, the International Statistical Classification of Diseases and Related Health Problems, produced by the World Health Organization (WHO), is another commonly used manual that includes criteria for mental health disorders.

Medication and Pharmaceutical Direction

To quote the Mental Health America article on access to medication,

> While medication is by no means the "be all and end all" of psychiatric treatment, for many if not most people, medication has played an essential role. This treatment technology by abating symptoms has enabled people with mental illness to take advantage of and benefit from the many other technologies (such as community-based case management, wrap around plans, supported employment and housing, and peer-led services) to build or rebuild the type and quality of life they desire. It is for this reason that "preserving open access," assuring that all medications for the treatment of mental illness are equally and easily available, is so critical. Unfortunately, open access has been under threat for a number of years and has intensified recently in many states. (Mental Health America 2012)

The community mental health programs are being affected by the following:

- Medicaid preferred drug lists, formerly called drug formularies. Many of these drug lists only contain one or two mental health medications and rarely include the newest or most effective drugs available. Providers must obtain prior authorization from the Medicaid agency, which frequently denies this authorization.
- There is an emphasis on drug therapy and the derived benefits of an individual being able to return and function in the community.
- Pharmaceutical companies are marketing their newer, more costly drugs to the mental health centers, while insurers are constructing barriers to medication access. Insurers fail to take into account the complexity of mental illness and the fact that an individual may have more than one illness, mental or medical, which may require the prescription of multiple medications, including newer, more effective drugs.

In the past, psychiatrists focused on identifying the cause of the problem and on developing associated treatment plans to treat the cause. With the increasing number of mental health patients, especially those with chronic mental illness conditions, psychiatrists do not have the time to focus solely on the treatment plan and the underlying cause of the mental illness. Instead, their focus has shifted to intake evaluations, case coordination, and medication checks. Use of medication has replaced the treatment plan and continues to play a much larger and more primary role in the treatment of most, if not all, patients. If medications are reduced, the end result is that these patients will require more costly treatment in the long run.

The United States Food and Drug Administration lifted restrictions against direct pharmaceutical advertising several years ago, enabling the representatives of these firms to market and advertise their drugs. Advertisers target both medical and mental problems, ranging from depression, anxiety, and attention deficit disorder, to acid reflux disease, high cholesterol, erectile dysfunction, and arthritis, to allergies, over-active bladder, and asthma. With the advent of marketing, many drugs are now being overprescribed and are becoming a component of spiraling healthcare costs.

In summary, these pharmaceutical issues are having an impact on community mental health centers—first as a cost issue, second because of the change-in-direction treatment modality, and third from the perspective of potential ethical issues involved in provider/pharmaceutical company relationships. There is a fine line between what is needed by the patient in the treatment of a mental health condition and what may result in unnecessary and costly drug interventions.

DECENTRALIZATION

The shift to the outpatient setting has been evident for several decades, and this has been demonstrated in the mental healthcare field by the increasing volume of patients seeking care in community mental health centers. This evolution has a positive impact on patients and their families as they are able to re-acclimate to society versus spending their waning years institutionalized. However, the increased volume of patients contributes to long wait times, increased costs, lower quality of care, and limited interaction times between providers and patients. This issue persists and will continue to persist until different revenue dollars, whether from the federal, state, or county levels or from insurance, can offset the rising operational costs.

INCREASED AND DIVERSIFIED PATIENT POPULATIONS

Patient populations at community mental health centers are on the rise, and this rise is associated with different groups or classifications of individuals. Some centers may or may not have experienced increases in these specific classifications previously; however, they are increasing in many centers today and will continue to do so in the future. There is an unprecedented number of older adults who are experiencing substance abuse issues, depression, anxiety, or dementia-related behavioral and psychiatric symptoms, along with a multitude of medical issues and complicated medication regimens, who frequent these centers across the United States. The clinic healthcare workforce is not prepared to address this influx of patients and their associated special needs. Another category of patients, children and teenagers, is also growing. This can be attributed to increased referrals by schools, more families seeking care for their children, greater emphasis on mental health treatments and medications, or a combination of these and other factors. Minorities, such as Hispanics, Latinos, African Americans, and others, are somewhat reluctant to seek behavioral health treatment because of the associated cultural stigma surrounding mental health issues. However, when these same individuals have combined physical and mental healthcare-related needs, they are seeking care at community centers. Finally, others seeking care have had terrorism scares, are veterans with post-traumatic stress disorder (PTSD) and other affiliated behavioral symptoms, or have been afflicted with a long-term mental or emotional issue from the impact of natural disasters, such as the loss of a loved one, home, pet, or job. Many of these individuals not only have mental health issues but also have one or more medical health issues, thus creating a complex case.

FACILITY PAYMENTS

Federal per diem base payment rates for facility payments (i.e., free-standing clinics or hospitals) are calculated by the Centers for Medicare and Medicaid Services using a separate marketplace basket to update payments and reimbursement. This payment process is called the Inpatient Psychiatric Facility Prospective Payment System (IPFPPS) and is determined by the following:

- Geographic factors based on geographic differences in wage levels
- Patient characteristics that includes Medicare's Severity Diagnosis-Related Groups (MS-DRGs) along with age, length of stay, and co-morbidity
- Facility characteristics such as rural, teaching hospital, etc.
- Other factors such as electro-convulsive therapy or other extraordinarily high-cost items

FUTURE OPTIONS FOR COMMUNITY MENTAL HEALTH CENTERS

With all the issues, especially those related to diminishing financial resources, that are affecting community mental health centers, state and county officials as well as directors of mental health centers are looking at options for survival. In general, public sector providers rely heavily on tax monies from state and federal governments, on health insurance, and to a lesser degree on private or self-pay funds. State appropriations for community mental health services are always among the first items cut in biennial budgets and are significantly reduced by administrative expenses at state and regional levels. Most insurance companies still find ways to restrict mental health benefits and the associated funding thereof. In addition, prior to the adoption of the PPACA, insurance reimbursement, such as from Medicaid, has always been inadequate, and cuts were made in Medicaid reimbursement and in other state programs serving the poor—programs on which community mental health services are heavily dependent. As a consequence, the community mental health centers find themselves continually re-aligning internal cost priorities and struggling with financial viability, which has resulted in many program closures.

Throughout the years, even for private sector providers, the funding is no better and patients often have significant out-of-pocket expenses. Health insurance companies reimburse only licensed providers and severely limit the amount of service that can be provided (for instance, by limiting the number of psychotherapy sessions). Medicare funding is available only to older adults and to some disabled persons, and the elderly typically have not sought mental health treatment because of the stigma attached. As for Medicaid, many private practitioners have refused to accept Medicaid's reimbursement because it is so inadequate compared to Medicare, private insurance, or managed care reimbursement.

There are four options available for the survival of community mental health centers. An internal reorganization is one solution that can create more operational efficiencies in some centers. Another solution includes the provisions of the PPACA. The more promising solution for survival is a combination of PPACA benefits with either a combined medical–mental health center or privatization. There is a potential fifth option, which will be briefly described at the end. All options are detailed below.

INTERNAL REORGANIZATION

Internal reorganization is a solution, but one that requires the full support of every person within a community mental health center. Centers need to evaluate themselves internally and develop action plans that will organize, coordinate, direct, and manage all aspects of their internal operation.

The first step in this process is actually conducting interviews and gathering information. From this information, a center will need to focus on five things:

1. Identification and location of services presently offered, and nature of clients served
2. Operational processes from the time the patient enters the door until he or she leaves
3. Staffing capabilities, training, and qualifications
4. Funding sources
5. Issues, problems, and needs

Checklist 1 presents a typical list of questions that should be addressed. Through these questions and others, a community mental health center will be able to develop a detailed action plan that will lend itself to improving day-to-day operations, standardizing treatment protocols, improving scheduling, recruiting and retaining qualified staff, improving collaboration and coordination, increasing funding options, and improving insurance qualification and reimbursement.

The internal reorganization option requires a considerable amount of invested time, cost, and commitment from staff to make it truly effectual. Many centers are unwilling to invest the resources or cost to change; staff members are often reluctant to change their routines. Therefore, many centers choose other more immediate solutions.

PATIENT PROTECTION AND AFFORDABLE CARE ACT (PPACA)

This national health reform law enables many individuals who have previously been uninsured to obtain Medicaid coverage. In addition, PPACA works to achieve more medical and mental health parity, where mental health providers would be paid in a manner comparable to medical providers, enabling more equality. This law also creates a mandated benefit for the coverage of certain mental health and substance abuse disorders that, when adopted, will require insurance firms—Medicaid, Medicare, Managed Care, and private insurance—to cover these services. Those individuals who would have been precluded from obtaining insurance because of a pre-existing condition will now be able to obtain coverage. Likewise, certain preventive benefits will be included without associated restrictions, deductibles, co-insurances, or annual or lifetime coverage caps.

The PPACA does not immediately address all of the financial, staffing, or benefits issues, but it is a step in enabling patients without insurance coverage to have coverage and allowing clinics and providers to receive equitable reimbursement. The financial picture of a community mental health center could improve within several years but would still need state, federal, local, and grant subsidy.

COMBINED MENTAL AND MEDICAL HEALTH CENTERS

As alluded to previously in this chapter, many individuals who seek care in community mental centers, emergency rooms, urgent care centers, or provider offices have a combination of mental and medical conditions. It is well known that many private care providers do not have the skills and training to treat psychiatric problems nor to prescribe associated medications; likewise, mental health providers are not familiar with the current treatment and medication protocols to treat medical problems. It is further known that one condition could precipitate another and vice versa, and that initial evaluations and preventive treatment could eliminate potential chronic conditions, whether mental or medical.

One of the future recommendations for economies of scale and for integration of care is to co-locate the mental and medical health centers at one site. This will enable coordination of care plans between multiple specialties as well as enable patients to immediately see other specialists without having to obtain a referral with a provider across town. As everyone knows, if a patient has to wait to see another provider, that secondary visit may not occur. Secondarily with the existing process, providers are neither sharing their findings nor communicating with other providers, which can result in disjointed treatment efforts and poor outcomes. This newer model provides prevention and early intervention, coordination of care, improved patient outcomes and recovery, reduction or elimination of ongoing symptoms and mental/medical problems, and fewer repeat clinic visits. This represents a total healthcare package that includes both mental and medical components and can prevent the development of more serious mental health or medical conditions, improve quality of life, and be more cost-effective to the community center.

Pros	Cons
• Overhead costs are shared by combining two clinics.	• A great deal of time is required to plan, coordinate, move, and re-organize business processes.
• Both medical and mental care issues are addressed at one site.	• Staff may resist re-education and re-positioning of duties.
• Early prevention can reduce chronic conditions, saving more expensive treatment costs.	• The co-location may be cost-prohibitive to both the medical and mental clinics and may not be a feasible option.
• Providers collaborate on combined treatment plans.	
• Cross-specialty education occurs.	
• Resources and systems are shared.	

PRIVATIZATION

Privatization—where a private for-profit business takes over the processes of a traditional public government-provided service—is a continuing trend that has been used not only for mental health centers but also for other public services. This process shifts the funding and cost from the community-based organization to a privately managed behavioral healthcare organization that has operated similar functions in the past.

In today's economy, the government, especially with community mental health centers, is being asked to do more with less money, which has increased the cost and decreased the revenues. It has been demonstrated from other privatization efforts that the private sector can deliver quality products and services more efficiently and at a much lower cost to taxpayers. The components of privatization are:

- Alignment of expectations
  - What the agency thought they were getting from the RFP
  - What the firm said they would do in the proposal
  - What the contract committed both to do
  - Original alignment of expectations and outcomes
  - Modifications where necessary
  - Quarterly and annual performance meetings
- Staffing
  - Full or part time
  - Training
  - Compensation and benefit structure
  - Defined performance methods
- Process and procedures
  - Written policies and procedures
  - Training on processes and procedures
  - Continual communication
- Structure
  - Internal reporting structure
  - Role of agency and customer
  - Role of team
  - Defined roles and responsibility

Privatization can be accomplished in one of three ways:

1. Outsourcing: The government agency delegates some or all of its in-house operations or processes to a third party. It is a contracting transaction where the government agency purchases services from a private firm while keeping ownership and ultimate responsibility for the underlying processes. They inform the private firm of what they want and how they want the work performed. The private firm can be authorized to operate as well as redesign basic processes to ensure even greater cost and efficiency benefits.

2. Design, build, operate: The government negotiates with a private firm to design and construct a new facility that is fully operational. The project components are procured from the private sector in a single contract with financing secured by the public sector.
3. Public–private partnership: This is a cooperative arrangement between both parties where each assumes some responsibility for operating the program.

More specific techniques are outlined in Table 6.1.

Many states and counties are seeking to outsource, privatize, or contract with private entities, especially when it is reasonable to believe that those private entities can provide equivalent or better quality services at lower cost than the government agency. Note, however, that equating cost efficiency with the lowest bidder may be a mistake.

AN EXAMINATION OF THE PRIVATIZATION OPTION

A key to the successful privatization of government services is the use of a systematic decision-making process to guide actions taken. Such a process includes an analysis of various factors that will determine the success of privatization efforts. These factors include the following:

- Realistic and measurable goals and criteria
- Availability of qualified and capable competition
- An accurate cost or business analysis
- State employee and union decisions, especially regarding current staff
- Safeguards to mitigate risks
- Adequate management controls, monitoring, and evaluation
- Controls for maintaining and monitoring quality of service

As with all shifts in services, there are pros and cons that need to be considered when contemplating privatization of a community mental health center (Table 6.2).

TABLE 6.1
Privatization Techniques

Privatization Technique	Description
Asset sale	Ownership of government assets, commercial-type enterprises, or functions is transferred to the private sector through the selling of such assets.
Contracting out	Government enters contractual agreements with a private firm(s) to provide goods or services.
Franchising	Government grants a concession or privilege to a private sector entity to conduct business in a particular market or geographical area.
Managed competition	A public sector agency competes with private sector firms to provide public sector functions or services under a controlled or managed process.
Public–private partnership or joint venture	A contractual arrangement is formed between government and private sector partners that can include a variety of activities, including development, financing, ownership, and operating of a public facility or service.
Subsidies	Government encourages private sector involvement in accomplishing public purposes through direct subsidies, such as funding or tax credits.
Vouchers	Government subsidies are given to individuals for the purchase of specific goods or services from the private or public sector.

Source: Office of the Auditor, Report No. 99-11, Study of Privatizing Adult Mental Health Program Services, 1998.

TABLE 6.2
Pros and Cons of Privatization

Pros	Cons
Eliminates cost of staff, overhead, and operating cost to the community mental health center. This staff would be outsourced to the new firm.	The new arrangement may lack support from unions or exclude unions and staff covered by unions.
	Affects morale of both patients and staff because they fear change.
	New firm may reduce level of care or services as a cost-saving measure.
	A shift of cost and burdens to other agencies could occur.
Provides a managed care coverage concept.	Increases patient volumes per provider in managed care.
Leads to more efficient operations.	Tends to limit patient–provider interaction and increase fragmentation of treatment services by eliminating interdisciplinary teams.
Assumes quality of care with a quality run firm.	May resort to older, cheaper medications because the newer, more expensive medications are too costly to dispense.
Outsourcing becomes a management tool for the mental health center oversight team.	Limits the decision making of mental health professionals with regard to authorizations, length of treatments, treatment protocols, etc.
Reduces state and community liability.	Community will need to establish an oversight body and define performance standards to monitor private entity once contract is in place. Costs will increase, both in terms of time and of personnel.
Improves organizational efficiency and eliminates overlap of services and specialties.	May result in questionable performance from contracted firm.
Private sector management flexibility (recruiting, hiring, compensation, etc.).	Existing staff may not be hired, resulting in potential unemployment.
Private sector management experience of similar projects.	Qualifications may be stated, but company may not have quality performance requirements in place.
Improvements in patient outcomes and patient satisfaction.	Projected outcomes may suffer based on clinical protocols and treatments.

What are the prerequisite characteristics of an ideal partner when considering privatization?

• Understanding the needs of the agency and local community	• Long-term, low-cost solutions
• Project approach	• Competitive pricing
• Similar management and governance philosophies	• A tailored or customized operational process, not an off-the-shelf, one-size-fits-all model
• Ability to provide services	• Willingness to partner and consider long-term arrangement
• Operational background and experience	
• Financial solvency	• Open dialogue on issues
• Understand political issues	• No interest in cutting or restricting services
• Operations program strategy	• Service-oriented approach

Successful privatization results cannot be guaranteed; however, strong leadership can ensure that privatization efforts are adequately planned, implemented, and evaluated. To this end, the leaders in any drive towards privatization must prepare a thorough analysis of both the costs and the benefits. On the one hand, what is the potential for cost savings? On the other hand, what new costs might be involved in writing bid and contract requirements and in developing monitoring and oversight requirements? Table 6.3 outlines the cost components to be considered.

A business case assessing privatization should include the following elements:

- Description of service to be outsourced
- Description and analysis of agency's current performance
- Desired goals and rationale for each goal
- Options for achieving goals and advantages and disadvantages
- Description of current market conditions
- Cost–benefit analysis
- Current and expected performance standards
- Key benchmarks
- Contingency plan for contractor non-performance
- Transition plan

For assistance in preparing such an analysis, the following guidelines, studies, and reports may be helpful:

- *Annual Privatization Report 2010: State Government Privatization*, published by Reason Foundation (Gilroy et al. 2011)
- Reason Foundation, *Privatization Blog* (Reason Foundation 2013)
- *Privatization: Lessons Learned by State and Local Governments*, published by the General Accounting Office (Needham 1997)
- *Private Practices: A Review of Privatization in State Government*, published by the Council of State Governments (Chi and Jasper 1998)
- *Effective Bidding System and Monitoring System to Minimize Problems in Competitive Contracting*, published by the Reason Foundation (Refhuss 1993)
- *How to Compare In-House and Contracted Services*, published by the Reason Foundation (Martin 1993)
- *Designing a Comprehensive State-level Privatization Program*, published by the Reason Foundation (Eggers 1993)
- *Social and Health Services Privatization: A Survey of County and State Governments*, published by the Reason Foundation (Eggers and Ng 1993)

Once the decision is made to proceed with privatization, the process should include, at a minimum, the establishment of a privatization oversight committee to assure systematic progress. The process should include implementation of a method for identifying potential privatization opportunities, development of privatization guidelines to promote accountability, and the identification and analysis of the services to be privatized. Internally, staff must assemble necessary information, including the following:

- Organization chart
- Job descriptions of all staff, including the Director
- Summary of patient volumes by day, by month, by category
- Insurance distribution, including a reimbursement summary by month
- Budget versus actual summary of monthly and annual cash flows
- Listing of any outsourced services
- Union regulations in place and information on whether the union agreed to privatization
- Detailed outline of treatment protocols currently in use
- Details of problems and issues
- Operations manual of policies and procedures
- Referral services

TABLE 6.3

Cost Components of Privatization

Cost Component	Description
Total in-house (fully allocated) costs	**Direct costs:** 100 percent chargeable to service targeted for privatization. This can include salaries, wages, fringe benefits, supplies, materials, travel, printing, rent, utilities, communications, and other costs such as interest costs, pension costs, and facility and equipment costs.
	Indirect or overhead costs: benefit the target service and at least one other government service, program, or activity.
	This can include salaries, wages, fringe benefits, supplies, materials, travel, printing, rent, utilities, communications, interest, pension, and depreciation that benefit the target service and at least one other government service, program, or activity. State and local governments frequently develop overhead or indirect cost rates that are simply applied to the personnel or total direct costs of a target service.
Total contracting costs	**Contractor cost:** cost to perform target service.
	Administration costs: procurement, contract negotiation, contract award, amendment and change order processing, dispute resolution, contractor invoice processing, and contract monitoring and evaluation.
	Conversions costs: personnel, material, and other costs resulting from the conversion from in-house to contracted service, and off-setting revenue (new or enhanced revenue stream resulting from contracted service).
Total avoidable costs	Costs that will not be incurred if a target service or portion of a service is contracted out.
	All direct costs are avoidable; however, determining what portion of indirect/overhead costs is avoidable requires professional judgment and largely depends on three factors:
	• how effectively resources are reallocated
	• the time period in which resource allocation will occur
	• the extent of the privatization effort
Potential savings	Subtract total contracting costs from total avoidable costs.

Source: Reason Foundation, Massachusetts Office of the State Auditor and Texas Council on Competitive Government, 2013.

Community center and county officials must also determine the criteria for selecting a service provider and establish bid and contract requirements. Appendix 1 provides an example of a bidder evaluation form.

Finally, county officials should establish performance outcomes that are specific in terms of service quality, service levels, timeframe, reporting requirements, and tolerance ranges. Strong oversight of privatization efforts is critical. This should include periodic inspections, citizen questionnaires, complaint resolution, review of performance standards, and cost–benefit analyses to determine whether identified savings are realized and maximized.

Appendix 2 provides an RFP outline form to be presented to private firms bidding on services that have been identified for privatization.

Once the RFPs are received, an evaluation process must be established. This process should be under the direction of the center's Director, and the evaluation process and evaluation of RFPs should be done collectively by the oversight committee along with a report to the Director. The following list outlines the steps that should be followed in this process:

• Evaluation of mandatory requirements: Have mandatory requirements of RFP been agreed to? Evaluate each RFP as pass or fail.

- Evaluation of technical proposal: A team of qualified members should evaluate the proposal using standardized evaluation tools and forms. The technical details should be scored using a point system.
- Evaluation of pricing/cost for each firm and comparison of each firm's cost to center's current operational cost.
- Oversight committee review and recommendations: Interview applicants and decide on a scoring process (probably a point system that assigns points to specific criteria such as background, experience, qualifications, scope of work, project organization and staffing, and project management).
- Rank the proposals: Points for technical proposal are added to points for cost proposal and ranked highest to lowest.
- Announce the proposal award.
- Publicize the appeal process.

In summary, the important point to stress is that the community mental health center needs to define its criteria for an RFP, evaluate each firm against the criteria, and select the firm that aligns most closely with those criteria and will provide the quality of services, operational structure, and efficiency that the center desires. Without this process in place, privatization may not be better for the center than their own reorganization efforts.

ANOTHER POTENTIAL OPTION: FEDERAL QUALIFIED BEHAVIORAL HEALTH CENTERS (FQBHC)

This is a concept that would replace the current criteria for a community mental health center and would be established out of SAMHSA as a block grant. Services include screening, assessment, diagnosis, risk assessment, person-centered treatment planning, outpatient mental health services, outpatient primary care services, crisis mental health services, case management, psychiatric rehabilitation, and peer and family support. This would require that services funded by the block grant be provided through appropriate qualified community programs and would require that an entity be certified as an FQBHC by the SAMHSA Administrator at least every five years on the basis of specified criteria.

CONCLUSION

In conclusion, community mental health programs face financial, re-direction, morale, staffing, and organizational issues today and will more so in the future. These issues will have an impact on the clinic's viability. Each community mental health program needs to determine if it can provide the quality of care needed for the community with its existing structure and budget; if not, changes *will* need to be made.

Those responsible for the management of these programs need to evaluate each of the critical components compared to one or both of the options presented to determine which would provide the most positive outcome for the community it serves.

ACKNOWLEDGMENTS

To Hope Rachel Hetico, RN, MHA, CMP™, of the Institute of Medical Business Advisors, Inc., of Atlanta, Georgia.

APPENDIX 1

BIDDER EVALUATION

Bidder Information

Name _____

Contact _____

Phone _____

Fax _____

Cell _____

E-mail _____

Background

\# Years in business _____

\# Years in mental health_____

\# Years Medicaid experience_____

Medicaid gross billings × 3 years_____

References

Nearest county mental health center

State board

Bank

Trade accounts

Financial	Yes	No
Nearest county mental health center		
State board	o	
Bank	o	
Trade accounts		
Two years financial statements	o	o
Audited for accuracy?	o	o
Two years tax returns	o	o
Credit report	o	o
Dun & Bradstreet report	o	o

Technical

	Yes	No
Financial software used	o	o
Practice management software used	o	o

APPENDIX 2

REQUEST FOR PROPOSAL

Purpose of the Request for Proposal

_____

_____

_____

Overview of the organization and operation of the county mental health program

_____

_____

_____

Scope of services to be outsourced or privatized with a description of each service

_____

_____

_____

Contract Duration—period of performance and option years_____

Non-discrimination statement_____

_____

_____

Schedule of Events
   Date RFP issued

   Due date for written questions_____

   Due date for answers to questions_____

   Closing date and time for receipt of proposals_____

   Date for opening proposals_____

   Oral presentations _____

   Award and contract start date _____

Issuing officer and address _____

_____

_____

Targeted individual for questions and Internet address_____

_____

_____

Proposal submittal guidelines

   Format and content (specify font size, margins, spacing, etc.) _____

   Preparation costs (specify responsibility of respondent) _____

   Opening of proposals (specify date officially opened) _____

   Criteria for acceptance of proposal (specify review and acceptance criteria)

_____

   Criteria for rejection of proposal (specify criteria for rejecting a proposal) _____

_____

   Disposition of proposals (specify that proposals will be on the public record unless designated as confidential) _____

_____

Incorporation into the Contract—record including for disclosing and for using information incorporated in the proposal

_____

Subcontracting guidelines (number of subcontractors, if any, that can be included in the response)

_____

Minority business policy_____

Prohibited solicitation—those rules following a breach of ethical standards, such as commission, brokerage fees, etc.

_____

RFP amendments (specify the procedure for making amendments) _____

RFP rules of withdrawal (outline the withdrawal process) _____

Respondent's contact person (name and telephone number) _____

Awarding of contract (explain the process in detail)

_____

Notification (how will respondents be notified of the results) _____

Rules of procurement (specify general rules) _____

Restrictions on communications with state staff (specify limitations on talking with state or county officials until RFP awarded)

Technical proposal requirements

Cover sheet (format and what to include, usually name and number of RFP and name and address of respondent)

_____

_____

Table of contents

_____

Statement of acknowledgment of RFP (acknowledgment of key facts from the respondent such as minority vendor, no previous fraud, authorized individuals, use of subcontractor, no separate cost nor pricing data included, etc.)

_____

Disclosure of litigation (acknowledgment of whether any existing litigation could affect the project or contract)

_____

Approach and process to scope of service (respondent's plan for meeting the objectives of the contract)

_____

Respondent's background

   date established_____

   ownership _____

   number of employees _____

   number of full-time equivalents in similar contracts_____

Respondent's experience

   letters of recommendation_____

   right to contact references_____

Respondent's qualifications

   evidence of qualifications and credential_____

   number and description of similar projects worked on successfully_____

   responsibility and experience on each project, etc._____

Technical proposal response

   Executive summary (provide a condensed summary of the contents of the technical proposal)

   _____

   _____

   _____

   Project organization and staffing

   organization charts_____

   lines of supervision_____

   identification of key personnel_____

   _____

   Target population (specify area and patient population served)_____

   Needs assessment (function proposed in project)_____

   Incorporation of union support and staff_____

   Project management (specify project control methods)_____

   Financial disclosures (provide respondent's evidence of financial status and ability to carry out the project) _____

   _____

   _____

Reimbursement methodology (specify method of payment for services or whether private firm will independently bill insurers)_____

_____

_____

Vendor number _____

Proof of licensure _____

Performance and outcome measurements (demonstrate success of program through qualitative and quantitative goals) _____

_____

Reports (required and ad hoc) _____

CASE MODEL

THE DOWNHOME MENTAL HEALTH CENTER: POISED FOR PRIVATIZATION

Strong rumors about privatization of the Center abound, since the enactment of the Patient Protection and Affordable Care Act (PPACA). The Administrator sees this as a potentially good transition and decides to prepare the Center internally for the inevitable Request for Proposals (RFPs) that will be presented to the private sector.

Therefore, the Administrator establishes the following goals:

1. Maintain quality and scope of service to existing clients of the Center.
2. Maintain jobs and benefits for employees of the Center.
3. Extend Center mental health services to currently underserved classes of clients (e.g., Latino migrant population, rural shut-ins, etc.).

She also requires the following financial analysis from her staff:

1. Translate governmental accounting:
   a. Consider the impact of privatization on current revenues.
   b. Consider the impact of privatization on current expenditures.
2. Improve profitability:
   a. Consider the impact privatization might have on increasing revenues.
   b. Consider the impact privatization might have on decreasing expenditures.

Strategies and Solutions

The Administrator sets out her long-term strategies for the Center:

1. Ensure strong financial standing of bidders. Although this is outside the Administrator's authority, she wants to be prepared to give input. Staff turnover

is traumatic, so the Administrator wants to get it right the first time. The state may require bidders to be intra-state. She knows some of the local mental health organizations have financial problems. Start-up funds or transitional reserves are an issue.

2. Ensure strong Medicaid experience of the bidders. The Center is not motivated by profit, and profitability under Medicaid requires existing expertise.

3. Ensure strong managerial track record of bidders in the mental health field. The bulk of the initial revenues for the bidder will be Medicaid at 84 percent. The county will probably keep the case management aspect of the Center intact for quality assurance. The successful bidder should provide the bulk of the currently outsourced services, for which the Center gets a 16 percent case management fee. However, the current outpatient revenue of the Center, not subject to the 16 percent fee by the Center, will also be subject to the 16 percent fee for the bidder.

4. Make the Center attractive, but realistic, for bidders by showing potential sources of increased revenues and potential cost-cutting strategies.

Project

The Administrator and her staff gather information to put together an RFP, an auxiliary help list for bidders, and a form/process to evaluate bidders.

Statement of Net Assets

The Center does not have a significant amount of assets or even capital asset needs. The computers may or may not be part of the sale.

Statement of Revenues, Expenses, and Changes in Net Assets

Last year's charge for services consists of two lines: services rendered, for $2.6 million, and case management, for $0.6 million. Case management fees are 16 percent of the Medicaid outsourced reimbursement the Center monitored. Internal records show Medicaid totaled $1.8 million of the services rendered.

The total of outpatient revenues from last year, translated into bidder revenue, is $2.3 million [($1.8 million Medicaid revenue × 84% = $1.5 million) + ($0.8 million non-Medicaid sources)]. The 84 percent reflects the expected 16 percent fee that the county will take for ongoing case management of previously non-fee Center (outpatient) revenue.

The Administrator estimates the bidder can perform 90 percent of the currently outsourced client services in house. Last year's revenue, from performed services that the Center outsourced, is $2.8 million [($0.6 million/16%) × 90%].

The operating expenses section must be:

1. Reduced:
   a. By the salaries of the case managers: $180G [6 × $30G/y]
2. Increased:
   a. by the equivalent cost of county-provided rent; space to accommodate the previously outsourced client services must be added on, and the current space for the six case managers can be eliminated
   b. by the equivalent cost of county-provided janitorial service
   c. by the equivalent cost of county-provided printing
   d. by the equivalent cost of county-provided utilities
   e. by the equivalent of county-provided technological support

Expense	Estimated Current Amount (in $)	By	Space/Volume Multiplier	Expected Amount (in $)
Rent	1,475	Realtor	2.1	3,098
Janitorial	650/month	3 estimates	2.1	1,366
Printing	1,200	Kinko's	2.6	3,128
Electric	625	By SF-county	2.1	1,391
Water	250	By SF-county	2.1	525
Repair/ Maintenance	3,180	By SF-county	2.1	6,678
Tech Support	22,600	County tech	1.0	22,600

The non-operating revenues (expenses section) must be:

1. Decreased:
   a. by interest expense: this expense is irrelevant to the bidder
   b. by depreciation expense: most of this is for the building

The Administrator assumes the county will charge a fair market rent if the bidder elects to stay in this location. The Administrator deems the remainder of the depreciation expense, for a few copiers and computers, to be immaterial.

Capital contributions and transfers out are both irrelevant to the bidder.

Statement of Cash Flows

The Administrator feels the bidders will concentrate on the Statement of Revenues, Expenses, and Changes in Net Assets and decides to forego proactive translation of the Statement of Cash Flows into bidder terms. The only item really affected is the interest paid, described above.

Increasing Revenues

The Administrator knows the local mental healthcare providers well. She does not feel the bidder would lose current non-Medicaid clients to these other providers. She feels the Center, after a bidder's upgrades, would attract additional non-Medicaid patients, drawn from the existing providers and attracted by an increased awareness secondary to the bidder's expected marketing.

In the past, the Center could not engage in health maintenance organization (HMO) contracts because of logical county prohibition. Any bidder that can turn a profit at an 84 percent level of Medicaid reimbursement could probably afford to take on these potential contracts.

The Administrator feels there will be cost savings by increasing the efficiency of internal processes.

Decreasing Expenditures

Because of the cost of technology, the Center uses manual systems for appointments, for billing private payers, and for performing and collecting transcriptions into medical records. Billing for Medicaid, Medicare, and Blue Cross/Blue Shield uses their programs because they are free, but this results in a fragmented billing system. The Administrator feels any solid bidder would already have appropriate practice management and billing software.

Summary

Despite multiple constraints, governmental mental health administrators can make a difference in how the facility is run, and thus more positively affect their community. A facility does not have to face privatization to improve in multiple parameters.

Governmental accounting focuses on stewardship of public funds. Public accounting focuses on performance. For internal purposes, the savvy administrator utilizes the best of both worlds.

Key Issues

1. Can the Administrator achieve all her goals?
2. How might these goals be achieved?
3. What strategies might be used?
4. What is the impact of the financial statement(s) on the Center?
5. Will the RFP meet the Administrator's near- and long-term needs?

CHECKLIST 1: Analyze Your Mental Health Center	Yes	No
Have I determined the volume of patients using the mental health center?	o	o
What is the volume of patients on a daily basis? _____		
What is the volume of services for each of the specialty mental health services, such as marriage counseling? _____		
Is the volume of patients projected to increase in the next couple of years?	o	o
Do you have a sufficient number of providers to cover care?	o	o
If not, is it financially feasible for others to be added?	o	o
Could any programs be outsourced?	o	o
Specialty mental health services?	o	o
Crisis services?	o	o
Residential services?	o	o
Other?	o	o
Could patients be referred to other comparable programs in the community?	o	o
Have I identified the social service organizations in the community that provide mental health services? List services provided and hours of operation. _____ _____		
Have I identified all languages needed to converse with the patient population?	o	o
Are all providers' credentials in order?	o	o
Are providers continuing their professional education?	o	o
Do any of the providers in community private practice accept patients with Medicaid or without insurance?	o	o
Are detailed documented treatment protocols in place?	o	o
Are they used?	o	o
Have I identified and prioritized the major service needs for the mental health center?	o	o
What other services should be considered and how do they fit within the priority listing? _____ _____		
Is anyone your advocate to lobby the Legislature for additional mental health funds?	o	o

CHECKLIST 2: Analyze the Revenue Sources of Your Mental Health Center	Yes	No
Does the center receive funding from the following?	o	o
If yes, write the percentage in the space provided:		
Federal government? _____		
Direct state funding programs? _____		
Indirect state funding (via county)? _____		
County? _____		
Medicaid? _____		
Medicare? _____		
Grants from national foundations? _____		
Cash from patients? _____		
Co-pays? _____		
Private insurance? _____		
Have you broken down your revenue by insurer?	o	o
Is eligibility for insurance being identified at time of entry and pursued?	o	o
Is the state funding reimbursement for chronic patient care?	o	o
What funds, grants, etc., are currently being used?		
_____		
_____		
Are any other grants being pursued to help improve revenue?	o	o
Can any of the patients qualify for Medicaid?	o	o
Is that possibility being pursued?	o	o
Is the center aware of all the benefits, non-covered services, and/or required billing processes to improve reimbursement?	o	o
Are laboratory services a source of revenue?	o	o

CHECKLIST 3: Prepare for the RFP	Yes	No
Has an oversight committee been established?	o	o
Does the committee include a representative distribution of staff who can effectively evaluate various firms against the criteria set forth in the RFP?	o	o
Has a financial person been added to the oversight committee to evaluate and compare the cost of the firms, and has the cost of the firms been compared to the internal cost of the existing operations?	o	o
Are the job descriptions representative of the skill sets needed to be filled by the private firm?	o	o
Have the Director and the oversight committee agreed to all the criteria set forth in the RFP?	o	o
Does each member of the oversight committee know the steps in the evaluation process?	o	o
Has the Director developed a process for rescinding the RFP if none of the firms meets the criteria or cost?	o	o
Are all of the staff in the center aware of and knowledgeable of the RFP and the associated process?	o	o
Have the unions been contacted and made aware of the RFP process?	o	o
Have the unions agreed to the RFP?	o	o
Is a process in place to help current staff find new positions or new training once the RFP has been awarded?	o	o
Has an evaluation form been developed to record the oversight committee's evaluation of the RFP firms?	o	o

CHECKLIST 4: Prepare for Clinical Treatment Programs	Yes	No
Typically, mental health services include treatments for various disorders. Do you have programs available in your mental health center for the following disorders?		
Anxiety disorders	o	o
Attention deficit hyperactivity disorders (ADHD, ADD)	o	o
Autism spectrum disorders (pervasive developmental disorders)	o	o
Bipolar disorder (manic-depressive illness)	o	o
Borderline personality disorder	o	o
Depression	o	o
Eating disorders	o	o
Generalized anxiety disorders	o	o
Obsessive-compulsive disorder (OCD)	o	o
Panic disorders	o	o
Post-traumatic stress disorder (PTSD)	o	o
Schizophrenia	o	o
Social phobia (social anxiety disorder)	o	o
Suicide prevention	o	o
Are you familiar with the *Diagnostic and Statistical Manual of Mental Disorders, Fourth Edition–Text Revision*, also known as the DSM-IV-TR?	o	o
Are you familiar with the coding definitions and the system utilized by DSM-IV?	o	o
Are you familiar with, and do you track, emerging mental health parity laws?	o	o

MENTAL HEALTH SUPPORT GROUPS

American Association for Marriage and Family Therapy
American Counseling Association
American Family Therapy Academy
American Group Psychotherapy Association
American Nurses Association
American Psychiatric Association
American Psychiatric Nurses Association
American Psychoanalytic Association
American Psychological Association
Clinical Social Work Federation
National Association of Alcoholism and Drug Abuse Counselors
National Association of Social Workers
National Depressive and Manic-Depressive Association
National Mental Health Association
Therapeutic Communities of America

MENTAL HEALTH PROFESSIONAL PUBLICATIONS

Academic Psychiatry
American Journal of Psychiatry
American Journal of Psychotherapy
Applied and Preventive Psychology
Archives of General Psychiatry
Behavior Research Methods, Instruments, and Computers
Behavior Therapy
Biological Therapies in Psychiatry
Biological Therapies in Psychology
British Medical Journal

Bulletin of the Canadian Psychiatric Association
Bulletin of the Canadian Psychological Association
Canadian Journal of Psychiatrics
Canadian Journal of Psychoanalysis
Clinical Psychiatry News
Clinical Psychology: Science and Practice
CyberPsychology & Behavior, catchword
CyberPsychology & Behavior, liebertpub
International Journal of Psychopathology, Psychopharmacology, and Psychotherapy
Journal of Addictive Diseases
Journal of American Academy of Child & Adolescent Psychiatry
Journal of the American Pharmaceutical Association
Journal of the American Psychoanalytic Association
Journal of Behavioral Health Services & Research
Journal of the California Alliance for the Mentally Ill
Journal of Clinical Psychiatry
Journal of Health Politics, Policy and Law
Journal of Information Technology in Medicine
Journal of Internet Law
Journal of Law, Medicine & Ethics
Journal of Neuropsychiatry and Clinical Neurosciences
Journal of Psychiatry & Neuroscience
Journal of Telemedicine and Telecare
Journal of Virtual Environments Journal of Addictive Diseases
Morbidity and Mortality Weekly Report
Psychiatric News
Psychiatric Services
Psychiatric Times
PsychNews International
Psycoloquy
Social Science Computer Review
Studi di Psichiatria
U.S. Pharmacist

MENTAL HEALTH PROFESSIONAL ORGANIZATIONS

Administrators in Academic Psychiatry
Adult Children of Alcoholics
Albert Ellis Institute
Alliance for Psychosocial Nursing
American Academy of Child & Adolescent Psychiatry
American Academy of Experts in Traumatic Stress
American Academy of Neurology
American Academy of Psychiatry and the Law
American Academy of Psychotherapists
American Association for Geriatric Psychiatry
American Association for Marriage and Family Therapy
American Association of Community Psychiatry
American Association of Suicidology
American Board of Psychiatry and Neurology
American College Counseling Association
American College Health Association
American College of Mental health Administration
American College of Neuropsychopharmacology
The American College of Psychiatrists
American College Personnel Association
American Counseling Association

American Family Therapy Academy
American Foundation for Suicide Prevention
American Medical Association
American Medical Informatics Association
American Mental Health Counselors Association
American Neurological Association
American Neuropsychiatric Association
American Pain Society
American Psychiatric Association
American Psychiatric Nurses Association
American Psychoanalytic Association
American Psychological Association
American Therapeutic Recreation Association
American Psychological Society
American Psychotherapy Association
American School Counselors Association
American Society of Addiction Medicine
American Society of Clinical Psychopharmacology
APA Division 28 (Psychopharmacology)
APA Division 46 (Media Psychology)
Associação Brasileira de Psicólogos e Profissionais de Saúde Mental On Line
Association for Academic Psychiatry
Association for Advanced Training in Behavioral Science
Association for Advancement of Behavior Therapy
Association for Advancement of Philosophy and Psychiatry
Association for the Study of Dreams
Association for University and College Counseling Center Directors
Association of Psychology Postdoctoral and Internship Centers
Biofeedback Foundation of Europe
Canadian Psychiatric Association
Center for Mental Health Services Research
Centers for Disease Control (and Prevention)
Chicago Institute for Psychoanalysis
Chicago Psychoanalytic Society
Citizens' Council on Health Care
Citizens for Responsible Care and Research
Depression and Bipolar Support Alliance
Epilepsy Foundation of America
European College of Neuropsychopharmacology
Healthcare Information and Management Systems Society
Illinois Psychiatric Society
Illinois Psychological Association
Institute for Behavioral Healthcare
International Association of Counseling Services
International Association of Group Psychotherapy
International Association for the Study of Pain
International Medical Informatics Association
International Society for Mental Health Online
International Society for the Study of Dissociation
International Society for Traumatic Stress Studies
International Stress Management Association
International Transactional Analysis Association
Internet Healthcare Coalition
InterPsych
K. Rice Institute
Mental Health America
Murray Research Center
National Alliance for the Mentally Ill

National Alliance for Research on Schizophrenia and Depression
National Association for the Advancement of Psychoanalysis
National Association of Boards of Pharmacy
National Association of Cognitive-Behavioral Therapists
National Association of School Psychologists
National Association of Social Workers
National Association of State Mental Health Program Directors
National Board of Certified Counselors
National Center for Complementary and Alternative Medicine
National Center for Post-Traumatic Stress Disorder
National Chronic Fatigue and Immune Dysfunction Syndrome Foundation
National Council on Community Behavioral Health Care
National Depressive and Manic-Depressive Association
National Institute of Mental Health
National Institutes of Health
National Library of Medicine National Mental Health Association
National Psychological Association for Psychoanalysis
Obsessive-Compulsive & Spectrum Disorders Association
Obsessive-Compulsive Foundation
Pharmaceutical Research and Manufacturers of America
Physicians for Social Responsibility
Psychiatric Society for Informatics
Royal Australian & New Zealand College of Psychiatrists
Royal College of Psychiatrists
Sociedad Española de Psiquiatría
Sociedad Española para la Investigación de las Diferencias Individuales
Società Italiana di Psichiatria
Società Psicoanalitica Italiana
Society of Biological Psychiatry
Society for Computers in Psychology
Substance Abuse and Mental Health Services Administration
Texas University & College Counseling Directors Association
UK Council for Psychotherapy
World Federation for Mental Health
World Health Organization
World Psychiatric Association

REFERENCES

American Psychiatric Association. *The Diagnostic and Statistical Manual of Mental Disorders* (fourth ed., text revision). Arlington, VA: American Psychiatric Association, 2000.
American Psychiatric Association. *The Diagnostic and Statistical Manual of Mental Disorders* (fifth edition). Arlington, VA: American Psychiatric Association, 2013.
Angoff, J. "Building a Better Insurance Marketplace: Setting the Stage for 2014." HealthCare Blog. http://HealthCare.gov (accessed July 2010).
Chi, K., Jasper, C. *Private Practices: A Review of Privatization in State Government.* Council of State Governments, 1998.
Eggers, W. *Designing a Comprehensive State-Level Privatization Program.* Reason Foundation, 1993. http://reason.org/news/show/designing-a-comprehensive-stat.
Eggers, W., Ng, R. *Social and Health Service Privatization: A Survey of County and State Governments.* Los Angeles, CA: Reason Foundation, 1993.
Flannery, F., Adams D., O'Connor, N. "A Community Mental Health Service Delivery Model: Integrating the Evidence Base within Existing Clinical Models." *Australasian Psychiatry.* 19(1): 49–55. 2011.
Gardner, A. "Aging Boomers' Mental Health Woes Will Swamp Health System: Report." *Health Day*, July 2012.
Gillette, H. "Minority Mental Health Month: Focusing on Issues of Hispanics." *Mental Health*, July 2012.
Gilroy, L., Kenny, H., Snell, L., Ybarra, S., Millhouse, T. *Annual Privatization Report 2010: State Government Privatization.* Reason Foundation. http://reason.org/files/state_annual_privatization_report_2010.pdf

Gleaton, D. "Report Points to Need for Mental, Physical Health Link." *The Times and Democrat*, July 2012.

HealthCare.gov. "Read the Law." 2013. http://www.healthcare.gov/law/full.

Hogan, M. F. "Will We Need a Separate Mental Health System in the Future?" *National Council Magazine*, 2010. Revised February 2012.

Hyde, P. S. "The Affordable Care Act & Mental Health: An Update." *HealthCare Blog*. http://HealthCare.gov (accessed August 2010).

Lebovici, S. *The Future of Public Mental Health Centers, Part I*. American Mental Health Foundation, 2011.

Machado, M. B. *Privatization of Public Services: A Research Project*. Shasta Voices, August 2009. http://shastavoices.com/.

Martin, L. *How to Compare In-House and Contracted Services*. Reason Foundation, 1993.

Mental Health Advocacy Coalition and Center for Community Solutions. "By the Numbers: Developing a Common Understanding for the Future of Behavioral Healthcare." January 2011. http://mentalhealthadvocacy.org/

Mental Health American. "Issue Brief: Access to Medications." 2012. http://www.mentalhealthamerica.net/farcry/%E2%80%A2/go/action/policy-issues-a-z/access-to-medications/access-to-medications-issue-brief/issue-brief-access-to-medications.

National Conference of State Legislatures (NCSL). State Laws Mandating or Regulating Mental Health. December 2011. http://www.ncsl.org/issues-research/health/mental-health-benefits-state-mandates.aspx.

Needham, J. *Privatization: Lessons Learned by State and Local Government*. Report to the U.S. General Accounting Office, February 1997.

O'Connor, J. "State Pushes to Privatize Services: Proposed Change to Mental Health Department Raises Concerns." *The Post and Courier*, May 2011. Update March 2012.

Refhuss, J. *Effective Bidding System and Monitoring System to Minimize Problems in Competitive Contracting*. Reason Foundation, 1993.

Reason Foundation. Privatization Blog. 2013. http://reason.org/blogs/privatization.

Substance Abuse and Mental health Services Administration (SAMHSA). "Resource Center to Promote Acceptance, Dignity, and Social Inclusion with Associated Mental Health" June 2012. http://stopstigma.samhsa.gov/archTelPDF/ADS_Brouchure_508.pdf

Substance Abuse and Mental health Services Administration (SAMHSA). "Health Reform: Overview of the Affordable Care Act. What Are the Implications for Behavioral Health?" *Substance Abuse and Mental Health Services Administration (SAMHSA) News*, 2012.

Sundararaman, R. "Behavioral Health Care in Health Care Reform Legislation." Congressional Research Service, December 2009. http://www.crs.gov.

Thayer, B. "Evidence-Based Practice and Clinical Social Work." *Evidence Based Mental Health*. 5 (2002): 6–7.

U.S. Department of Health and Human Services. *Mental Health U.S., 1999*. U.S. Department of Health and Human Services, Substance Abuse & Mental Health Services Administration, 2009.

7 Internal Audit Control Measures for Medical Practices and Clinics

Gary L. Bode and David Edward Marcinko

CONTENTS

In accounting, internal controls are affected by a healthcare organization's structure, work and authority flows, people, and HIT systems, and they are designed to help the entity accomplish specific goals or objectives. Internal controls are a means by which an organization's resources are directed, monitored, and measured. They play an important role in preventing and detecting fraud and protecting the healthcare organization's resources, both physical (e.g., machinery and property) and intangible (e.g., reputation or intellectual property, such as trademarks).

At the organizational level, internal control objectives relate to the reliability of financial reporting, timely feedback on the achievement of operational or strategic goals, and compliance with laws and regulations.

At the specific transaction level, internal control refers to the actions taken to achieve a specific objective (e.g., how to ensure the organization's payments to third parties are for valid services rendered). Internal control procedures reduce process variation, which leads to more predictable outcomes.

Internal control is a key element of the Sarbanes-Oxley Act of 2002, which required improvements in internal control in United States public corporations. Internal controls within healthcare business entities are also referred to as healthcare entity operational controls.

Internal controls have existed from ancient times. In Hellenistic Egypt there was a dual administration, with one set of bureaucrats charged with collecting taxes and another with supervising them. Without internal controls, a medical practice, clinic, or any health entity would never reach peak efficiency or profitability.

PURPOSE

Internal controls designed and implemented by the healthcare entity, medical clinic, or physician-owner help prevent bad things from happening. Embezzlement protection is the classic example.

Internal controls also help ensure good things happen, at least most of the time. A procedural manual that teaches employees how to deal effectively with common patient complaints is one example. Operating efficiency, safeguarding assets, quality patient care, compliance with existing laws, and accuracy of financial transactions are common goals of internal controls.

Internal controls, albeit in publicly held companies, came to national attention with the Enron scandal. Congress subsequently enacted the Sarbanes-Oxley Act in 2002, overseen by the Public Practice Accounting Oversight Board. This legislation demanded certain internal controls be put in place in publicly held companies and made provisions to hold top management personally responsible for these controls. The primary goal was to ensure accuracy of the financial statements. It also stripped away much of the accounting industry's self-regulation.

HEALTHCARE FRAUD DEFINED

According to editors Marcinko and Hetico (2007), *fraud* may be defined as any illegal healthcare activity where someone obtains something of value without paying for or earning it. In healthcare, this usually occurs when someone bills for services not provided by a physician. Healthcare *abuse* is the activity where someone overuses or misuses services.

According to the Center for Medicare and Medicaid Services (CMS), "Although some of the practices may be initially considered to be abusive, rather than fraudulent activities, they may evolve into fraud" (CMS 2013).

Example

Healthcare abuse may occur when a physician sees the patient for treatment more times than deemed medically appropriate. If there are reported issues or actions from other sources, such as the National Practitioner Data Bank (NPDB) or a medical board, a health insurance program can take that opportunity to review healthcare providers' activities. Most participation agreements allow for this type of scrutiny.

After a workable definition of healthcare fraud and abuse has been determined, and we have some definitional clarity, any preliminary billing, invoice review, or internal control program will usually request a sampling of specific medical records. This may progress to an on-site review of any and all medical records of patients that participate in a CMS program. These activities can be generated by the plan's quality assurance or quality improvement program and often are tied to the credentialing process for a provider's participation.

PREVENTIVE INTERNAL CONTROLS

On the other hand, employee theft in a clinic or medical practice is often underreported as a business issue. The emotional trauma of such an event often transcends the financial loss. Opportunity is the main causative factor in embezzlement, and a scenario can be constructed under which any one would feel justified in "borrowing" money. Perceived need, rationalization, and opportunity comprise the commonly accepted model used in ethics classes.

Be careful to manage employee's perceptions of internal practice accounting controls. Implementation and maintenance of them can be seen as oppressive to some employees. Proactively setting up internal controls may not only prevent embezzlement, but this can make honest employees feel more comfortable in that it is harder to be falsely suspected. Preventive internal controls include:

- Daily inspection of the practice's online checking, savings, and credit card accounts by the owner. This is the vital first line of defense against most embezzlement scenarios.

- Separation of duties in all financial matters. This makes embezzlement only possible with collusion of at least two employees. This can be hard to implement in smaller medical practices with less personnel. Only management should have check-signing privileges. A staff member may prepare them and present the checks, along with all appropriate documentation, for management's perusal and signature. Only preprinted checks should be used; avoid using check creation programs that allow printing of blank checks. Voided checks and subsequent sequential numbering should be retained. The checking statement should be sent to the physician-owner's home, and this statement and the checks should be inspected thoroughly. A different staff member can reconcile the checking statement if you choose not to do it yourself.
- Rotation of duties, as most prolonged embezzlement schemes will be uncovered if a different person periodically performs the duty. The "perfect" office employee, who refuses to take a vacation, may in fact be hiding such a scheme. Rotation of duties has the side benefit of cross-training employees, an important factor in small and medium practices.
- Bonding of key employees. Bonding companies pursue criminal matters as a matter of policy, once you prove guilt. The fear of certain prosecution is sometimes a deterrent.
- Do not let the staff order anything with a practice credit card. If you do, have the statement sent to your home and check it against documentation.
- Physical safeguards. Lock up or otherwise secure items prone to theft.
- Enable software audit trails. If your software tracks corrective entries and deletions, use it. In addition to documenting possible fraud, this allows examination of which things go wrong and how to (and how not to) fix them.
- Internal mini-audits with frequent random checks of theft-prone systems can easily be set up and quickly performed.
- Security cameras.
- Computer monitoring programs that allow real-time, key-stroke, or logged inspection of the employee's computer screen.

COMMON EMBEZZLEMENT SCHEMES

1. The physician-owner pockets cash "off the books." The IRS views this scheme as embezzlement because it is intended to deliberately defraud it out of tax money.
2. Employees pocket cash from cash transactions. This is why you see cashiers following protocol that seems to take forever when you are in the grocery checkout line, and why you see signs offering a reward if the customer is not offered a receipt. This is also one of the reasons that security cameras are installed.
3. Bookkeepers write checks to themselves. This is easiest to do in flexible software programs like QuickBooks, Peachtree Accounting (http://na.sage.com/sage-50-accounting-us), and other financial software. This is one of the hardest schemes to detect. The bookkeeper self-writes and cashes the check in their own name, and then the name on the check is changed in the software program to a vendor's name. So a real check exists and looks legitimate on checking statements unless a picture of it is available.
4. Employees order personal items on practice credit cards.
5. Bookkeepers receive patient checks and illegally deposit them in an unauthorized, pseudo practice checking account, which they have set up in a bank different from that used by the practice. They then withdraw funds at will. If this scheme uses only a few patients, who are billed outside of the practice's accounting software, this scheme is hard to detect. Executive management must have a good knowledge of existing patients to identify when some are not listed in the practice records. Monitoring the bookkeeper's lifestyle might raise suspicion, but this scheme is generally low profile and protracted. Checking the

accounting software audit trail will turn up the required original invoice deletions or credit memos in a less sophisticated version of this scheme.
6. Bookkeepers write payroll checks to non-existent employees. This scheme works well in larger practices and medical clinics with high seasonal turnover of employees, and in practices with multiple locations that are infrequently visited by the physician-owner.
7. Bookkeepers write inflated checks to existing employees, vendors, or subcontractors. Physician-owners should be aware of romantic relationships between the bookkeeper and other practice-related parties.
8. Bookkeepers write checks to false vendors. This is another low-profile, protracted scheme that exploits the physician-owner's indifference to accounts payable.

Positive Internal Controls

1. Standards flow from the top down; high ethical standards of physician-management set the tone for the practice. This may seem rather philosophical, but it is true: Human standards often follow those of their executive leaders.
2. A standard operational procedural (SOP) manual is a must for every practice. With a word processor, organize this into small sections that can be easily updated and reprinted whenever changes occur. This should include how things should be done, and why. Give examples of common problems and how to avoid or solve them. This should include the practice's human resources policies, an important legal concern in any business.
3. Establish regular reporting. Each employee should submit regular reports, such as a daily transaction log, which becomes part of the managerial report.

Spot Audits

Spot audits are an important internal control for a medical practice. With this method, physician-owners use their expertise with the logistics and dynamics of their practice to devise a series of regular inspections to see if anything is going wrong and to assure that everything is going right. Frequent, small spot audits, possibly differing in nature from time to time, work best. Implementation and application of such non-disruptive spot audits can make the difference between them being perceived (by employees, patients, and vendors) as prudent and responsible versus petty and mistrusting. Nothing erodes a practice's efficiency faster than physician indifference, and nothing demoralizes a practice more quickly than a petty, mistrusting doctor.

Examples of possible spot audit components include:

1. Payroll monitoring. Follow the complete payroll process sporadically for an employee chosen at random:
   - Is the time clock accurate?
   - Can it be manipulated?
   - Is this a real employee?
   - Is the correct number of employee days being paid?
   - Is the correct number of employee hours being paid?
   - Is the compensation level accurate?
   - Is petty cash reimbursement fully documented?
   - Are withheld funds appropriate?
   - Do the net pay figures in the accounting software agree with the bank records?
   - Are payroll tax and liability (e.g., child support checks) accurate and timely?
   - Are payroll reports being properly generated and submitted?

2. Employee log monitoring. Reports can be two edged. They can document activity and generate data vital to managerial decision making. They can also be oppressive and demoralizing, like the "TPS" reports in the movie *Office Space* (Judge 1999).[*]

3. Patient audits.
   - Accounting firms may ask if their submitted report of your status with another firm is accurate. This can detect some embezzlement schemes.
   - Patient satisfaction surveys, properly done, can reveal surprising patient perceptions. Patient satisfaction occurs when their perceptions exceed their expectations. Perceptions can be influenced.
   - Sporadically check the complete accounts receivable cycle for random patients: internal billing data, timeliness of patient invoices, documentation, write-offs, credit memos, payment process, consistent accounts receivable collections guidelines enforcement, accuracy of accounting software to bank records, etc.

4. Quality checks for manufactured products and maintenance inspection of practice equipment.

5. Sporadic physical inventory counts of random stock items.

6. Monitor the list of approved vendors.

7. Monitor the list of patients. Remember to try and re-activate old patients.

8. Sporadically check the accounts payable cycle for random vendors.
   - Follow the purchase order protocol.
   - Cross-reference invoices.
   - Check for late fees and interest.
   - Check accuracy of payment.
   - Check timeliness of payment.
   - Are payment internal guidelines being followed?
   - Does the software "audit trail" exhibit any anomalies?
   - Do the bank records reconcile themselves?

ASSESSMENT

The Certified Fraud Examiner (CFE) credential denotes proven expertise in fraud prevention, detection, and deterrence. CFEs are trained to identify the warning signs and red flags that indicate evidence of fraud and fraud risk (ACFE 2013). CFEs, forensic accountants, and attorneys focus on detecting fraud and providing litigation support.

CONCLUSION

A clinic or medical practice needs to ensure that the chances of detrimental financial events occurring are minimized and that the chances of positive events occurring are maximized. A pre-requisite to optimizing this is a thorough understanding of the financial and non-financial aspects of the underlying practice logistics.

Internal controls are the systems implemented to make this optimization happen. In a healthcare practice, internal controls can be extended to assure quality patient care and prevent malpractice suits. Internal controls are long-standing business practices and do not need to be re-invented. They do, however, need to be formally addressed for the practice to reach peak economic efficiency. Thus the internal fraud control checklist shown at the end of this chapter may prove useful to all medical practitioners.

---

[*] The "TPS report" has come to denote pointless, mindless paperwork after its use in the comedy film *Office Space*. In the story, a primary character is reprimanded by several of his superiors for forgetting to put the new cover sheet on his TPS report. It is said that the abbreviation means "toilet paper sheet."

MEDICAL PRACTICE/CLINIC INTERNAL CONTROL AUDITING CHECKLIST

CHECKLIST 1	Yes	No
Check that super bills (patient encounter forms) are pre-numbered and accounted for on a daily basis.	o	o
Ensure that the person who posts payments to patient accounts does not open the mail or prepare the deposit slip.	o	o
Reconcile the patients listed on the sign-in sheet to the appointment book and either the daily report of charges (computerized system) or the day-sheet (pegboard system).	o	o
Review the daily report of payments (computerized system) or the day-sheet (pegboard system) to detect any payments by patients that may not have been posted. Be reasonable after taking into account the practice's payer mix.	o	o
Take a sample of patient charges and trace the information on the related explanation of benefits (EOB) to each individual ledger sheet. Trace payment per EOB to the deposit slip. Investigate any discrepancies.	o	o
Review all patients' ledger cards to detect if any balances were written off in their entirety.	o	o

CHECKLIST 2	Yes	No
Make sure that the practice has a policy in place so that an account cannot be written off as a bad debt without the authorization of a physician.	o	o
Implement password access for the computer system. Supply the password only to authorized practice personnel.	o	o
For a pegboard system, reconcile the accounts receivable balance per the day-sheet to the individual ledger cards.	o	o
Are all practice employees bonded?	o	o
Is a physician the only employee authorized to sign checks?	o	o
Does a physician review and approve vendor invoices before signing checks?	o	o

CHECKLIST 3	Yes	No
Review endorsements of canceled checks and investigate any irregularities.	o	o
Compare month end collections per medical billing software management report to actual amount deposited per monthly bank reconciliation(s). Review related reconciliations.	o	o
Ensure that the person who posts payments to patient accounts does not open the mail or prepare the deposit slip.	o	o
Take a sample of daily deposits and compare to computer Daily Report of Posted Payments. Investigate differences.	o	o
Review a selected sample of canceled checks for appropriate vendor endorsement.	o	o
Scan a list of cash disbursements to identify possible false vendor relationships.	o	o

CHECKLIST 4	Yes	No
Review monthly contractual adjustments posting for reasonableness.	o	o
Review monthly practice charges for reasonableness. Investigate decreases in production.	o	o
Take samples of charge tickets and determine if any charge tickets (or charge ticket numbers) are missing. Investigate discrepancies.	o	o
Conduct on-site visits to review cash and disbursement procedures in place, including related employee interviews.	o	o
Review the practice's contractual adjustments for the period and year to date.	o	o

CHECKLIST 5	Yes	No
Review adequacy of current accounts payable procedures and related approval for vendor payment system.	o	o
Review sample of petty cash reconciliations.	o	o
Review access controls to medical billing software system.	o	o
Ensure that all patient account statements are prepared and mailed each month.	o	o
Ensure that all available vacation time has been taken by related billing, collection, and management personnel.	o	o
Ensure that all appropriate personnel are bonded.	o	o

BIBLIOGRAPHY AND REFERENCES

Association of Certified Fraud Examiners (ACFE). 2013. Home. http://www.acfe.com/

Bode, G.B. 2012. Internal Medical Practice Controls. In *Business of Medical Practice* (p. 503), Marcinko D.E., ed. New York: Springer Publishing.

Bragg, S.M. 2009. *Accounting Control Best Practices*. New York: Wiley.

Centers for Medicare and Medicaid Services. 2013. Medicare Carrier Manual (14-3-14001); Part B Medicare Fraud. http://www.cms.gov/Regulations-and-Guidance/Guidance/Manuals/index.html?redirect=/Manuals/.

Grant, B.J. 2007. Fundamentals of Healthcare Accounting and Finance. In *Practicing Medicine in the 21st Century* (p. 323), Nash, D.B., ed. Tampa, FL: American College of Physician Executives.

Marcinko, D.E., Hetico, H.R. 2007. *Dictionary of Health Economics and Finance*. New York: Springer Publishing Company.

Judge, M. (Director). 1999. *Office Space* [Motion picture]. United States: Twentieth Century Fox.

Tinsely, R.E. 2004. *Medical Practice Management Handbook*. New York: Aspen Publisher.

Turner, L., Weickgenannt, A. 2008. *Accounting Information Systems: Controls and Processes Accounting for Decision Making and Control*. New York: McGraw-Hill.

Young, D. 2008. *Management Accounting in Health Care Organizations*. New York: Jossey-Bass Public Health.

Zimmerman, J. 2008. *Accounting for Decision Making and Control*. New York: McGraw-Hill.

8 The Early Promise of Health 2.0 to Enable Wellness, Improve Care, and Reduce Cost in Support of Population Health Management

Jennifer Tomasik, Carey Huntington, and Fabian Poliak

CONTENTS

INTRODUCTION

The United States must transform its costly, fragmented healthcare system to a new paradigm of healthcare delivery—one that is integrated, takes accountability for the sickness of individuals as well as their wellness, and provides better value for patients, providers, and payers. Care providers of all types are already working to redesign care models, improve quality, and slow the rise in costs in their centers of care, but these changes will only go so far to change the current model. The transformation we are talking about will require changes beyond what's happening in the provider realm alone—it requires changes in how patients and their families and friends participate in their care (when sick) and in their overall well-being (when healthy).

This chapter will explore this cultural transformation and the emerging role of Health 2.0—healthcare with a renewed participatory role for patients—in making change possible. We will start by examining why change is needed in the healthcare industry.

We then move to a discussion of the fairly significant shifts that are taking place in care delivery, with an emphasis on the need to engage patients more actively in their health. The remainder of this chapter explores the potential of Health 2.0 in supporting behavior change to help people become more able to manage their health, including some results of early Health 2.0 efforts.

THE CASE FOR CHANGE: WHY BOTHER?

A CRISIS OF VOLUME AND COST

"Fee-for-service" has been the dominant financial dynamic in the U.S. healthcare system for decades, whereby providers are reimbursed for the quantity of visits, tests, or procedures that are performed, often without adequate regard for the cost of the interventions relative to patient outcomes. This focus has arguably fueled incredible advances in medical devices, diagnostic tests, pharmaceuticals, and other innovations. Dr. Atul Gawande, MD, surgeon and author, describes how far medicine has come since the days before penicillin, when convalescence in the shelter of a hospital was the best of only a few treatment options and, therefore, "when what was known you [as a doctor] could know. You could hold it all in your head, and you could do it all."[1] The surge in the number of diagnoses and treatments that physicians have access to today is transforming their profession from a field of autonomous craftsmen wielding basic tools to what Gawande suggests should be like race-car pit crews that together can deliver on the scientific promise of 4,000 medical and surgical procedures and 6,000 drugs.[2] This is a double-edged sword, as the autonomous mentality on which the field developed is now often at odds with the machine-like functioning expected of an effective and efficient pit crew. Together with the fee-for-service incentive structure, these realities have collided in a perfect storm propelling tremendous growth in healthcare spending characterized by fragmentation and high volume, high cost per episode, and inconsistent quality. We are now witnessing the costly "failure of success" from focusing so heavily on sick care while ignoring well care to keep individuals and populations healthy from the start.

THE FAILURE OF SUCCESS

As a result of what we have just described, healthcare now makes up 17 percent of the U.S. gross domestic product.[3] Other industrialized nations achieve the same or better health outcomes at a significantly lower cost per capita—for example, the $8,362 spent per capita on health in the United States in 2010 was more than twice what was spent in the United Kingdom ($3,503).[4]

International benchmarks aside, one could argue that the extra cost is worthwhile if it produces great outcomes. Unfortunately, this is not the case. A recent study of chronic care patients in the United States showed that, while regions ranked in the highest fifth of spending were providing as much as 60 percent more care than regions in the lowest fifth of spending, the increased outlay resulted in negligible improvement of outcomes or patient satisfaction.[5] It is no wonder that a 2012 Commonwealth Fund report concludes, "The findings make clear that, despite high costs, quality in the U.S. healthcare system is variable and not notably superior to the far less expensive systems in the other study countries."[6] This expense competes with other national priorities, yet the Congressional Budget Office expects the cost of Medicare and Medicaid to continue to rise rapidly as a percent of gross domestic product (GDP), while other programs except Social Security will shrink. (See Table 8.1.)[7]

As the U.S. population ages, numerous forecasts agree that Medicare and Medicaid will rise sharply in the coming decades and, together with Social Security, will consume nearly all annual federal revenues. At the current rate, our healthcare spending will come at the cost of other public

TABLE 8.1

Spending and Revenues as a Share of GDP

Source: Center on Budget and Policy Priorities. Spending and revenues as a share of GDP. Congressional Budget Office. http://www.cbpp.org. 2012.

goods like education, infrastructure, and security. Even if problems of sustainability feel too far off in the future to worry about today, we know that employers and families are already clamoring for greater value for their healthcare dollars.

According to a recent poll of U.S. corporate executives conducted by the staffing company Adecco, 55 percent named healthcare benefits as their biggest current business challenge, up from 35 percent in 2007.[8] The 2012 Employer Health Benefits Survey by the Kaiser Family Foundation and the Health Research and Educational Trust found that employer-based family health insurance premiums had risen for the thirteenth consecutive year. Premiums have increased nearly 100 percent since 2003, growing faster than wages (up 33 percent) and overall inflation (28 percent).[9,10] For the time being, employers continue to serve as the primary vehicle through which average Americans receive their healthcare coverage, and we have heard business leader after business leader say "enough is enough." At a recent strategy retreat, we heard a sampling of what we know is happening in boardrooms across the country. The health system's board members—many prominent businesspeople in the region—demanded lower costs, better outcomes, and more choices for their employees.

These challenges have been brewing for decades and, despite a number of attempts to correct the course, waste remains a huge problem—in the forms of duplicative testing, lost results, medication errors, inefficient processes, poor care coordination, etc. PricewaterhouseCoopers' Health Research Institute estimates the waste at $1.2 trillion of the $2.2 trillion spent nationally—more than half of all health spending.[11]

All of these issues have culminated in a problem that feels big enough and with potential consequences that are real enough to promote widespread change across the industry. Numerous experiments are underway to reduce cost and increase quality and safety—and, in so doing, to create greater value for patients and their families, and for the providers and payers who have traditionally masked individuals' own "skin in the game" by footing most of the bill. Many of these experiments, such as Accountable Care Organizations, are inviting providers across the country to make care more efficient and less costly—but how?

IDENTITY SHIFTS IN HEALTHCARE ORGANIZATIONS

FROM SICKNESS TO HEALTH: POPULATION HEALTH MANAGEMENT

An identity shift is taking place in hospitals and health systems across the country in response to the challenges we have described above. Organizations and their leaders who have spent decades honing their skill at providing acute inpatient care services are being asked to think very differently about the business that they are in and their role relative to other parts of the continuum of care (e.g., preventative outreach, outpatient care, etc.). Physician authors David Asch and Kevin Volpp suggest—and we agree—that the U.S. healthcare industry is moving from the business of "sickness" to the business of "health."[12]

Asch and Volpp posit that many ailing companies have a fatal misunderstanding of the industry that they are in as that industry seemingly shifts beneath their feet.

- Recently bankrupt Eastman Kodak failed to realize that, after 131 years, it was no longer in the film and camera business but rather was in the image business. Digital cameras made film practically obsolete in the consumer market, but Kodak did not adapt its offerings accordingly.
- The eclipse of railroads resulted from the view that they were in the railroad industry rather than the transportation industry, competing not simply with other railroads, but with trucking and airlines.

Asch and Volpp propose that these leaders missed some key signals to the broad changes taking place in their industries and urge healthcare leaders to take heed of similar signals. Payment systems that promote holistic health and that will not reimburse for poor-quality outcomes (like preventable re-admissions) are increasing in prominence in both the public and private sectors. Moreover, we are slowly taking to heart the fact that social factors are significant determinants of health and illness. In fact, McGinnis et al. find that traditional healthcare delivery determines as little as 10 percent of a person's overall health. (See Table 8.2.)[13]

If we believe we are focusing on better health, and our current healthcare delivery system only contributes 10 percent to health, what must we do to influence some of the other 90 percent? We face

TABLE 8.2
Determinants of Individuals' Overall Health

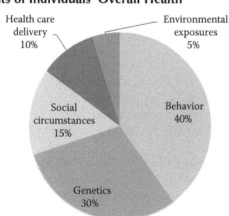

Source: McGinnis J.M., Williams-Russo P., Knickman J.R., *Health Affairs* 21, 2, 2002.

a significant shift in bridging the gap between how things work today and a system that can reliably deliver comprehensive health.

What Is "Health"?

What do we even mean when we say "health"? The 1978 International Conference on Primary Health Care in Alma-Ata (now Almaty, Kazakhstan) provides one of the most succinct if not sophisticated definitions we have found. The conference conceptualized health as "a state of complete physical, mental, and social well-being, and not merely the absence of disease or infirmity."[14] Those gathered at Alma-Ata sought to advance primary healthcare to the forefront of international efforts, a task that is still underway more than 30 years later. The work the conference produced to define "health" remains a noble aim and is taking on new relevance today as health systems across the United States take up this challenge within the frame of population health management. How, then, do we move from an understanding of health within each individual to something that is more collective?

What Is Population Health Management?

The Care Continuum Alliance, an alliance of stakeholders across the continuum of care, is working precisely toward the goal of improving the health of populations. The alliance espouses a detailed set of principles and a model of "population health management." It can be summed up, in the broadest sense, as the care provider community, in partnership with patients and their families, conducting proactive and collective monitoring of the patient's healthcare quality, adherence, access, and outcomes with the goal of improving the health of an entire patient population. As such, population health management stresses wellness and prevention through lifestyle and disease management and complex case management to remove the gap between zero care and costly chronic or emergency care. It emphasizes the full spectrum of needs from prevention and wellness to keeping healthy people and at-risk people healthy, to better managing the care of those with chronic conditions, and to still being ready to provide emergent or acute care services. In most cases, it also includes the involved providers taking on accountability for the financial risk and quality of care provided.[15]

We have been working with administrative and physician leaders across the country to grapple with what it will mean to actually foster valuable population health management in the different communities they serve. It is clear that this is a new paradigm and that the years of experience and training that have brought them to where they are today may not have sufficiently prepared them for what is to come. It requires a well-coordinated and complete continuum of care, with new metrics and advanced analytics. As one might expect, while clusters of resistance to the idea remain, most have flung themselves into learning mode and are beginning to act their way into new thinking. However, we also see a big risk in powering ahead without revisiting the role of a key stakeholder group—patients and their families, whose experience and perspective are often left behind, but whose actions will have a profound effect on the future success of population health management efforts.

FROM PATIENT TO PARTNER: A NETWORKED APPROACH

As one of our clients has said, "This population health management stuff is great, but how in the world are we going to get enough of our patients to do the right thing—especially when so many of those choices are deeply entrenched in their culture?" While there is an incredible amount of work to do to build out fully functioning, well-coordinated systems of care that focus on both illness and well-being, population health management can only go so far without enabling patients to more actively engage in their own health. If we are asking our health system to become more accountable for the overall health of populations, should we not also ask the populations in question to become more accountable for their own health? If we do, how will they do it, and what is their motivation?

Patient Behavior and Lifestyle Choices Drive Cost

We focused earlier on the rising cost of healthcare in the United States and the tremendous amount of waste represented in that cost. We have not yet considered the similarly mind-numbing role that disease brought on by behavior-mediated causes plays in these numbers. Numerous studies suggest that upwards of 50 percent of health problems in the United States can be attributed to lifestyle issues, from high stress and smoking to sedentary activity and improper nutrition (leading to excess weight and obesity), to name a few.[16]

Safeway Chief Executive Officer Steven Burd, like many employers, has been feeling the pinch of ballooning healthcare costs. In 2010, he embarked on a mission to engage his employees in programs designed to curb those costs. Citing numerous studies, he focused on two key statistics to highlight the role that behavioral choices contribute to the problem:

- 70 percent of all healthcare costs are attributable to behavioral choices (like reaching for an extra slice of pizza rather than a salad).
- 74 percent of all healthcare costs are related to four chronic conditions (i.e., cardiovascular disease, cancer, diabetes, and obesity), all of which, at least to some degree, can be attributed to behavioral or environmental factors.[17]

If this is the case, then we have a lot of work to do to influence those behavioral choices in the service of promoting health.

We know that changing individual behavior is not easy. Even with the best of intentions, launching a change to behavior is much easier than sustaining those changes over time. For example, many smokers attempt to quit by themselves over and over again, most to no avail—the American Cancer Society has estimated the success rate of smoking cessation without medicines or other help as 4 to 7 percent.[18] Individuals with weight problems struggle to keep the pounds off, even when they have successfully reduced their weight. Given how important we believe it will be to help large-scale populations become more engaged in and accountable for their health, and knowing how difficult it will be to do so, we set out to answer the question, "What might make it easier for people to take greater ownership of their health so they can successfully transform from passive patients to active partners?"

The day-to-day social networks in which individuals live out their lives hold an important key to this behavioral change. In the book *Connected*, Professors Nicholas Christakis of Harvard University and James Fowler of the University of California (San Diego)[19] study the relationship between people's social networks and their health, happiness, wealth, tastes, and beliefs. They observe that smoking decreased from 45 percent of U.S. adults to 21 percent since the 1970s. Interestingly, they found that people tend to quit successfully together—in effect, as a community of friends and acquaintances. Social ties have an impact on obesity as well. They suggest that behaviors like weight gain might be seen as "contagious" in that they can spread from person to person in a network. Furthermore, these calculated changes in risk of "contracting" weight, happiness, depression, etc., can travel to indirect acquaintances within the network—as far as friends of friends of friends—posing even more value for interventions aimed at measurably improving the well-being of entire communities than previously anticipated.[20] With reports estimating that upwards of 43 percent of adults in the United States will be obese by 2018, adding nearly $344 billion to the nation's healthcare costs, the potential to curb the obesity epidemic through more social network channels looks promising.[21]

We have summarized what is behind the growing healthcare cost crisis in the United States, including the resulting shift from a focus on "sickness" to a focus on "health" and the critical role of individual behavior and lifestyle choices. Next, we shall explore Health 2.0 as a promising subset of interventions that promote healthier individuals through healthier populations, and vice versa.

WHAT IS HEALTH 2.0?

Health 2.0 is participatory health care. Enabled by information, software, and community that we collect or create, we the patients can be effective partners in our own health care, and we the people can participate in reshaping the health system itself.

Dr. Ted Eytan, Director, Permanente Federation, LLC[22]

Health 2.0's potential lies in enabling, catalyzing, and sustaining changes in the practice of healthcare. Dr. Ted Eytan, a nationally recognized proponent of digitally enhanced patient care with a particular interest in preventive care, has blogged the above "declaration of health care independence," which we will use as our own working definition of Health 2.0.[23] We see Health 2.0 as a human space defined by engagement, aided by technology, in which information and accountability can flow between individuals and their care teams and between individuals and their social networks.[24]

The "practice" of healthcare can be understood as a set of "behaviors" that becomes embedded in daily life, plus the "supports" that provide the appropriate resources to achieve the desired outcomes. Thus, changing a current practice (in pursuit of a different outcome) requires enabling the behavior you want to encourage by providing the necessary supports to make it happen. Health 2.0 has made new supports available for people to embed health-seeking behaviors and sustain practices that increase their involvement in their own health.

Consider this chapter's case model. ShapeUp, Inc., an international employee wellness company, uses Health 2.0 technology to utilize what they describe as a "social approach to wellness that drives maximum engagement, outcomes, and return on investment."[25] ShapeUp has incorporated the social network research of Christakis and others as the basis of an innovative approach to wellness. They use proprietary software as a support that combines social networking, social gaming, and financial incentives to make wellness fun, drive behavior change, and help employers cut their healthcare costs. With clients like Cleveland Clinic, Highmark Blue Cross Blue Shield, and Sprint witnessing unparalleled voluntary employee engagement in these programs, and some projecting savings in the millions of dollars, ShapeUp's forays into population health management offer a promising glimpse into the future of healthcare. ShapeUp provides a vehicle to lead a set of effective wellness strategies, engage targeted participants, and motivate action to achieve desired results—for both the participants and their employers.

CREATING PULL: HOW HEALTH 2.0 WORKS

When we work with organizations, we help them "create pull"—develop and implement a strategy for identifying, developing, and building out the supports that need to be in place to change organizational behavior and practices. In this chapter's case model, ShapeUp creates pull by nurturing a (virtual) community and providing the rewards of peer support with the discipline (and transparency) of social accountability to guide exercise participants toward better health outcomes.

Creating pull—rather than trying to "push" a new behavior—begins with understanding the interests of each person at the table. The health and wellness interests of individuals are particularly difficult to work toward, not least because people tend to dismiss the importance of their well-being and become invested in these interests only upon becoming acutely ill (a noticeable loss of well-being). Even when the risks and benefits are communicated effectively, complying with lifestyle regimens without immediate results remains difficult. Health 2.0 can aid in the shift from hierarchically prescribing patients a treatment plan and hoping for long-term compliance, to interesting patients in taking small, incremental actions on their own behalf—in effect, having them convince *themselves* of the benefits and making it easier to take those actions. The goals are to have the patients seek effective tools to better manage their own care and to ensure that such tools are made available. This new paradigm can be described as creating pull for each individual to become an engaged partner in his or her own health.

Based on what we know about what it takes to influence and support behavior change, the following are four tips for creating pull, with examples of Health 2.0 programs and software applications that show why they work.

1. Fill a void—for people in need of a service to which they do not have access
2. Triangulate—to mobilize the group with the most interest in change to influence other players
3. Remove barriers and engage patients—to increase buy-in
4. Enlist a critical mass—so that others can join an already-winning effort

Fill a Void

Target people in need of a service that they do not have access to. Perhaps the best way to create pull for a new practice is to offer a solution to a problem that a group has been struggling with. For example, the demand for mental health services far surpasses what providers can handle, and access to mental healthcare is often complicated by meager insurance coverage.[26]

One particular diagnosis in the *Diagnostic and Statistical Manual of Mental Disorders,* 4th edition (DSM-IV-TR),[27] post-traumatic stress disorder (PTSD), affects 7.8 percent of Americans, and approximately 30 percent of those who have been in combat.[28] Treatment for the condition usually consists of cognitive behavioral therapy and prescribed antidepressants, which require in-person visits. Although the current administration has authorized the hiring of a significant number of staff for psychiatric treatment at Department of Veterans Affairs hospitals, there are additional barriers to seeking treatment—in a 2009 study, 29 percent of U.S. Army soldiers reported embarrassment as a factor in their decision to forgo mental health treatment.[29] This indicates high potential for patients to privately take ownership of their care.

Virtual solutions alone are unlikely to suffice for acute mental health conditions, but people are beginning to find some help for PTSD through mobile software applications (or "apps"). The Veterans Affairs website itself features one such app, *PTSD Coach,* which helps veterans in ways that are confidential and convenient. Veterans can assess their PTSD symptoms and learn techniques to alleviate them. Having this resource available can pull people to seek treatment who might not otherwise do so, because it provides free information on the disorder and suggests small, manageable steps for addressing symptoms. In other words, it contributes to filling the void of convenient, accessible, timely mental healthcare in a private setting.

Triangulate

Mobilize the group with the most interest in change to influence others. The previous strategy for creating pull relies on someone assessing a need and gravitating toward a resource that addresses that need. Triangulation operates on a similar principle—having people pulled toward fulfilling their own needs—but it incorporates the need to change other people's behaviors as well. For instance, while some reforms in population health will depend on patients changing their own practices (e.g., lowering sodium intake), other innovations will depend on groups, such as payers and providers, making changes. Triangulation creates change by having the group that will benefit the most do the legwork.

Medical errors are a well-documented issue and a ripe area for changing providers' practices. A 2001 study of seven Veterans Affairs medical centers estimated that, for roughly every 10,000 patients admitted to the subject hospitals, one patient died who would have lived for three months or more in good cognitive health had "optimal" care been provided.[30] Preventing medical errors is in the best interest of everyone involved, from payers who are less likely to have to cover the cost of follow-up treatment, to providers who want to ensure high-quality care for their patients as part of their own professional identity—and avoid litigation and negative effects on their reputation. In the end, however, the patients clearly benefit the most from preventing harmful errors.

If, as we said, triangulation creates pull by activating the group most interested in attaining the new outcome, triangulation works in preventing medical errors by mobilizing patients and their families to change provider behaviors. Campaign Zero, an organization that "delivers safety strategies to patients and their family-member advocates to prevent medical errors,"[31] is guided by this principle. Campaign Zero has created online resources, such as checklists, to educate patients and their families on specific ways that they can contribute to avoiding hospital-acquired infections and other medical errors. While educating patients and their families about preventative measures is important, the checklists also provide encouragement for changing behaviors that get in the way of actually preventing medical issues, like a family member's anxiety about overstepping bounds with providers. The checklists contain information about simple elements of monitoring the care of a family member, such as detecting early signs of bed sores, as well as context for what a family member can let nurses know and what they can ask them to do. The checklist becomes a tool for creating pull by encouraging specific actions and doing so in a way that helps normalize the behavior—reminding the family member of their agency and their responsibility in preventing medical errors, even if it means telling a provider something that he or she should already know.[32] The combination of having a motivated clinical partner in the family member, and the supports in place in the form of a checklist with information and encouragement, creates the conditions for triangulation to succeed.

REMOVE BARRIERS AND ENGAGE PATIENTS

Increase patient buy-in. Patients are not the only group that has been frustrated by the lack of information in the current healthcare system, or that could benefit from having more evidence-based insights on practices that work. Providers know that patients have clear reasons to help identify interventions that work, but providers often find it difficult to meet all of the requirements and commitments needed for outpatient trials. They also may experience resistance to following regimens because trials do not usually take patients' ideas about their own care into account. Providers are beginning to create pull for patients to partner in their own care by using Health 2.0 techniques that remove previous barriers to sharing information and create a collaborative space for problem solving.

In the traditional healthcare system, patients with comparatively rare diseases and their providers often have trouble finding evidence-based interventions and solutions. Knowledge sharing across providers can be irregular, may happen through journals and association conferences, and may depend on projects that do not necessarily link closely to one another. Some providers have taken the lead on innovating ways to share data and stories about clinical methods that work, reaching out to patients to source specific data in ways that are convenient for the patient. At least one online community has taken this further: actively engaging patients in suggesting interventions to study on themselves.

The Collaborative Chronic Care Network is a virtual partnership of more than 300 pediatric gastroenterologists dedicated to advancing remission rates of chronic conditions like inflammatory bowel disease. Their first step into the online space was to create a network where they could share information and advice on interventions. They realized that mobile capabilities like texting could help them gain more insight into what was actually working for their patients by setting up systems for patients to report daily on specific questions about the efficacy of certain treatments via text message. This worked because it removed barriers for patients to participate—patients did not have to be available at a certain point in the day for a call and spend time on the phone, nor did they have to come into an office to fill out questionnaires or have interviews. It was also more precise to have daily submissions because, as one physician put it, "when you have chronic symptoms, every day blurs." And yet, remission rates were not dropping as significantly as expected.[33]

The network of physicians soon realized that they had an opportunity to create more pull for the program by involving patients in decisions about which interventions would be studied. At this point, the Collaborative Chronic Care Network shifted its focus from answering physicians' questions about treatment to listening to patient's ideas about paths to explore. Eliciting the patient's voice in the projects has been successful to date, and the network now has 6,800 registered patients at 33 care centers participating. Physicians in the network are cautiously optimistic that these mini-trials, targeted to levers that patients perceive as significant, will lower remission rates further over time by creating pull for patients to participate and for providers to share what works more efficiently.

Enlist a Critical Mass

Show that others can join an already-winning effort. We know that people reach out to one another in times of crisis, benefiting from support and advice from peers, and that in times of illness people seek others who have been through similar ordeals. Just as the Internet has made it possible for providers to collaborate more closely and constantly, patients are seizing on Health 2.0 to create online communities based on shared experiences. The Collaborative Chronic Care Network established a community of practitioners and has built a platform where patients can share information on interventions and give each other a sense of community and emotional support. Patients are also taking the lead in creating these online communities, which are especially powerful for those with rare diseases who would have had less of a chance of speaking with others in their situation in the traditional healthcare era. Patients then had few ways of meeting one another or sharing information from their perspectives about symptoms, procedures, medications, workarounds, and providers.

The Internet is beginning to make a dramatic impact on the lives of people suffering from obscure and more prevalent conditions alike, through a kind of snowball effect. PatientsLikeMe is a social-networking site that connects people who are battling the same illnesses, while also encouraging openness of medical information to understand outcomes and drive at solutions more quickly.[34] It puts the data in patients' hands and gives them a platform to discuss it. When patients meet, they can create pull for change together by doing things as simple as communicating about interventions that work, sharing their own medical data and results, or launching larger undertakings, such as lobbying the government to fund research for their condition or convincing pharmaceutical companies to develop drugs that have a life-saving impact on a relatively small number of worldwide sufferers.

HEALTH WEBSITES AND APPS: NOT JUST A FAD

Information technology may have arrived slowly into clinics and insurance companies, but the pace of innovation and adoption in consumer electronics today is astounding (and accelerating). Devices are quickly penetrating every facet of our lives in the form of laptops, smartphones, tablets, and beyond. Thousands of health and wellness websites and software apps already exist, and we believe their role will become increasingly important in healthcare. Some are crucial elements of health organizations' programming, such as the online platform that ShapeUp uses to manage its business functions. Many are stand-alone tools without an organization or programming per se (e.g., apps for counting calories, monitoring glucose levels, or tracking sleep). Are websites and applications effective means of engaging individuals in their own health? And if so, what separates the good ones from the bad ones?

A 2009 meta-analysis of web-based smoking cessation programs found the pooled quit rate for participants to be 14.8 percent after follow-up conducted three months out, and 11.7 percent after six months out.[35] These figures are an improvement over the rate of people attempting to quit without any help or resources, as previously cited. From our own study of health websites and applications, we are beginning to see that high-quality digital resources share many characteristics with effective products and services in the physical world. They create pull by engaging users via explicit reward structures. They enable teamwork and foster social accountability. Their content is interactive, informative, and often individualized. Their use is intuitive, convenient (e.g., accessible via the Internet on a laptop or tablet and by smartphone mobile apps), and even effortless to the user (e.g., automatically collecting, synchronizing, and analyzing information).

The fragmented world of websites and applications is not without its problems. In today's app market, the void that many websites and applications fill is not necessarily in the best interest of health consumers, and the quality of products or services is often questionable. We see such issues as a reality of any market in its early stages. We are optimistic, however, that greater consultation with medical professionals, greater investment and competition among health organizations, and improved regulation can help this new market mature into an indispensable virtual ecosystem of resources for health-seeking individuals.

EARLY RESULTS FOR HEALTH 2.0

Despite the growth in Health 2.0 interaction since 2010, we still see Health 2.0 as being in its infancy relative to the potential it holds for engaging patients in managing and being more accountable for their own health. There is further hard evidence that its strategies are already improving patients' quality of life, expanding providers' expertise, and helping health systems and payers financially. (Sprint estimated more than one million dollars in savings for a challenge that lasted only twelve weeks.) If Health 2.0 can, as we have discussed, enable people to reduce smoking, become more fit, and more actively participate with their providers in the management of chronic disease, we posit that these factors will combine to result in a better sense of health and well-being for those involved. One would logically conclude that these kinds of interventions result in fewer interactions with the healthcare system, an issue that Harrison et al. tackled in a study from 2012 that was published in *Population Health Management*.[36] It looked at the relationship between self-reported individual wellbeing and future healthcare utilization and cost. They found that higher self-reported well-being was associated with fewer hospitalizations, visits to the emergency room, and use of medications. Overall, the authors concluded that improving well-being (or what we would refer to as a perceived sense of health) holds tremendous promise in reducing future use of healthcare services and the costs associated with that care. We see Health 2.0 as an effective way to enable people to improve their well-being and suggest that its impact will continue to grow over time in terms of better outcomes and reduced cost.

Health 2.0 offerings are looking at a variety of ways to measure their impact beyond cost and quality. The Collaborative Chronic Care Network, for example, is reporting on number of participants, response rates via text, and pilot projects undertaken, but not yet on the clinical or financial impact of its patient partnerships. Even well-known companies, such as PatientsLikeMe, are not currently reporting their specific impact on influencing organizations and institutions to drive toward standards of care and other cost-reduction solutions in healthcare—rather, they are reporting their impact on individual lives, through testimonials on the power of connection. Their vision of results rings true for many components and actors in Health 2.0:

> We envision a world where information exchange between patients, doctors, pharmaceutical companies, researchers, and the healthcare industry can be free and open; where, in doing so, people do not have to fear discrimination, stigmatization, or regulation; and where the free flow of information helps everyone. We envision a future where every patient benefits from the collective experience of all, and where the risk and reward of each possible choice is transparent and known.[37]

This description does not mention economics, but it also does not mention illness. We know that clients of companies like ShapeUp are working in the background to compile their own estimates of the savings that these programs and other interventions are likely to have on their healthcare costs. This is the kind of data that will "triangulate" out to other organizations and help build momentum for Health 2.0.

As we shift from a system that addresses sickness to one that promotes health, we may experience that the more interesting promise of Health 2.0 is less about economics and more about accelerating a sweeping cultural shift that focuses our collective and individual energy on wellness. We know that tools alone—the supports that can help catalyze behavior change—will not be totally responsible for the change in outlook, but the tools and other supports in Health 2.0 will serve as some of the key catalysts, ushering in a new era that foregrounds prevention, wellness, and better management of chronic disease, and works to reduce the economic burden on health systems, governments, and individuals themselves.

CONCLUSION

The promise of Health 2.0, while substantial, has yet to be realized on a large-scale basis. New technology, programs, and apps are being introduced to the market on a daily basis, yet we know that these technologies are not accessible to all who need them, and it can be difficult to evaluate their effectiveness. We read one study that looked at a diabetes group on Facebook, where nearly one-third of the posts were related to some type of promotional activity for non–FDA-approved natural products.[38] With examples like this, it is important to be clear that we do *not* see Health 2.0 as a substitute for physicians or other members of the care team.

Instead, we view Health 2.0 as a currently underutilized enabler to more effectively engage patients in understanding how they can take greater ownership of their own health. Reaching back to the beginning of this chapter, Health 2.0 has the potential to help patients become part of the "pit crew" that Gawande describes. This would enable tighter coordination among individuals and their care providers and support networks in scalable ways that promote wellness at great value (in terms of health gains per dollar spent). When considering the potential for behaviors to spread in social networks, the influence that some aspects of Health 2.0 could have seems particularly potent. We envision a day when Health 2.0 spreads from somewhat grassroots programs targeting segments of populations to an industry-wide, organization-driven paradigm where Health 2.0 is simply part of effective population health management.

CASE MODEL

ShapeUp, Inc. is an employee wellness company, founded in 2006 by two entrepreneurial doctors, that uses social networking and friendly competition to incentivize healthy behaviors including weight loss, increased physical activity, conscientious eating, and preventive care. ShapeUp's online social networking platform was built on research showing the link between achieving and sustaining positive behavior change like losing weight or quitting smoking and significant help and support from social networks. ShapeUp's health interventions have been clinically shown to improve the health of employee populations and have been used by more than 200 employers internationally.

To use ShapeUp, employees form teams but log on individually to enroll and participate in the wellness program online. There they can track individual and team progress for up to three daily metrics: steps walked (as measured by a provided pedometer), minutes of exercise, and weight. At its core, the program is structured around social accountability to encourage reporting on a regular basis and to deter misreporting (i.e., inflating numbers). While metrics are generally tracked on an honor system, the platform also offers integration with fitness devices, such as the Fitbit, that directly submit data.

Participants are able to add each other as "supporters" to create a larger, more engaging wellness network, beyond the team structure. Encouragement and suggestions can be exchanged within these networks via a team chat tool, through one-click options to send motivating emails and reminders to track data, and even by virtual "high fives" to recognize individuals who have done a great job. In addition to the team goals and overall rankings, participants can invite one another to perform spontaneous "quick challenges"—for example, challenging a friend to do 30 sit-ups today.

Sprint is one of the largest American telecommunications companies, with 40,000 national employees working in more than 1,000 retail stores across the country. Sprint sought a wellness program that would excite and engage a diversified, tech-savvy workforce while providing measurable outcomes and return on investment.

To that end, Sprint partnered with ShapeUp in 2012 to run a 12-week fitness challenge that asked employees to form teams and see which teams could walk the farthest, exercise the most minutes, and lose the most weight. Individuals were asked to track their daily fitness activities through the ShapeUp platform, enabling co-workers across the country to virtually connect with one another with a common goal in mind. This online support encouraged participants to stay engaged in the program and in their exercise and weight loss plans.

The results:

- Sprint enjoyed a 40 percent engagement rate for the program, involving 16,000 employees.
- Participants completed nearly 22,000 minutes of exercise, logged almost 4.8 billion steps, and lost over 40,000 pounds over the 12-week challenge.
- Sprint estimates that the total healthcare cost savings as a result of the program is over $1.1 million.

CHECKLIST

As we have discussed, the shift in focus from sickness to health can be enabled by providing supports for the behavior changes that will drive population health management. Our research shows that elements of infrastructure and support, or strategies to "create pull," rarely work alone—any tool or process requires a few of these elements to work in tandem to be successful. Whether you are using mobile applications and online communities, or engaging patients in using Health 2.0 resources, here are some ways to think about whether a platform will help foster the change you need.

CHECKLIST:	Yes	No
Fill a void		
Does it meet an expressed or tacit need to keep people healthy?	o	o
Does it do something that's never been done before for prevention, care, or wellness—or just do it better?	o	o
Track progress and results data		
Does it automatically show people what they have accomplished?	o	o
Does it motivate people through tying their progress to results and reasons to achieve them?	o	o
Remove barriers		
Does it remove issues and problems—technical, emotional, logistical, communicative, or other—that keep people from making the behavior change?	o	o
Pilot patients' ideas		
Does it gather new ideas about symptoms, treatment, side effects, outcomes, and other experiential measures from first-hand accounts?	o	o
Does it involve the patient in decisions?	o	o
Triangulate		
Does it mobilize the people who will feel the biggest impact, and who have the most incentive to make the change happen?	o	o

Enlist a critical mass		
Does it help people to form coalitions and share information to gain headway on developing and allowing access to clinical information or procedures, pharmaceutical options, or governmental processes?	o	o
Create accountability		
Does it create expectations for self-reporting, ask people to compare their progress to others', or otherwise drive accountability?	o	o
Provide social support		
Does it create a community of common experience or provide mechanisms for peer support?	o	o
Give people an incentive		
Does it reward people economically, or through respect and recognition?	o	o
Ensure ease of use		
Is it fairly easy and intuitive for people to adopt?	o	o

REFERENCES

1. Gawande A. Atul Gawande: How do we heal medicine? 2012. *TED* (Blog). http://www.ted.com/talks/atul_gawande_how_do_we_heal_medicine.html (accessed October 10, 2012).
2. Gawande A. Atul Gawande: How do we heal medicine? 2012. *TED* (Blog). http://www.ted.com/talks/atul_gawande_how_do_we_heal_medicine.html (accessed October 10, 2012).
3. Darzi A., Beales S., Hallsworth M., King D., Macdonnell M., Vlaev I. 2011. The five bad habits of healthcare: How new thinking about behaviour could reduce health spending. World Economic Forum, White paper.
4. World Health Organization. 2012. Per capita total expenditure on health at average exchange rate (US$), 2012. World Health Organization Global Health Observatory. http://gamapserver.who.int/gho/interactive_charts/health_financing/atlas.html?indicator=i3&date=2010 (accessed October 31, 2012).
5. Fisher E.S., Wennberg D.E., Stukel T.A., Gottlieb D.J., Lucas F.L., Pinder E.L. 2003. The implications of regional variations in Medicare spending. Part 1: The content, quality, and accessibility of care. *Ann Intern Med* 138(4):273–287.
6. Squires D. 2012. Explaining high health care spending in the United States: An international comparison of supply, utilization, prices, and quality. *Commonwealth Fund* 1595(10). http://www.commonwealthfund.org/Publications/Issue-Briefs/2012/May/High-Health-Care-Spending.aspx.
7. Center on Budget and Policy Priorities. 2012. Spending and revenues as a share of GDP. Congressional Budget Office. http://www.cbpp.org.
8. Zieminski N. 2012. Healthcare costs top U.S. executives' concerns: Adecco survey. *Reuters*. http://www.reuters.com/article/2012/10/22/us-adecco-election-survey-idUSBRE89L12T20121022 (accessed October 25, 2012).
9. *Employer health benefits 2012 annual survey.* 2012. Kaiser Family Foundation and Health Research & Educational Trust. http://ehbs.kff.org/pdf/2012/8345.pdf.
10. Pugh T. 2012. Health-care premiums rise three times faster than wages. *CSMonitor*. http://www.csmonitor.com/Business/Latest-News-Wires/2012/0912/Health-care-premiums-rise-three-times-faster-than-wages (accessed September 12, 2012).
11. *The price of excess: Identifying waste in healthcare spending.* 2008. PricewaterhouseCoopers' Health Research Institute.
12. Asch D.A., Volpp K.G. 2012. What business are we in? The emergence of health as the business of health care. *N Engl J Med* 367(10):888–889.
13. McGinnis J.M., Williams-Russo P., Knickman J.R. 2002. The case for more active policy attention to health promotion. *Health Affairs* 21(2):78–93.
14. Primary health care: Report of the International Conference on Primary Health Care, Alma-Ata, USSR, September 6–12, 1978. Geneva: World Health Organization.
15. Population health: Advancing the population health improvement model. 2012. Care Continuum Alliance. http://www.carecontinuumalliance.org/phi_definition.asp (accessed October 25, 2012).

16. George B. 2012. September virtual HC roundtable: Transforming healthcare through integrated leadership. Presentation to Harvard Business School Health Industry Alumni Association. http://hbr.org/case-studies (accessed November 1, 2012).

17. Moussa M., Tomasik J.L. 2011. The business case for cultural change: From individuals to communities. In *Population health: Creating a culture of wellness* (p. 137), ed. Nash D.B. et al. Sudbury, MA: Jones and Bartlett Learning.

18. Guide to quitting smoking: A word about quitting success rates. American Cancer Society. 2012. http://www.cancer.org/acs/groups/cid/documents/webcontent/002971-pdf.pdf (accessed November 1, 2012).

19. Christakis N.A, Fowler J.H. 2009. *Connected: The surprising power of our social networks and how they shape our lives.* New York: Little, Brown and Co.

20. Christakis N.A, Fowler J.H. 2009. *Connected: The surprising power of our social networks and how they shape our lives.* New York: Little, Brown and Co.

21. Moussa M., Tomasik J.L. 2011. The business case for cultural change: From individuals to communities. In *Population health: Creating a culture of wellness* (p. 137), ed. Nash D.B. et al. Sudbury, Mass: Jones and Bartlett Learning.

22. Eytan T. 2008. The Health 2.0 definition: Not just the latest, the greatest! Blog. http://www.tedeytan.com/2008/06/13/1089 (accessed November 1, 2012).

23. Hawn C. 2009. Take two aspirin and tweet me in the morning: How Twitter, Facebook, and other social media are reshaping health care. *Health Affairs* 28(2):361–368.

24. Moussa M, Tomasik JL. 2011. Doctor–patient relationships in the modern era: Can we talk—a collaborative shift in bedside manner. In *The business of medical practice: Transformational health 2.0 skills for doctors* (p. 195), eds. Marcinko D.E., Hope R. Hetico. New York: Springer Publishing Co.

25. ShapeUp. 2011. ShapeUp introduces social game to encourage employees to get flu shots. http://www.shapeup.com/news/article/shapeup-introduces-social-game-to-encourage-employees-to-get-flu-shots/ (accessed June 12, 2013).

26. Wang P.S., Lane M., Olfson M., Pincus H.A., Wells K.B., Kessler R.C. 2005. Twelve-month use of mental health services in the United States. *Arch Gen Psychiatry* 62(6):629–640.

27. American Psychiatric Association. *The Diagnostic and Statistical Manual of Mental Disorders* (fourth ed., text revision). Arlington, VA: American Psychiatric Association, 2000

28. PTSD Frequently Asked Questions. 2012. Military.com Benefits. http://www.military.com/benefits/veterans-health-care/ptsd-frequently-asked-questions.html (accessed November 4, 2012).

29. Mental Health Advisory Team (MHAT) VI Report. 2009. Office of the Surgeon of Multi-National Corps-Iraq and Office of the Surgeon General United States Army Medical Command.

30. Hayward R., Hofer T. 2001. Estimating hospital deaths due to medical errors: Preventability is in the eye of the reviewer. *JAMA* 286(4):415–420.

31. CampaingZero. 2011. Our goals. http://www.campaignzero.org/about/our-goals/.

32. CampaignZERO. 2011. Our goals. http://www.campaignzero.org/about/our-goals/ (accessed October 3, 2012).

33. Marcus A.D. 2012. Patients as partners: An online network for sufferers of inflammatory bowel disease provides some clues to the power of collaboration. *The Wall Street Journal,* April 16, 2012. http://online.wsj.com/article/SB10001424052702304692804577281463879153408.html (accessed October 25, 2012).

34. PatientsLikeMe. 2013. About us. http://www.patientslikeme.com/about (accessed 12 Oct 2012).

35. Myung S.K., McDonnell D.D., Kazinets G., Seo H.G., Moskowitz J.M. 2009. Effects of web- and computer-based smoking cessation programs: Meta-analysis of randomized controlled trials. *Arch Intern Med* 169(10):929–937.

36. Harrison P.L., Pope J.E., Coberley C.F., Rula E.Y. 2012. Evaluation of the relationship between individual well-being and future health care utilization and cost. *Popul Health Manag* 15(6)325–330.

37. PatientsLikeMe. 2012. Corporate FAQ: What is the future of healthcare in a PatientsLikeMe world? http://www.patientslikeme.com/help/faq/Corporate (accessed October 12, 2012).

38. Greene J.A., Choudhry N.K., Kilabuk E., Shrank W.H. 2011. Online social networking by patients with diabetes: A qualitative evaluation of communication with Facebook. *J of Gen Intern Med* 26(3):287–292.

Section III

Institutional and Professional Benchmarking

Advanced Applications

9 Interpreting and Negotiating Healthcare Contracts

David Edward Marcinko and Hope Rachel Hetico

CONTENTS

INTRODUCTION

In the distant fee-for-service past, an independent private physician, hospital, or healthcare entity would raise fees if more income was desired. Correspondingly, income increased and volume changed very little, if at all. This occurred because patients (or insurance payers) were willing to pay almost any price and because medical fees were considered inelastic, within the relevant price range.

Economists call this relationship the **elasticity of demand** and define it as a ratio of the percentage change in quantity (patient volume) demanded of a service resulting from each 1 percent change in the price of the service (Hyman 2000).

Demand is considered elastic if the price of the service exceeds 1.0 unit, and is deemed inelastic if equal to or greater than zero, but less than 1. In other words, demand for medical services is elastic if revenues increase only by lowering price. Conversely, raising the price will decrease revenues if demand is elastic, because consumers (patients) will seek medical services at lower prices elsewhere.

Medical care has an elasticity ratio of about 0.35. Inelasticity occurs in a growth industry, such as wireless Internet, where a fee increase will also increase revenues in the relevant range, while elasticity occurs in a mature (non-growth) business, such as medicine, where revenues are increasing but profits are stagnating or decreasing. The marketplace becomes resistant to price pressure, as it has done with health maintenance organizations (HMOs) (Marcinko 2000).

HOSPITALISTS AND PHYSICIANS

The term "hospitalist" was coined in 1996 by Dr. Robert M. Wachter, of the University of California at San Francisco (UCSF), and L. Goldman to describe physicians who devote much of their professional time and focus to the care of hospitalized patients (D.E. Marcinko, pers. comm.). It denotes a hospital-based and hospital-employed specialist in inpatient medicine (Wachter's World 2013).

In the most prevalent American model of hospitalist care, several doctors practice together as a group and work full time caring for inpatients. Hospitalists are familiar figures today and produce a leading peer-reviewed publication, known as the *Journal of Hospital Medicine*. Doctors specializing in intensive care have long taken care of patients admitted to the intensive care unit by primary care doctors, geriatricians working in nursing homes have often admitted patients to the care of their hospital-based colleagues, etc. Thus, according to Harold C. Sox, "the hospitalist model (of care) is not new (in the United States), but it is growing rapidly as a result of the role of managed care organizations, the increasing complexity of inpatient care, and the pressures of busy outpatient practices" (Sox 1999).

At the center of a hospitalist's responsibility is the understanding of an integrated model of low-cost, comprehensive, broad-based care in the hospital, hospice, or even extended care setting. If well designed, hospitalist programs can offer benefits beyond the often cited inpatient efficiencies they may bring (DeNelsky 1998). On the other hand, some managed care organizations have mandated that patients are to be treated by their own hospitalists. Patients may also be assigned to hospitalists who are unknown to the primary care physician or to hospitals other than those that the primary care physician typically uses.

Before the advent of hospitalists, the usual role of inpatient care in the United States saw primary care or admitting physicians caring for hospitalized patients. Although this method of patient care had the advantage of continuity, and perhaps personalization, it often suffered because of the limited knowledge base of the physician, as well as a lack of familiarity with the available internal and external resources of the hospital. Furthermore, the limited time spent with each patient prevented the physician from becoming the quality leader in this setting.

These shortcomings have led hundreds of hospitals around the United States to turn to hospitalists as dedicated inpatient specialists. The National Association of Inpatient Physicians, now the Society of Hospital Medicine, reports the desire for hospitalist programs to grow to 75,000 new hospitalists by the year 2015 (Society of Hospital Medicine 2012).

For example, using standard treatment protocols (STPs), the average length of stay for patients on the medical service at UCSF's Moffitt-Long Hospital fell by 15 percent compared to concurrent and historical controls adjusted for case mix. There was no reported decrease in patient satisfaction or clinical outcomes.

MEDICAL OFFICE PROFITS

A cost-volume-profit relationship exists in any healthcare entity and emphasizes the point that the goal of an efficient emerging healthcare organization (EHO) should be profit optimization, rather than revenue or volume maximization. The profit of any healthcare facility is what's left after all financial outflows are removed from all financial inflows. This optimization is reached at the point where patient volume, fee per patient, and costs per patient produce highest profit, not the highest revenue. This is the point of maximum efficiency—this is where you want to be. It can be described in the equation below.

THE PROFIT EQUATION

Medical profit can be defined by the equation:

$$\text{Profit} = (\text{Price} \times \text{Volume}) - \text{Costs}$$

$$or \; P = (P \times V) - C$$

whereas:

$$\text{Revenue} = \text{Price} \times \text{Volume}$$

$$\textit{or } R = PV$$

To increase profits, the doctor must increase price (if possible), increase volume (if possible), or decrease costs (if possible); ideally the doctor should perform all three maneuvers simultaneously. If one assumes that only costs are under the doctor's control (this is not altogether valid as a strategic mindframe), any strategic financial planning process that ignores them will be detrimental to the viability of the practice.

A more efficient practice addresses cost and volume together; at some point, however, more volume does not equal more profit. This point is known as the average cost per patient and should be determined and known for each doctor, service segment, clinic, or hospital. If visually graphed, the curve would be U-shaped, with both arms extending upward and the hump pointed downward at its most efficient point on the long-range average cost curve. This tangent is the point of maximum efficiency, and this is where the healthcare entity should be, as seen diagrammatically in Figure 9.1.

Working harder by taking on more patients, performing additional procedures, or working additional hours in this scenario will not get the clinic, hospital, or medical practice ahead, only further behind and less economically efficient. Thus, the main goal for all EHOs is profit improvement, not just revenue growth.

Once the fixed and variable costs of a medical practice or hospital clinic are known, the effects of changes in volume on its cost structure can easily be determined. This is known as the cost–volume relationship, as seen diagrammatically in Figure 9.2.

For example, the effects of varying volume decreases on an average internist's medical practice are demonstrated below:

Capacity	Total Fixed Costs ($)	Variable Costs per Visit ($)	Visits	Total Variable Costs ($)	Total Costs ($)	Average Cost per Visit ($)
70%	150,000	20	3,500	70,000	220,000	62.86
60%	150,000	20	3,000	60,000	210,000	70.00
50%	150,000	20	2,500	50,000	200,000	80.00
40%	150,000	20	2,000	40,000	190,000	95.00
30%	150,000	20	1,500	30,000	180,000	120.00
20%	150,000	20	1,000	20,000	170,000	170.00

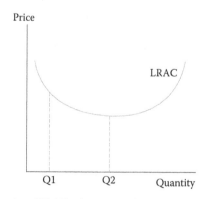

FIGURE 9.1   Average cost per patient. LRAC = long-run average cost.

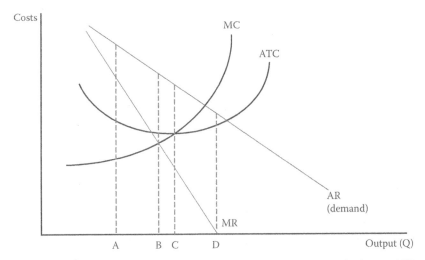

FIGURE 9.2 Cost–volume relationship. ATC = average total costs; MC = marginal costs; MR = marginal revenue. (From Tutor2U, http://tutor2u.net/quiz/economics/diagrams/a2_test_3.gif, 2013.)

If the cost structure remains unchanged in the face of declining volume, the consequences will be higher average costs, reduced profitability, and an overall deterioration in the financial profitability and flexibility of the healthcare entity. In fact, the increased average cost per visit accelerates faster in the downward capacity direction than it decreases in the upward capacity direction.

However, the effects of a volume increase are quite the opposite and much more pleasing. For example, at 70, 80, 90, and 100 percent capacity rates, the average cost per visit decreases to $62.86, $57.50, $53.33, and $50.00, respectively, when calculated in a similar fashion. Theoretically, at 110 percent of capacity, for a limited time, the average cost per visit decreases to $47.27, but at a slower rate. Nevertheless, this is an unrealistic expectation in a capitated or managed care environment that encourages lower utilization rates.

If the cost structure described above—$150,000 total fixed costs and $20 variable costs per visit (VC/visit)—is more realistically transformed to $100,000 total fixed costs and $34.29 VC/visit, the total practice cost at 70 percent capacity remains at $220,000:

$$\$150,000 + (\$20 \times 3,500) \approx \$220,000$$

$$\$100,000 + (\$34.29 \times 3,500) \approx \$220,000$$

In fact, the next table demonstrates how the fixed cost decrease responds using the new, reduced fixed cost formula.

Capacity	Total Fixed Cost ($)	VC/Visit ($)	Visits	Total VC ($)	Total Cost ($)	Average Cost/Visit
70%	100,000	$34.29	3,500	120,015	220,015	$62.86
60%	100,000	34.29	3,000	102,870	202,870	67.62
50%	100,000	34.29	2,500	85,725	185,725	74.29
40%	100,000	34.29	2,000	68,580	168,580	84.29
30%	100,000	34.29	1,500	51,435	151,435	100.96
20%	100,000	34.29	1,000	34,290	134,290	134.29

Note that, at 60 percent capacity, in comparison to the old cost structure, the practice has a total savings of $7,125 and a reduction of $2.38 in average costs. At 50 percent capacity, there is a total savings of $14,275, and average cost drops $5.71.

MARGINAL PROFIT

Recalling the equation, Profit = (Price × Volume) − Total Costs, we could amend it to say:

$$\text{Total Profit} = \text{Price} \times \text{Volume} - (\text{Fixed Costs} + \text{Variable Costs})$$

$$or\ \text{Total Profit} = P \times V - (FC + VC)$$

However, most HMO contracts today are based not on total profit, but on additional or marginal profit, because overhead costs always remain and clinic fixed costs are not important in contracted medicine. For other pricing decisions, the profit equation can again be rewritten to emphasize variable costs:

$$\text{Marginal Profit} = (P \times V) - VC$$

COST-VOLUME-PROFIT ANALYSIS

Once a basic understanding of medical cost behavior has been achieved, the techniques of cost-volume-profit analysis (CVPA) can be used to further refine the managerial cost and profit aspects of the office business unit. They can also help illustrate the important differences between the traditional office net income statement and the more contemporary contribution margin income statement (CMIS). CVPA is thus concerned with the relationship among prices of medical services, unit volume, per unit variable costs, total fixed costs, and the mix of services provided.

TRADITIONAL NET INCOME STATEMENT

In financial accounting, the traditional net income statement incorporates office medical costs organized by function:

Example

January revenues	$12,000
Less costs	6,000 (variable and fixed costs)
Gross margin less operating expenses	5,000
Net income	**$1,000**

CONTRIBUTION MARGIN INCOME STATEMENT

The CMIS approach of managerial accounting is more useful than a traditional income statement approach in CVPA.

Example

The following is a CMIS for Dr. Smith, a solo independent hospitalist, for last month.

	Total ($)	VC per (Unit) Patient ($)	Proportion of Revenues (%)
Revenues (500 patients)	25,000	50	100
Less variable expenses	15,000	30	60
Contribution margin	10,000	20	40
Less fixed expenses	8,000		
Net income	**2,000**		

Recognize that the revenues (net of variable expenses) contribute toward covering fixed expenses and then toward profits. Also, the per unit contribution margin remains constant as long as the office visit price and the variable expenses per unit do not change.

To illustrate the powerful effects that volume change can have in CVPA, a CMIS is presented for monthly revenues generated by treating 1, 2, 400, and 401 patients, respectively.

	Total Cost ($)	Per (Unit) Patient ($)	Proportion of Revenues (%)
Revenues (1 patient)	50	50	100
Less variable expenses	30	30	60
Contribution margin	20	20	40
Less fixed expenses	8,000		
Net income (loss)	**(7,980)**		

	Total Cost ($)	Per (Unit) Patient ($)	Proportion of Revenues (%)
Revenues (2 patients)	100	50	100
Less variable expenses	60	30	60
Contribution margin	40	20	40
Less fixed expenses	8,000		
Net income (loss)	**(7,960)**		

	Total Cost ($)	Per (Unit) Patient ($)	Proportion of Revenues (%)
Revenues (400 patients)	$0,000	50	100
Less variable expenses	12,000	30	60
Contribution margin	8,000	20	40
Less fixed expenses	8,000		
Net income (break-even)	**0**		

	Total Cost ($)	Per (Unit) Patient ($)	Proportion of Revenues (%)
Revenues (401 patients)	20,050	50	100
Less variable expenses	12,030	30	60
Contribution margin	8,020	20	40
Less fixed expenses	8,000		
Net income (profit)	**200**		

If Dr. Smith treats exactly 400 patients a month, he breaks even (no profit or loss).

The break-even point can be defined either as the point where total revenue equals total expenses (variable and fixed), or as the point where total contribution margin equals total fixed expenses.

Once the break-even point is reached, net income (profits) is increased by the amount of the unit contribution margin for each additional patient seen. The clinic should be able to increase its patient volume with little or no corresponding increase in its fixed costs.

CONTRIBUTION MARGIN RATIO

The contribution margin ratio (CMR) is the ratio of contribution margin to total revenues, expressed as a percentage (i.e., contribution margin/revenues). The CMR can also be calculated using per unit figures (patient contribution margin/per patient revenue).

The CM in the following example is 40 percent ($10,000 ÷ 25,000 = 40 percent, or 20/50). The CMR demonstrates how the contribution margin will be affected by a given change in total revenues:

Example

Assume that revenues for Dr. Smith increase by $15,000 next month. We can now inquire what the effects on the contribution margin and net income might be.

(1) Effect on Contribution Margin
    Increase revenues $15,000
    Multiplied by CM   × 40%
    Increase in Contribution Margin: **$6,000**
(2) Effect on Net Income

If fixed expenses do not change, Dr. Smith's net income will again increase $6,000.

	Present	Expected	Change
Revenue (patients)	50	80	30
Revenues ($)	$25,000	40,000	15,000
Less variable expenses	15,000	24,000	9,000
Contribution margin	10,000	16,000	6,000
Less fixed expenses	8,000	8,000	0
Net income	**2,000**	**8,000**	**6,000**

As long as the revenue received from the practice is above the variable costs of providing the medical service, the contribution margin is positive and contributes to fixed costs (Hogan et al. 2004).

In the real world of managed care, any managed care organization contract that is below a doctor's or clinic's variable costs will lower its profit and should never even be considered.

STANDARD COST PROFILES

The standard cost profile concept is not new in the industrial sector, but it is still considered quite innovative in the healthcare sector. For our purposes, its two key elements include the direct or indirect service units or diagnosis-related groups (DRGs) being costed, and the resource required to produce or serve the DRG (human resources is typically the cost driver here).

Example

INDIRECT COST PROFILE FOR HOSPITAL PATIENT FOOD SERVICE

Category	Patients	Fixed Cost	Unit Cost	Variable Cost	Average Fixed Cost	Average Total Cost
Material						
Labor						
Overhead						
Allocation						
– Housekeeping						
– Facility						
– Administration						
Total costs						

Currently, indirect costs are more than 50 percent in many healthcare settings, but this could be reduced with better tracking, bar coding, radio frequency identification devices (RFIDs), etc. Of course, this identification of services is the heart of activity-based medical cost management.

CAPITATION REIMBURSEMENT

According to Richard Eskow, CEO of Health Knowledge Systems of Los Angeles, capitated medical reimbursement has been used, in one form or another, in every attempt at healthcare reform since the Norman Conquest (Eskow 2007). Some even say an earlier variant existed in ancient China.

Initially, when Henry I assumed the throne of the newly combined kingdoms of England and Normandy, he initiated a sweeping set of healthcare reforms. Historical documents, though muddled, indicate that soon thereafter at least one "physician," John of Essex, received a flat payment honorarium of one penny per day for his efforts. Historian Edward J. Kealey opined that sum was roughly equal to that paid to a foot soldier or a blind person (Kealey 1981).

Clearer historical evidence suggests that American doctors in the mid-19th century were receiving capitation-like payments. No less an authoritative figure than Mark Twain, in fact, is on record as saying that during his boyhood in Hannibal, Missouri, his parents paid the local doctor $25/year for taking care of the entire family regardless of their state of health (*New York Times* 1902).

Capitation payments made a comeback in the managed care field during the 1980s and 1990s because fee-for-service medicine created perverse incentives for physicians. As the public, physicians, and stakeholders understand, fee-for-service medicine pays more for treating illnesses and injuries than it does for preventing them or even for diagnosing them early and reducing the need for intensive treatment later.

Nevertheless, the managed care industry's experience with capitation was not initially a good one. The 1980s and 1990s saw a number of HMOs attempt to put independent physicians, especially primary care doctors, into a capitation reimbursement model. The result was often negative for patients, who found that their doctors were far less willing to see them—and saw them for briefer visits—when they were receiving no additional income for their effort.

Attempts were also made to aggregate various types of health providers—including hospitals and physicians in multiple specialties—into capitation groups that were collectively responsible for delivering care to a defined patient group. These included healthcare facilities and medical providers of all types: physicians, osteopaths, podiatrists, dentists, optometrists, pharmacies, physical therapists, hospitals and skilled nursing homes, etc.

The healthcare industry, however, is not collective by nature, and these efforts tended to be too complicated to succeed. One lesson that these experiments taught is that provider behavior is difficult to change unless the relationship between that behavior and its consequences is fairly direct and easy to understand.

Today, the concept of pre-payment and medical capitation is intended to uncouple compensation from the actual number of patients seen, or treatments and interventions performed. This is akin to a fixed price restaurant menu, as opposed to an à la carte eatery. This model is based on the CVPA calculations outlined below.

Cost-Volume-Profit Analysis

One factor for determining profitability in CVPA is the accuracy range of estimated utilization rates for each managed care contract. Too much patient utilization of the doctor's resources means little or no profit, while less utilization means more profit (at-risk contract).

Example

A primary care clinic has 20,000 patients under a per member per month (pm/pm) contract and is offered a capitation rate of 0.12 pm/pm. The estimated variable cost for the service is $2.50 per patient. The gross revenue for the 12-cent contract is $2,400 a month (20,000 × 0.12). What is the profitability range against different utilization rate assumptions, and can the group afford to take the contract?

A	B	C	D	E	F
Annual Revenue	Utilization Ratio/1000 (estimate)	Utilization (per/20,000)	Variable Cost (patient)	Total Cost (increased)	Profit Contract
$2,400 × 12		(B × 20)		(C × D)	(A – E)
28,800	20	400	$2.50	1,000	$27,800
28,800	50	1,000	2.50	2,500	26,300
28,800	90	1,800	2.50	4,500	24,300
28,800	100	2,000	2.50	5,000	23,800

The spreadsheet shows that this contract is profitable over the entire range of utilization rates (20, 50, 90, and 100). However, the clinic might determine that it cannot manage additional patients beyond a utilization rate of 50 without more staff, office space, or other resources (i.e., no excess capacity). At this rate, the contract would be rejected because the annual increase in these overhead costs would begin to erode the estimated profit of $26,300. Contract risk is now quantified, and the group can investigate other "what if" scenarios regarding increased variable costs per patient (e.g., costlier injections, X-rays, dressings, or lab tests) or other parameters, such as a new capitation rate.

As an example, the spreadsheet below demonstrates the same scenario, but with a new and increased variable cost rate of $10, rather than the $2.50 rate used above.

A	B	C	D	E	F
Annual Revenue	Utilization Ratio/1000 (estimate)	Utilization (per 20,000)	Variable Cost (patient)	Total Cost (increased)	Profit Contract
2,400 × 12		(B × 20)		(C × D)	(A – E)
$28,800	20	400	$10	4,000	$24,800
28,800	50	1,000	10	10,000	18,800
28,800	90	1,800	10	18,000	10,800
28,800	100	2,000	10	20,000	8,800
28,800	120	2,400	10	24,000	4,800
28,800	150	3,000	10	30,000	(1,200)

Profits decrease as variable costs increase, by $3,000, $7,500, $13,500, and $15,000, respectively, at the relevant utilization rates of 20, 50, 90, and 100. Moreover, at a utilization rate of 150, with the new VC factor of $10, the clinic actually loses money (−$1,200) because profit becomes negative beyond some utilization or variable cost point. This break-even point can be calculated by finding the utilization or variable cost rate that produces zero profit.

To determine the break-even point using the above scenario, use the following formula:

$$B = (UR \times VC) - \text{Annual Revenue}$$

$$B = (20 \times 10) - 28,800$$

$$B = 144$$

Thus, capitation CVPA seeks to determine at what volume capacity does the clinic maximize profits, but not necessarily revenue. The clinic wants to see the optimal number of patients for profitability, but not the greatest number of patients. It wants to maximize its profits, not gross revenues. In terms of HMO contract negotiations, the group can now leverage this information by trying to do one of the following:

- Increase the pm/pm capitation rate
- Control utilization rates (ration care)
- Carve out certain services
- Sacrifice the contract

However, gross variances in CVPA might warrant further investigation or contract consideration when:

- Actual dollar compensation (profit) exceeds established guidelines
- Variance does not exceed an acceptable range of compensation (profit)
- The anticipated benefits of CVPA are more than expected profits
- Past CVPA benchmarks warrant a further review

CAPITATION ECONOMICS

According to Hogan, Gordon, and Herron of Phoenix Healthcare Consulting, LLC, a capitation scheme can be illustrated by the baseline office example of an independent physician (Tinsley, 2002).

One first assumes that payment for services is from traditional fee-for-service sources, including indemnity insurance, some discounted rate plans, self-pay patients, and Medicare. To analyze the potential financial impact of a shift in payer mix to or from capitation, it is necessary to establish a few key statistics from the practice's most recent 12-month period. Total net patient revenue and total operating expenses can be easily identified. Next, identify fixed operating expenses, which are those costs that generally do not change with volume within a defined range of capacity, such as space, most staffing, and utilities. Subtracting fixed expenses from total operating expenses provides total variable expenses, or those costs that are directly related to patient volume, such as medical supplies. Average variable expense per visit is calculated by dividing the total variable expenses by the number of patient visits. A baseline practice profile is illustrated in Table 9.1.

In the baseline example, the practice needs 2,028 annual visits to break even. Any additional visits contribute $81.38, or the difference between net revenue and variable expenses, to net income.

TABLE 9.1
Baseline Practice Profile

	Total Annual	Average per Visit
Patient visits fee-for-service	4,800	
Total net revenue	$480,000	$100.00
Fixed expenses	$165,000	$34.38
Variable expenses	$89,400	$18.62
Total practice expenses	$254,400	$53.00
Net income	$225,600	$47.00
Break-even visits	2,028	
Contribution to net income after break-even		$81.38

We can now develop scenarios to help evaluate the impact of changes in payer mix. In each scenario, we assume that the practice is at capacity with 4,800 visits, so new capitated patients represent a shift from fee-for-service business and are not incremental business to the practice.

Payer Mix Scenario 1: Shift to Capitation

Let's assume that 333 of the practice's patients shift to a capitated plan, and that a capitated patient has an average of three visits per year, for 1,000 total visits. The physician receives a capitation payment of $12 per member per month. The average revenue per visit under the capitated agreement is $48 ($12 per month times 12 months, divided by three visits), a substantial reduction from the fee-for-service average of $100. Therefore, the break-even number of visits for the practice increases to 2,339, as the overall average net revenue per visit decreases to $89.17. To maintain the fee-for-service break-even level of 2,028, the practice would need to reduce total costs significantly. However, even modest reductions in operating expenses can help compensate for the downward pressure of capitated contract rates on net revenue. In this scenario, total expenses are reduced by 10 percent through a combination of fixed and variable cost reductions. Scenario 1 is shown in Table 9.2.

As a medical practice shifts back from capitation to better paying fee-for-service business, it is important to remember two things:

1. Increasing revenue per visit does not mean costs should increase.
2. Be careful to maintain enough capitated business to average out the effect of a few high utilizers, or get out of capitation entirely.

TABLE 9.2
Shift to Capitation

	Total Annual with No Expense Reductions	Average per Visit with No Expense Reductions	Total Annual with Expense Reductions	Average per Visit with Expense Reductions
Patient visits: fee-for-service	3,800		3,800	
Patient visits: capitation	1,000		1,000	
Total net revenue	$428,000	$89.17	$428,000	$89.17
Fixed expenses	$165,000	$34.38	$148,500	$30.94
Variable expenses	$89,400	$18.62	$80,440	$16.76
Total practice expenses	$254,400	$53.00	$228,940	$47.70
Net income	$173,600	$36.17	$199,060	$41.47
Break-even visits	2,339		2,051	
Contribution to net income after break-even		$70.55		$72.41

Payer Mix Scenario 2: Maintain Practice Cost Savings

Hogan, Gordon, and Herron assume that the hospitalist or physician is able to decrease operating expenses by 10 percent. With the shift to capitated business, the practice's net income is $199,060. What happens if the practice's business shifts back to fee-for-service? If the costs revert back to the levels before cost savings were implemented, the practice's net income and break-even volume are the same as they were originally under the baseline scenario (see Table 9.1). If the practice is able to maintain the cost savings it experienced, however, then net income increases by $25,460, break-even volume decreases by 244 visits, and each visit above the break-even point contributes $83.24 to the bottom line. This is shown in Table 9.3.

Payer Mix Scenario 3: Manage the Level of Capitated Business

Physicians are paid a fixed amount per member per month to care for capitated patients. Capitation rates paid to the practice are determined actuarially based on demographics of the patient population covered, including their anticipated utilization of resources. When a practice has a significant number of capitated patients, the effects of a few high utilizers are usually offset by the utilization patterns of the rest of the population.

For example, if the average number of visits per year for a capitated patient is three, it is likely that a few patients will have more visits, but that most patients will visit the physician less frequently. In a practice with a large capitated population, the patients who visit the physician less frequently offset the additional use of resources (cost) required to care for the higher utilizers.

Assume the practice's capitated enrollment shifts mostly back to fee-for-service, so that only fifty capitated patients remain. Ten of those fifty are high utilizers, requiring ten visits per year. The contribution to net income drops by nearly half, from $31.24 to $15.97. As an extreme example, assume that only fifteen capitated patients remain and that ten of them are high utilizers. The contribution drops to only $2.02 per visit, barely enough to cover variable costs. The impact of this is shown in Table 9.4.

TABLE 9.3
Shift from Capitation to Fee-for-Service

	With Old Cost Structure	With New Cost Structure
Total visits	4,800	4,800
Net revenue	$480,000	$480,000
Total expenses	$254,400	$228,940
Net income	$225,600	$251,060
Break-even visits	2,028	1,784
Contribution to net income after break-even	$81.38	$83.24

TABLE 9.4
Revised Shift from Capitation to Fee-for-Service

	333 Capitated Patients	50 Capitated Patients	15 Capitated Patients
Capitated patient visits	1,000	220	115
Average visits per capitated patient	3.00	4.40	7.67
Annual capitation revenue	$48,000	$7,200	$2,160
Capitation revenue per visit	$48.00	$32.73	$18.78
Variable expense per visit	$16.76	$16.76	$16.76
Contribution to net income after break-even	$31.24	$15.97	$2.02

BREAK-EVEN ANALYSIS FOR CAPITATED CONTRACTS

Break-even analysis can be illustrated using Dr. Smith's office data:

	Per Patient	Percent
Revenue price	50	100
Variable expenses	30	60
Contribution margin	20	40

Equation Method:
X = *Break-even point in patients*
Revenues = Variable Expenses + Fixed Expenses + Profits
$\$50X = 30X + 8{,}000X + 0$
$\$20X = 8{,}000$
$X = 400$ patients or, in terms of revenue dollars, $\$50 \times 40 = \$20{,}000$

X = *Break-even point in dollars*
Revenues = Variable Expenses + Fixed Expenses + Profits
$X = 0.6X + \$8{,}000 + 0$
$0.4X = \$8{,}000$
$X = \$20{,}000$

Unfortunately, break-even analysis does not recognize cash flow. Cash break-even point (units) is equal to fixed costs minus non-cash outlay/contribution margin per unit, and cash break-even point (dollars) is fixed costs minus non-cash outlay/contribution margin ratio. Contribution margin per unit of the constrained resource is used to determine the most profitable short-term decisions.

Another critical business and moral issue in break-even analysis is the existence of multiple contribution margin ratios (see above) for different medical services. This means that multiple break-even points exist within each medical clinic for its unique service mix.

Net Target Profit Analysis

The above formulas used to compute the break-even point can also be used to determine the revenue volume needed to meet net target profit analysis figures.

Example

Assume that Dr. Smith would like to earn a minimum profit of $7,000 each month from his hospitalist practice. How many patients must be treated each month, at $50/patient, to reach his net target profit goal?

Equation Method:
X = *Number of patients to attain the target net profit*
Revenues = Variable Expenses + Fixed Expenses + Target Profits
$\$50X = 30X + \$8{,}000 + \$7{,}000$
$\$20X = 15{,}000$
$X = 75$ patients or, in terms of total revenue dollars, $\$50 \times 75 = \$3{,}750$

Margin of Safety

The **margin of safety** is the excess of budgeted or actual revenues over the break-even point in revenues. It demonstrates the amount by which revenues can drop before losses begin to be incurred.

The margin of safety can be expressed in either dollar form or percentage form, as seen in the following two equations:

$$\text{Total Revenues} - \text{Break-Even Revenues} = \text{Margin of Safety (dollars)}$$

or

$$\text{Margin of Safety (dollars) Divided by Total Revenues} = \text{Margin of Safety (percentage)}$$

OFFICE OPERATING LEVERAGE

Medical office operating leverage is a measure of the mix of variable and fixed costs in a medical practice. The formula to calculate the degree of operating leverage at a given level of revenues is as follows:

$$\text{Degree of Operating Leverage} = \text{Contribution Margin/Net Income}$$

The degree of operating leverage is useful when comparing two or more satellite medical clinics.

	Satellite Clinic #1		Satellite Clinic #2	
Revenues	$50,000	100%	$50,000	100%
Less variable expenses	35,000	70	10,000	20
Contribution margin	15,000	30	40,000	80
Less fixed expenses	9,000		34,000	
Net income	6,000		6,000	
Degree of leverage	**2.5**		**6.7**	

Furthermore, the degree of leverage can be used to predict the impact on net income of a given percentage revenue increase. For example, if the degree of leverage is 2.5 and there is a 10 percent increase in revenues, then net income will increase by 25 percent (i.e., 2.5 × 10 = 25%).

Example

Assume that each satellite clinic experiences a 10 percent increase in revenue.

	Satellite Clinic #1		Satellite Clinic #2	
Revenues	$55,000	100%	$55,000	100%
Less variable expenses	38,500	70	11,000	20
Contribution margin	16,500	30	44,000	80
Less fixed expenses	9,000		34,000	
Net income	7,500		10,000	
Degree of leverage	**2.2**		**4.4**	
Increase in net income	**22%**		**44%**	

Note: Be aware that the degree of leverage is not constant and changes with the level of revenues. Ordinarily, the degree of leverage declines as revenues increase. When profits, but not necessarily revenue, increase at a faster rate than costs, a high degree of leverage is said to exist.

STANDARD TREATMENT PROTOCOLS

Standard treatment protocols (STPs) are guidelines that reduce unnecessary variations (price rate, efficiency, volume, and intensity) in medical care and surgical treatment. They improve outcomes, eliminate redundancy, establish a clear line of communication for all caregivers, help reduce length of stay in hospitals, and reduce bad practices in outpatient care as well.

Goals and Objectives of STPs

- Raise quality and lower hospitalization costs by defining and standardizing best practices for a typical patient in a given DRG, or new medical severity-DRG (MS-DRG) category.
- Redesign care for patients within selected diagnoses meeting minimum structure standards.
- Eliminate unnecessary tests, procedures, interventions, and drugs, with standardized quality and cost limits.
- Integrate management of quality and cost to reach (charge/cost) models.
- Establish a benchmark that can be used to calculate actual cost, so contracting and negotiating can involve less guesswork.

Targeted Procedures

- High-volume procedures
- High-cost procedures
- High-risk procedures
- Multiple specialties involved
- Multiple nursing unit work
- Niche programs

In many respects, there is a similarity between medical contract break-even analysis, STPs, and standard job-costing sheets used in manufacturing accounting systems. In such a job-order cost system, a separate cost sheet is completed for each specific job, because each job is different from those performed in the past, or those that will be performed in the future. The cost sheet then serves as a bill or customer invoice.

Hospitals also operate in a job-cost setting, as patient bills vary significantly and reflect actual medical services rendered. Note, however, that in a typical manufacturing job-order cost setting, standards may not always be applied, as customers pay directly and there is no third-party payer incentive to do so. Of course, the private pay exceptions today are concierge medicine, consumer-directed healthcare plans, and retail health clinics.

Today, private pay is not the norm, as the majority of hospitals, medical providers, and healthcare firms are paid a fixed fee or negotiated fee schedule. Those who have accepted capitation contracts face the additional problem of total costs because it is now a function of both utilization and episodic care. Like a manufacturer's warranty, healthcare entities must now determine both the frequency and average cost of medical claims.

CAPITATION IMPACT ANALYSIS: EXPERIENCES, ATTITUDES, AND PREDICTORS

Given the explosive expansion of capitated reimbursement for the services of primary care physicians, a national survey of practitioners was undertaken in the early 2000s to measure attitudes toward capitated payment and to identify predictors of important attitudes. Descriptive, factor analysis, and regression analysis techniques were used. The response rate was 54 percent.

As measured by scales derived from factor analysis, perceptions were strong that capitation was costly to professional and patient relationships. Patients' access to care was perceived by all concerned to be slightly reduced. Actual participation in capitation attenuated feelings of lack of access but not those of capitation's costly effects.

Interestingly, physicians' attitudes toward capitation remain negative today, as its economic burden is shifted back to them, yet patients now perceive their access to appropriate medical care as reasonable; hence its re-emergence.

Evolution of the Domestic Healthcare Payment System

Self-Pay	→	Indemnity Insurance	→	Capitation
1st Party		3rd Party		2nd Party
Patients		*Governments/Insurance Companies*		*Providers*

Finally, as third-party health insurance premiums climb, and as first-party private-pay concierge and retail medicine models evolve, employers continue to compress payer reimbursements. For example, capitation interest is robust in states like California, New York, Florida, Texas, Ohio, Pennsylvania, Maryland, and Michigan because of the politically democratic view that the domestic healthcare system needs to be overhauled. Healthcare costs on the west coast are substantially lower than on the east coast, while the health of the population is marginally better. Corporate America is taking notice that the amount of money spent is not proportional to services received from second-party medical providers.

As consultants like Rachel Pentin-Maki, RN, MHA, of Atlanta, Georgia, say, "Healthcare organization CXOs [chief-level officers] who think that budgets [fixed or flexible] are not necessary are not realistic. There is nothing more sacred to any business entity than a budget, where costs can be estimated, predicted, and benchmarked—and that's called medical capitation" (pers. comm.).

NEGOTIATION AND MANAGED CARE CONTRACTING

The need for contracting and negotiating proficiency is a concept integrated with CVPA, and CXOs of all mature healthcare facilities and EHOs should embrace this idea for its impact on profitability.

Few doctors or EHOs negotiate directly with managed care organizations (MCOs). Rather, they allow managers, medical networks, independent physician associations, CXOs, or other third parties to negotiate for them. Unfortunately, this usually results in low compensation and a lump sum monthly payment to the network, which is then divided among the participating providers on a distributed or pro rata basis. Even more unfavorable is the fact that this mechanism merely accentuates the concept of "managed competition," as the practitioners work feverishly in true competitive fashion to acquire a larger share of a diminishing pie. As a result, the per-patient unit revenue for each procedure performed is actually reduced, using this so-called "capitated risk pool" methodology.

CONTRACT NEGOTIATION OBJECTIVES

Objectives of the medical contract negotiating process are threefold:

1. Acquiring and maintaining a long-term relationship with your MCO, HMO, or insurance payer
2. Exerting some control over the manner in which the contract is constructed
3. Receiving maximum cooperation and a fair price for medical services rendered

Although prioritized as last, the concept of price is the real emotional "trigger point" for almost all medical contract negotiation, and most sophisticated physician executives and administrators realize that it is merely one component of the entire payer–provider relationship.

Obviously, the above concepts suggest that over 90 percent of the time involved in a successful negotiation must be invested in preparing for the actual deliberation. For example, the physician executive (seller of medical services) must:

- Have a technical understanding of all anticipated provided medical services
- Conduct a cost analysis of these services with the use of managerial accounting principles

- Analyze the payer's relative bargaining position by means of a classic marketing concept known as a SWOT evaluation; in this technique, the insurance payer's (S)trengths, (W)eaknesses, (O)pportunities, and (T)hreats are objectively considered in relation to your own

TYPES OF CONTRACTS

The type of contracts obtained from an MCO or insurance company might include sub-capitation, self-tracking, or a discount plan.

Sub-Capitated Contract

The often contentious dilemma of "carve-outs" from capitated managed care contracts is abating in some parts of the country, just as it is accelerating in others. Under this scenario, medical services or products such as surgery, trauma, physical therapy, eye care, immunizations, certain tests, wound care, or prosthetic devices may be excluded from a managed care contract in favor of another, often sub-capitated, provider. However, if your organization is contemplating a sub-capitated contract, consider the following scenarios.

For example, an orthopedic group notes that foot surgery is listed in a new capitation contract that it is considering. The group is not comfortable with such surgery, and they ask that these services be excluded. Because the contract provider will not exclude the surgery, the orthopedist group either has to accept it and perform unfamiliar surgery, or reject the contract provider.

In another example, a primary care group notes that allergy testing and related services are included in their contract proposal. Because these services are not in their area of expertise, they negotiate to have them deleted, reducing the capitation rate accordingly (Figure 9.3).

Thus, the following are conditions considered important for carved or sub-capitated risk contracts:

- Equivalent risk for the provider and sub-capitated specialist
- Fixed expenses for the sub-capitated specialist
- Predictable and low cost of care, per specialty episode
- High episodes of specialty care (not unusual or unpredictable events)
- Definable and understood responsibilities of the specialist

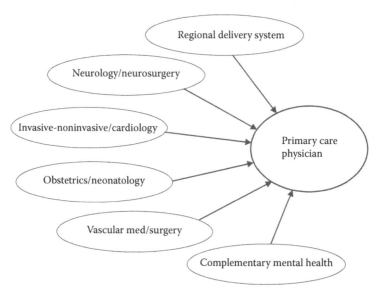

FIGURE 9.3   Medical care carve-outs in a sub-capitated reimbursement system contract.

- Profit and cost savings potential for both the referring and specialty provider
- Existence of re-insurance

Self-Tracking Managed Care Plans

A self-tracking managed care plan is similar to an incentive bonus payment for achieving targets in certain key areas, such as patient satisfaction, access to care, emergency room utilization, mammography rates, diabetes testing, well-baby care with immunizations, colorectal cancer screening rates, etc.

To meet quality targets and hit bonus levels (typically 5 to 10 percent) of self-tracking plans, a new practice philosophy is required. This might include using computerized patient databases to track patients, sending reminder notices to patients, or partnering with plans to obtain lists of patients needing care, along with flow sheets, guidelines, patient education materials, and other tools. Simple fee-for-service methodology includes:

- Recording patient payment charges at the usual office rate
- Posting patient and plan payments to the specific client ledger account
- Posting withholding amounts, which represent adjustments to the account, and a credit (if any) to an account for the specific plan
- Posting the remaining amount as a contractual adjustment from the patient account
- Making the patient account balance zero out, as the account is increased by the amount of any withholdings
- Calculating collection percentages for the plan and benchmarking them with other financial classes

Example

PATIENT ACCOUNT

	Charges	Payments	Adjustments	Balance
	$50	$10		$40
Payment		$23	$2 withholding	$15
			$15 disallowed	
Plan account:	($2)	$2		

CAPITATION DISCOUNT PAYMENTS

Under the earlier fee-for-service payment scheme, doctors were compensated in the traditional fee-for-service, indemnity insurance system, which included:

- Payment per patient visit, per procedure, and per treatment
- Payment per hospital visit, per surgical and diagnostic intervention
- À la carte medical menu

In this system, patients are regarded as assets, not as liabilities; doctors are their advocates, and costs are not controlled. Now, compare and contrast how doctors are compensated under a capitated payment system. Financial danger and opportunity are joined for doctor, facility, and hospital alike:

- Per member/per month/per year/per contract/per life
- Fixed price medical menu

In this system, patients represent liabilities; doctors may become adversaries of patients, not advocates, and costs are controlled.

MANAGED CARE CONTRACT PITFALLS

There are several key pitfalls to watch out for when evaluating a managed care organization contract, as noted and continually revised by the Advisory Board Company (*Capitation strategy,* 1995).

- **Profitability:** Less than 52 percent of all senior physician executives know whether their managed care contracts are profitable. *Many simply sign up and hope for the best.*
- **Financial data:** 90 percent of all executives said the ability to obtain financial information was valuable, yet only 50 percent could obtain the needed data.
- **Information technology (IT):** IT hardware and sophisticated software are needed to gather, evaluate, and interpret clinical and financial data, yet it is typically *unavailable to the solo or small group practice.*
- **Underpayments:** This rate is typically between 3 to 10 percent and is usually "left on the table."
- **Cash flow forecasting:** MCO contracting will soon begin yearly (or longer) compensation disbursements, *causing significant cash flow problems to many physicians.*
- **Stop-loss minimums:** These are one-time, up-front premium charges for stop-loss insurance. However, if the contract is prematurely terminated, you may not receive a pro rata refund unless you ask for it.
- **Automatic contract renewals:** These "evergreen" contracts automatically renew unless one party objects. This is convenient for both the payer and payee, but it may result in overlapping renewal and re-negotiation deadlines. Hence, a contract may be continued on a sub-optimal basis, to the detriment of the providers.
- **Eliminate retroactive denials:** Eliminate the rejection of claims that were either directly or indirectly approved initially. Example: The MCO reserves the right to perform utilization review (prospective, retrospective, or concurrent) and to adjust or deny payments for medically inappropriate services.
- **Define "clean" and "dirty" claims:** Eliminate the rejection of standard medical claim formats like CMS-1450, CMS-1500, or UB-92 for non-material reasons. Make payment of appropriate clean claims within some specific time period, such as 30 days, to enhance free cash flows.
- **Reject silent or faux HMOs or preferred provider organizations (PPOs), etc.:** Eliminate leased medical networks or affiliates and reject further payment discounts to larger subscriber cohorts than originally anticipated.
- **Include terms for health IT:** Eliminate the economic risk of leading edge electronic advancements like electronic medical records, personal health records, computerized provider order entry systems, and so on.
- **Establish ability to recover payments after contract termination:** Eliminate financial carry forward for an excessive period of time.
- **Preserve payment ability:** Provide medical services if requested by patients, who are then billed directly.
- **Minimize differentials:** Establish a standardized rate structure (fee schedule) for all plans and then grant discounts for administrative or other efficiencies, rather than have different schedules for each individual plan.

APPEALING DISENROLLMENT DECISIONS

The decision by an HMO or managed care plan to not include your healthcare organization in their plan or network, or dis-enroll you if already included, is not irrevocable. You may not have been included, or may have been rejected, for any number of reasons, including clinical or economic re-credentialing, malpractice history, unfavorable patient survey, certification, or a host of other tangible or intangible reasons. Therefore, to appeal the decision, the following guidelines are suggested in any request for a reconsideration process.

- Obtain a letter of explanation from the medical or clinical executive director.
- Ensure your initial application went through the proper channels of consideration.
- Contact your local plan representative, in person, if possible.
- Make sure your state and national medical affiliations are current, as well as hospital and surgical center staffing applications and credentials.
- Write a letter to the medical director and send it by U.S. Postal Service with a return receipt or by private carrier.

Inform the director of the actions you are taking to become more attractive to the plan or what you have done to correct the deficiencies that initially caused your non-inclusion.

USEFUL PATTERNS AND TREND INFORMATION

Knowing your contract negotiation objectives, gathering information on the choices of contract and discount payment system you may need, and understanding the pitfalls to watch for when evaluating a contract are the keys to any successful negotiation process. According to the *Managed Care Digest Series* for 2004–2005, the following pattern and trend comparative information has been empirically determined and may provide a basic starting point for the process for three or more practitioners to share business management, facilities, personnel, and records (Managed Care Digest Series 2012).

Procedural Utilization Trends
- Among all physicians in a single-specialty group practice, invasive cardiologists averaged the most encounters with total hospital inpatient admissions, down from the prior year. However, encounters rose for cardiologists in multi-specialty group practices.
- Echocardiography was the most commonly performed procedure for HMO seniors, followed by coronary artery bypass graft surgery. Group practices performed cardiovascular stress tests for circulatory problems most often.
- Computed tomography imaging of the brain and chest were the most common studies for HMO seniors, while magnetic resonance imaging of the head was the most common diagnostic test performed for commercial HMO members.
- Colonoscopy was the most common digestive system procedure for senior HMO members, while barium enemas were more common for commercial members.
- Hospital admission volume decreased for allergists, family practitioners, internists, obstetricians/gynecologists (OB/GYN), pediatricians, and general surgeons.
- Internists ordered more in-hospital laboratory procedures than any other physicians in single-specialty groups.
- Non-hospital medical doctors and doctors of osteopathy used in-hospital radiology services most frequently, continuing a three-year upward trend.
- Pediatricians averaged the most ambulatory encounters, down from the prior year.
- Non-hospitalist internists ordered a higher number of in-hospital laboratory procedures than any other single medical specialty group, but allergists and immunologists increased their laboratory usage.
- The number of ambulatory encounters increased for general surgeons, while group surgeons had the most cases. Capitated surgeons, of all types, had a lower mean number of surgical cases than surgeons in groups without capitation. Surgeons in internal medical groups also had more cases than those in multi-specialty groups.

- The average number of total office visits per commercial and senior HMO visits fell, along with the number of institutional visits for both commercial and senior HMO members.
- The average length of hospital stay for all commercial HMO members increased to 3.6 days, but for all HMO members this statistic decreased to 6 days.
- The total number of births increased for commercial HMO members served by medical group practices, and decreased for solo practitioners.

Treatment, Protocol, Quality, and Satisfaction Trends

- More than one-third of all medical groups use STPs, an increase from the year before. Multi-specialty groups were more likely to use them than single-specialty groups, who often develop their own protocols. The use of industry benchmarks to judge the quality of healthcare delivery also increased.
- Outcome studies are most common at larger medical groups, and multi-specialty groups pursue quality assurance activities more often than single-specialty groups.
- Provider interaction during office visits is increasingly coming under scrutiny. Patients approve of cardiologists more frequently than allergists and ophthalmologists.

Mid-Level Provider and Staffing Trends

- Mid-level provider use increased among multi-specialty groups, especially in those with more than half of their revenue from capitated contracts. Use also rose with the size of the practice and was highest with OB/GYN groups.
- Medical support staff for all multi-specialty groups fell and was lowest in medical groups with fewer than ten full-time equivalent physicians. However, groups with a large amount of capitated revenue actually added support staff. Smaller groups limited support staff.
- Compensation costs of support staff increased, and the percentages of total operating costs associated with laboratories, professional liability insurance, IT services, and imaging also increased. Support staff costs increase with capitation levels, and more than half of all operating costs are tied to support staff endeavors.

Managed Care Activity and Contracting Trends

- More medical group practices are likely to own interests in PPOs than in HMOs, and the percentages of groups with managed care revenue continues to rise. Multi-specialty and large groups also derive more revenue from MCOs than single-specialty or smaller groups.
- Managed care has little effect on physician payment methods that are still predominantly based on productivity. Physicians were paid differently for at-risk managed care contracts in only a small percentage of cases.
- Most medical groups (75 percent) participating in managed care medicine have PPO contracts. Group practices contract with network HMOs more often than solo practices. Single-specialty groups more often have PPO contracts.
- Capitated lives often raise capitation revenues in large group practices. Group practices are more highly capitated than smaller groups or solo practices. Almost 30 percent of highly capitated medical groups have more than fifteen contracts, and 22 percent have globally capitated contracts.
- Higher capitation is linked with increased risk contracting. Larger groups have more risk contracting than smaller groups.

Financial Profile Trends

- Medicare fee-for-service reimbursement is decreasing. Highly capitated groups incur high consulting fees.
- The share of total gross charges for OB/GYN groups associated with managed care at-risk contracts is rising, while non-managed care or not-at-risk charges are declining.

- Capitated contracts have little effect on the amount of on-site, office non-surgical work. Off-site surgeries are most common for surgery groups, not medical groups.
- Half of all charges are for on-site non-surgical procedures.
- Highly capitated medical groups have higher operating costs and lower net profits.
- Groups without capitation have higher laboratory expenses than those with capitation.
- Physician costs are highest in orthopedic surgery group practices. Generally, median costs at most specialty levels are rising and profits shrinking.

Obviously, the above information is only a gauge because regional differences, and certain medical sub-specialty practices and carve-outs, do exist. For example, after a period of time on any specific MCO contract, you may wish to perform your own annual utilization summary, as shown in this example.

Example

To more effectively evaluate the financial potential of a managed care contract, the following simple spreadsheet may be employed.

Patient Visits/Net Revenue	$ Amount Estimated	$ Amount Received
Current patients		
New patients		
Old patients		
Total visits or procedures		
Visits/current patients		
Total net revenue		
Net revenue		
Current patient		

THE NEGOTIATION PROCESS

Once the numbers are crunched, the formal negotiation process with the MCO consists of a five-step sequence, according to Professors Bruce Patton and William Ury of the Harvard Business School:

1. Do not bargain over positions. Taking them only makes matters worse because egos often become identified with positions. Is it harder to rob a friend or a stranger?
2. Separate the people from the process before considering the substantive problem. Figuratively, if not literally, both parties should come to see each other as working side by side, attacking the problem, not each other.
3. Invent options for mutual gain, because having a lot at stake narrows your vision and inhibits creativity. Brainstorm possible solution options that advance shared interests and creatively reconcile differences.
4. Insist on using objective criteria rather than discussing what the parties are willing, or not willing, to accept. These standards can be a matter of custom, law, informed opinion, or market value.
5. Know your bottom line limit, and recognize that you do not have to come to an agreement in each and every situation. Therefore, you must know your best alternative to a negotiated agreement, and be prepared to say "no" and walk away. (Ury, Fisher, and Patton 1991)

Furthermore, financial steps to successfully negotiating capitated medical contracts will involve the following key elements: developing a pricing model; using effective negotiation skills; incorporating protective contract clauses; and monitoring, implementing, and renegotiating the contract as needed.

DEVELOP AN ACCURATE PRICING MODEL

MCOs use a number of methods to pay capitated medical contracts.

- **Per member/per month (pm/pm):** The best known, if not most popular, method. The Advisory Board Company reported their results of a survey of 60 percent commercial HMO pm/pm rates. Compare them with current rates today and then project them into the near future for your specialty (Managed Care Digest Series 2012). The following spreadsheet example illustrates how different capitation rates may be determined:

A	B	C	D	E
Utilization Rate	Charge/Service	Cost /1000 Members	Cost/Member (annual)	pm/pm
	(A × B)	(C/1000)	(D/12)	
20%	$32	$640	$0.64	$0.053
50%	$88	$4,400	$4.40	$0.366
90%	$88	$7,920	$7.92	$0.666

For full risk-capitated care, the following comprehensive healthcare pm/pm of $120/month for the average commercial HMO plan breaks down into costs divided into components something like this:
- $10–$20 for office and administration expenses
- $8–$12 for carve-outs and stop-loss insurance
- $5–$10 for drugs and pharmaceuticals
- $80–$90 for medical care:
    - primary physicians and/or specialists: $20–$40
    - surgery centers and hospitals: $35–$50

Obviously, payments to all of the above cost drivers are decreasing over time.

- **Percent (net) of premium method:** Medical service payment is directly proportional to the MCO insurance premium and indexed for inflation or deflation. This is analogous to a Social Security Cost of Living Allowance (COLA) for the medical provider, whose compensation will increase or decrease in proportion to the medical coverage premium charged to the insureds (i.e., a form of risk sharing with the MCO).
- **Single or family coverage:** Family size, medical acuity, and other assumptions are compared to the entire MCO contract and pro-rated accordingly.
- **Average blended HMO population:** A subset of small group assumptions is integrated within the larger MCO entity and pro-rated accordingly.

USE EFFECTIVE NEGOTIATION SKILLS

The general negotiation skills advocated by the Harvard Business School are effective when beginning to negotiate an MCO contract. The following suggestions are also excellent tips for effectively negotiating payment agreements.

- **Do not get emotional, upset, or angry ... stay cool!:** Although financial negotiations are a vitally important matter to you, it is probably just another job to your MCO opponent. She will likely negotiate with many doctors, and you are not important enough for her to get upset about. Do the same with her, and stay cool.
- **Do not get personal or lose your dignity:** No one will respect an angry, loud, or abusive doctor. This type of behavior will not only fail to get you a raise, but you may be delisted

from the plan because one can reasonably infer that your patients might be treated in the same impolite manner as your MCO counterpart.

- **Do not share your information:** If you have good results or outcomes with a particular treatment protocol, do not share them with the plan unless they sign a non-disclosure, non-compete, or no-sale agreement with you. Get information before you give information that might later be used against you.

- **The first offer should not be the last offer:** Even if you "split the price difference," you might not receive a better financial deal. On the other hand, the initial offer was likely so low that even a "split" would benefit the MCO, so be careful. Splitting the difference is not negotiation.

- **Stand firm and await counteroffers:** Once you have performed the calculations to determine your bottom line, do not settle for less because you will likely be offered less next time. Be aware of your best alternatives.

- **Leave something on the table:** If you give something in return for getting something, you will foster a continuing relationship with your MCO plan. For example, you might accept a slightly lower pm/pm rate in exchange for a "diabetic carve-out." In an older geographic neighborhood, this might be a better deal for you because wound or ulcer care is expensive. Your opponent can then go back to his or her supervisor and brag about "putting one over on you" by getting a lower capitation rate! In other words, you both get bragging rights.

- **Do not be afraid of calculated risks:** Partial or full risk, fixed based medical capitation is the wave of the future. So is the corporate practice of medicine seen in professional practice management corporations. Do not be foolhardy, but those who take calculated and informed risks will prosper, while conservative types will not.

- **Do not give your MCO opponent too much credit:** Your opponent may know nothing about your area of medical specialty, so do not give him information about your practice or profession to use against other colleagues. You might just know more about managed care than he does.

- **Take your time—time is usually on your side:** Unless you have no practice accounts receivable reserves, are a new practitioner, cannot get a line of credit, or are really destitute, you probably have time on your side to negotiate a deal in your favor. Simple procrastination will often increase your capitation or fee rates.

- **Use a professional negotiator or Certified Medical Planner™ advisor if you are uncomfortable:** Although professional negotiators and business specialists may be expensive in the short run, you may gain much more in the long run by using them, especially if they are knowledgeable. If you have been unhappy with your own results to date, by all means get professional assistance.

INCORPORATE PROTECTIVE CONTRACT CLAUSES

Protective or "safe harbor" contract clauses are designed to help clarify the appropriateness of percentage-based MCO contract arrangements and include termination, renegotiation, catastrophic, solicitation, non-disclosure, non-compete, gag order, and solicitation clauses.

The anti-kickback or "safe harbor" clauses make it a criminal offense to knowingly and willfully offer, pay, solicit, or receive any remuneration to induce the referral of business covered by a federal healthcare program (Medicare and Medicaid).

According to the Office of Inspector General (OIG), in Opinion 98-4,* a percentage-based MCO contract would only qualify for the personal services and management contracts "safe harbor," and it would be suspect if it did not meet all six of the following "safe harbor" regulations:

---

* Opinion 98-4 was generated by a request from a single physician. All medical practitioners are entitled to seek an OIG opinion on individual contract arrangements.

1. The agreement is set out in writing and signed by the parties involved.
2. The agreement specifies the services to be performed.
3. If the services are performed on a part-time basis, the schedule for performance is specified in the contract.
4. The agreement is for not less than one year.
5. The aggregate amount of compensation is fixed in advance, based on fair market value in an arms-length transaction, and not determined in a manner that takes into account the volume or value of any referrals or business otherwise generated between the parties for which payment may be made by Medicare or a state healthcare program.
6. The services performed under the agreement do not involve the promotion of business that violates any federal or state law.

Other important clauses to consider include: indemnification clauses, procedural carve-outs, low enrollment guarantees, utilization rate kick-outs, drug or formulary clauses, risk pool limitation clauses, doctor/member ratio requirements, "all or none" group clauses, stop-loss re-insurance, as well as arbitration and mediation clauses in your home state.

MONITOR, IMPLEMENT, AND RENEGOTIATE THE DEAL

Ongoing total quality improvement and management evaluation, payment schedules, medical and economic credentialing, as well as financial ratio analysis should be done quarterly with MCO administrators to ensure that the contract you originally signed is meeting the expectations of all concerned. For example, the following scheme may be used to assess your contract(s) utilization and net revenue(s).

Projected Utilization and Net Revenue	
First step: Calculate potential available patients	
Total patients covered	30,000
Total patients in service perimeter	12,000
Potential available patients	12,000
Second step: Determine (MD) provider competition	
Total panel of MD providers	6
Total MDs in service perimeter	2
Potential MD options (competition)	2
Third step: Determine estimated patient volume	
Visits/1000 patients/year	50
× Potential available	12
= Total visits/patients	600
Total visits/potential patients	600
Divided by potential MD options	2
= Potential patient volume (visits/year)	300
Fourth step: Calculate projected net $ revenue	
Potential Utilization (visits/year)	300
× Projected net revenue/visit	$50
= Projected net revenue/year	$15,000

Source: InterStudy, *Modern Physician*. January 2000.

As HMOs are themselves increasingly coming under their own cost pressures, many are willing to negotiate complementary or alternative healthcare modalities as part of a benefits program (e.g., weight and stress management, nutritional services, biofeedback, herbal medicines, meditation, and yoga) (InterStudy 2000).

Other benefits programs include:

- **Acupuncture:** Treatment of a condition by influencing points on meridians, or "lines of energy" known as the chi, which interconnect across the body surface and relate to major organs of the body; performed by the insertion of fine needles.
- **Alexander technique:** Movement awareness and the re-education of that movement to relieve long-term muscular stresses.
- **Aromatherapy:** Specialized technique incorporating essential oils that are individually chosen for each treatment.
- **Biomagnetics:** Electronic magnetic intervention.
- **Bowen technique:** A treatment consisting of a specific sequence of gentle, rolling "moves" done across superficial muscles, tendons, and nerves that realign the body and balance and stimulate energy flow.
- **Chinese medicine/herbalism:** One of the oldest systems of herbal therapy in the world; treats a wide range of conditions with the use of raw herbs as well as a vast array of prepared or patent medicines available in pill and powder form.
- **Dietary:** Treatment of disorders and diseases using specific substances to correct or prevent an imbalance and to correct daily nutrition; it allows for biochemical balance to be achieved through supplementation that can be maintained with the daily diet.
- **Homoeopathy:** A form of natural healing based on the Law of Similars, which states "like cures like"; for example, a homoeopathic remedy that could produce sick symptoms in a healthy person might cure those same symptoms in a sick person.
- **Hydrotherapy:** Water-based treatment for muscular strains and sprains, muscular fatigue, and backache; also useful in physiotherapy because patients who exercise in a buoyant medium can move weak parts of their bodies without contending with the strong force of gravity.
- **Hypnotherapy:** A method of lulling the conscious mind to reach the subconscious. When the subconscious is spoken to directly, old patterns and conditioning are re-programmed and new ideas and positive suggestions are introduced; these positive suggestions are then used to help make the desired changes.
- **Kinesiology:** The study of body movement that identifies factors that block the body's natural healing process; dysfunctions are treated at reflex and acupressure points, and treatment uses specific body movements.
- **Manual healing:** See massage therapy.
- **Massage therapy:** A system of physical treatment aimed at alleviating tissue congestion.
- **Myotherapy:** A method of relaxing muscle spasm, improving circulation, and alleviating pain; to defuse "trigger points," pressure is applied to the muscle for several seconds by means of fingers, knuckles, and elbows.
- **Naturopath:** A wide range of diagnostic techniques used to assess causative factors; treatment may involve dietary changes, herbal medicines, homeopathy, or nutritional supplements.
- **Reflexology:** A system of manipulation of pressure points in the feet; it is believed that, by stimulating these points, healing mechanisms can be activated.
- **Remedial massage:** A blend of approved, scientific massage techniques promoting efficiency in the body's systems that in turn enhances the functioning of the entire person.
- **Shiatsu:** The traditional Japanese technique of diagnosis and treatment in which the thumbs and the palms of the hand are used to apply deep pressure to certain points to stimulate specific areas, clearing blockages and restoring the flow of energy to the body.
- **Western herbalism:** Classical herbal medicine utilizes the Hippocratic principles of treating the person, not the disease. It evaluates the patient's lifestyle and the emotional, circumstantial environment of the patient, not just the physical symptoms. Individually applicable herbal extracts and tinctures are then prescribed.

If you do not inquire about these types of complementary and alternative healthcare methods, you will not be able to negotiate for them in your next MCO insurance contract (Harvard Pilgrim Health Care 2012).

MEDICAL CONTRACT STANDARDS

The conversion to managed healthcare and capitation financing is a significant marketing force and not merely a temporary business trend. More than 60 percent of all physicians in the country are now employees of an MCO, and more the 5 percent are members of a professional practice management corporation. Those that embrace these forces will thrive, while those opposed will not.

After you have evaluated the HMOs in your geographic area, you must then make your practice more attractive to them, because there are far too many physicians in most regions today. The following issues are considered by most MCO financial managers and business experts as they decide whether to include any doctor or practice in their network:

GENERAL STANDARDS

- Is there a local or community need for your practice, with a sound patient base that is not too small or large? Remember, practices that already have a significant number of patients have some form of leverage because MCOs know that patients do not like switching their primary care doctors or pediatricians, and women do not want to be forced to change their OB/GYN specialist. If the group leaves the plan, members may complain to their employers and give a negative impression of the plan.
- A positive return on investment from your economically sound practice is important to MCOs because they wish to continue their relationship with you. This often means it is difficult for younger practitioners to enter a plan, because plan actuaries realize that there is a high attrition rate among new practitioners. They also realize that more established practices have high overhead costs and may enter into less lucrative contract offerings just to pay the bills.
- A merger or acquisition is a strategy for the MCO internal business plan that affords a seamless union should a practice decide to sell out or consolidate at a later date. Therefore, a strategy should include considerations such as strong managerial and cost accounting principles, a group identity rather than individual mindset, profitability, transferable systems and processes, a corporate form of business, and a vertically integrated organization if the practice is a multi-specialty group.
- Human resources, capital, and IT service should complement the existing management information system framework. This is often difficult for the solo or small group practice and may indicate the need to consolidate with similar groups to achieve needed economies of scale and capital, especially in areas of high MCO penetration.
- Consolidated financial statements should conform to generally accepted accounting principles (GAAP), Internal Revenue Code (IRC), Office of the Inspector General (OIG), and other appraisal standards.
- Strong and respected medical doctor leadership in the medical and business community is an asset. MCOs prefer to deal with physician executives with advanced degrees. You may not need a MBA, CMP™, or CPA, but you should be familiar with basic business, managerial, and financial principles. This includes a conceptual understanding of horizontal and vertical integration, cost principles, cost–volume analysis, financial ratio analysis, and cost behavior.
- The doctors on staff should be willing to treat all conditions and types of patients. The adage "more risk equates to more reward" is still applicable, and most groups

should take all the full risk contracting they can handle, providing they are not pooled contracts.

- Are you a team player or solo act? The former personality type might do better in a group or MCO-driven practice, while a fee-for-service market is still possible and may be better suited to the latter personality type.
- Each member of a physician group, or a solo doctor, should have a valid license, U.S. Drug Enforcement Administration narcotics license, continuing medical education, adequate malpractice insurance, board qualification or certification, hospital privileges, and agree with the managed care philosophy; each partner in a group practice should meet all the same participation criteria. Be available for periodic MCO review by a company representative.

SPECIFIC MEDICAL OFFICE STANDARDS

MCOs will require that the following standards are maintained in the medical office setting:

- It is clean and presentable with a professional appearance.
- It is readily accessible and has a barrier-free design (see Occupational Safety and Health Administration [OSHA] requirements).
- There is appropriate medical emergency and resuscitation equipment.
- The waiting room can accommodate five to seven patients with private changing areas.
- There is an adequate capacity (e.g., 5,000–10,000 member minimum), business plan, and office assistants for the plan.
- There is an office hour minimum (e.g., 20 hours/week).
- Round the clock, on-call coverage is available, with electronic tracking.
- There are MCO-approved sub-contractors.

STANDARD MANAGED CARE CONTRACT QUESTIONS

The nine following managed care contracting questions should be answered before any negotiations or re-negotiations are considered.

Question 1

What does the practice or medical clinic do really well?

Is there a particular procedure the practice or clinic is really good at, and, because it is so good at it, can the practice or clinic save a managed care payer certain healthcare costs?

What are those healthcare cost savings, if known?

Question 2

How cost effective is the practice or clinic in the delivery of its medical care to a managed care payer's patients?

Example: lower length of stay in the hospital; fewer surgeries as a percentage of office visits because the practice tries to manage care first before going to the operating room; fewer orders for ancillaries and drugs; fewer complications after surgery; etc.

Question 3

Does the practice or clinic receive the majority of referrals from a managed care payer's primary care physicians?

If so, how many patients from the payer did the practice or clinic treat in 2012?

We are trying to find out a percentage of the payer's enrollees that are actually treated by the practice's physicians.

Question 4

Are there any clinical services that can only be rendered by a physician in the practice? Please provide a list of these sub-specialty services.

We are looking for sub-specialty services here. In other words, is this practice or clinic the only place a patient can obtain care for a certain specialty problem?

Question 5

Does the practice or clinic have or use sub-specialists? If so, please provide a name or names.

Are there any other sub-specialists in the service area who are not members of the practice? If so, please provide their names.

If sub-specialty care is not provided, where would the patients have to be sent for care (city and hospital, if known)?

Question 6

Are there any problems with patient access to the clinic or practice? How quickly can a patient get in to see a doctor?

If access can be provided, what is the practice's patients' attitude towards it?

Have you recently conducted a patient satisfaction survey? If so, please provide a summary of the results.

Question 7

If the practice or clinic were to terminate a managed care contract, do you think the payer would still have enough specialty doctors remaining on its panel to service its enrollees?

If yes, would a patient have any difficulty gaining access to these competitors of the practice?

For example, would a patient have to drive very far to see one of these doctors; would a patient have trouble making an appointment with a competing practice or clinic?

Question 8

Are there any other benefits the practice thinks it brings to a managed care payer's provider network not mentioned above? Please list.

Question 9

In a contract negotiation, what Current Procedural Terminology (CPT®) code reimbursement rates are of the most concern to you? Please list and prioritize.

Which contract terms are most important to you?

MICRO-CAPITATION

More than a few medical providers and healthcare facilities have a natural aversion to capitated reimbursement, as it has always been associated with the worst components of managed care: hurried office visits and soul less physicians.

In the early 2000s, astute physician executives and healthcare administrators were averse to the idea that they should accept pre-payment for unknown commitments to provide an unknown amount of services. It seemed to create an unnatural and difficult set of incentives where fewer patients were seen and less care rendered for more compensation.

Curiously, Stark Laws I, II, and III were created to eliminate concerns that self-referral could lead to excessive care and fee-for-service payments, though this system had long been perfectly acceptable. Many also never understood how a commitment could be made with little or no actuarial information. Hence frustration was the initial reaction of many medical providers to capitated reimbursement.

Since that time, it can be seen that capitation has some advantages, as our cost accounting information has demonstrated. For example, it can create and align incentives that help patients, providers, and payers by limiting their contingent fiscal liabilities. Capitation might be viewed in a more positive way going forward.

MEDICAL CARE PACKAGES

When capitation is focused on discrete medical conditions, or on subsets of clinical conditions rather than through CPT or MS-DRG activities, it is delivered in more discrete "medical care packages." This creates a true healthcare marketplace where price, quality, and medical outcomes can be compared side by side, or provider by provider, or facility by facility.

The discrete services provided by vertically or virtually integrated medical teams would enable a new level and degree of expertise. High-volume providers would develop additional experience, which would enable them to introduce innovations and efficiencies in a classic economies-of-scale cycle. With the additional delivery and outcomes experience, providers would be much more willing to put out a set fee for a set grouping of clinical services, because they would have some confidence in their ability to deliver care for that price. Philosophically, this is still capitation, but it is a finer "micro-capitation" at the medical condition level (lowest common unit of care delivery that can be measured), not at the gross CPT code or MS-DRG level.

To emphasize the concept, the term *micro-capitation* was coined by Dr. Scott L. Shreve in 2008. It makes sense because it is for a definable, controllable, and limited set of clinical activities in which providers can, with confidence, provide services for a set fee. Micro-capitation delivered in smaller care packages will be a critical new clinical service product as we make the transition toward a futuristic competitive marketplace (D.E. Marcinko pers. comm.).

Micro-capitation around specific medical conditions or acute episodes of care also provides a manageable unit of healthcare delivery in which we can develop the appropriate care linkages across all provider lines and form a team to deliver a full episode of care. It represents a properly sized clinical effort in which the appropriate healthcare infrastructure allows for better outcomes measurement, monitoring, comparison, and ultimately consumption in a competitive healthcare marketplace.

The marketplace today is taking a fresh look at capitation exposure and is attempting to control economic risk by moving to discrete micro-capitated care packages or bundles that can be understood, measured, and marketed.

ACUTE EPISODES OF CARE

A related packaged medical care concept, called "acute episodes of care," is also being studied. For example, in June 2008 the Centers for Medicare and Medicaid Services (CMS) outlined a planned demonstration beta project that would combine payments for both hospital and physician services for a select number of acute episodes of care, with the intent of seeing whether such an approach would be more efficient and improve the quality of care. The project, called the Acute Care Episode (ACE) Demonstration, is testing whether a global payment model will better align the incentives for both types of providers and lead to better quality and greater efficiency.

Although the project is not yet complete, some healthcare organizations are voicing early support for the concept, which holds the promise of providing more transparent pricing for healthcare episodes. Currently, patients are often confused by receiving multiple bills from separate provider groups that provided services during a traditional medical or surgical care episode.

The hospitals and physicians selected to participate in the ACE Demonstration would see their payments combined for certain cardiac and orthopedic inpatient surgical services. CMS plans to select as many as fifteen ACE sites in Colorado, New Mexico, Oklahoma, and Texas.

The selected sets of procedures included in the bundled payment demonstration are 28 cardiac and 9 orthopedic inpatient surgical services. According to CMS, these elective procedures were selected because profit margins and volume have historically been high, there is sufficient marketplace competition to ensure interested demonstration applicants, the services are easy to specify, and quality metrics are available for them.

Nevertheless, the ACE Demonstration reflects an ongoing commitment to actively pursue the best medical care for Medicare beneficiaries through value-based purchasing by testing whether an approach of bundling payment for both hospital and physician services will work. Pending positive preliminary results, the private sector is sure to follow.

COMPREHENSIVE PAYMENT REFORM: AN EMERGING THEORETICAL CONSTRUCT

Yet another new look at capitation reimbursement involves an emerging theoretical construct where incentives are created for physicians to provide effective and efficient primary care. A team of physicians led by Alan H. Goroll, MD, of Massachusetts General Hospital, reported on how their proposed system avoids the problems of previous capitation systems, which merely bundled together inadequate fee-for-service payments, substantially increasing payments for primary care in return for greater accessibility, quality, safety, and efficiency (Goroll et al. 2007).

Under their model, medical practices would receive monthly payments for each patient under their care, with adjustments made according to the patient's needs and risks. Over two-thirds of the payments would be designated to pay for multidisciplinary healthcare teams (e.g., nurse practitioners, nutritionists, and social workers) and for information systems to monitor safety and quality, including interoperable electronic health records. Fifteen to 25 percent of payments would be linked to performance in meeting benchmarks of cost-effectiveness, efficiency, health outcomes, and patient-centered care.

Payments for hospital and specialist services, laboratory tests, imaging studies, and other ancillary services would remain unchanged and would continue to be paid under a resource-based, relative-value scale system. Appropriate use of such services would be promoted through reliance on evidence-based guidelines and performance incentives linked to efficiency.

ADVANTAGES OF COMPREHENSIVE PAYMENTS

This proposed comprehensive payment system moves away from payments based solely on discrete face-to-face patient encounters. Instead, primary care medical practices would be paid for providing coordinated, well-organized primary care—which in turn would lead to a healthier, more productive population and reduced need for hospitalizations and other costly services.

These comprehensive payments differ from capitation systems since the early 2000s in three important ways:

1. Payments would be adjusted according to patient levels of risk and need
2. Outcome and patient satisfaction measures would ensure that health services would not be underused
3. Funds would be provided to support healthcare teams and infrastructure

It is thought that these features would avoid the pitfalls of earlier capitation systems, which had the effect of erecting barriers to necessary care and encouraging providers to avoid complex patients.

ECONOMIC ASSESSMENT

Under one projected scenario, medical practices might receive an average of $800 per patient per year rather than the usual fixed payment system of per member/per month compensation. This would increase total healthcare spending for a given population by 2 to 3 percent. While in the short run such a comprehensive payment system would represent a net investment in primary care, in the long term it is projected that reductions in waste and improvements in care would ensure the system would pay for itself.

In addition, the comprehensive payment system would free up time that primary care practices now devote to claims billing, coding, and other administrative tasks embedded in the current system. By separating income from volume of patient visits, the new system would enable practices to tailor care to the particular needs of patients—from customized office visits with members of the healthcare team to e-mail and web-based communications, group visits, and even visits in patients' homes.

SAMPLE FINANCIAL PRO-FORMA PAYMENT SCHEME

Sample Allocation Formula for Comprehensive Payment System

25%	Primary care physician reimbursement: $250,000 before bonus/fringe benefits
60%	Staff, fringe, rent, office expense (assumes hiring of multidisciplinary office team charged with timely delivery of personalized comprehensive care): $600,000

- nurse practitioner: $100,000
- nurse: $90,000
- 0.5 full-time equivalent nutritionist: $35,000
- 0.5 full-time equivalent social worker: $35,000
- receptionist: $60,000
- medical assistant: $50,000
- rent: $40,000
- office expenses: $50,000
- insurance: $50,000
- physician fringe benefits: $75,000–$90,000

10%	IT/patient safety/quality monitoring: $100,000
	purchase/lease/setup of electronic health record and quality monitoring system: $35,000
	data manager: $35,000
5%	Performance bonus, annual meeting mutually established goals: $50,000

Note: This example assumes an average comprehensive payment of $800/year per patient, an average panel size of 1,250 patients/full-time primary care physician and team, 30 percent fringe benefit unless otherwise specified, and gross revenue of $1 million/full-time equivalent primary care physician and team.

Source: A. H. Goroll, R. A. Berenson, S. C. Schoenbaum et al., *Journal of General Internal Medicine,* March 2007 22 (3) 410–415.

ABUSE POTENTIAL

Abuse is possible in this system, so certain safeguards are necessary. For example, disbursement guidelines must ensure the appropriate use of funds targeted for healthcare team salaries and systems. Objective, validated measures of risk and need as well as independent audits might prevent participants from "gaming" the risk-adjustment process. To prevent practices from "dumping" patients onto specialists, the per-capita payments should follow patients when specialists assume most of the responsibility for their care.

REDUCED FEE-FOR-SERVICE MODEL

Under the reduced fee-for-service model, the provider receives a fee for every patient treated and a fee for every procedure performed. The provider can increase revenue by increasing the number of patients treated and procedures performed. Under this scenario, there is no decreased liability risk, or it may actually increase, for several reasons.

More patients are treated and more procedures are performed. Each individual patient encounter carries with it a degree of risk. By increasing the number of encounters, the risk is increased. It would appear that the risk would increase arithmetically, but in fact it has the potential to increase exponentially. The reason is that the provider only has a certain amount of time in which to provide the service. In the current environment, the provider must squeeze more encounters into the same time period than was the case in the past. The increased workload may increase stress and fatigue on the provider. With increased stress and fatigue, mistakes are more likely. Therefore, the increased liability risk is not only due to the increased number of patients, but also the increased fatigue levels that may result in medical error. Under the reduced fee-for-service model, there is also the possibility of undertreatment. The reimbursement for certain procedures may be determined by the provider to be unreasonably low, which might encourage the provider to avoid such procedures. To the extent that the provider performs a lesser procedure, the possibility of increased liability exists.

HYBRID CAPITATED/REDUCED FEE-FOR-SERVICE MODEL

The hybrid capitated/reduced fee-for-service model is commonly used with a group of specialists, as opposed to primary care physicians. An entire group of specialists will be capitated with a fixed dollar amount (risk pool). The allocation to the individual specialist will be based on a function of the allowed rate of all procedures performed by the individual, compared with the allowed rate of all procedures by the group. Although the entire group of specialists is capitated such that the MCO's liability is limited, each individual provider still acts on a (reduced) fee-for-service basis. Unless there are disincentives, this forces each provider to compete for a smaller share of the monetary disbursement. By performing more services/procedures, the individual provider can increase the share of the total allocated capitation. However, by increasing the number of services performed, in aggregate, the total reimbursement per service/procedure is reduced.

Unlike the pure at-risk capitation model, which gives an incentive to reduce the number of services/procedures, this hybrid capitated/fee-for-service model actually creates incentives, up to the point of diminishing marginal (marginal cost > margin benefit) returns, for the individual to increase the number of services. The increase in services will continue until the individual perceives that the per-procedure reimbursement has fallen to levels that make the addition or continuation of certain services/procedures unprofitable.

This model has several advantages for the MCO. First and foremost, the MCO's liability is limited and definite. Second, specialists will individually seek to increase the number of patients treated. Consequently, MCO patients have access to needed specialist care. However, this model also has the potential for the drawbacks of both the at-risk capitated model and the reduced fee-for-service model: There is incentive both for undertreatment in certain instances and for increased patient encounters in other instances.

CONCLUSION

Astute physician executives and administrators realize that CVPA and managed care contracting and negotiation represent free-market enterprise in its purest form. These techniques match the skills of determined payers against medical executives. All explore ways to achieve objectives that tend to optimize the self-interest of their respective positions. By rewarding efficiency and penalizing inefficiency, MCOs can, and often do, determine the medical reimbursement structure for the entire medical healthcare industrial complex. The reviewed techniques will help equalize the struggle for CVPA needs of hospitals and EHOs.

CVPA depends on the following economic assumptions, which may or may not be true in every case, and negotiating strategies:

- Volume, not acuity or quality, is the sole cost driver, and the relevant range will not change.
- The behavior of revenue and cost is linear (i.e., proportional to volume). In practice, variable costs and revenues are affected by output levels, which may result in non-linear relationships. In addition, the relationship of past data may not be representative of the changing future.
- Costs can be accurately divided into fixed and variable elements. CVPA is only useful if mixed (micro) costs are stable and can be separated and measured.
- There is a constant service mix in multi-service offices. If the actual medical service mix provided differs from the service mix used in the analysis, there will be a divergence percentage between expected profit and profit actually realized.
- Doctor, hospitalist, or clinic treatments remain the same. Therefore, the number of patients seen equals the number of unit revenues received. This is ideal for a capitated service contract.
- CVPA assumes short-term profit planning and does not consider the timing of revenues and costs, nor the time value of money. The value of a dollar today is the same as the value of a dollar in the future. This is also true in a low interest rate climate, rather than a high one.
- Phony facts about contracts, providers, patients, venues, demographics, prices, utilization rates, or services may occur. Some insurance companies may even offer a fee-for-service fee schedule as enticement into the plan. Usually, fees are dramatically reduced once the initial enrollment period has elapsed.
- Do not assume ambiguous authority regarding negotiating intentions or power. Once the deal is done and a firm agreement has been made, do not allow the other side to take the agenda to a higher authority for final approval (and another shot at your resistance).
- The "good guy–bad guy" routine is a psychological tactic where one partner appears to be hard-nosed and the other appears more yielding. Small concessions result that, upon repetition, become larger in aggregate.
- The "take it or leave it" tactic can be easily avoided by knowing your best alternative to the negotiated agreement. More formally, this is known as a unilateral contract of adhesion.
- Escalating or increasing demands occur when the opponent increases his or her demands or re-opens old demands. Call the bluff on this one by pointing it out to the MCO negotiator and replying that you are aware of its use.
- Avoid beginning the negotiating process when you are in stressful personal situations. Do not negotiate when you feel ill, your personal life is in shambles, your child or spouse is sick, or you feel too mentally exhausted or "psyched out."

These negotiation and CVPA accounting principles represent powerful techniques for increasing physician, hospital, or healthcare facility profits in the competitive marketplace. Their prudent use may result in improved profits, better care, and less provider stress—the ultimate successful outcome in any healthcare organization.

CASE MODEL 1

TO JOIN OR NOT TO JOIN: EVALUATING AN MCO CONTRACTING PROPOSAL

A managed care organization (MCO) wants a multi-specialty medical group to contract with them to provide medical services to all subscribers. Compensation would be in the form of a fixed-rate capitated payment system (i.e., per member/per month [pm/pm]). The medical group practice administrator reviewed their request for proposal (RFP) very carefully but is still not sure what to do.

Key Issues

Facts to know for an informed pm/pm capitated reimbursement decision:
- Annual frequency (office visits) or service rate per 1,000 patients
- Unit cost of medical services per unit-patient
- Co-payment dollar amount per patient
- Co-payment frequency rate per 1,000 patients
- Variable cost per patient
- Under-capacity medical group office utilization rates
- Fixed overhead office cost coverage (+/−)

Solution

There are several issues to resolve.

1. Be sure that all office fixed costs are paid, because revenues are fixed and costs vary with patient volume.
2. Be sure there is sufficient unused office capacity for the additional patients. Additionally, one must determine the maximum amount of services provided under the pm/pm rate that will make it possible to still break even.
3. Expected costs per patient must be estimated. If total pm/pm cost is less than the pm/pm compensation premium, the capitated contract might make economic sense for the medical group. If not, it should be rejected or re-negotiated.

CHECKLIST 1: CVPA for Prospective Payment System Contracts	Yes	No
If you are a financial manager responsible for negotiating, implementing, and maintaining a managed care contract for the organization, you should address the following concerns.		
Do I have contracting power of authority?	o	o
Have I determined the contract patient mix?	o	o
Am I aware of the capitation rate and contract terms?	o	o
Is the capitation rate a fixed amount, adjusted for age, gender, and medical condition acuity differences?	o	o
Do I know what day of the month capitation payments are made?	o	o
Are there any contract low-enrollment guarantees or high-enrollment maximums?	o	o
Are provisions in place for retroactive contract changes?	o	o
Is a bonus structure in place for self-tracking or other plans?	o	o
Do I know how bonuses, if any, are paid and how frequently?	o	o
Do I know of any penalties or deductions from the capitated contract?	o	o
Does management support the capitated contract process?	o	o
Do I know how often the contract is renegotiated?	o	o
Do I know of any restrictions or billing limitations for non-covered services?	o	o
Does the contract reimburse for supplies, bandages, injectibles, durable medical equipment, etc.?	o	o
Do I know the financial responsibilities of call coverage for the capitated contract?	o	o
Do I know how each plan relates to other plans?	o	o

Do I understand all operative definitions, such as care, treatments, inclusions, exclusions, urgent vs. emergent care, medical necessity, enrollee, in-service vs. out-of-service area, pharmacy and risk pools, locale and geography, etc.?	o	o
Do I understand how much control over business decisions the doctor or medical provider retains?	o	o
Do I know the reputation of the contract or how employees, patients, and other doctors feel about the contract?	o	o
Do I understand the physicians, referring specialists, durable medical equipment providers, and para-professionals?	o	o
Do I know if there is any independence in the medical decision-making process?	o	o
Is pre-certification still necessary (oral or written)?	o	o
Is pre-certification worthwhile or tied to payment?	o	o
Can the doctor refer directly to a specialist?	o	o
Do I know how fluid the availability of medical records will be?	o	o
Must medical records be electronic?	o	o
Does the primary care doctor control the specialist?	o	o
Is there a graduated appeals process in place?	o	o
Do medical providers participate in the process?	o	o
Are quality improvement reports required?	o	o
Do I know what is expected from the MCO, plan, or the patient?	o	o
Is the contract exclusive or inclusive to other MCOs or providers?	o	o
Do I know about the carve-outs, withholdings, or ancillary bonus structures?	o	o
Are doctors penalized economically for treating patients?	o	o
Do I know how quickly providers are paid (turnaround time)?	o	o
Does the number of patients promised offset reductions in payment?	o	o
Is there a guaranteed number of patients, such as 3,000 members ($250 month × 12 months), because a lower number may not economically justify the extra administrative costs to service the plan?	o	o
Is there a fail-safe floor, such as an 85 percent fee-for-service equivalent rate, if the minimum number of patients is not enrolled?	o	o
Do I understand that Medicare risk enrollee rates are usually four to six times more than commercial rates because Medicare+C risk plans are now so out of favor?	o	o
Do I know how much total capital is available in the plan, and is it enough to run the program?	o	o
Do I know what relative value system is used, and do I know the conversion factors?	o	o
Do I know the impact and return on investment, operating costs, revenues, and profit of the plan, thus far?	o	o
Do I understand the annual utilization (frequency) and actuarial rates and claims history for the last three years (e.g., new demographic groups are riskier than known groups)?	o	o
Do I know if the doctors spend more time with patients, utilization review, quality assurance, or case managers?	o	o
Do I know about the plan's sales force, advertising channels, or marketing initiatives compared to other plans?	o	o
Am I informed about changes in the rules and am I kept informed?	o	o
Do I know administrative cost ranges?	o	o
Do I know about sub-capitated contracts?	o	o
Do I know the equivalent risk for the primary medical doctor/doctor of osteopathy and sub-capitated specialist?	o	o
Do I know the fixed expenses for the sub-capitated specialist?	o	o
Do I know if there is a predictable and low cost of care, per specialty episode?	o	o
Have I tracked high episodes of specialty care (not unusual or unpredictable events)?	o	o
Can I define and understand the responsibilities of the medical specialist?	o	o

	Yes	No
Am I aware of the profit and cost savings potential for both the referring doctor and specialty doctor?	o	o
Do I know if there is re-insurance?	o	o
Do I know about doctor credentialing (board certification or qualification)?	o	o
Do I know which medical credentialing boards are involved?	o	o
Do I understand patient stream?	o	o
Do patient stream numbers justify the capitated or HMO discount?	o	o
Do I understand about restrictive covenants, gag orders, restrictions, and termination clauses?	o	o
Are arbitration or negotiation clauses in place?	o	o
Do I know about audit rights and non-compliant patients?	o	o
Are there medical standards, guidelines, and indemnification clauses in the contract?	o	o

CHECKLIST 2: Pitfalls of Evaluating CVPA

Make sure you are aware of the pitfalls of evaluating CVPA in managed care contracts.

	Yes	No
Do I know whether the managed care contracts are profitable?	o	o
Do I simply sign up and hope for the best?	o	o
Do I have the ability to obtain the needed financial information?	o	o
Is the IT hardware and sophisticated software needed to gather, evaluate, and interpret clinical and financial data available to the practice?	o	o
Although the underpayment rate is typically 3–10 percent, do I allow contract underpayments to be left on the table?	o	o
Would I allow yearly (or longer) compensation disbursements to cause significant cash flow problems to my physicians and clinics?	o	o
If the contract is prematurely terminated, will I receive a pro-rata refund of my stop-loss minimums only if I ask for it?	o	o
Do I allow an automatic renewal or evergreen contract, which may result in overlapping renewal and renegotiation deadlines, to be continued on a sub-optimal basis?	o	o
Have I determined a cutoff point at which such an evergreen contract would work to the detriment of the medical providers?	o	o

CHECKLIST 3: HMO Managed Care Needs

Document what HMOs seek in managed care contracts.

	Yes	No
Is there a local or community need for the medical practice, with a sound patient base that is not too small or large?	o	o
Is a positive return on investment from an economically sound practice possible so the HMO can continue its relationship with you?	o	o
Is there a merger or acquisition strategy for the MCO internal business plan that affords a seamless union should a practice decide to sell out or consolidate at a later date?	o	o
Will the human resources, capital, and IT services complement the existing management information systems framework?	o	o
Are consolidated financial statements conforming to generally accepted accounting principles, IRC, OIG, and other appraisal standards available?	o	o
Is there a sense of strong and respected physician leadership in the medical and business community?	o	o
Does the practice or clinic have a willingness to treat all conditions and types of patients?	o	o
Are valid medical licenses, DEA narcotics licenses, CME, adequate malpractice insurance, board qualifications/certifications, and hospital privileges in place?	o	o
Do all members of the practice agree with the managed care philosophy?	o	o
Have partners in the group practice, clinic, or healthcare entity met all the same participation criteria?	o	o
Are you and the physicians available for periodic MCO review by a company representative?	o	o

CHECKLIST 4: Medical Office Standards for HMO Contracts	Yes	No
Ensure you are familiar with Medical Office Standards for HMO contracts		
Is the office clean and presentable, with a professional appearance?	o	o
Is there a readily accessible and barrier-free design that meets OSHA standards?	o	o
Is appropriate medical emergency and resuscitation equipment available?	o	o
Does the waiting room accommodate five to seven patients with private changing areas?	o	o
Is there adequate capacity (e.g., 5,000–10,000 member minimum), a business plan, and office assistants for the plan?	o	o
Do office hours meet the required minimum (e.g., 20 hours/week)?	o	o
Is there 24/7 on-call coverage with electronic tracking?	o	o
Are there MCO-approved sub-contractors?	o	o

CHECKLIST 5: Appealing MCO Disenrollment Decisions	Yes	No
In order for you to appeal an MCO disenrollment decision, have you done the following in your request for reconsideration?		
Obtain a letter of explanation from the medical or clinical executive director.	o	o
Ensur your initial application went through the proper channels of consideration.	o	o
Contact your local plan representative, in person, if possible.	o	o
Make sure your state and national medical affiliations are current, as well as hospital and surgical center staffing applications and credentials.	o	o
Write a letter to the medical director and sent it by U.S. Postal service with a return receipt or by private carrier.	o	o
Inform the director of the actions you are taking to become more attractive to the plan.	o	o
Inform the director of what you have done to correct the deficiencies that caused your non-inclusion initially.	o	o

CHECKLIST 6: Capitation Rate and Contract Terms	Yes	No
One important consideration is the actual capitation rate and the factors that can affect that rate, either up or down. It is also important to have a sense of "market comparison" on the capitation rate provided under the contract. Here are specific questions the financial manager, director, or physician executive should ask.		
Do I know which health plans can access this contractual arrangement?	o	o
Is the health plan limited to just the one negotiating the contract or are there silent or affiliated plans that can access the agreement?	o	o
Do I know the monthly capitation rate paid to the physicians?	o	o
Do I know what various third party administrators are keeping from the health plan's payments to cover the cost of their services?	o	o
Do I know if the capitation rate is a fixed amount per member per month, or will it be age-/sex-adjusted based on the actual blend of patients who are assigned to the physician?	o	o
Do I know what day of the month the capitation payment will be paid?	o	o
Do I know if the contract stipulates that the third party administrators must pay interest charges for late payments?	o	o
Am I aware of any low enrollment guarantees built into the contract to provide for minimum payment amounts in the early stages of contract enrollments?	o	o
Are there provisions for retroactive changes in the enrollment assigned to the practice, and are there specific time limits on those provisions, such as 30 days or 60 days?	o	o
Do I understand how bonuses, if any, are earned and paid?	o	o

	Yes	No
Do I know what penalties and deductions from the capitation payment can be imposed for actions such as "inappropriate referrals" or for referrals to non-contracted providers?	o	o
Do I know how often the capitation rates can be re-negotiated?	o	o
Do I understand the clinic's or physician's financial obligations upon termination of the contract?	o	o
Do I know if the contract converts to a fee-for-service agreement or if continuing care for the patient is covered under the existing capitation rate?	o	o
If so, do I know what the contract time limit is for providing continuing care?	o	o

CHECKLIST 7: Managed Care Negotiations and Renegotiations	Yes	No
Have I obtained a current copy of the payer's existing contract?	o	o
Have I obtained the payer's existing reimbursement schedule for the contract?	o	o
If the reimbursement schedule is not based on resource-based relative value units, have I compared it to new MS-DRG or Medicare/Medicaid rates and determined percent of Medicare being reimbursed?	o	o
Have I obtained a CPT® frequency report?	o	o
Have I developed a contracting strategy?	o	o
Have I contacted the payer and made a contract negotiation proposal?	o	o
If so, have I obtained the payer's response to the proposal?	o	o
If so, have I reviewed and analyzed the payer's response and decided whether to accept the contract or offer a counter proposal?	o	o
Did I assess antitrust concerns and consult hospital legal counsel, if necessary?	o	o
If the decision was made to accept the contract:		
Has the proposal been submitted to the chief-level officers or board of director members for review and acceptance?	o	o
Did I notify the payer and document this notification?	o	o
Have I obtained a written contract change and executed it?	o	o
Have I made sure that future reimbursements agree with new contract terms, conditions, and rates?	o	o
If the decision was to counter-propose:		
Have I adjusted the proposal and submitted it to the payer?	o	o
Have I maintained a strict follow-up schedule with "ticklers"?	o	o
If necessary, have I communicated with the payer contact's superiors?	o	o
Have I obtained the payer's final response to the counter-proposal?	o	o
Have I analyzed the payer's response and decided whether to accept or reject?	o	o
Have I discussed the response with chief-level officers or board of director members, etc.?	o	o
If the counter-proposal is accepted:		
Have I notified the payer and documented the acceptance?	o	o
Have I obtained the written contract change and execute?	o	o
Have I made sure future reimbursement agrees with new rates and terms?	o	o
If the counter-proposal is rejected:		
Have I decided whether or not to terminate the payer contract?	o	o
Have I analyzed the potential financial impact as a result of contract termination?	o	o
If chief-level officers or board of director members decide not to terminate, does negotiation end?	o	o
Do I intend to contact payer again, to determine if they are willing to reconsider?	o	o

CASE MODEL 2

OFFSETTING COSTS FOR CARDIO-THORACIC SURGICAL SERVICES

A new MCO asks the Hospital of Saint Mackenzie the Hopeful to provide coronary artery bypass graft (CABG) surgical services, with catheterization, for its insured patients. The CFO at Saint Mackenzie is pleased to review their request for proposal (RFP), as this is the exact type of patient that is needed to help offset the costs of the new cardio-thoracic surgical services wing at the hospital.

After some preliminary discussions, the MCO offers to pay the hospital $34,805 for a normal triple-artery CABG without complications (MS-DRG 233).

The CFO reviews the standard treatment protocol (STP) and standard cost profile (SCP) for this MS-DRG procedure. To her dismay, she discovers that the hospital's cost would be $36,000 with a six-day average length of stay (LOS) in the new wing. What should she do?

Key Issues

Facts must you know to make an informed decision:

- MS-DRG code number
- MS-DRG reimbursement rate from Medicare/MCO payer
- Fixed cost elements per MS-DRG
- Variable cost elements per MS-DRG
- Review of facility STPs and SCPs for same MS-DRG
- Average LOS for same procedure

Solution

Hopefully, the STP for MS-DRG 233 allocates costs into fixed and variable portions at Saint Mackenzie. If the variable cost is less than $34,806, the hospital may earn some marginal profit from the additional business. In this case, it may not. However, it is also important to closely examine the STP. There may be some patient management issues and follow-up care differences to consider.

For example, the six-day LOS might result in even higher or lower costs, if able to adjust +/− day(s); thus profit would adjust upward or downward, accordingly.

An agreement on the STPs with the MCO should also be negotiated.

CASE MODEL 3

MICRO-CAPITATION: A CHRONIC DIABETIC CARE PACKAGE IN DRIGGS, IDAHO

A family practice doctor in rural Driggs, Idaho (population ~5,000) cared for a fairly sizable population of diabetic patients. Driggs is the county seat for Teton County. It is nestled at an elevation of 6,200 feet between the majestic Teton Mountains and the beautiful Big Hole Mountains, in an incorporated area of nearly 350 acres.

In reviewing several paper charts, the doctor recognized that many patients were not getting the care they needed. In questioning these patients, he learned it was difficult for them to receive proper care because busy schedules created seasonal encounter difficulties. The physician decided to bolster his sparsely attended diabetic clinic by creating a new micro-capitated diabetic care package (DCP).

Coordination of Care

To deliver this diabetic care package, the family practice physician entered into conversations with other medical providers to determine a pricing schedule, how care was to be coordinated, and how the virtual team would work together to deliver care. They agreed to revenue splits, performance metrics, and a mechanism to market the micro-capitated service. Contingencies were even made for patient needs that extended beyond the initial DCP provider agreement.

Value-Added Medical Care

Because an entire year of routine care was included for a single discounted fee, given the efficiencies gained through care coordination, patients saw the clinical and financial value added. The physician immediately signed up 50 percent of his current patient population (250 people). An additional 100+ patients signed up within the first 90 days, as word-of-mouth marketing and positive local press reports made the program more widely known.

Key Issues

1. Coordination: A single program coordinator would help schedule appointments and provide outcomes measurements.
2. Staffing: All participating medical providers were staffed and organized to deliver their component services, and, because they were all working under capacity, no new equipment or staffing would be required.

Solution:

The DCP included the following medical services:

- Four routine medical office visits
- A bi-annual podiatric visit for foot care
- An annual optometric eye examination
- Four additional in-home nutritional/medication consultations

Multiple side effects emerged from initiation of the DCP, including a spontaneous patient support group that met bi-monthly to discuss nutrition, insulin regimens, and related diabetic healthcare issues. The program coordinator participated actively with the group and recognized the opportunity for the various component providers to present the latest treatment options on a monthly basis. These meetings built additional rapport and patient confidence, and served as a recruiting mechanism for other diabetics in the community.

Within two years, three other physicians began selling modified versions of the DCP with new features, functions, and capabilities. The average community hemoglobin A1C metric, which was assembled by the patient support group, dropped from 9.5 to less than 7.0 for the 472 known diabetic patients in the Driggs community.

Source: Modified courtesy of Scott L. Shreve, MD.

REFERENCES

Arnst, Catherine. 2008. "Hospitals and Insurers Try Flat Fees Again." *BusinessWeek*, September 15.
Capitation strategy. 1995. Washington, DC: Advisory Board Company, Governance Committee.
Clemens, S. *Autobiography of Mark Twain,* C. Nieder, ed. Perennial Classics (pub. date unknown).

Bader, B. and Matheny, M. 1994. "Understanding Capitation and At-Risk Contracting." *Health Systems Leader,* 1(1): 4–16.

Baum, N. 1996. "Putting 'Managed' Into Managed Care." *Take Care of Your Medical Practice* (p. 505), N. Baum, ed. Gaithersburg: Aspen Publishers.

Berlin, M.F. 1998. "Budget Variance Analysis Using RVUs." *MGMA Journal,* December, 50–52.

Bazzoli, Fred. 2008. "CMS Announces Demo for Bundled Hospital-Physician Payment." *Healthcare Financial News,* May 19.

Cykert, S., Hansen, C., Layson, R., and Joines, J. 1997. "Capitation; Experiences, Attitudes and Predictors" *Journal of General Internal Medicine,* 12(3) (March 1997): 192–194.

DeNelsky, S.J. 1998. "Then Came the Hospitalists." *Managed Healthcare News,* 14:10.

Eskow, R. 2007. "A Brief History of Capitation." *Sentinel Effect.* sentineleffect.wordpress.com

Finkler, S. 1994. *Essentials of Cost Accounting for Healthcare Organizations* Gaithersburg: Aspen Publishers.

Goroll, A.H., Berenson R.A., Schoenbaum, S.C., and Gardner L.B. 2007. "Fundamental Reform of Payment for Adult Primary Care: Comprehensive Payment for Comprehensive Care." *Journal of General Internal Medicine,* 22(3):410–415.

Grab, E.L. and Caesar, N.B. 1993. "Negotiating Profitable Managed Care Contracts for Your Group." *Group Practice Journal,* 42(5): 28–30.

Guo, Z. 1995. "Chinese Confucian Culture and the Medical Ethical Tradition." *Journal of Medical Ethics,* 21(4): 239–246.

Harvard Pilgrim Health Care. 2012. Home. https://www.harvardpilgrim.org/portal/page?_pageid=1391,1&_dad=portal&_schema=PORTAL.

Hogan, J., Gordon, A., and Heron A. 2004. "Basic Capitation for Internists and other Specialists," In *The Advanced Business of Medical Practice,* D.E. Marcinko, ed., New York: Springer Publishing.

Hultman, J. 1995. *Here's How, Doctor.* Los Angeles: Medical Business Advisors.

Hyman, D. 2000. *Economics.* Boston: Irwin.

InterStudy. 2000. "HMO Enrollment Stabilizing." *Modern Physician.* January, 1.

Kealey, E.J. 1981. *Medieval Medicus: A Social History of Anglo-Norman Medicine.* Baltimore: Johns Hopkins University Press.

Living with Managed Care (A View from the Front). 1995. Englewood, CO: Medical Group Management Association.

Managed Care Digest Series (1998). 1998. Kansas City, MO: Hoechst Marion Roussel.

Managed Care Digest Series. 2012. Home. https://www.managedcaredigest.com/default.aspx.

Marcinko, D.E. 2000. "Advanced Office Cost Behavior Techniques." In *The Business of Medical Practice* (p. 201). Marcinko, D.E. and Hetico, H.R., eds. New York: Springer Publishing.

Marcinko, D.E. 2007. *Dictionary of Health Insurance and Managed Care.* New York: Springer Publishing.

Marcinko, D.E. 2008. *Dictionary of Health Economics and Finance.* New York: Springer Publishing.

Marcinko, D.E. 2012. "Analyzing and Negotiating Cost Volume Profit Medical Contracts: Profit Maximization versus Revenue Maximization." In *The Business of Medical Practice* (p. 347). Marcinko, D.E. and Hetico, H.R., eds. New York: Springer Publishing.

Medical Management Institute. 1994. *Negotiating Managed Care Contracts.* New York: McGraw-Hill.

New York Times. 1902. "Mark Twain on Medicine." Accessed at http://www.twainquotes.com/19020309.html.

Senterfitt, B. 2008. "States Decide Business of Insurance." *Managed Healthcare Executive,* July 1.

Society of Hospital Medicine. 2012. Home. http://www.hospitalmedicine.org/.

Sox, H.C. 1999. "The Hospitalist Model: Perspectives of the Patient, the Internist, and Internal Medicine." *Ann Intern Med,* 130: 368–372.

Spiro, G.W. 1993. *The Legal Environment of Business.* New York: Prentice Hall.

Tinsley, R. 1998. "Negotiating, or Re-Negotiating Managed Care Contracts." *MGM Journal,* October: 6.

Tinsley, R. 2002. *Medical Practice Management Handbook.* New York, Aspen Publisher.

Ury, W. 1993. *Getting Past No: Negotiating Your Way from Confrontation to Cooperation.* New York: Bantam Books.

Ury, W., Fisher, R., and Patton, B. 1991. *Getting to Yes.* New York: Bantam Books.

Wachter R.M., and Goldman L. 1996. "The Emerging Role of 'Hospitalists' in the American Health Care System." *NEJM,* 335(7): 514–517.

Wachter R.M., Katz, P., Showstack, J., Bindman, A.B., and Goldman, L. 1998. "Reorganizing an Academic Medical Service: Impact on Cost, Quality, Patient Satisfaction, and Education." *JAMA,* 279: 1560–1565

Wachter R.M., and Flanders S. 1998. "The Hospitalist Movement and the Future of Academic General Internal Medicine." *Journal of General Internal Medicine* 13: 783.

Wachter's World. 2013. Blog. http://community.the-hospitalist.org/

Walker, T. 2008. "Ohio Mandate Calls for Contract Transparency." *Managed Healthcare Executive*, July 15.

Youngberg, B.A. 1996. *Managing the Risks of Managed Care*. Gaithersburg: Aspen Publishers.

10 Investment Policy Statement Benchmark Construction for Hospital Endowment Fund Management

Perry D'Alessio and David Edward Marcinko

CONTENTS

INTRODUCTION

Dr. Malcolm T. MacEachern, Director of Hospital Activities for the American College of Surgeons, presciently observed that:

> Our hospitals are now involved in the worst financial crisis they have ever experienced. It is absolutely necessary to all of us to put our heads together and try to find some solution. If we are to have effective results we must have concerted and coordinated immediate action. . . . Repeated adjustments of expenses to income have been made. Never before has there been such a careful analysis of hospital accounting and study of financial policies. It is entirely possible for us to inaugurate improvements in business methods which will lead to greater ways and means of financing hospitals in the future. . . . It is true that all hospitals have already trimmed their sales to better meet the financial conditions of their respective communities. This has been chiefly through economies of administration. There has been more or less universal reduction in personnel and salaries; many economies have been affected. Everything possible has been done to reduce expenditures but this has not been sufficient to bring about immediate relief in the majority of instances. The continuance of the present economic conditions will force hospitals generally to further action. The time has come when this problem must be given even greater thought, both from its community and from its national aspect.[1]

Many health administration and endowment managers would agree that Dr. MacEachern accurately describes today's healthcare funding environment. Although they might be startled to learn that Dr. MacEachern made these observations in 1932, there is the old truism that there is nothing new under the sun.

Healthcare statistics after the 2012 presidential election and Patient Protection-Affordable Care Act confirmation suggest that the financial crises are much the same for today's hospitals as they were for hospitals during the Great Depression. The American Hospital Association recently reported a number of gloomy statistics for hospitals: [2]

- Hospitals provided $39 billion in uncompensated care to patients in 2010 representing 5.8 percent of their expenses.
- Technology costs are soaring as traditional technologies such as X-ray machines (available for $175,000) are being replaced by contemporary technologies such as computed tomography (CT) scanners (available for $1 million), which are in turn being replaced by CT functional imaging with positron emission tomography scans (available for $2.3 million). Even a "simple" instrument like as a scalpel that costs $20 is being replaced by equipment for electrocautery, which costs $12,000, and that is then being replaced by harmonic scalpels that cost $30,000.

A further review added more daunting numbers:[3]

- In 2010, 22.4 percent of hospitals reported a negative total margin.
- From 1997 through 2009, hospitals saw a small net surplus from government payments from sources such as Medicare and Medicaid deteriorate into a deficit approaching $35 billion.
- Emergency departments in 47 percent of all hospitals report operating at or over capacity, partially reflecting an approximately 10 percent decline in the number of emergency departments since 1991.
- The average age of hospital plants has increased 22.5 percent from 8.0 years to 9.8 years in just 15 years.
- From 2003 through September 2007, hospital bond downgrades have outpaced hospital bond upgrades by 19 percent.

In a time when so much seems different yet so much seems the same, hospitals are increasingly viewing their endowments as a source of help. But what is an endowment? The same Latin words that give rise to the word *dowry* also give rise to the word *endowment*.[4] Interestingly, the concepts of a dowry and an endowment are similar in many ways. Both are typically viewed as gifts for continuing support or maintenance. With respect to the healthcare entity, an endowment is generally used to smooth variations in operating results and to fund extra programs or plant purchases. Any entity that enjoys the support of an endowment also encounters the conflicting objectives between current income and future growth.

Dean William Inge, a nineteenth century cleric and author, aptly noted, "Worry is interest paid on trouble before it falls due."[5] When managing an endowment, it is important that the institution focus its attention on those items that it can control rather than worrying about those it cannot control. Successful endowment managers seem to agree that there are at least two major areas subject to the endowment's control: asset allocation (also known as investment policy) and payout policy.

ASSET ALLOCATION

Since a 1986 study of large pension funds suggested that investment policy, rather than market timing or security selection, was the primary determinant of portfolio performance,[6] investors have seized upon asset allocation as the Holy Grail of investing. Although there has been ongoing debate regarding the original study's methodology and conclusions, David Swensen, the Chief Investment Officer of Yale University, made the following observation with respect to asset allocation: "Investors often treat asset allocation's central role in determining portfolio returns as a truism. It is not. The Brinson, Singer, and Beebower study describes investor behavior, not finance theory."[7]

It is its ability to control investor behavior that makes asset allocation so valuable. But what is asset allocation? In simple terms, asset allocation is the process of combining or blending investment asset classes in an attempt to obtain the highest possible return at the lowest possible risk. Because this is a laudable pursuit, an endowment should have a process to guide its behavior in establishing investment allocation.

DEVELOP A PROPER PERSPECTIVE

It has been said that the most difficult single feat in professional sports is hitting the major league pitch that can arrive at the plate in as few as 0.4 seconds after being thrown. Perhaps the most difficult feat in investing is setting an asset allocation. For the endowment manager (and most other investors), maintaining proper perspective of risk and return is likely the most difficult aspect of setting investment policy. Although investing carries many risks, William Spitz, CFA (Chartered

Financial Analyst), the treasurer of Vanderbilt University School of Medicine, and manager of the team that provides day-to-day management of Vanderbilt's $2.25 billion endowment, succinctly summarized the risks that should represent the primary areas of concern:

1. The endowment could suffer an unacceptable market loss
2. There could be a decrease in the amount of support the endowment could provide to the sponsoring institution
3. The endowment could fail to preserve its real purchasing power[8]

When balancing these divergent risks, the endowment manager must remember that an endowment is a matter of "inter-generational equity," meaning that the future generation cannot and must not be harmed by actions taken on behalf of the current generation. When establishing the allocation for an endowment, the concept of inter-generational equity means that the manager must take a long-term perspective. Such a strict long-term perspective would likely require an almost complete equity allocation. However, because most healthcare institutions have immediate needs, an endowment manager's investment allocation must also remain sensitive to the needs for current period funding.

To put endowment management into a more personal perspective, liken it to investing an individual retirement account (IRA) for a 65-year-old Methuselah who is preparing for 904 golden years of retirement bliss. His dilemma involves satisfying a need for current income while ensuring that he preserves the purchasing power of his portfolio.

ASSET CLASS CONSIDERATIONS

The 2006 Commonfund Benchmarks Healthcare Study surveyed 202 public and private healthcare institutions with total investment assets of $105.8 billion. The average asset allocation reported by those institutions is shown in Table 10.1.[9] Note that this study included pension, operating, and insurance reserve assets. Because most institutions invest their insurance reserves more conservatively than their pension or operating (endowment) assets, the data will likely appear to be somewhat more conservative than is actually the case for endowment assets. However, even allowing for this enhanced conservatism, the average annual returns of 6.3 percent for the year ending June 30, 2006, does not seem particularly healthy.

Domestic Equity

Historically, domestic equities have represented a significant portion of a typical endowment's assets because they have generated favorable long-term returns relative to cash and bonds. Of course, this greater return has also entailed greater risk as compared to those same lower return investments. As shown in the Commonfund survey, the average healthcare entity continues to place heavy reliance on domestic equities. However, survey participants have reduced their allocations to domestic equities by 7 percent in just two years in favor of international equities and alternative investments.

TABLE 10.1
Average Asset Allocations

Total domestic equities	30%
Fixed income	34%
International equities	12%
Alternative investments	15%
Cash/short-term securities	9%
Total	100%

Fixed Income

Most endowments will use fixed income or bond positions to provide more stable sources of income, greater portfolio diversification, and a hedge against unanticipated spending needs. Although many fixed income investments have historically exhibited less volatility or risk than other investment alternatives, they have also generally tended to have lower long-term returns. When determining the size of the endowment's fixed income position, the manager will want to remember that the inter-generational nature of endowments is such that long-term returns remain important. In addition, a substantial body of research suggests that the risk of higher-returning investments such as stocks diminishes substantially over longer holding periods. Endowments may desire to hedge their long-term liabilities with long-term bonds. However, they should consider research compiled by Dimensional Fund Advisors showing that longer-term bonds may not provide significantly higher return relative to their risk. As shown in the following chart, the average annual return of twenty-year bonds is virtually identical to that of five-year bonds, but the risk (as measured by standard deviation) is 75 percent higher.[10]

	U.S. Treasury Obligations 1964–2012		
	One-Year U.S. Treasury Bills	Five-Year U.S. Treasury Notes	Twenty-Year U.S. Government Bonds
Annualized compound return (%)	0.73	5.17	5.46
Annualized standard deviation (%)	2.24	3.13	3.96

Foreign Equity

Exposure to foreign equity can enhance the overall diversification of the endowment portfolio. Perhaps more importantly, some foreign equity markets are substantially less efficient than the domestic equity market, which affords the portfolio manager the opportunity to earn above market returns. Within the foreign equity class, emerging markets are often viewed to be especially attractive because their rapidly growing and changing economies provide the skillful manager with an opportunity to add value.

Absolute Return

This class of investment seeks to exploit market inefficiencies and generate positive returns regardless of broader market performance. Investments in this class often are made through the use of hedge funds. Hedge funds will often employ leverage, short-selling, and arbitrage to take advantage of pricing distortions in their targeted strategy area.

When investing an endowment's assets in this category, the manager should be aware of fee structures that commonly include performance-related incentive fees, hurdle rates, and clawback clauses. The endowment manager should also remember that these types of investments generally have much less transparency than other asset classes with which they may be more familiar. Finally, because many of these investments are offered only to accredited investors, the investment manager is often free to pursue much more aggressive strategies than would otherwise be pursued for retail customers.

Private Equity

As with absolute return investments, private equity is generally available only to accredited investors. The relative lack of efficiency in this market allows the endowment to seek superior risk-adjusted returns by participating in such investments as venture capital and leveraged buy-out funds. When investing in this asset class, the endowment manager would be well served to partner with managers who "emphasize a value-added approach to investing. Such firms work closely with the portfolio companies to create entities that are fundamentally more valuable, relying only secondarily on financial engineering to generate returns."[11] Although this class of investments has handsomely rewarded many large endowments, the manager must also remember that the very nature of this class is such that liquidity may be very limited.

Real Assets

Also known as "hard assets," this class includes such investments as real estate, gas and oil, and timber. Many successful endowments have found this to be an attractive class of investments because they provide strong returns and can serve as an inflationary hedge. The Yale Endowment's allocation to real assets is almost six times the average for other similar institutions, and since 1978 this allocation has returned an average 15 percent per year.[11] As further illustration, since 1987 timber has provided average annual returns of approximately 15.6 percent* as compared to 13.1 percent for domestic equities (as measured by the Wilshire 5000 Index). During this time period, timber had only three negative return quarters[12] and significantly lower volatility than domestic equities. However, investing in assets such as timber requires that an endowment accept the approximate fifteen-year time frame and the limited liquidity it represents (William Spitz, pers. comm.).

COMBINING THE ASSET CLASSES

Combining the disparate information into a workable asset allocation is as much art as it is science, perhaps more so. Most endowments will use a combination of quantitative and qualitative analyses to develop their allocations. The quantitative portion of the analyses generally uses a variety of statistical techniques to develop a top-down approach to the general allocation. After developing a general sense of their desired range of returns, many endowments will use one of several "optimizer" techniques to assist in constructing an allocation. Commonly used optimization techniques include mean variance optimization (MVO) and Monte Carlo simulation (MCS).

Mean Variance Optimization

MVO has at its core modern portfolio theory (MPT), which seeks to find the "efficient frontier" that defines the minimum risk for any given level of return. To find this frontier, MVO will consider the expected returns, standard deviations (i.e., volatility), and correlation coefficients of individual asset classes. All things being equal, the endowment manager would generally choose the investments with the highest expected long-term return. However, the current funding needs placed upon endowments require that they be sensitive to the volatility of asset classes.

Expected volatility is often defined as "risk" and is measured by the standard deviation of investment returns around an expected average return for that same investment. In other words, an asset class with an expected return of 10 percent and standard deviation of 5 percent would have its returns range from 5 percent to 15 percent approximately two-thirds of the time. This assumes that returns are normally distributed around a mean, although a fair amount of evidence suggests that they are not. Table 10.2 summarizes periodic returns and standard deviations for selected classes of assets.

Cross-asset correlation is measured by the correlation coefficients between two categories of investments. Correlation coefficients range from −1.0 to +1.0. A correlation coefficient of −1.0 means two investment classes move exactly inversely to one another. On the other hand, a +1.0 correlation coefficient means that two asset classes have totally positive correlation. A 0.0 correlation coefficient means that movement in one asset class cannot be used to predict the level of return in another asset class. By holding asset classes with imperfect correlation, volatility in the portfolio can be reduced as classes with higher returns balance those with low or negative returns. Table 10.3 summarizes correlation coefficients for the same asset classes described in Table 10.2.

The MVO optimizer will then mathematically plot a series of portfolio options that represent the maximum level of return for a given level of risk. By definition, there can be only one such efficient frontier of portfolios. Also explicit in MPT is the idea that a portfolio below the efficient frontier is

---

* Data from the National Council of Real Estate Investment Fiduciaries (2013); calculations by author J. Wayne Firebaugh.

TABLE 10.2

Average Annual Returns and Standard Deviations for Selected Asset Class Returns, 2006–2011

Benchmark/Asset Class	Return	Standard Deviation
Wilshire 5000	1.15%	19.24%
MSCI EAFE	−5.37%	22.69%
MSCI EAFE Emerging Markets	−1.7%	29.01%
Hedge Fund	2.95%	9.20%
Timber	6.39%	25.67%
Real Estate	6.77%	6.41%
Long-term U.S. Government	11.21%	1.01%
Intermediate U.S. Government	6.34%	1.40%
Short-term U.S. Government	2.69%	1.50%
Medical Inflation	4.20%	1.14%

Sources: Index data for the Wilshire 5000 data were obtained from Wilshire Associates. Index data for the MSCI EAFE and MSCI EAFE Emerging Markets were obtained from Morgan Stanley Capital International, Inc. Index data for the HFRI Fund Weighted Composite Index was obtained from Hedge Fund Research, Inc. Index and return amounts for timber and real estate were obtained from the National Council of Real Estate Investment Fiduciaries. Returns and standard deviations for the Long-term U.S. Government, Intermediate U.S. Government, and Short-term U.S. Government asset classes were calculated by the author using thirty-year Treasury Bond, five-year Treasury Note, and thirteen-week Treasury Bill average annual yields. Medical Inflation was obtained from the Bureau of Labor Statistics and represents the rate of inflation for medical care of all urban consumers. All annual returns and standard deviations were calculated by the principal author.

inefficient, whereas a portfolio above the efficient frontier is impossible to sustain on a long-term basis. Figure 10.1 provides a graphic representation of the efficient frontier and portfolios that would be considered either inefficient or impossible to attain.

Monte Carlo Simulation

Named after Monte Carlo, Monaco, which is famous for its games of chance, MCS is a technique that randomly changes a variable over numerous iterations to simulate an outcome and develop a probability forecast of successfully achieving an outcome. In endowment management, MCS is used to demonstrate the probability of "success" as defined by achieving the endowment's asset growth and payout goals. In other words, MCS can provide the endowment manager with a comfort level that a given payout policy and asset allocation success will not deplete the real value of the endowment.

The problem with many quantitative tools is the divorce of judgment from their use. Although useful, both MVO and MCS have limitations such that they should not supplant the endowment manager's experience. As noted, MVO generates an efficient frontier by relying upon several inputs: expected return, expected volatility, and correlation coefficients. These variables are commonly input using historical measures as proxies for estimated future performance. This poses a variety of problems. First, the MVO will generally assume that returns are normally distributed and that this distribution is stationary. As such, asset classes with high historical returns are assumed to have high future returns. Second, an MVO optimizer is not generally time sensitive. In other words, the optimizer may ignore current environmental conditions that would cause a secular shift in the returns of a given asset class. Finally, an MVO optimizer may be subject to selection bias for certain asset classes. For example, private equity firms that fail will no longer report results and will be eliminated from the index used to provide the optimizer's historical data.[13]

TABLE 10.3
Selected Asset Class Correlations' Annual Returns

	Wilshire 5000	MSCI EAFE	MSCI EAFE Emerging Markets	Hedge Fund	Timber	Real Estate	Long-term U.S. Government	Inter U.S. Government	Short-term U.S. Government	Medical Inflation
Wilshire 5000	1.00									
MSCI EAFE	0.71	1.00								
MSCI EAFE Emerging Markets	0.41	0.67	1.00							
Hedge Fund	0.70	0.60	0.82	1.00						
Timber	0.38	0.18	0.32	0.58	1.00					
Real Estate	0.07	0.16	−0.42	−0.38	−0.59	1.00				
Long-term U.S. Government	0.08	−0.26	0.01	0.25	0.63	−0.65	1.00			
Intermediate U.S. Government	0.07	−0.32	−0.20	0.13	0.42	−0.34	0.91	1.00		
Short-term U.S. Government	0.10	−0.30	−0.36	0.01	0.09	0.04	0.64	0.89	1.00	
Medical Inflation	−0.30	−0.40	0.12	0.02	0.30	−0.80	0.73	0.55	0.30	1.00

Note: Historical data presented for illustrative purposes only.

Sources: Index data for the Wilshire 5000 data were obtained from Wilshire Associates. Index data for the MSCI EAFE and MSCI EAFE Emerging Markets were obtained from Morgan Stanley Capital International, Inc. Index data for the HFRI Fund Weighted Composite Index were obtained from Hedge Fund Research, Inc. Index and return amounts for timber and real estate were obtained from the National Council of Real Estate Investment Fiduciaries. Returns for the Long-term U.S. Government, Intermediate U.S. Government, and Short-term U.S. Government asset classes were calculated by the author using thirty-year Treasury Bond, five-year Treasury Note, and thirteen-week Treasury Bill average annual yields. Medical Inflation was obtained from the Bureau of Labor Statistics and represents the rate of inflation for medical care of all urban consumers. All annual returns and correlations were calculated by the principal author.

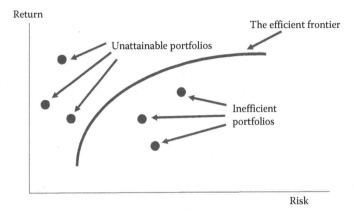

FIGURE 10.1 The efficient frontier.

Table 10.4 compares the returns and standard deviations for large- and small-cap stocks for the twenty-year periods ending in 1979 and 2010.

David Nawrocki identified a number of problems with typical MCS models as being that most optimizers assume "normal distributions and correlation coefficients of zero, neither of which are typical in the world of financial markets." Dr. Nawrocki subsequently described a number of other issues with MCS, including non-stationary distributions and non-linear correlations. Finally, Dr. Nawrocki quotes Harold Evensky, who eloquently noted that "[t]he problem is the confusion of risk with uncertainty. Risk assumes knowledge of the distribution of future outcomes (i.e., the input to the Monte Carlo simulation). Uncertainty or ambiguity describes a world (our world) in which the shape and location of the distribution is open to question. Contrary to academic orthodoxy, the distribution of U.S. stock market returns is far from normal."[14] Other critics have noted that many MCS simulators do not run enough iterations to provide a meaningful probability analysis.

Some of these criticisms have been addressed by using MCS simulators with more robust correlation assumptions and with a greater number of iterative trials. In addition, some simulators now combine MVO and MCS to determine probabilities along the efficient frontier.

The Role of Judgment

Despite their limitations, optimizers are useful tools for developing asset allocations for endowments. They represent another tool in ensuring rational and consistent investor behavior. Most endowments will also use bottom-up analysis to examine the opportunities within a given asset class and to make adjustments to the allocations across asset classes.

TABLE 10.4

Twenty-Year Risk and Return Small-Cap versus Large-Cap (Ibbotson Data)

	1979			2010		
	Risk	**Return**	**Correlation**	**Risk**	**Return**	**Correlation**
Small-Cap Stocks	30.8%	17.4%	78.0%	18.1%	26.85%	59.0%
Large-Cap Stocks	16.5%	8.1%		13.1%	15.06%	

Note: IA Micro-Cap Value 14.66, 17.44, 24.69, 0.44

Source: Reproduced from Loeper, D. 2001. Asset Allocation Math, Methods and Mistakes. Wealthcare Capital Management White Paper. CIMA, CIMC

OTHER ASSET CLASS CONSIDERATIONS

Liquidity

Many investors seek significant liquidity in their investments, and many professionally managed investments make arrangements to accommodate this desire. The endowment manager, however, should be sensitive to the diminished portfolio return that may result from requiring excess liquidity. Several studies have supported Harvard's Jeremy Stein in his observation that on-demand liquidity exposes "arbitrageurs to the risk of large withdrawals if they perform poorly in the short run. This risk in turn makes it dangerous for them [investment managers] to put on trades that are attractive in a long-run sense, but where convergence to fundamentals is unlikely to be either smooth or rapid" (J. Wayne Firebaugh, pers. comm.).

To take one leading example, open-end funds are unlikely to want to bet against something like the Internet bubble of the late 1990s.[15] It could be argued that competition for investor funds among managers makes mediocrity preferable to the chance of failure. Verne Sedlacek of Commonfund termed this phenomenon "time frame arbitrage" and noted that endowments that could have a longer-term investment horizon routinely cede this benefit by unnecessarily insisting on liquidity.[16] When the performance of less liquid asset classes such as real assets and private equity are compared to that of more liquid classes such as domestic equity, the endowment manager seeking superior long-term performance would do well to incorporate less liquid classes into the portfolio.

Other Asset Classes

Some analysts believe that the focus on asset classes may have gone too far as investors have sought to "over-optimize" their portfolios. David Loeper, CEO of Wealthcare Capital Management, explained this concept as follows:

> Where things have really got off track has been the insistence on breaking asset classes into sub-classes by style, market capitalization, etc. The unpredictability of all the inputs into our optimizers, even over long periods of time, has been ignored. We have attempted to take efficient portfolios of stocks, bonds and cash and make them even more efficient by breaking the unpredictable asset classes into even less predictable sub-classes. This has all been done into the pursuit of "efficiency" as the proposal was validated by the Brinson and Beebower study, which purports to find that over 90 percent of the investment return variance is explained by asset allocation. The risk that you produce inefficient portfolios INCREASES if you increase the number of "asset classes" for which you must forecast not only the risk and returns but also each asset class' correlation to the others. The results of the optimizer and your resulting portfolio's efficiency is based on the accuracy of the inputs and NOT THE NUMBER OF THE INPUTS.[17]

Organizational Expertise

Some organizations have significant tenures of experience with certain asset classes. For example, William Spitz noted that Vanderbilt's endowment has over twenty-five years of experience investing in private equities (William Spitz, pers. comm.). Breadth of experience with a particular asset class helps ensure that an endowment understands its true risks, the proper analysis of potential additional investments, and its interactions with other elements of the portfolio.

Groupthink

Several endowment fund managers have noted that they commonly compare their endowment allocations to those of peer institutions and that, as a result, endowment allocations are often similar to the "average" as reported by one or more surveys or consulting firms. One endowment fund manager expanded this thought by presciently noting that expecting materially different performance with substantially the same allocation is unreasonable. It is anecdotally interesting to wonder whether the seminal study "proving" the importance of asset allocation could have even had a substantially different conclusion. It seems likely that the pensions surveyed in the study had very similar allocations given the human tendency to measure one's self against peers and to use peers for guidance.

Although peer comparisons can be useful in evaluating your institution's own processes, groupthink can be highly contagious and dangerous. For example, in the first quarter of 2000, net flows into equity mutual funds were $140.4 billion as compared to net inflows of $187.7 billion for all of 1999. February's equity fund inflows were a staggering $55.6 billion, the record for single month investments. For all of 1999, total net mutual fund investments were $169.8 billion,[18] meaning that investors "re-balanced" out of asset classes such as bonds just in time for the market's March 24, 2000 peak (as measured by the S&P 500). Of course, investors are not immune to poor decision making in upward trending markets. In 2001, investors withdrew a then-record amount of $30 billion[18] in September, presumably in response to the September 11 terrorist attacks. These investors managed to skillfully "re-balance" their ways out of markets that declined approximately 11.5 percent during the first several trading sessions after the market re-opened, only to reach September 10, 2001 levels again after only 19 trading days. In 2002, investors revealed their relentless pursuit of self-destruction when they withdrew a net $27.7 billion from equity funds[19] just before the S&P 500's 29.9 percent 2003 growth.

Although it is easy to dismiss the travails of mutual fund investors as representing only the performance of amateurs, it is important to remember that institutions are not automatically immune by virtue of being managed by investment professionals. For example, in the 1960s and early 1970s, common wisdom stipulated that portfolios include the Nifty Fifty stocks that were viewed to be complete companies. These stocks were considered "one-decision" stocks for which the only decision was how much to buy. Even institutions got caught up in purchasing such current corporate stalwarts as Joe Schlitz Brewing, Simplicity Patterns, and Louisiana Home & Exploration. Collective market groupthink pushed these stocks to such prices that price/earnings ratios routinely exceeded 50. Subsequent disappointing performance of this strategy only revealed that common wisdom is often neither common nor wise.

More recently, the *New York Times* reported on June 21, 2007, that Bear Stearns had managed to forestall the demise of the Bear Stearns High Grade Structured Credit Strategies and the related Enhanced Leveraged Fund. The two funds held almost $2 billion in mortgage-backed debt securities, many of which were in the sub-prime market. To compound the problem, the funds borrowed much of the money used to purchase these securities. The firms who had provided the loans to make these purchases represent some of the smartest names on Wall Street, including JP Morgan, Goldman Sachs, Bank of America, Merrill Lynch, and Deutsche Bank.[20] Despite its efforts, Bear Stearns had to inform investors less than a week later that these two funds had collapsed.

Amount of Support Endowment Needs to Provide

The endowment manager will certainly want to consider the proportion of the institution's operating budget that is funded by the endowment. For example, an institution whose operating budget is funded 30 percent by the endowment may need to make fundamentally different decisions regarding the risk/return parameters of the portfolio than an institution whose operating budget is funded 5 percent by the endowment.

TACTICS FOR IMPLEMENTING THE ALLOCATION POLICY

The Efficient Market Hypothesis

An efficient capital market is one in which security prices rapidly change to reflect the arrival of new information and where the prices of securities reflect all information about the securities. The efficient market hypothesis (EMH) includes assumptions regarding the strength of the markets' efficiency.

For example, if the markets fully reflect all security-market information such as historical pricing trends, the efficiency is deemed to be of at least the weak form. If, on the other hand, security prices reflect all public and private information, the efficiency is deemed to be of the strong form. If the EMH is true in its strongest form, investors cannot hope to achieve risk-adjusted returns in excess of those for the applicable market. In other words, if the EMH is true in its strongest sense, endowment managers would wisely seek to employ a passive form of investing in which the endowment purchases baskets of investments designed to replicate a given market index.

Numerous research studies have been conducted regarding the strength of the market's efficiency, and the results suggest that the domestic markets are efficient to some degree. However, the manager considering a purely passive approach to endowment management should consider several additional items. First, passive investing may be an unattractive strategy in protracted bear or flat markets. For example, the Dow Jones Industrial Average fell approximately 9.7 percent over the fifteen-year period between 1966 and 1981. Second, although domestic equity markets are generally believed to have some efficiency, other asset classes are believed to be much less efficient.

Managing for Alpha

Alpha measures non-systematic return, or the return that cannot be attributed to the market. It shows the difference between a fund's actual return and its expected performance given the level of systematic (or market) risk (as measured by beta). For example, a fund with a beta of 1.2 in a market that returns 10 percent would be expected to earn 12 percent. If, in fact, the fund earns a return of 14 percent, it then has an alpha of 2, which would suggest that the manager has added value. Conversely, a return below that expected given the fund's beta would suggest that the manager diminished value. In a truly efficient market, no manager should be able to consistently generate positive alpha. In such a market, the endowment manager would likely employ a passive strategy that seeks to replicate index returns. Although there is substantial evidence of efficient domestic markets, there is also evidence to suggest that certain managers do repeat their positive alpha performance. In fact, a 2002 study by Roger Ibbotson and Amita Patel found that "the phenomenon of persistence does exist in domestic equity funds." The same study suggested that 65 percent of mutual funds with the highest style-adjusted alpha repeated with positive alpha performances in the following year.[21]

Additional research suggests that active management can add value and achieve positive alpha in concentrated portfolios. A recent study of actively managed mutual funds found that "on average, higher industry concentration improves the performance of the funds. The most concentrated funds generate, after adjusting for risk . . . the highest performance. They yield an average abnormal return [alpha] of 2.56 percent per year before deducting expenses and 1.12 percent per year after deducting expenses."[22]

FutureMetrics, a pension plan consulting firm, calculated that in 2006 the median pension fund achieved record alpha of 3.7 percent compared to a 60/40 benchmark portfolio, the best since the firm began calculating return data in 1988.[23] Over longer periods of time, an endowment manager's ability to achieve positive alpha for his or her entire portfolio is more hotly debated. Dimensional Fund Advisors, a mutual fund firm specializing in a unique form of passive management, compiled FutureMetrics data on 192 pension funds for the period of 1988 through 2005. Their research showed that, over this period of time, approximately 75 percent of the pension funds underperformed the 60/40 benchmark.[24] The end result is that many endowments will use a combination of active and passive management approaches with respect to some portion of the domestic equity segment of their allocation. One approach is known as the "core and satellite" method, in which a "core" investment into a passive index is used to capture the broader market's performance while concentrated satellite positions are taken in an attempt to "capture" alpha. Because other asset classes such as private equity, foreign equity, and real assets are often viewed to be less efficient, the endowment manager will typically use active management to obtain positive alpha from these segments.

The Tactical Approach

Many successful endowments will establish a "strategic" allocation policy that is intended to guide long-term (greater than one year) investment decisions. This strategic allocation reflects the endowment's thinking regarding the existence of perceived fundamental shifts in the market. Most endowments will also establish a target range or band for each asset class. The day-to-day managers then have the flexibility to make tactical decisions for a given class so long as they stay within the target range. The term "tactical" when used in the context of investment strategy refers to the manager's ability to take advantage of short-term (under one year) market anomalies such as pricing discrepancies between different sectors or across different styles. Historically, tactical decisions with respect to asset allocation were derided as "market timing." However, market timing implies moving outside of the target ranges, whereas tactical decision making simply addresses the opportunistic deployment of funds within the asset class target range.

PAYOUT POLICY

Although an endowment is intended to provide an institution with continuing support and as such is a long-term investment, the institution's needs for current support dictate that some level of income be drawn from the endowment. The original payout policies had their roots in federal tax regulations that prescribed certain minimum payout standards for private foundations. Although these rules are not generally applicable to healthcare endowments, the 5 percent payout currently required under these rules seems to be a starting point for many endowments. After an extended bull market in which institutions could simultaneously raise their level of endowment distributions and increase the asset base of the endowment through market growth, the three-year bear market forced many endowments to re-examine their payout policies.

SUSTAINABLE WITHDRAWALS

Spending policies, which have a different yet as important a role in overall investments policy as asset allocation, are focused on the concept of providing for inter-generational equity; that is, current [patients and programs] should be neither advantaged nor disadvantaged relative to future [patients and programs]. To maintain this inter-generational equity, the endowment must maintain its value in real terms (i.e., adjusted for inflation) over a period of time. Thinking of it in another way, the endowment at a minimum should cover an institution's spending and then grow by at least the rate of inflation.[25]

In other words, if the applicable long-term rate of inflation is 3 percent and the rate of withdrawal is 5 percent, the long-term rate of return cannot be less than 8 percent in order to avoid depleting the real value of the portfolio. The difficulty arises when market volatility causes the rate of return during discreet time periods to fluctuate significantly from the long-term average. This phenomenon can cause an endowment to meet its long-term return objectives but still to deplete the portfolio.

COMMON PAYOUT METHODS

Recognizing the risk that market volatility represents to long-term portfolio health, endowments utilize a variety of methods to calculate periodic payouts.

- **Investment yield:** An endowment using this method spends only its dividends and interest and re-invests any unrealized and realized gains. There would appear to be two primary disadvantages of this method. First, the payout amount will be extremely volatile as yields on equity and fixed income investments fluctuate. Second, the endowment manager could be encouraged to adopt a short-term focus on yield to the detriment of purchasing power preservation.
- **Percentage of the prior year's ending market value:** An endowment using this method would withdraw some fixed percentage of the prior year's market value. As with the investment yield method, disbursements from the endowment can be somewhat volatile under this method.
- **Moving average:** This approach, which is most common among educational institutions, generally involves taking a percentage of a moving average of the endowment market value. The percentage commonly approximates 5 percent over a three-year period.

- **Inflation-adjusted:** This method simply adds some factor to the applicable rate of inflation for the institution.
- **Banded inflation or corridor:** This method is similar to the inflation-adjusted method except that it establishes a corridor or band of minimum and maximum increases in an attempt to limit the volatility of the disbursement amounts.

Table 10.5 compares the year-end endowment balances under each of these payout methodologies over a twenty-year period assuming a 60/40 equity/fixed income allocation to roughly mirror the average allocation described earlier. Table 10.6 compares annual disbursements from the endowment (see note to Table 10.5 for details). Equity returns are approximated using the S&P 500 index returns while fixed income returns are approximated using five-year Treasury bill yields.

TABLE 10.5
Payout Policy Comparison Ending Portfolio Balance (in Thousands)

	Spend Yield	Spend Percentage	Moving Average	Inflation Adjusted	Banded Inflation	Medical Inflation
1984	$101,170	$101,085	$101,085	$99,474	$99,585	$106,111
1985	$103,268	$102,181	$102,217	$98,301	$99,171	$113,288
1986	$106,576	$103,290	$103,382	$96,216	$98,760	$122,017
1987	$109,668	$104,410	$104,561	$96,007	$98,544	$129,098
1988	$112,625	$105,543	$105,754	$94,732	$98,135	$138,021
1989	$115,671	$106,688	$106,961	$91,968	$97,727	$149,758
1990	$118,841	$107,845	$108,181	$88,288	$97,322	$164,113
1991	$122,610	$109,015	$109,416	$86,227	$96,918	$177,110
1992	$127,017	$110,198	$110,664	$85,329	$96,515	$188,846
1993	$132,142	$111,393	$111,927	$85,492	$96,700	$199,030
1994	$136,611	$112,601	$113,204	$86,059	$97,341	$208,826
1995	$141,489	$113,823	$114,495	$87,467	$98,935	$217,071
1996	$146,590	$115,058	$115,802	$89,695	$100,997	$223,666
1997	$151,886	$116,306	$117,123	$92,176	$103,103	$229,971
1998	$158,036	$117,567	$118,459	$94,175	$105,252	$237,827
1999	$164,117	$118,843	$119,811	$95,977	$107,267	$246,557
2000	$170,110	$120,132	$121,178	$97,335	$108,785	$256,838
2001	$177,438	$121,435	$122,561	$98,176	$109,725	$268,962
2002	$185,622	$122,752	$123,959	$98,703	$110,313	$282,541
2003	$194,738	$124,084	$125,373	$100,556	$112,384	$293,016
2004	$206,585	$131,634	$133,002	$106,674	$119,222	$305,432
2005	$219,158	$139,644	$141,095	$113,165	$126,477	$318,526
2006	$232,493	$148,141	$149,680	$120,051	$134,172	$329,874

Note: All calculations were performed by the principal author and assume an initial $100 million endowment portfolio and a 60/40 split between domestic equities and fixed income. Domestic equity returns are assumed to be entirely appreciation in nature and to be approximated by increases in the S&P 500 index. Fixed income returns are assumed to be approximated by average annual yields reported for U.S. five-year Treasury notes. The analysis assumes cost-free annual re-balancing to the asset allocation. The Spend Yield method assumes that only the yield (interest) is spent each year. The Spend Percentage method assumes that a consistent 5 percent of the prior year's ending balance is spent each year. The Moving Average method assumes that 5 percent of the average of the prior three year's ending balance is spent. The Inflation-Adjusted method assumes that ½ percent is added to the rate of medical inflation to determine each year's spending rate. The Medical Rate of Inflation was obtained from the Bureau of Labor Statistics CPI for Medical Care for All Urban Consumers. The Banded Inflation method utilizes the same assumptions as the Inflation Adjusted method except that annual spending cannot be less than 4 percent or more than 6.5 percent. Table 10.6 compares the annual disbursements from the endowment under these alternative methodologies.

TABLE 10.6
Payout Policy Comparison Annual Endowment Payouts (in Thousands)

	Spend Yield	Spend Percentage	Moving Average	Inflation Adjusted	Banded Inflation
1984	$4,914	$5,000	$5,000	$6,611	$6,500
1985	$4,058	$5,054	$5,018	$7,226	$6,473
1986	$2,977	$5,109	$5,055	$8,066	$6,446
1987	$3,393	$5,164	$5,111	$6,064	$6,225
1988	$3,716	$5,221	$5,169	$7,116	$6,405
1989	$3,807	$5,277	$5,228	$8,529	$6,379
1990	$3,868	$5,334	$5,288	$9,275	$6,352
1991	$3,463	$5,392	$5,348	$7,434	$6,326
1992	$3,053	$5,451	$5,409	$6,145	$6,300
1993	$2,603	$5,510	$5,471	$5,028	$5,688
1994	$3,571	$5,570	$5,533	$4,635	$5,243
1995	$3,435	$5,630	$5,597	$3,828	$4,330
1996	$3,508	$5,691	$5,660	$3,095	$3,957
1997	$3,624	$5,753	$5,725	$2,977	$4,040
1998	$3,092	$5,815	$5,790	$3,610	$4,124
1999	$3,535	$5,878	$5,856	$3,928	$4,390
2000	$3,993	$5,942	$5,923	$4,482	$5,009
2001	$3,023	$6,007	$5,991	$5,081	$5,679
2002	$2,612	$6,072	$6,059	$5,448	$6,088
2003	$2,179	$6,138	$6,128	$4,153	$4,641
2004	$2,666	$6,204	$6,198	$4,763	$5,324
2005	$3,350	$6,582	$6,372	$5,107	$5,707
2006	$4,151	$6,982	$6,657	$4,598	$5,138

Source: All calculations were performed by the principal author using assumptions that are the same as those used in Table 10.5.

STRESS TESTING

The numerical results indicate that spending must be set substantially lower than the long-term growth rate of the portfolio, in order to produce an acceptable probability of preserving real value of the original [principal]. As a very crude rule of thumb, the spending rate must be set at 200 basis points lower than the expected growth rate of the fund itself in order to secure a less than 20% chance of having a negative real return after 20 years. Thus, if a fund is expected to grow by 6% in real terms—a generous equity premium in today's environment—spending should be set at less than 4% of current assets.[26]

In other words, even if an endowment achieves its expected long-term real return of 6 percent, it is possible for the endowment to fail to meet the goal of long-term principal preservation. Table 10.7 summarizes the diminution in real value of the $100 million endowment under the alternative payout methods described and illustrated in the previous section.

AVOIDING MISTAKES

Among the best of the numerous books analyzing the causes of the crisis in the financial markets is *Too Big to Save?*,[27] written by Robert Pozen, chairman of MFS Investment Management and member of The Commonwealth Fund's board of directors and its investment committee.

In *Too Big to Save?*, Pozen describes how the Federal Reserve set interest rates too low from 2001 through 2006, leading dollar investors across the world to search for higher yields from

TABLE 10.7

Payout Policy Comparison Erosion of Purchasing Power (in Thousands)

	Spend Yield	Spend Percentage	Moving Average	Inflation Adjusted	Banded Inflation
1984	−$4,940	−$5,026	−$5,026	−$6,636	−$6,526
1985	−$10,020	−$11,107	−$11,071	−$14,987	−$14,117
1986	−$15,442	−$18,728	−$18,635	−$25,801	−$23,258
1987	−$19,430	−$24,688	−$24,537	−$33,091	−$30,554
1988	−$25,396	−$32,478	−$32,267	−$43,289	−$39,886
1989	−$34,087	−$43,070	−$42,797	−$57,790	−$52,030
1990	−$45,271	−$56,267	−$55,931	−$75,824	−$66,791
1991	−$54,500	−$68,095	−$67,694	−$90,883	−$80,192
1992	−$61,829	−$78,648	−$78,182	−$103,517	−$92,331
1993	−$66,888	−$87,637	−$87,103	−$113,538	−$102,330
1994	−$72,215	−$96,225	−$95,623	−$122,767	−$111,485
1995	−$75,582	−$103,248	−$102,575	−$129,603	−$118,136
1996	−$77,076	−$108,609	−$107,865	−$133,972	−$122,669
1997	−$78,085	−$113,665	−$112,848	−$137,795	−$126,868
1998	−$79,792	−$120,260	−$119,368	−$143,653	−$132,575
1999	−$82,440	−$127,714	−$126,746	−$150,579	−$139,290
2000	−$86,728	−$136,706	−$135,660	−$159,503	−$148,053
2001	−$91,524	−$147,527	−$146,402	−$170,786	−$159,237
2002	−$96,919	−$159,789	−$158,582	−$183,838	−$172,228
2003	−$98,278	−$168,933	−$167,643	−$192,461	−$180,633
2004	−$98,844	−$173,798	−$172,430	−$198,757	−$186,209
2005	−$99,368	−$178,882	−$177,431	−$205,361	−$192,049
2006	−$97,381	−$181,733	−$180,194	−$209,823	−$195,702

Source: All calculations were performed by the principal author using assumptions that are the same as those employed in
Table 10.5.

mortgage-backed securities than were obtainable with U.S. Treasuries. This global demand,
given lax regulation of many mortgage lenders and the excessive leverage allowed in Wall Street
banks, drove housing prices to bubble heights. Pozen documents how the spread of new financial
instruments such as collateralized debt obligations and credit default swaps introduced significant
unappreciated risks into the financial system, a problem compounded by the trading of such securities outside regulated exchanges and by the conflicted position of credit-rating agencies, whose
compensation depended on favorable ratings for securities they were supposed to score objectively.
In the debate on legislation to address these flaws, there is wide agreement on the need for the
following reforms: a systemic risk monitor, higher capital requirements for financial institutions,
more transparent and better organized markets for financial derivatives, as well as expansion of the
federal government's resolution authority to cover insolvent non-bank financial firms. Passage of
reform legislation, however, has been delayed by major points of disagreement, including the scope
of the Federal Reserve's authority, the proper agency for regulating consumer financial products,
and the supervisory framework for mega-financial institutions in the system—how to insure their
accountability and define a contained, low-cost role for government when these institutions get into
trouble.

Along with all Americans, foundation endowment managers have a great deal riding on the outcome of the ongoing financial system reform debate in the U.S. Congress. The modest investment
returns forecast through 2020, noted above, are predicated on at least a modest economic recovery
and average annual inflation of 2.5 percent.

However, as documented by Carmen M. Reinhart and Kenneth S. Rogoff in a recently published landmark study of financial crises, the typical aftermath of a major bank-centered financial crisis involves a protracted period of falling gross domestic product, often lasting two years or more.[28] In their review of eight centuries of financial crises, with special focus on those in this century, these scholars label the current turmoil as the "Second Great Contraction," ranking just below the one that produced the Great Depression. Thus, there is substantial risk that the nation may face slow growth and high unemployment for an extended period. This risk puts a premium on getting financial system reforms "right," and in place as soon as possible. As Rogoff notes, "If we don't re-regulate the banking system properly, we'll either get very slow growth from overregulation, or another financial crisis in just ten to fifteen years."[29]

Added to these risks are those posed by the state of U.S. finances—the level of government debt and persistent international balance of payments (current account)—deficits that threaten long-term growth and stability.

RETHINKING THE MANAGEMENT OF FOUNDATION ENDOWMENTS: THE COMMONWEALTH FUND 2009 ANNUAL REPORT

In *Too Big to Save?*, Pozen lays out the mistakes made by many modelers responsible for the introduction of the complex financial instruments, such as mortgage-backed securities and credit default swaps, that played key roles in bringing the financial system to its knees in 2008. Reinhart and Rogoff similarly identify recurring fallacies and lessons to be drawn from the history of financial crises. These two bodies of work can help foundations avoid mistakes in managing their endowments.

1. **Simple extrapolations of the past are dangerous:** Pozen cautions that "the differences between past and future trend lines can be as important as the similarities."[30] For example, given the gravity of the current financial crisis, foundations should be careful about assuming that the historical average of market returns will prevail over the next several years.
2. **Be patient in riding out financial bubbles:** As Pozen reminds us, investment bubbles can last for years, but economic fundamentals ultimately win out. In safeguarding against bubbles, foundations should base their budgeting and investment strategies on what they perceive to be long-term realities. As Jeremy Grantham points out, this means in practice that, in a financial bubble like that of 2003–2008, perpetual foundations should allow their spending rate (spending as a percentage of endowment average market value) to fall— thereby setting aside "fat years" funds for use in the lean years that are inevitably to come (Jeremy Grantham, pers. comm.). More difficult, of course, is sticking to fundamentally sound investment strategies that produce below-benchmark returns in periods of market excess. As Pozen concludes, "The timing of the burst of any bubble is impossible to predict, so be very patient."[30]
3. **The frequency of extreme events is greater than people think:** Major global banking crises have occurred, on average, every twelve years since 1900, as Reinhart and Rogoff document, and every eleven years since 1945. For perpetual foundations, the occurrence within a forty-year period of two endowment-shaking crises like the financial crisis and oil shock–induced stagflation of the 1970s (when it was not unusual for the inflation-adjusted market value of foundation endowments to decline by 60 percent) and the 2008 global financial disorder indicates that such crises are not "black swan" events. Foundation managers would be wise to heed Pozen's advice: Pay more attention to low-probability events and hedge or insure against them if possible.
4. **Beware of the "This Time Is Different" syndrome:** As Reinhart and Rogoff describe, the thinking of the mid-2000s in the United States was, "Everything is fine because of globalization, the technology boom, our superior financial system, our better understanding

of monetary policy, and the phenomenon of securitized debt."[31] In their research covering multiple centuries, these authors find that similar thinking preceded virtually every financial crisis. Foundation managers should conclude that the siren call of "This Time Is Different" is a sure signal to lower the risk profile of the endowment.

5. **Be knowledgeable of the predictors of financial crisis:** Reinhart and Rogoff present a convincing body of evidence that markedly rising asset prices (particularly housing bubbles), slowing real economic activity, large current account deficits, and sustained debt build-ups (public or private) generally precede a financial crisis. Attention to such systemic risk measures can help foundations position their endowments to better weather financial crises.

6. **Understand how the origins of a financial crisis can greatly affect the depth and duration of its impact on economies and markets:** Reinhart and Rogoff's research informs us that bubbles are far more dangerous when they are fueled by debt, as was the case with the global housing bubble of the early to mid-2000s. Their study reveals that global financial crises arising from excess leverage are typically followed by very severe multi-year slowdowns in economic activity accompanied by high unemployment. Just as such crises produce major bear markets in stocks, so they entail bear market rallies followed by resumed slumps. Endowment managers ignore this pattern at considerable risk.

7. **Ignore liquidity risk at your peril:** With their deep endowment pockets and significant fixed-income holdings, foundations generally do not worry much about liquidity. With increasing commitments to private equity and hedge fund partnerships, however, liquidity risk was a real concern for many endowments before the recent financial crisis. The crisis demonstrated that this risk rises significantly as leverage increases within the financial system. Thus, foundations should keep necessary reserves on hand and take increasing care that they are cautiously invested as financial storms gather. As yields fall on short-term investments, foundations will be lured to higher-yielding alternative products, but the risks and liquidity profiles of such products require very close examination. In light of recent experience, a number of foundations have taken out lines of credit, and more should consider doing so.

8. **Be ready to question the experts:** Adapting Pozen's advice on how banks and investment firms should manage their expert modelers, a primary role of a foundation's investment committee is to understand the limitations of the foundation's financial staff, consultants, and investment managers. Committee members should ask questions that push the so-called experts to explore fully the risks involved in each strategy and the assumptions underlying any quantitative model.

OTHER CONSIDERATIONS

Management Models

Solo Investment Committee Model

In this common approach, typically employed by very small foundations but also by many small and even midsize ones, the investment committee of the board has virtually all strategic and operational responsibility for the endowment—working with little or no internal staff or consultant support, although generally delegating portfolio management to a brokerage firm, mutual funds, or external investment managers (typically using commingled funds shared with other investors).

In this model there is no question where accountability lies, provided performance is tracked and the board holds the committee accountable.

The weaknesses are that it can be difficult to recruit members with sufficient investment experience and the ability to commit the required time and attention to successful investment, and there is significant risk of conflict of interest. There are challenges in achieving consensus while avoiding "groupthink," and no investment company research is available.

Investment Committee-Investment Consultant Model

As foundation size and investment strategy complexity increase, many investment committees recognize the need for an investment consultant to help inform and guide their decisions, and sometimes to help implement them. The amount of responsibility delegated by the committee ranges significantly under this model, depending on the capacities and preferences of the committee and the ability and services offered by the consultant.

The strength in this model is provided by advice a consultant can bring on asset allocation based on a wide range of contacts and experience, as well as a strong financial research base. A consultant can provide an independent voice that helps build a consensus and avoids conflicts of interest.

This model has weakened accountability by diffusion of responsibility resulting from difficulties in attributing performance. There is difficulty in verifying the past performance of the consultant, and the entity must compete with many other clients requiring consultant's attention. Effective management of the consultant can also be an issue.

Investment Committee-Internal Financial Staff-Investment Consultant Model

Any foundation with assets of $250 million or more is likely to pursue a sophisticated diversified investment strategy. Under these circumstances, the day-to-day responsibilities of managing the endowment require qualified staff; moreover, barring an investment committee member with the time, inclination, and expertise to work closely with the consultant on strategic and operational issues like manager searches, a professional staff member is needed to ensure the best use of the time and skills of the consultant and committee members. Thus, this model entails still higher de facto (if not formal) levels of responsibility delegation by the investment committee.

The model provides better oversight of and more effective use of the consultant. More accountability exists and there are safeguards from conflict of interest. This model, however, relies heavily on the ability of internal staff and the entity's ability to pay competitive wages to attract capable staff to add value.

Internal CIO Model

Once a foundation reaches the $2 billion level in endowment assets, it becomes economical and feasible to hire a full-time, highly trained, experienced chief investment officer (CIO) and recruit a sizeable, dedicated professional investment team, compensated at the necessary competitive levels. As described by Lawrence E. Kochard and Cathleen M. Rittereiser,[32] a number of very large foundations, including the Carnegie Corporation and the William and Flora Hewlett Foundation, use this model and have achieved considerable success.

Outsourced CIO (O-CIO) Model

Given the shortcomings of the solo investment committee, committee-consultant, and committee-financial staff-consultant models discussed above, the trend in recent years is for endowments with less than $2 billion dollars in assets to fully outsource the management of their endowment to a firm that essentially offers a packaged set of services comparable to those that very large foundations obtain with an in-house CIO. The O-CIO firm—the best being the creation of a stellar former CIO of a large university endowment or pension fund—assumes most of the responsibility for managing the endowment. While the amount of delegated authority varies from foundation to foundation, most investment committees using this model have an essentially advisory role and, beyond consultation on broad strategy, leave decisions on managers and tactical moves to the O-CIO. The spectrum of actual services offered by O-CIOs is wide, ranging from somewhat customized portfolios to one-size-fits-all proprietary portfolios.

This method provides a high level of investment experience and expertise and is a potential solution to the problem of a "missing CIO" for endowments with less than $2 billion. Weaknesses of this approach are the limitations on customization of strategy, the "key person risk," and inadequate oversight by the investment committee.

Controlling Risks

By definition, investment risk means uncertainty. As John Griswold, Executive Director of the Commonfund Institute noted, however, risk can be managed, but it takes "top-down commitment to risk management and a tough attitude." An endowment must understand its risks and put someone in charge of regularly assessing risk and reporting to the committee (John Griswold, pers. comm.). In 1994, Orange County in California filed for bankruptcy after its treasurer invested significant portions of its $7.5 billion investment pool in various leveraged or derivative securities. It is quite likely that this bankruptcy would not have occurred had the Orange County treasurer, Robert Citron, been subject to independent, informed oversight and a comprehensive risk management strategy.[33]

If the ultimate measure of performance is achieving the endowment's goals, the ultimate measure of risk is failing to achieve those same goals. Unfortunately, the inter-generational nature of endowments is such that ultimate performance and risk are difficult to measure in discreet time increments. In fact, fixation solely upon the long-term risk would often obscure short-term risks that would actually result in long-term failure. In managing endowment risk, there seem to be several best practice steps that successful endowments follow.

Understand the Risk

Although the broad risk facing endowments can be quickly summarized as "the failure to achieve spending and inflation-adjusted growth goals," the endowment portfolio and the individual assets may face any number of the following subsidiary risks.

- Call risk: The risk faced by a holder of a callable bond that a bond issuer will take advantage of the callable bond feature and redeem the issue prior to maturity. This means the bondholder will receive payment on the value of the bond and, in most cases, will be re-investing in a less favorable environment (one with a lower interest rate).
- Capital risk: The risk an investor faces that he or she may lose all or part of the principal amount invested.
- Commodity risk: The threat that a change in the price of a production input will adversely affect a producer who uses that input.
- Company risk: The risk that certain factors affecting a specific company may cause its stock to change in price in a different way from stocks as a whole.
- Concentration risk: Probability of loss arising from heavily lopsided exposure to a particular group of counterparties.
- Counterparty risk: The risk that the other party to an agreement will default.
- Credit risk: The risk of loss of principal or loss of a financial reward stemming from a borrower's failure to repay a loan or otherwise meet a contractual obligation.
- Currency risk: A form of risk that arises from the change in price of one currency against another.
- Deflation risk: A general decline in prices, often caused by a reduction in the supply of money or credit.
- Economic risk: The likelihood that an investment will be affected by macroeconomic conditions such as government regulation, exchange rates, or political stability.
- Hedging risk: Making an investment to reduce the risk of adverse price movements in an asset.
- Inflation risk: Uncertainty over the future real value (after inflation) of your investment.
- Interest rate risk: Risk to the earnings or market value of a portfolio due to uncertain future interest rates.
- Legal risk: Risk from uncertainty due to legal actions or uncertainty in the applicability or interpretation of contracts, laws, or regulations.
- Liquidity risk:[34] The risk stemming from the lack of marketability of an investment that cannot be bought or sold quickly enough to prevent or minimize a loss.

It would seem self-evident that a risk that is not fully understood cannot be consciously managed or mitigated. As such, the endowment board should consider asking the chief investment officer to delineate the risks associated with each asset class and determine whether options exist for mitigating or eliminating those risks (John Griswold, pers. comm.).

Measure the Risk

In addition to the listed risks that may be relevant to particular investments or classes, most endowments will use one of the following broad measures of risk:

- **Beta:** Beta is a measure of systematic or market risk for either an individual asset or an entire portfolio. In other words, beta measures a given security's sensitivity to market movements. For example, a beta of 1.0 means that a 1 percent change in the market will result in a 1 percent change in the security's price. A beta of 1.5 means that a 1 percent change in the market will result in a 1.5 percent change in the price of the security. Beta is calculated using a regression model that compares fluctuations in the security's return to that of the market. Many endowments will seek to maintain a beta that is substantially less than that of some broad market index.
- **Standard deviation:** In statistical terms, standard deviation measures a normal distribution around a mean or average. For investment purposes, standard deviation is used to measure "risk" or, more literally, volatility. As with beta, standard deviation can be measured at either the asset or the portfolio level.
- **Value at risk (VAR):** VAR[35] as a risk measure has been gaining in popularity for several reasons. First, portfolio managers and their clients intuitively evaluate risk in monetary terms rather than standard deviation. Second, in marketable portfolios, deviations of a given amount below the mean are less common than deviations above the mean for that same amount.[36] Unfortunately, measures such as standard deviation assume symmetrical risk. VAR measures the risk of loss at some probability level over a given period of time. For example, a manager may desire to know the portfolio's risk over a one-day time period. The VAR can be reported as being within a desired quantile of a single day's loss. In other words, assume a portfolio possesses a one-day 90 percent VAR of $5 million. This means that in any one of ten days the portfolio's value could be expected to decline by more than $5 million. Note that VAR is only useful for the liquid portions of an endowment's portfolio and cannot be used to assess risks in classes such as private equity or real assets.

Contingency Plan

Many quantitative methods would have suggested that the October 1987 crash was impossible. Mark Rubenstein, a professor at University of California at Berkeley, noted that if annualized stock market volatility is assumed to be approximately 20 percent, "(the historical average since 1928), the probability that the stock market could fall 29 percent in a single day is 10^{-160}. So improbable is such an event that it would not be anticipated to occur even if the stock market were to last for 20 billion years. . . . Indeed, such an event should not occur even if the stock market were to enjoy a rebirth for 20 billion years in each of 20 billion big bangs."[37] Although it was statistically impossible for it to happen, it did. The nature of crises is such that many are unanticipated events with unexpected precipitators. As such, a contingency plan cannot address every conceivable event. A contingency plan should address the process for confronting these events. Most importantly, the plan should assign responsibility for actions and contain provisions to limit the ability of panic to impair long-term decisions.

Endowments have at their core donor trust. As such, it is important for an endowment's contingency plan to include provisions for communicating promptly and forthrightly with the public. One only has to look at the Red Cross performance during the aftermath of the September 11, 2001, tragedy to receive a lesson on an inappropriate approach. After donating more than $550 million to the Liberty Fund, donors learned that less than $175 million had been spent on direct aid for victims and that the Red Cross was allocating a large portion of the funds to other programs. After public outcry and congressional hearings, the Red Cross announced that all donations would be spent on direct victim relief. Unfortunately, Dr. Bernadine Healy, the president of the Red Cross, resigned at least in part because of this controversy.[38] These violations of public confidence can have long-term impacts on an endowment's donor base. Consider also the United Way, whose national leader, William V. Aramony, was accused of fraud, embezzlement, and other charges in 1992. Even a decade later, inflation-adjusted contributions are lower than they were before the scandal, even though charitable giving in general has doubled.[39]

The very nature of crises is such that pre-determined contingency plans generally allow more rapid and appropriate reaction. For an endowment, a well-considered contingency plan will include both an action (or standstill) plan and a public relations plan.

Re-balance

Re-balancing the endowment portfolio contradicts conventional market "wisdom" that you allow your winners to run. Perhaps in speculation this is true, but for investing such a view can be deadly. Take, for example, the Cleveland Clinic's experience with its endowment. In 1999, the Cleveland Clinic Foundation reported $1.2 billion in investments. Unfortunately, by the end of 2002, the Foundation's investments were valued at $650 million, a loss of approximately 50 percent. Its losses reflected its substantial allocation into technology stocks during the technology boom of the late 1990s. As a result of these investment losses, the Clinic had to postpone a planned $300 million cardiology center, and certain debt financing had to be re-structured. In addition, both Moody's and Standard & Poor lowered their ratings on the Clinic.[40]

Because re-balancing by definition requires an endowment to take money from more successful investment classes and invest it into underperforming classes, it will always cause some measure of anguish. There will always be some reason why re-balancing should not take place. In 1987, the unprecedented single-day decline in the market could have been presented as an argument against moving into equities. In 1998, the seemingly endless number of world financial crises could have provided a useful excuse to avoid re-balancing into emerging markets. Current bond prices could provide similar reasons for not re-balancing into an appropriate fixed income position. However, because the whole reason for asset allocation policy decisions is to mitigate the negative impact that irrational behavior can have on an endowment's investment performance, the endowment should include a process for periodic re-balancing of its assets.

WRITE IT DOWN

As described earlier, the primary lesson of asset allocation studies seems to be that investor behavior is arguably the primary determinant of investment success. No one would dream of building a new house without a blueprint. Although the homeowner might make change orders throughout the process, the blueprint will always be used to ensure that the actual house floor plan matches the homeowner's expectation and, more importantly, that the house is structurally sound. The Investment Policy Statement (IPS) is the endowment manager's equivalent of a blueprint. One consultant notes that an IPS must possess three characteristics:[41]

- **Detailed and specific:** The more detail and specificity an IPS embodies, the more useful and measurable it will be.
- **Sound rationale:** The IPS should answer many of the "why" questions that could arise when someone with perfect hindsight looks to question the endowment manager's approach.
- **Logically consistent:** The IPS should function as a cohesive document in which the provisions do not contradict one another.

Jay Yoder, CFA, Director of Investments at Smith College, noted that an IPS must have the following seven components:[41]

- Return objectives
- Definition and tolerance of risk
- Asset allocation guidelines
- Asset class rationales
- Provisions for periodic re-balancing
- Benchmarks at both the portfolio and asset class level
- Policy regarding indexing

A well-considered endowment IPS will also likely address such issues as payout policy, descriptions of roles and responsibilities, and any investment restrictions. See a sample of an IPS at the end of this chapter.

COMMITTEES AND STAFF

The failures of corporate governance have been well-publicized, with such examples as Enron, MCI WorldCom, Adelphia, the Bear Stearns hedge funds, and even the New York Stock Exchange. That such failures could happen despite the number of intelligent and talented people at each of these entities suggests that the problems of corporate governance could easily afflict the committee running an endowment. Although Sarbanes-Oxley does not yet directly impact the boards of non-profit organizations such as endowments, Verne Sedlacek, the former CEO of the Harvard Management Company and current CEO of Commonfund, suggests that it does provide some considerations for best practices. In particular, Verne Sedlacek notes that endowments should consider the following minimum items with respect to their boards:[42]

- **Structure:** One of the key considerations with respect to structure is the board's size. Verne Sedlacek notes that the trend is towards smaller, more active boards. Larger boards can devolve in such a way that little is accomplished.
- **People:** Although it may be enticing to have only investment professionals on the board, the endowment may actually find a board composed of individuals with varying experience to be more valuable. Investment professionals are not immune to believing that their approach or knowledge of a particular market segment represents the best option for the endowment.
- **Relationships:** It is becoming increasingly important that endowment boards have a number of independent voices.
- **Compensation:** Although most board members are volunteers, the potential liability and degree of work required by service might lead the endowment to consider paying board members to ensure that it attracts the best possible talent.
- **Roles and Responsibilities:** The endowment should try to carefully delineate the responsibilities of the board and its members in relation to internal staff and the external managers. Indecisive or conflicting actions by the board can make it difficult for the endowment to retain quality staff.

SELF-ASSESSMENT

Successful healthcare endowments often attribute part of their success to a consistent investment policy. The elements of a formalized policy that are best known include the IPS, the asset allocation, and the payout policy. Until recently, few tools existed to help endowments assess and benchmark their investment processes, particularly the less publicized elements of an appropriate process. The Foundation for Fiduciary Studies publishes a guide, *Prudent Practices for Investment Stewards,* that could be helpful to endowment fiduciaries seeking to understand best practices in managing an investment process. The Foundation also publishes a *Self-Assessment of Fiduciary Excellence for Investment Stewards,* which allows endowment fiduciaries to ask a number of questions about their own processes.[43]

OTHER RESOURCES

There are many resources on investment theory and analysis. Although a growing number of consultants will either fully or partially outsource endowment management, relatively fewer resources offer unbiased advice regarding the controllable aspects of endowment management. Fortunately, at least three resources provide general assistance to the endowment manager seeking additional broad coverage of these topics.

Commonfund Institute: http://www.commonfund.org
Swensen, D.F. 2003. *Pioneering Portfolio Management: An Unconventional Approach to Institutional Management.* New Haven: The Free Press.
Foundation for Fiduciary Studies: http://www.fiduciary360.com

CONCLUSION

Hospital and major healthcare entity endowment fund management needs aim for accountability on the part of each major player who shares responsibility for the endowment, and for a management model likely to make the most of their resources while protecting against major risks.

In periods of extreme uncertainty, like the recent economic downturn, endowments should give heightened attention to the composition of their investment committees and to the skills and time priorities of members. They should also reassess the extent to which their investment committee is adequately staffed to do its job and whether external resources need to be tapped to ensure strong endowment management.

Just as the field of medicine continuously changes, so too does the field of endowment management. Endowment managers continue to increase their knowledge of the science and expand their skill in the art. However, successful endowment managers will continue to focus on the areas that they can control in order to minimize the risk of the areas they cannot.

CASE MODEL 1

The Initial Investment Allocation

After conducting a comprehensive fundraising program, the Hoowa Medical Center received initial gifts of $50 million to establish an endowment. Its status as the community's only trauma center and neonatal intensive care unit causes it to provide substantial amounts of unreimbursed care every year. This phenomenon, together with the declining re-imbursements and an estimated 6 percent increase in operating costs, leaves the Center with a budgeted cash shortfall of $4 million for the next fiscal year. Although the new endowment's funds are available to cover such operating shortfalls, the donors also expect their gifts to provide perpetual support for a leading-edge medical institution.

Bill, the Center's treasurer, has been appointed to supervise the day-to-day operations of the endowment. One of his initial successes was convincing his investment committee to retain a consultant who specializes in managing endowment investments. The consultant has recommended a portfolio that is expected to generate long-term investment returns of approximately 10 percent. The allocation reflects the consultant's belief that endowments should generally have long-term investment horizons. This belief results in an allocation that has a significant equity bias. Achieving the anticipated long-term rate of returns would allow the endowment to transfer sufficient funds to the operating accounts to cover the next year's anticipated deficit. However, this portfolio allocation carries risk of principal loss as well as risk that the returns will be positive but somewhat less than anticipated. In fact, Bill's analysis suggests that the allocation could easily generate a return ranging from a 5 percent loss to a 25 percent gain over the following year.

Although the committee authorized Bill to hire the consultant, he knows that he will have some difficulty selling the allocation recommendation to his committee members. In particular, he has two polarizing committee members around whom other committee members tend to organize into factions. John, a wealthy benefactor whose substantial inheritances allow him to support pet causes such as the Center, believes that a more conservative allocation that allows the endowment to preserve principal is the wisest course. Although such a portfolio would likely generate a lower long-term return, John believes that this approach more closely represents the donors' goal that the endowment provide a reliable and lasting source of support to the Center. For this committee faction, Bill hopes to use mean variance optimization to illustrate the ability of diversification to minimize overall portfolio risk while simultaneously increasing returns. He also plans to share the results of the Monte Carlo simulation stress testing he performed, which suggests that the alternative allocation desired by these "conservative" members of his committee would likely cause the endowment to run out of money within 20–25 years.

Another polarizing figure on Bill's committee is Marcie, an entrepreneur who took enormous risks but succeeded in taking her software company public in a transaction that netted her millions. She and other like-minded committee members enthusiastically subscribe to the "long-term" mantra and believe that the endowment can afford the 8 percent payout ratio necessary to fund next year's projected deficit. Marcie believes that the excess of the anticipated long-term rate of return over the next year's operating deficit still provides some cushion against temporary market declines. Bill is certain that Marcie will focus on the upside performance potential. Marcie will also argue that, in any event, additional alternative investments could be used as necessary to increase the portfolio's long-term rate of return. Bill has prepared a comparative analysis of payout policies to illustrate the potential impact of portfolio fluctuations on the sustainability of future payout levels. Bill is also concerned that Marcie and her supporters may not fully understand some of the trade-offs inherent in certain of the alternative investment vehicles in which they desire to increase the allocated funds.

Key Issues

1. Given the factors described in the case study (anticipated long-term investment return, anticipated inflation rate, and operating deficit), how should Bill recommend compromise with respect to maximum sustainable payout rates?
2. How should Bill incorporate the following items into his risk management strategy?
   a. educating the committee regarding types of risk affecting individual investments, classes, and the entire portfolio
   b. measuring risk and volatility
   c. provisions for periodic portfolio re-balancing
   d. using tactical asset allocation
   e. developing and implementing a contingency plan
3. What additional steps should Bill take to form a group consensus regarding the appropriate level of endowment investment risk?
4. What additional elements should Bill add to his presentation to target the concerns of the "conservative" and "aggressive" committee members, respectively?

CHECKLIST 1: Hospital Endowment Fund Asset Allocation	Yes	No
Have you developed estimates of expected returns for individual asset classes?	o	o
Have you developed estimates of expected volatility for individual asset classes?	o	o
Have you developed estimates of the expected correlation co-efficiencies among the various asset classes?	o	o
Have you used some form of simulation to develop a top-down preliminary asset allocation:		
To determine whether risk could be reduced without sacrificing return?	o	o
To determine the likelihood that your allocation will yield a "successful" result?	o	o
Have you performed bottom-up analysis of each asset class to refine the preliminary allocation?	o	o
Does your institution have any specialized knowledge with respect to a given asset class?	o	o
Does your organization place any restrictions on the types of assets in which the endowment can invest?	o	o
With respect to each asset class, have you:		
Considered whether the class provides opportunity for managers to add value through active management?	o	o
Considered whether the class has liquidity constraints that should limit the amount of its allocation?	o	o
Developed an understanding of the risks particular to individual security positions and the class as a whole?	o	o
Determined whether the risks particular to that class can be mitigated or quantified?	o	o
Have you compared your proposed asset allocation to that of peer organizations and evaluated the reasons for any material differences?	o	o
Does your analysis of the allocation suggest that you will be able to meet the desired payout levels?	o	o

CHECKLIST 2: Hospital Endowment Fund Payout Policy	Yes	No
Does your organization require annual support from its endowment to meet operating needs?	o	o
If so, is that support a significant portion of your operating budget?	o	o
Have you identified a target payout rate as a starting point for your payout policy determination?	o	o
Have you compared the anticipated annual distributions under various payout methods given your target allocation?	o	o
Have you developed an estimate of inflation for your institution?	o	o
Have you estimated an expected long-term rate of return given your asset allocation?	o	o
Have you estimated a long-term sustainable payout rate given your inflation and return estimates?	o	o
Have you used modeling to "stress-test" the portfolio given the target payout rate?	o	o
If so, does the stress-testing suggest that you modify your target payout rate or smoothing methodology?	o	o
If so, does the stress-testing suggest that you modify your target asset allocation to allow for greater long-term returns or less short-term volatility?	o	o
Does your analysis suggest that you modify your payout targets to ensure that the real purchasing value of the endowment portfolio is preserved?	o	o

CHECKLIST 3: Hospital Endowment Fund Investment Policy Statement (IPS)	Yes	No
Does your endowment have a written IPS?	o	o
If so, does it contain:		
Written return objectives?	o	o
Definition and tolerance for risk?	o	o

Asset allocation guidelines?	o	o
Asset class rationales?	o	o
Provisions for periodic re-balancing?	o	o
Portfolio level benchmarks?	o	o
Asset class level benchmarks?	o	o
Description of payout policy?	o	o
Description of team member roles/responsibilities?	o	o
Description of any investment restrictions?	o	o
Provisions for voting proxies?	o	o
Limitations on concentrations of any particular security or investment position?	o	o
Do you periodically review and update your IPS?	o	o

CASE MODEL 2

Sample Hospital Endowment Fund Investment Policy Statement

Goals and Objectives

Objective of the Policy Statement

In recognition of the inter-generational character of the fund, the Plan has as its objective the attainment of real growth on the total asset value after current spending. The principle purpose of the Investment Policy Statement (IPS) is to protect the portfolio from ad hoc revisions of sound long-term policy. The written policy will serve to guide and direct various investment managers in the investment of funds when short-term market outlooks are troubling. The Board wants to detail, to the extent reasonably possible, the goals and objectives of the investment plan, as well as the performance measurement techniques that will be used to evaluate the services rendered by the managers. Realizing that our overall objective is best accomplished by using a variety of management styles, we will adjust our asset tolerances and permissible volatility to incorporate specific manager styles. The Board hopes that the net result of the process used to develop investment policy and formalize that policy into a written statement will increase the likelihood that the Plan can meet the inter-generational needs of the sponsoring organization.

Performance Objectives and Goals

The Plan's target performance, on an annualized basis net of fees, will be expected to:

- Equal or exceed the spending rate plus inflation over the market cycle
- Equal or exceed the average return of the appropriate capital market index weighted by the asset allocation target percentages

Interim fluctuations in the value of the fund will be viewed in perspective because the Plan is considered to have a long-term horizon. However, within an individual asset class, the fund's short-term performance and volatility should not be materially worse than those of the appropriate benchmark for that class.

Investment Philosophy

The Plan will allocate its investments in accordance with the belief that it has a long-term investment horizon. We believe that long-term investment success requires discipline and consistency of approach. The Plan will be managed on a total return basis, recognizing the importance of capital preservation while remaining cognizant that real returns require the assumption of some level of investment risk. The Plan shall seek appropriate compensation for the risks that must inevitably be assumed while using prudent investment practices to mitigate or eliminate those risks that can be diversified without sacrificing return. The basic tenets of the Plan's management include the following:

- The portfolio as a whole is more important that any individual asset class or investment.
- At any given level of risk, there is an optimal combination of asset classes that will maximize returns.
- Equities and similar investments generally offer higher long-term returns than fixed income investments while also generally having higher short-term volatility.
- Overall portfolio risk can be decreased by combining asset classes with low correlations of market behavior.

Investment Policies and Procedures

Investment Program Policy

The investment program is intended to result in a policy that allows the greatest probability that the goals set forth in the Objective of the Policy Statement can be met. This process includes the following broad actions:

- Projecting the organization's spending needs
- Maintaining sufficient liquidity for near-term spending commitments
- Assessing expected market returns and risks for the individual asset classes

The policy recognizes that diversification among and across asset classes can result in lower portfolio risk while simultaneously providing higher portfolio returns. Modeling and simulation are used to identify the asset classes the Plan will use as well as the approximate percentage of the Plan that each class will represent. It is recognized that fluctuation in market values will occur or that tactical movements can be made to recognize temporary market inefficiencies. As such, the asset allocation provides ranges around each asset class target. It is generally anticipated that the investment program that gives rise to the asset allocation will be periodically repeated and that asset class target ranges will be modified or affirmed.

Asset Allocation Targets and Ranges

As a result of the above investment process, the Board has adopted the following asset allocation policy with the indicated targets and ranges.

Asset Class	Minimum Weight	Target Weight	Maximum Weight
Domestic equities	xoxox%	xoxox%	xoxox%
Fixed income	xoxox%	xoxox%	xoxox%
International equities	xoxox%	xoxox%	xoxox%
Absolute return	xoxox%	xoxox%	xoxox%
Private equity	xoxox%	xoxox%	xoxox%
Real assets	xoxox%	xoxox%	xoxox%

It is expected that the fund's daily management team will utilize external managers to implement areas within individual asset classes for which those managers have the requisite expertise, resources, and sustainable investment selection process. These external managers will have discretion over matters related to security selection and timing within their area of mandate.

Spending Policy

It is the organization's intent to distribute ___ percent annually based on the ___ payout methodology. This intent is subject to the understanding that the spending rate plus the organization's rate of inflation will not normally exceed the rate of return. It is understood that the total return basis for calculating spending as sanctioned by the Uniform Management of Investment Funds Act (UMIFA) allows the organization to spend an amount in excess of the current yield (interest and dividends earned), including realized and unrealized appreciation. However, it is also understood that the inevitable volatility in the portfolio occasionally may require payouts to be reduced to preserve the purchasing power of the fund.

Rebalancing Policy

The organization recognizes that a disciplined approach to investing is the best way to secure consistent performance. As such, the fund should be re-balanced within target ranges on no less than an annual basis in a manner consistent with not incurring inappropriately excessive costs.

Investment Management Policies and Procedures

Equity Securities

Both domestic and international securities are intended to provide capital appreciation and current income to the Plan. It is generally recognized that the higher return potential of equities entails higher market volatility and potential for loss. This asset class shall include domestic and international common stocks or equivalents (American Depository Receipts plus issues convertible into common stocks). The equity portfolio shall be well diversified to avoid undue exposure to any single economic sector, industry group, or individual security. No more than 5 percent of the equity portfolio based on the market value shall be invested in securities of any one issue or corporation at the time of purchase. No more than 10 percent of the equity portfolio based on the market value shall be invested in any one industry at the time of purchase. Capitalization/stocks must be of those corporations with a market capitalization exceeding $50,000,000. Common and convertible preferred stocks should be of good quality and traded on a major exchange, including NASDAQ, with requirements that such stocks have adequate market liquidity relative to the size of the investment.

Fixed Income Securities

Fixed income securities are intended to provide additional diversification to the Plan and to provide dependable sources of income to the Plan. It is anticipated that the Plan will include fixed income investments of various maturities and durations. Allowable types of such securities include marketable debt securities issued by the United States Government or an agency of the United States Government, foreign governments, domestic corporations, mortgages and asset-backed securities, and high yield debt. These investments should be managed actively to take advantage of opportunities presented by such factors as interest rate fluctuations and changes in credit ratings. These investments are subject to the following limitations:

- No issues may be purchased with more than 30 years until maturity.
- Investments of single issuers other than direct obligations of the United States Government or its agencies may not represent more than 5 percent of the Plan's assets.
- No more than 25 percent of the fixed income securities portion of the Plan's assets may be allocated to below investment grade debt issues.

Cash and Equivalents

All cash and equivalent investments shall be in pooled investment vehicles, such as money market funds, where the fund's share price is intended to remain constant and the yield is comparable to the then current risk-free rate of return. The Plan is also permitted to purchase United States agency-guaranteed certificates of deposit or short-term United States Government securities. Cash and equivalents are not generally considered to be appropriate vehicles for purposes of investment return. As such, these investments should typically be limited to serving as temporary placements for funds awaiting distribution to the sponsoring organization or investment into an approved asset class.

Other Securities

- **Private capital partnerships:** Investments may be made into venture capital, leveraged buy-out, or other private equity managed pools. Such investments should only be made through managers having the requisite experience, resources, and track record of superior performance with the given type of private equity.
- **Real estate:** Investments in real estate should be in the form of professionally managed, income-producing commercial or residential properties. Such investments should be made only through pooled investment real estate funds as managed by professionals with track records of superior long-term performance.
- **Natural resources:** Investments may include timber, oil, or gas interests held in the form of professionally managed pooled limited partnership interests. Such investments should only be made through managers having the requisite experience, resources, and track record of superior performance with the given type of natural resource.
- **Absolute return investments:** Investments may include equity-oriented or market-neutral hedge funds (e.g., long/short, event-driven, arbitrage, etc.).
- **Derivatives and derivative securities:** Derivatives are securities whose value depends upon the value of some other security or index. Examples of such investments include futures, options, options on futures, interest-only or principal-only strips, etc. Certain managers may be permitted to use derivatives. However, no derivative positions can be utilized if such positions would cause the portfolio to fall outside of portfolio guidelines. In addition, such derivative positions must be fully collateralized. Examples of appropriate derivative strategies include hedging a position; maintaining exposure to an asset class while making changes to the allocation, where maintaining the derivative position is more cost-effective than holding a cash position; or changing the duration of a fixed income position. Such investments should only be made through managers having the requisite experience, resources, and track record of superior performance with the given type of derivative. The manager must also be able to demonstrate that such derivatives are integral to their mandate and that the counterparty to the derivative strategy can fulfill their obligations.

Restrictions

The Board is authorized to waive or modify any of the restrictions in these guidelines after thorough investigation of the manager and the rationale for the deviation.

Roles and Responsibilities

To achieve our overall goals and objectives, we want to identify the parties associated with our accounts and the functions, responsibilities, and activities of each with respect to the management of fund assets. Our investment managers are responsible for the day-to-day investment management of the Plan assets, including specific security selection and timing of purchases and sales. The custodian is responsible for safekeeping the securities, collections, and disbursements and periodic accounting statements. The prompt credit of all dividends and interest to our accounts on payment date is required. The custodian shall provide monthly account statements and reconcile account statements with manager summary account statements. The investment consultant is responsible for assisting the client in developing the investment policy statement and for monitoring the overall performance of the Plan and the specific investment managers.

Duties of the Board

The Board's primary duties shall include, but not be limited to, the following items:

- Hiring and evaluating the members of the management team
- Approving the investment policy as prepared by the management team
- Reviewing, no less than annually, the Plan's allocation and performance

Duties of the Management and Staff

Management and staff will be primarily responsible for the day-to-day administration of the Plan. It is anticipated that their primary duties shall include, but not be limited to, the following items:

- Selecting, retaining, and terminating investment managers as necessary to implement the investment policy
- Selecting, retaining, and terminating consultants as necessary to prepare the asset allocation, hire and evaluate managers, perform topical research, and review performance
- Developing investment policy for the Board's review and approval
- Implementing investment policy within the target ranges set forth by the Board
- Reviewing no less than quarterly the Plan's investment performance
- Administering the Plan's investments in a cost-effective manner
- Developing a contingency Plan for the protection of the Plan's assets and ensuring appropriate communication with the public in the face of a catastrophic event
- Selecting an appropriate custodian to hold and safeguard the Plan's securities investments
- Maintaining sufficient records to allow for the necessary oversight and management of the Plan's investments

Duties of External Investment Managers

Management and staff will be primarily responsible for the day-to-day administration of the Plan. It is anticipated that their primary duties shall include, but not be limited to, the following items:

- Complying with the provisions of this policy statement
- Staying within the style and risk parameters of their respective mandates
- Providing proof of liability and fiduciary insurance coverages
- Maintaining necessary risk controls
- Using best possible execution for trades made on the Plan's behalf to ensure the most timely, cost-effective execution
- Reconciling transaction data no less than monthly with the custodian
- Disclosing material changes in personnel, processes, investment outlook, financial condition, or other matters that could be reasonably deemed to be of interest to the Plan

Other Considerations

Trading Guidelines

All trading in accounts shall be done through a recognized national or regional brokerage firm. Additionally, it is understood that block transactions or participation in certain initial public offerings might not be available through a primary broker. In this case, the manager should execute those trades through the broker offering the product and service necessary to best serve the account. It should be the responsibility of the manager to see that duplicate trade confirmations and duplicate monthly statements are mailed to the consultant.

Proxy Voting

The investment manager shall have the sole and exclusive right to vote any and all policies solicited in connection with securities held by the client.

Performance Review and Evaluation

Performance results for the investment managers will be measured on a quarterly basis. Total fund performance will be measured against a balanced index composed of commonly accepted benchmarks weighted to match the long-term asset allocation policy of the Plan. Additionally, the investment performances specific for individual portfolios will be measured against commonly accepted benchmarks applicable to that particular investment style and strategy. The consultant will be responsible for complying with this section of our policy statement. The managers shall report performance results in compliance with the standards established by the Association for Investment Management and Research. Reports shall be generated on a quarterly basis and delivered to the client with a copy to the consultant within four weeks of the end of the quarter.

ACKNOWLEDGMENT

To J. Wayne Firebaugh, CPA, CFP®, CMP™, for assistance in the preparation of this chapter.

SUGGESTED READINGS

Coons, J., Cunnings, C. 204. Introduction to investment concepts. In *Financial planning for physicians and advisors*, Marcinko, D.E., ed. Sudbury, MA: JB Publishing.

Craig, J.E. Jr. 2009. Rethinking the management of foundation endowments. In *The Commonwealth Fund 2009 annual report*. New York: The Commonwealth Fund.

Marcinko, D.E., Firebaugh, W.F. 2010. *Hospital endowment fund management*. Norcross, Ga: iMBA, Inc. Press.

McIntire, C. 2003. Whither self-portfolio management? In *Financial planning for physicians and healthcare professionals*, Marcinko, D.E., ed. New York: Aspen Publishers.

REFERENCES

1. MacEachern, M.T. 1932. Some economic problems affecting hospitals today and suggestions for their solution. *The Bulletin of the American Hospital Association*, 7(8): 58–67.
2. Steinberg, C. 2003. *Overview of the U.S. healthcare system*. Chicago: American Hospital Association.
3. American Hospital Association. Trends affecting hospitals and health systems. 2010. *TrendWatch Chartbook 2010*. Chicago: American Hospital Association.
4. Merriam-Webster Online. http://www.merriam-webster.com/.
5. Inge, W.R. n.d. Great Quotes. http://www.great-quotes.com/quote/1372086.
6. Brinson, G.P., Hood, R., and Beebower, G.L. 1986. Determinants of portfolio performance. *Financial Analysts Journal*. July/August.
7. Swensen, D.F. 2000. *Pioneering portfolio management*. New Haven, CT: The Free Press.
8. Spitz, W.T. 2001. I know I don't want too much of it, but what is it? *Principles of endowment management*. https://www.commonfund.org/InvestorResources/Publications/Brochures/Principles%20of%20Endowment%20Management.pdf.
9. Doody, D. 2007. *Measuring up investment policies and practices in not-for-profit healthcare: Investment management is an area that lends itself to quantitative analysis to produce information that can inform and guide your decision making*. New York: Healthcare Financial Management Association and Gale Group.
10. Dimensional Fund Advisors. 2006. Evaluating the maturity risk/return tradeoff. Quarterly: 1964–2006, PowerPoint. http://www.dimensional.com/.
11. The Yale Endowment. 2012. http://investments.yale.edu/images/documents/Yale_Endowment_12.pdf.
12. National Council of Real Estate Investment Fiduciaries. 2013. http://www.ncreif.org/.
13. Clark, S.E., and Yates, T.T., Jr. 2003. How efficient is your frontier? Commonfund Institute White Paper. November.
14. Nawrocki, D. 2001. The problems with Monte Carlo simulation. *FPA Journal*. November, 106–118.
15. Stein, J.C. 2004. Why are most funds open-end? Competition and the limits of arbitrage. *Harvard University and NBER Working Paper No. w10259*. February.
16. Sedlacek, V. 2004. Currents and commentary enter the matrix. *CFQ*. Commonfund.
17. Loeper, D.B. 2001. Asset allocation math, methods and mistakes. Wealthcare Capital Management White Paper. June.
18. Investment Company Institute. 2001. *2001 Investment Company fact book*, 41st ed. Washington, DC. Investment Company Institute.
19. Investment Company Institute. 2003. *2003 Investment Company fact book*, 41st ed. Washington, DC. Investment Company Institute.
20. Bajaj, V., and Creswell, J. 2007. Bear Stearns staves off collapse of 2 hedge funds. *New York Times*. June 21, 5–6.
21. Ibbotson, R.G., and Patel, A.K. 2002. *Do winners repeat with style? Summary of findings*. Chicago: Ibbotson & Associates.
22. Kacperczyk, M.T., Sialm, C., and Zheng, L. 2002. On industry concentration of actively managed equity mutual funds. University of Michigan Business School, Case Model, p. 3.
23. 2007 annual U.S. corporate pension plan best and worst investment performance report. 2007. *FutureMetrics*, April 20.
24. Dimensional Fund Advisors. 2006. Basic 60/40 balanced strategy vs. company pension plans results of 192 corporate pension plans. Annual: 1988–2006, PowerPoint. http://www.dimensional.com/.
25. Sedlacek, V.O., and Clark, S.E. 2003. Why do we feel so poor? How the overspending of the '90s has created a crisis in higher education. Commonfund Institute White Paper. December.
26. Milevsky, M.A. 2003. A new perspective on endowments. http://www.ifid.ca/pdf_workingpapers/WP2003MAR10.pdf.
27. Pozen, R. 2009. *Too big to save?* New York: Wiley.
28. Reinhart, C.M., and Rogoff, K. 2011. *This time is different: Eight centuries of financial folly*. Princeton: Princeton University Press.
29. Reinhart, C.M., and Rogoff, K. 2011. *This time is different: Eight centuries of financial folly* (p. 35). Princeton: Princeton University Press.
30. Pozen, R. 2009. *Too big to save?* (p. 15). New York: Wiley.
31. Reinhart, C.M., and Rogoff, K. 2011. *This time is different: Eight centuries of financial folly* (p. 121). Princeton: Princeton University Press.
32. Kochard, L.E, and Rittereiser, M. 2008. *Foundation and endowment investing: Philosophies and strategies for top investors and institutions*. New York: Wiley.

33. ERisk Services. 2010. Orange County: An ERisk.com case study. http://www.eriskservices.com/

34. Commonfund. 2013. *Risk management considerations for senior managers and trustees.* https://www.commonfund.org/Pages/default.aspx.

35. Gloria-Mundi. 2013. All about vaue at risk. http://gloria-mundi.com/.

36. Schachter, B. 1997. *An irreverent guide to value at risk.* http://www.gloriamundi.com/.

37. Rubenstein, M. 2000. Comments on the 1987 stock market crash: Eleven years later. *Risks in Accumulation Products.* Society of Actuaries, p. 11.

38. Red Cross defends handling of September 11 donations. November 6, 2001. http://archives.cnn.com/2001/US/11/06/rec.charity.hearing/.

39. Strom, S. 2002. Questions arise on accounting at United Way. *The New York Times.* November 19.

40. DeLucia, M.S. 2004. Sarbanes-Oxley and the impact on NH nonprofit organizations. *New Hampshire Bar Journal* 45:2. http://www.nhbar.org/publications/archives/display-journal-issue.asp?id=13.

41. Yoder, J. 2001. Investment policy: Start on course stay on course. *Commonfund Quarterly.* Winter.

42. Sedlacek, V. 2003. Your board: Dynamic or dysfunctional? *Commonfund Quarterly.* Spring/Summer.

43. FI360 Conference. 2013. Global fiduciary insights. http://www.fiduciary360.com.

11 Valuation of Hospitals in a Changing Reimbursement and Regulatory Environment

Robert James Cimasi, Todd A. Zigrang,
and Anne P. Sharamitaro

CONTENTS

INTRODUCTION

The valuation of hospitals can be examined within the framework of the "four pillars" of the health-care industry, i.e., regulation, reimbursement, competition, and technology (Figure 11.1). These four drivers of the healthcare market serve as a conceptual construct to analyze the forces and stakeholders of the healthcare industry and provide a framework for analyzing the viability, efficiency, and productivity of hospitals and other healthcare enterprises, assets, and services.

This chapter will examine recent changes affecting these aspects of the healthcare arena that exhibit the potential to have a dramatic impact on the valuation of hospital enterprises.

The current economic conditions and trends in the regulatory, reimbursement, competitive, and technology aspects of the healthcare environment facilitated the emergence of a historical healthcare reform initiative: the Patient Protection and Affordability Care Act (Public Law 111-148, enacted March 23, 2010) and the Health Care and Education Reconciliation Act of 2010 (Public Law 111-152, enacted March 30, 2011), collectively referred to as the ACA, which was mostly upheld (with the exception of the Medicaid expansion becoming voluntary) by a five to four vote by the U.S. Supreme Court on June 28, 2012.[1] The ACA marks the beginning of a new era in the long history of healthcare reform and will have a monumental impact on many aspects of healthcare delivery in the United States, affecting healthcare providers, insurers, employers, and individual citizens, and resulting in a dynamic healthcare marketplace that presents an unpredictable milieu of new provider configurations, strategies, and tactics. The extensive legislation has resulted in, and will continue to bring about, changes in both the operational and financial aspects of healthcare enterprises, assets, and services. Supportable business valuation engagements for healthcare enterprises, assets, and services should include an evaluation of expected economic conditions and events resulting from increasing regulatory pressures, shifting payor and reimbursement scenarios, changing competitive landscape, emerging technological and clinical advancements, and other factors specific to the industry, such as rising healthcare expenditures as a percentage of the gross domestic product

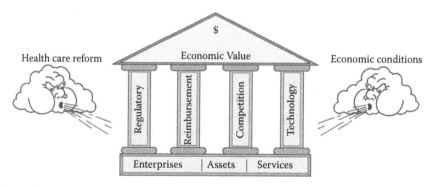

FIGURE 11.1   The four pillars of valuing healthcare enterprises.

(GDP) and changing patient and provider demographics; all of these factors may be altered and transformed by the ACA.

Despite trends in out-of-pocket spending growth, the "demographic time bomb" of changing patient population demographics and shifts in age and ethnic distribution will likely contribute to the projected increase in demand of healthcare services.[2] The 65 years and older population is expected to grow from 40.2 million in 2010 to 88.5 million in 2050, an increase from 13 percent to 20.2 percent of the total population.[3] Increased life expectancy suggests increased prevalence of chronic conditions common among the elderly.[4] The ethnicity of the U.S. patient population is also changing, with the 2000 census figures indicating an increasing degree of racial and ethnic diversity.[5]

To a great extent, the scope of an investor's understanding and perception of the various risks related to the several fundamental underlying factors discussed above, and the resulting impact of each factor on the future economic feasibility and financial performance of hospitals, will drive the investor market's perception of the financial value of these enterprises.

HOSPITAL INDUSTRY: HISTORY, BACKGROUND, AND OVERVIEW

The hospital industry continues to face many challenges in the changing healthcare environment,[6] including workforce shortages, rising healthcare costs to provide care, and difficulty acquiring needed capital.[6] With consistent financial stresses, hospitals in some areas appear to be struggling. However, general acute-care hospitals recorded record high profits of $35.2 billion in 2006, an increase of more than 20 percent from 2005. Total net revenues for general acute-care hospitals were $587.1 billion, resulting in an average profit margin of 6 percent (the highest since 1997, when the average profit margin was 6.7 percent).[7]

While the demand for healthcare continues to rise, the site of service also continues to evolve as more procedures are performed on an outpatient basis and by freestanding facilities rather than by inpatient acute-care hospitals. As evidence of this trend, the number of freestanding ambulatory care surgery centers increased from 2,864 in 2000 to 5,197 in 2006.[8]

Healthcare costs in the United States are again increasing after their rate of growth slowed in the mid-1990s.[8] In 2009, total national health expenditures in the United States grew to $2.5 trillion, a 5.7 percent increase from 2008.[9] Meanwhile, the nation's GDP shrank by 1.1 percent; as a result, national health expenditures increased from 16.2 percent to 17.3 percent of the GDP, the largest one-year increase in history.[10] Additionally, healthcare spending has been projected to grow to 19.6 percent by 2016.[11] The potential impact of the 2010 healthcare reform legislation to reduce rising healthcare expenditures is still uncertain.

According to a 2002 study conducted by the Blue Cross and Blue Shield Association, inpatient costs are responsive to hospital market organization. Each 1 percent increase in for-profit hospital market share is associated with a 2 percent increase in inpatient expenditure per person. Conversely, each 1 percent increase in network hospital* market share corresponds to a 1 percent decrease in inpatient expenditures.[12]

PATIENTS AND SERVICES

The acute care level of healthcare may be defined as involving the treatment of patients suffering from severe episodes of illness due to trauma or disease.

> An acute hospital is defined as a short-term hospital that has facilities, medical staff, and all necessary personnel to provide diagnosis, care, and treatment of a wide range of acute conditions, including injuries.[13]

---

* Network hospitals are hospitals that are joined into cooperative contractual arrangements for purchasing supplies and sharing other resources, but do not necessarily share the same ownership.

The impact of an increased proportion of the population at high risk for acute illness, combined with the evolution of many chronic diseases into manageable living conditions, has brought acute-care hospitals to the forefront of healthcare's competitive market.[14]

Shift to Outpatient Care

One of the most important phenomena affecting hospital departments is the continued shift from inpatient to outpatient care. In 1980, 16 percent of surgical procedures were performed on an out-patient basis. This number grew to 57.7 percent in 2007, according to a statistical brief published by the Agency for Healthcare Research and Quality.[15] The growth in outpatient procedures has been driven by advances in medical technology and changes in payment arrangements, which have allowed the ambulatory/outpatient surgery to become more feasible in recent years.[16]

Technological and medical advances, such as improvements in the administration of anesthe-sia and the development of minimally invasive or noninvasive procedures, have also driven the observed increase in outpatient procedures. For example, minimally invasive arthroscopic proce-dures require smaller incisions and less cutting of soft tissues, result in less blood loss, and decrease recovery times as compared to less advanced surgical procedures.[17] Advances in medical devices and pharmaceuticals have also contributed to reduced recovery times, further facilitating migration of surgical procedures from inpatient to outpatient care.[18]

Demographic Changes Affecting Hospital Utilization

The changing age and ethnic distribution of the population substantially impacts the demand for healthcare reform, and the projected growth of the elderly population in the United States plays an important role in the anticipated demand for healthcare services. The U.S. Census Bureau projects that the portion of the American population over age 65 will increase from 39 million in 2010 to more than 69 million in 2030. The most rapidly growing broad age group is projected to be those 85 years old and older, doubling its current size by 2025 and increasing five-fold by 2050.[19] In addition, the elderly population typically has a greater per capita use of healthcare services.[20]

The ethnicity of the U.S. patient population is also changing, with the 2000 Census figures indi-cating an increasing degree of racial and ethnic diversity.[20] As the minority population increases, the demand for the services tailored to this population may also increase. It is estimated that physi-cian patient-care hours devoted to minority patients will have increased to 40 percent by 2020 from an estimated 31 percent in 2000.[20] The healthcare delivery system will need to identify disparities in access to care and differences in culture that impact the provision of care to adjust the availability of healthcare workers adequately trained to meet the healthcare needs of this growing segment of the U.S. population.[20]

Reimbursement

Hospitals are reimbursed on an inclusive per diem or per case basis, based historically on Medicare's diagnosis-related group (DRG) system. More recently, outpatient charges are based on ambula-tory payment classifications (APCs), a payment system launched by the Centers for Medicare and Medicaid Services (CMS) on August 1, 2000.[21] However, various methods exist and are used by commercial payers:

- Discounts
- Per diems
- Sliding scales for discounts and per diems
- Differential by day in hospital
- DRGs
- Differential by service type

- Case rates
- Institutional only
- Package pricing or bundled rates
- Capitation
- Percentage of premium revenue
- Bed leasing
- Periodic interim payments or cash advances
- Performance-based incentives
- Penalties and withholds
- Quality and services incentives
- Outpatient procedures
- Discounts
- Ambulatory patient group

MEDICARE AND MEDICAID

Hospitals have faced a series of ongoing Medicare budget cuts over many years. Reimbursement pressures mounted for hospitals over the decade of the 1980s that saw the introduction of the Medicare prospective payment system (PPS) for hospitals in 1983. By 1990, the American Hospital Association called Medicaid reimbursements "inadequate," and there were proposals to cut Medicare payment levels.[22] The Omnibus Budget Reconciliation Act of 1990 included $17 billion in Medicare hospital payment reductions over a five-year period.[23]

The Balanced Budget Act of 1997 cut payments for fiscal year 1998[24] and permanently reduced capital payments by 15.7 percent, with an additional 2.1 percent reduction for fiscal years 1998–2002.[25] Over the five years between 1998 and 2002, this law was intended to save Medicare $115 billion. The progression of payment cuts was to occur as shown in Table 11.1.

Industry projections were for another $42 billion cut in Medicare payments by 2002,[26] but Congress granted hospitals some relief by passing the Balanced Budget Refinement Act in 1999 and the Benefits Improvement and Protection Act of 2000. With only $16 billion dollars of assistance over five years from the Balanced Budget Refinement Act and $35 million from the Benefits Improvement and Protection Act, however, relief from hospitals' financial strain remains limited.[26] Losses incurred from the direct costs of treatment for Medicaid patients rose by 68 percent from 1999 to 2000. Of the 64 hospitals that closed in 2000 (1.4 percent of all U.S. hospitals), however, only two reported reductions in Medicare and Medicaid payments as a reason for closure.[27]

The Balanced Budget Act required that CMS implement a PPS for hospital outpatient services. The hospital outpatient PPS classifies outpatient procedures into APC groups. Each APC is assigned a relative payment weight based on the median cost of the services within the APC. The APC is then adjusted by geographic area depending on the area's wage level. Under the Balanced Budget Refinement Act, APC weights are updated annually. The new payment system became effective August 1, 2000.[28] The Balanced Budget Refinement Act eased the transition to the new payment methodology by setting payment floors effective through 2003 and adding an outlier policy to compensate for extremely high-cost cases.[29]

TABLE 11.1

Progression of Payment Cuts under the Balanced Budget Act of 1997

1998	1999	2000
$6.7 billion	$16.1 billion	$29.9 billion

As a part of the 2010 reform legislation, the Medicare program is required to provide a productivity adjustment and slight reductions to market basket updates for several providers; make concessions to expand primary care; support quality, transparency, and fraud and abuse enforcement initiatives; enforce provisions to continuously reduce the gap between generic and brand-name drugs by 2020; and add restrictions to revenue spending for Medicare Advantage plans, among other topics.[30] Reform initiatives related to the Medicaid program began in 2010 and will be phased in through 2014. They include several provisions related to expanding enrollee eligibility, prescription drug coverage, and primary care and preventive services coverage, among others. Medicaid will also be required to designate new matching payments for eligible individuals and increase Medicaid payment rates for primary care physicians.[30]

Hospital Inpatient Prospective Payment System

Medicare payments for acute inpatient services are based on a PPS. Medicare pays hospitals predetermined per-discharge rates (Table 11.2) based on two factors: the patient's condition and related treatment strategy, and the market conditions in the facility's location (Tables 11.3 and 11.4).[31] The inpatient PPS calculations detail how hospital inpatient reimbursement is determined.

Inpatient PPS Calculations[32]

Federal rate for operating costs =	DRG relative weight × [(Labor-related large urban standardized amount × geographic MSA wage index) + nonlabor-related national large urban standardized amount] × (1 + IME + DSH)
Federal rate for capital costs =	DRG relative weight × federal capital rate × large urban add-on × geographic cost adjustment factor × (1 + IME + DSH)

Outpatient Prospective Payment System

Medicare payments for outpatient services are based on a PPS. Originally, hospitals were paid for outpatient services based on the allowable incurred costs. Section 4523 of the Balanced Budget Act allowed CMS, then known as the Health Care Financing Administration (HCFA), to implement a PPS under Medicare for hospital outpatient services. Payments are based on a set of relative weights, a conversion factor, and an adjustment for geographic differences in input prices. The PPS

TABLE 11.2
The Capital Standard Federal Payment Rates

Fiscal Years	National Rate
2013[33]	$425.49
2012[34]	$421.42
2011[35]	$420.01
2010[36]	$429.56
2009[37]	$430.20
2008[38]	$424.17
2007[39]	$427.03
2006[40]	$420.65
2005[41]	$416.63
2004[41]	$413.83[42]
2003[43]	$407.01
2002[44]	$390.74
2001[45]	$382.03
2000[46]	$377.03

TABLE 11.3
The National Adjusted Operating Standardized Amounts

	Large Urban Areas		Other Areas	
Fiscal Year	Labor-Related	Nonlabor-Related	Labor-Related	Nonlabor-Related
2012[47]	$3,584.30	$1,625.44	$3,230.04	$1,979.70
2011*[48]	$3,552.91	$1,611.20	$3,201.75	$1,962.36
2010*[49]	$3,593.52	$1, 629.62	$3,238.35	$1,984.79
2009*[50]	$3,723.07	$1,618.50	$3,311.77	$2,029.80
2008*[51]	$3,478.45	$1,512.15	$3,094.17	$1,896.43
2007*[52]	$3,397.52	$1,476.97	$3,022.18	$1,852.31
2006*[52]	$3,297.84	$1,433.63	$2,933.52	$1,797.95
2005*	$3,238.07	$1,316.18	$2,823.64	$1,730.62
2004	$3,136.39	$1,274.85	$3,086.73	$1,254.67
2003	$3,022.60	$1,228.60	$2,974.75	$1,209.15
2002	$2,955.44	$1,201.30	$2,908.65	$1,182.27
2001	$2,864.19	$1,164.21	$2,818.85	$1,145.78
2000	$2,809.18	$1,141.85	$2,764.70	$1,123.76
1999	$2,783.42	$1,311.38	$2,739.36	$1,113.47

*Amounts from 2005–2011 are the full market basket updates, where the amounts listed under "Large Urban Areas" are
those for which the wage index is greater than 1, and those listed under "Other Areas" are those for which the wage index
is less than or equal to 1.
Source: "Medicare Payment Analysis: Hospital Inpatient Prospective Payment System," Research & Planning Consultants,
www.rpcconsulting.com/hipps.htm, 2005.

includes an outlier adjustment for extraordinarily high cost services and "pass-through" payments
for new technologies.[53] CMS grouped outpatient procedures into approximately 750 APCs.

The APCs group services and items that are clinically similar and use comparable resources.
The APC is "bundled," meaning it encompasses integral services and items with the primary service. The payment is intended to cover the hospital's operating and capital costs. The payment
is determined by multiplying the relative weight for the APC by a conversion factor.[54] The APC
groups and their relative weights are reviewed annually. CMS updates the conversion factor for
inflation using the hospital inpatient market basket index.[55] As mandated by the ACA, the market
basket update for both inpatient and outpatient hospital services was reduced by: (1) 0.25 percent for
fiscal year (FY) 2010–2011; (2) 0.1 percent for FY 2012–2013; (3) 0.3 percent for FY 2014; (4) 0.2
percent for FY 2015–2016; and (5) 0.75 percent for FY 2017–2019.[56]

Services provided are assigned current procedural terminology (CPT) codes and classified into
APCs, each being assigned a specific payment rate.[57] Hospitals have the ability to bill for various
services performed on an individual on a single day. However, if there are multiple surgical procedures performed on a single day, the APC payment is subject to a discount.[58]

Outpatient PPS Calculations

Federal Rate for Operating Costs =	APC relative weight × [(labor-related large urban standardized amount × inpatient PPS geographic MSA wage index) + nonlabor-related national large urban standardized amount][58]

The proposed hospital outpatient PPS (HOPPS) conversion factor for 2010 was set at $67.406, an
increase of 2.1 percent over the 2009 conversion factor amount of $66.059.[59] Refer to Table 11.5 for
the HOPPS conversion factors for 2000–2010.

TABLE 11.4
Determining the Prospective Payment

Patient Condition	Market Condition
• Medicare groups patients with similar clinical problems requiring similar treatments and medical resources into DRGs. Criteria used for determining DRG classification: • Principal diagnosis • Up to eight additional diagnoses • Up to six procedures performed during the stay • Age • Sex • Discharge status of the patient • **Current Classification:** • There are 503 DRGs (including one catchall and one invalid DRG). A patient is categorized by the following: • Major Diagnostic Categories: usually grouped by the organ system that is affected, although there are some exceptions. Patients are assigned according to their principal diagnosis. • Surgical: differentiated based on a hierarchy that orders individual procedures or groups of procedures by resource intensity • Medical: grouped on the basis of diagnosis and age • With or without operating room • Type of procedure (up to six procedures performed during the stay) • Presence of comorbidities (conditions present at admission) or complications (conditions developed during stay) • DRGs are assigned weights that indicate the relative costliness of a patient in the group to an average Medicare patient (i.e., above-average costs will yield higher weights).	• A national average base payment rate (the amount that would be paid for an average patient in a facility located in an average market) determines the price level of the local market. This standardized base payment rate falls into two categories: • Labor-related share: adjusted by the wage index applicable to the area • Nonlabor share: if the hospital is located in Alaska or Hawaii, the nonlabor share is adjusted by a cost of living adjustment factor[60] • This input price is then multiplied with the DRG relative weight (accounts for differences in the mix of patients treated across hospitals). • The following market factors will also influence the payment rates: • Disproportionate share of low-income patients (PPS): If the hospital is recognized as serving a disproportionate share of low-income patients, it receives a percentage add-on for each case paid through the PPS. This percentage varies depending on several factors, including the percentage of low-income patients served. It is applied to the DRG-adjusted base payment rate, plus any outlier payments received. • Teaching hospitals: If the hospital is an approved teaching hospital, it receives a percentage add-on payment for each case paid through the PPS. This percentage varies depending on the ratio of residents-to-beds.[60] • Outliers: additional payment is designated to protect the hospital from large financial losses due to unusually expensive cases. Any outlier payment is added onto the DRG-adjusted base payment rate.[60]

Emerging Reimbursement Trends

The ACA has ushered a flood of new changes into the healthcare reimbursement system; principal among these changes is the implementation of payment bundling systems.[61] Generally speaking, a "bundled" payment is a single payment for reimbursement to multiple providers (e.g., both hospitals and physicians) that covers all services involved in a patient's care.[62] CMS described the goal of payment bundling as ". . . align[ing] the incentives for both hospitals and physicians, leading to better quality and greater efficiency in the care that is delivered."[63] Section 3023 of the ACA calls for CMS to establish national payment bundling programs, with Medicaid's demonstration program established in 2012 and a Medicare pilot program slated for late 2013.[64] Section 3023 also gives the Secretary of Health and Human Services (HHS) authority to expand the pilot program if, after five years, the Secretary deems the program effective.[65]

Beginning in 2013 (based on discharges from October 1, 2012), Section 3001 of the ACA creates a new value-based purchasing (VBP) program for hospitals that will require a percentage of Medicare payments to be tied to quality, in the case of some common, high-cost procedures, such as

TABLE 11.5
Medicare HOPPS Conversion Factor

Year	Conversion Factor	Percent Growth
2000	$48.487[66]	1.90%
2001	$50.080[67]	2.3%
2002	$50.904[68]	2.3%
2003	$52.151[69]	3.5%
2004	$54.561[70]	3.4%
2005	$56.983[71]	3.3%
2006	$59.511[72]	3.7%
2007	$61.468[73]	3.4%
2008	$63.694[74]	3.3%
2009	$66.059[75]	3.6%
2010	$67.241[75]	2.1%
2011	$68.876[76]	2.35%
2012	$70.016[77]	1.9%
Average Annual Growth Rate (2000–2012):		**2.85%**

cardiac, surgical, and pneumonia care. Under the VPB program, hospital payments become financial incentives for providers to achieve high-quality outcomes, as determined by CMS-established benchmarks, for Medicare inpatient acute-care patients.[78] The quality measures to be included in the program (and in all other quality programs in this title) will be developed and chosen with input from external stakeholders.[79] Section 10335 clarifies that the hospital VBP program shall not include measures of hospital readmissions.[79] The Final Rule regulating the VPB program was published on May 6, 2011, and has already created tensions with the currently established Inpatient Quality Reporting (IQR) Program, which contains similar reporting requirements but different reporting schedules.[80] Both programs aim to increase transparency for hospital quality outcomes by publishing certain measures on the publicly accessible CMS "Hospital Compare" website (http://www.medicare.gov/hospitalcompare).

MERGERS AND ACQUISITIONS

The 1990s witnessed an enormous consolidation in the healthcare industry overall, including the hospital industry. The volume of hospital transactions peaked around 1997 and has generally declined since then, remaining fairly stable since 2004. Table 11.6 provides the number of hospital deals transacted from 1995–2010.

Trends in Hospital Employment of Physicians

Hospitals have recently returned to the 1990s trend of directly employing physicians and increasingly competing for physicians' time and loyalty as more physician-owned specialty hospitals open, allowing increasing numbers of physicians to refuse on-call emergency room duties and other traditional medical staff responsibilities.[96] While hospitals primarily employed primary care physicians during the 1990s, the recent employment trend has seen a rise in the number of specialists employed by hospitals.[97] In a study undertaken by the Center for Studying Health System Change, it was reported that thirty out of forty-three hospital systems had increased the number of employed physicians between 2005 and 2007, with a particularly notable increase in the incidence of employed specialists (83 percent of the systems).[98] A 2009 study by Medical Group Management Association, entitled *Physician Placement Starting Salary Survey: 2010 Report Based on 2009 Data*, projected that more than half (65 percent) of established physicians were placed in hospital-owned practices

TABLE 11.6
Mergers and Acquisitions
Transactions in the Hospital Sector

Year	Number of Deals
1997[81]	183
1998[82]	145
1999[83]	110
2000[84]	85
2001[85]	84
2002[86]	61
2003[87]	38
2004[88]	58
2005[89]	53
2006[90]	57
2007[91]	58
2008[92]	60
2009[93]	53
2010[94]	76
2011[95]	86

and that 49 percent of physicians hired out of residency or fellowship were placed within a hospital-owned practice.[99]

Hospitals in the United States have responded to healthcare reform implementation through increasing physician employment. More than 50 percent of practicing physicians in the United States are employed by hospitals or integrated delivery systems. The decline in independent practices appears to be primarily driven by increasing regulatory efforts to control rising healthcare costs.[100] Physician employment has shifted from freestanding practices to hospital employment.[101] Large corporate and hospital-owned systems are attractive employment opportunities for independent physicians, offering higher salaries, loan forgiveness programs, and little administrative responsibility.[102] Additionally, increasingly complex treatments, the high costs associated with implementing technological advancements, and physician desire for more flexible working hours have all contributed to the decline of the independent practice.[103]

In addition to changing trends in physician employment by hospitals, in recent years the hospital industry has undergone an increase in consolidation of healthcare delivery services. The driving force behind the formation of hospitals into larger centralized corporate entities can be attributed to several factors, including tighter reimbursement costs from payers, reductions in traditional hospital inpatient use, closer regulation from state and federal government, and higher costs of capital.[104] Consolidation into larger entities provides advantages to hospitals in the marketplace and in the legislature, thus helping hospitals overcome the barriers imposed in this new regulatory environment.[104]

Joint Ventures between Hospitals and Physicians

The move toward specialized inpatient and outpatient facilities, often owned by physicians, is a natural reaction to the significant reimbursement, regulatory, and technological changes described above and represents beneficial competition and innovations that allow healthcare services to be provided in a more cost-effective manner while maintaining and improving quality and beneficial outcomes.[105] In an attempt to strengthen relationships and align economic incentives to enhance market position and financial success between physicians and hospitals, many specialty providers, such as orthopedic surgeons and cardiologists, are entering into joint ventures with one another.[106]

As competition over ancillary service technical component revenue streams between physicians and hospitals remains intense, new forms of joint ventures and revenue sharing options are developing in an attempt to repair their recently contemptuous relationship and to offer patients increased quality of services and access.[107] *FutureScan*[108] predicts that the relationship between hospitals and physicians will stabilize by 2013, resulting in more physicians investing with hospitals and both parties being involved in management decisions. The economic benefits of a physician and hospital joint venture are significant. Collaboration between physicians and hospitals creates an economy of scale not achieved if each continues to operate independently, thereby increasing hospital and health system interest.[109]

Tax-exempt joint ventures and investment partnerships may experience new compliance challenges with the implementation of the new Internal Revenue Service (IRS) form 990, which tax-exempt organizations must file annually to maintain their not-for-profit status. Under the new form 990, organizations must report their distributive share of income and expenses from a joint venture in addition to a distributive share of assets based upon the organization's ending capital account. Although many of the revisions to form 990 are designed to clarify reporting requirements and alleviate some of the burdens on filing organizations, other changes are likely to affect some organizations' operations and policies.[110]

Co-Management Arrangements

Alignment, integration, and engagement of physicians comprise a key strategy for health systems seeking to create high-performing, high-quality, and high-efficiency organizations. Yet aligning physicians' interests with those of hospitals and health systems has been an ongoing struggle, given the shift from small, physician/provider-owned, independent private practices to captive practices within larger integrated health systems, i.e., the corporatization of the practice of medicine. Successful hospital enterprises have understood that, "to effectively respond to the economic incentives of reform, a hospital must achieve a deeper level of integration with the physicians that practice there."[111] One way physicians and hospitals are trying to achieve this common goal is through co-management arrangements, which have re-emerged in recent years as an alternative to joint ventures or strict employment arrangements between hospitals and physicians who share mutual interests to lower costs, increase efficiency, and improve quality.[112]

Under the new co-management model, a hospital may enter into a management agreement with an organization that is either jointly or wholly owned by a physician to provide the daily management services for the inpatient and/or outpatient components of a medical specialty service line.[113] A co-management arrangement incentivizes physicians for the development, management, and improvement of quality and efficiency, as well as for making the service line more competitive in the target market.[113] Co-management arrangements may result in healthcare entities that are value-driven and provide physicians and hospitals an opportunity to achieve safety, quality, patient satisfaction, and cost efficiency, which ultimately result in improvement in the delivery of patient care.

Accountable Care Organizations

Accountable care organizations (ACOs) are healthcare organizations in which a set of providers, usually large physician groups and hospitals, are held accountable for the cost and quality of care delivered to a specific local population.[114] ACOs aim to affect a provider's patient expenditures and outcomes by integrating clinical and administrative departments to coordinate care. Since their four-page introduction in the ACA, ACOs have been implemented in both the federal and commercial healthcare markets, with thirty-two Pioneer ACOs selected (on December 19, 2011),[115] 116 federal applications accepted (on April 10, 2012, and July 9, 2012),[116] and at least 160 commercial ACOs in existence today.[117] Federal ACO contracts are established between an ACO and CMS and are regulated under the CMS Medicare Shared Savings Program (MSSP) Final Rule, published November

2, 2011. ACOs participating in the Medicare Shared Savings Program are accountable for the health outcomes, represented by thirty-three quality metrics, and Medicare beneficiary expenditures of a prospectively assigned population of Medicare beneficiaries.[118] If a federal ACO achieves Medicare beneficiary expenditures below a CMS-established benchmark (and meets quality targets), they are eligible to receive a portion of the achieved Medicare beneficiary expenditure savings in the form of a shared savings payment.[119]

Commercial ACO contracts are not limited by any specific legislation, only by the contract between the ACO and a commercial payer. In addition to shared savings models, commercial ACOs may incentivize lower costs and improved patient outcomes through reimbursement models that share risk between the payer and the providers, i.e., pay-for-performance compensation arrangements or partial to full capitation.[120] Although commercial ACOs experience a greater degree of flexibility in their structure and reimbursement, the principles for success for both federal ACOs and commercial ACOs are similar.

Although nearly any healthcare enterprise can integrate and become an ACO, larger enterprises may be best suited for ACO status. Larger organizations are better able to accommodate the significant capital requirements of ACO development, implementation, and operation (e.g., healthcare information technology) and to sustain the sufficient number of beneficiaries to have a significant impact on quality and cost metrics.

REGULATORY ENVIRONMENT

The hospital industry is subject to a wide variety of regulation and legislation. With the passage of the 2010 healthcare reform legislation, providers face an even more extensive regulatory scheme, much of which focuses on increased rules and stricter prosecution of violations, particularly as an avenue to finance the healthcare legislation. Not only are providers subject to different regulations based on the state in which they are located (e.g., certificate of need), but also they are subject to differing regulations based on the types of services they provide, resulting in an inconsistent regulatory framework. The following are descriptions of the major types of current laws and proposed legislation that may affect the hospital industry.

Corporate Practice of Medicine

These restrictions vary on a state-by-state basis. In states with strong laws governing the corporate practice of medicine, corporations, including hospitals, are limited in their control of physician compensation, referral decisions, physician fees, payer contracts, and anything that may constitute fee splitting. This doctrine is intended to preclude hospitals, insurers, management companies, and other lay corporations from employing physicians to practice medicine or otherwise exercising undue influence over physicians.

Licensure and Accreditation

All hospitals are subject to numerous federal, state, and local statutes and regulations pertaining to licensure requirements. Although the licensing of healthcare enterprises is typically handled by state governments, there is significant interplay between state and federal government regulations, as most states require healthcare enterprises to meet the practice standards set forth by Medicare as a condition of licensure, and participation in the Medicare and Medicaid program requires certification through CMS and accreditation by a national accrediting agency.[121] Hospital regulations generally require an organized governing board, medical and nursing staff, and administration staff, as well as minimum services (e.g., radiology, pharmacy, laboratory, and emergency services).[122]

Accreditation is the process by which private organizations evaluate participating institutions and programs and issue accreditation certificates to institutions that meet their organization's requirements.[123] If a participating institution or program fails to maintain the requisite standards, they may not incur penalties other than the loss of their accreditation by the given organization. In most states, there is no link between accreditation and institutional licensure; however, some states will forego further inspection and accept accreditation by certain organizations, such as The Joint Commission, as the basis for the state licensure of certain providers.[123]

Accreditation can be beneficial to organizations for purposes of federal compliance. Medicare grants "deemed status" to hospitals accredited by The Joint Commission or the American Osteopathic Association.[124] Deemed status allows providers to be certified to participate in the Medicare and Medicaid Program unless a later validation survey finds noncompliance with the conditions of participation requirements set forth in the federal regulations.[125] Additionally, some payers will only enter into contracts with providers who have been accredited by a specific organization.[126] Major accrediting bodies in the United States include The Joint Commission on Accreditation of Healthcare Organizations (JCAHO), the American Osteopathic Association (AOA), and the National Committee for Quality Assurance (NCQA).

Certificate of Need Laws

Certificate of need legislation, which requires governmental approval for new healthcare facilities, equipment, and services, has been in place since 1975. State certification of need laws create a regulatory barrier to entry. New medical provider entrants commonly face substantial political opposition by established interests, which is manifested in the certification of need review process. As of 2011, twenty-seven states and the District of Columbia had certificate of need laws in place regulating the number of beds in acute-care hospitals.[127]

Health Insurance Portability and Accountability Act of 1996 (HIPAA)

While the Health Insurance Portability and Accountability Act of 1996 (HIPAA) serves many purposes, it is most widely used for safeguarding the privacy of protected health information (PHI), i.e., individually identifiable health information.[128] This protection extends to information related to the "past, present, or future physical or mental health condition of an individual; the provision of healthcare services to an individual; or the past, present, or future payment for the provision of healthcare to an individual."[129] As the healthcare industry makes the transition to electronic transactions, the current version of the HIPAA standards that regulate the transmission of specific healthcare information, known as the Accredited Standards Committee X12 Version 4010/4010AI, have become increasingly less functional for the coding and transactional updates providers are currently required to accommodate (i.e., the International Classification of Diseases, Tenth Edition update). To rectify any inefficiency, HHS approved ASC X12 Version 5010,[130] which includes improvements in technical, structural, and data content requirements; transactional business standardization; data transmission specifications; and delineation of various patient codes.[131] Although the final HIPAA rule introducing the changes was published on January 16, 2009, the CMS Office of E-Health standards and Services (OESS), responsible for enforcement of compliance with electronic transaction standards, delayed enforcement until July 1, 2012,[132] partially due to industry feedback suggesting that many covered entities would be unable to comply with the new transaction standards by the original January 1, 2012, deadline.[133]

The American Recovery and Reinvestment Act of 2009 (ARRA) made significant changes to HIPAA's health information privacy and security provisions.[134] The ARRA enacted the Health Information Technology for Economic Clinical Health (HITECH) Act to promote widespread adoption of health information technology, particularly electronic health records.[135] Provisions in the HITECH Act protect the privacy and security of PHI by:

1. Allowing patients to request an electronic copy of their records as well as an audit trail that shows all disclosures of their PHI
2. Prohibiting the sale of a patient's PHI without their authorization
3. Requiring individuals to be notified if there is an unauthorized disclosure or use of their PHI[136]

This latter provision requires public notification to the HHS website, prominent media outlets, and the Secretary of HHS when breaches affecting 500 patients or more occur.[137] Though these new notification requirements were effective as of September 23, 2009, enforcement was delayed until February 22, 2010.[138]

Significant attention has been given to the HITECH Act, with the passage of the ACA in regard to the adoption of electronic health records. For example, since 2011, more than 3,300 hospitals and 120,000 eligible healthcare professionals have qualified for participation in the Electronic Health Record Incentive Program, exceeding the government's target by approximately 23,000 individuals.[139]

Not-for-Profit Status

Section 501(c)(3) of the IRS code requires that an exempt entity be organized and operated exclusively for exempt purposes. Regulations interpret this standard as requiring that exempt organizations engage "primarily in activities that accomplish one or more . . . exempt purposes." If "more than an insubstantial" amount of the exempt organization's activities does not further the purpose of the exempt organization, the standard is violated. Exempt organizations can engage in joint ventures with for-profit organizations.[140] When a not-for-profit hospital enters into a joint venture with a for-profit medical group, the IRS states the focus should be on whether the arrangement serves a charitable purpose.

In 2004, the IRS implemented the Executive Compensation Compliance Initiative to review the compensation practices of public charities and private foundations. Many reporting errors and omissions were found through compliance check letters and examinations due to confusion about the instructions on Forms 990 and 990-PF.[141] In 2006, the Government Accountability Office reported that, of the sixty-five hospitals responding to a survey, forty hospitals had written executive compensation criteria, with the majority of reporting hospitals having a committee that approved the CEO's base salary, bonuses, and prerequisites. Examinations of twenty-five exempt organizations found excessive salary and incentive compensation, payment for vacation homes and personal automobiles, and payments for personal meals and gifts. Many organizations also incorrectly reported compensation on one or more forms.

In March 2007, the IRS reported that, of the 1,826 tax-exempt organizations involved in its Executive Compliance Initiative, 782 audits were conducted and $21 million in excise taxes was levied against forty individuals and twenty-five different organizations for engaging in excess benefits transactions. Several key issues were factors in causing these assessments, including excessive salary and incentive compensation; payments to an officer's for-profit corporation in excess of the value of the services provided by the corporation; and payments for personal legal fees, vacation homes, and personal automobiles not reported as compensation. The report also indicated that loans to officers and other executives will be the subject of single-issue compliance checks and audits in the next phase of the IRS's Executive Compliance Initiative.

In February 2010, the IRS began a payroll audit program of 6,000 companies, including approximately 1,500 tax-exempt organizations, such as non-profit hospitals. The program primarily focuses on the misclassification of employee status, which can cost nearly $200 million annually in unemployment costs, and excessive executive compensation. The 2010 audits are part of an agency-wide national research program of employee tax reports, the purpose of which is to collect data to help the IRS target future employment tax audits.[142] Additionally, companies that are found to have executive compensation plans or benefits exceeding fair market value, according to the auditors, will face strict application of the current code's sanctions. Such penalties include being subject to an excise tax and the possible revocation of an organization's tax-exempt status.[143]

In addition to the increased scrutiny of hospital executive compensation by the IRS, provisions in recently passed healthcare legislation will likely result in additional enforcement action taken against non-profit entities. Section 4959 of the ACA calls for a mandatory review of the tax-exempt status of non-profit hospitals, focusing on the adequacy of their community benefit activities,[144] the standard by which hospitals gain tax-exempt status subsequent to the removal of charity care requirements in 1969.[145] All investigative efforts by both state and federal agencies regarding executive compensation assist the IRS with insight into the procedures for setting executive salaries at tax-exempt organizations and how to regulate these practices.[146]

Fraud and Abuse Laws

Healthcare organizations face a range of state and federal legal and regulatory constraints, which affect their formation, operation, procedural coding and billing, investors, and sale. The categories of laws and regulations that healthcare organizations are most affected by are the Fraud and Abuse laws, specifically those dealing with the coding and billing of services and the anti-kickback and physician self-referral laws, known as the Stark laws.

The growing need for healthcare services provided to Medicare and Medicaid beneficiaries has prompted a movement for increased government scrutiny of healthcare providers in an effort to control increasing levels of fraud and abuse.[147] The ACA authorizes expanded funding ($250 million) and new rules that will aid the HHS in its expanded efforts to prevent and fight fraud, waste, and abuse in government programs.[148] The Health Care Fraud and Abuse Control Program (HCFAC), jointly governed by the U.S. Attorney General and the Secretary of HHS and enforced through the Office of the Inspector General, coordinates federal, state, and local law enforcement activities with respect to preventing, identifying, and prosecuting healthcare fraud and abuse. The Medicare Fraud Strike Force (Strike Force), a partnership between the Department of Justice and HHS, combats healthcare fraud by prosecuting individuals and entities that exist for the sole purpose of defrauding Medicare and other government healthcare programs.[149] The Strike Force supplements the criminal healthcare fraud enforcement activities of the U.S. Attorneys' Offices by targeting both incessant fraud and transient schemes committed by those posing as legitimate healthcare providers or suppliers.[149] Additionally, the ACA makes two changes to the intent standards relating to fraud and abuse. First, the legislation amends the Anti-Kickback Statute (AKS) by stating that a person need not have actual knowledge of (the AKS) or specific intent to commit a violation of (the AKS) for the government to prove a kickback violation. Secondly, the healthcare reform provides that a claim that includes items or services resulting from a violation (of the AKS) constitutes a false or fraudulent claim for purposes of the False Claim Act, which results in a law that any violation of the AKS is sufficient to state a claim under the False Claim Act.

Within the context of the Medicare Program, fraud is generally defined as the misrepresentation of material facts, and abuse is defined as the provision of excessive, inappropriate, harmful, or poor quality healthcare.[150] More specifically, Medicare abuse denotes an incident or practice, carried out by providers, physicians, or service suppliers, that is inconsistent with accepted medical, business, or fiscal practices, and which directly or indirectly results in one of the following: (1) unnecessary costs to the program; or (2) improper reimbursement for services that fail to meet professionally reorganized standards of care.[150] Prohibition of physician self-referral and anti-kickback legislation are generally concerned with the same issue: the financial motivation behind patient referrals. However, the self-referral prohibition addresses the financial incentives of the physician who makes a referral, while the anti-kickback statute is concerned with financial relationships and transfers between providers.[151] Another important difference between the regulations is that the self-referral prohibitions apply only to Medicare and Medicaid, whereas the anti-kickback legislation applies to all federal healthcare programs.[152] In addition, the anti-kickback statute provides for possible criminal penalties.[153]

Stark I and II

The physician self-referral prohibitions are commonly known as "Stark I" and "Stark II" after Congressman Fortney "Pete" Stark (D-CA), the legislation's chief supporter. In supporting the legislation, Congressman Stark relied on studies indicating that, despite the broad scope of the AKS, self-referrals were prevalent in the healthcare industry.[154] For example, the Office of the Inspector General published a study in 1989 on physician investments in healthcare facilities, reporting that patients at physician-owned laboratories received more services than other Medicare patients.[155]

The Ethics in Patient Referral Act of 1989, now referred to as Stark I, was part of the Omnibus Budget Reconciliation Act (OBRA) of 1989 and prohibits physicians from referring Medicare patients to clinical labs in which the physicians or their family members have a financial relationship.[156]

In August 1993, the federal self-referral prohibition was expanded through the Comprehensive Physician Ownership and Referral Act of 1993, or Stark II, as part of the Omnibus Budget Reconciliation Act of 1993 (OBRA '93). OBRA '93 changed the self-referral prohibition in several ways. Significantly, the Medicare self-referral prohibition was broadened not to all payers, but only to Medicaid services.

Self-referral was banned for additional "designated health services" (DHS), including:

1. Clinical laboratory services
2. Physical therapy
3. Occupational therapy
4. Radiology or other diagnostic services
5. Radiation therapy
6. Durable medical equipment
7. Parenteral and enteral nutrients, equipment, and supplies
8. Prosthetics, orthotics, and prosthetic devices
9. Home health services
10. Ambulance services
11. Outpatient prescription drugs
12. Inpatient and outpatient hospital services

On March 26, 2004, CMS published the final version of the Stark II regulations, entitled Phase II, which explained exceptions to the Stark law and redefined key terminology.[157] Referrals subject to Phase I Stark law included requests by radiologists for diagnostic radiology services and requests by radiation oncologists for radiation therapy, only if the request was the result of a consultation requested by another physician, and only if the tests or services were performed or supervised by a radiologist or radiation oncologist. Under the new Phase II law, however, supervision may be provided by another pathologist, radiologist, or radiation oncologist within the same group practice.[157]

Stark II, Phase III Regulations

On September 5, 2007, CMS issued the final rule establishing the Stark II, Phase III regulations, which contains many changes that are predicted to have a significant impact on existing, as well as future, healthcare provider relationships.[158] The changes with perhaps the most significant expected impact are those related to provider compensation arrangements.[159] To comply with the Stark regulations, entities with certain financial arrangements must be classified as having an indirect compensation arrangement or fall within one of the Stark exceptions. If a valid indirect arrangement agreement was signed prior to September 5, 2007, CMS will allow this arrangement to continue until the term of the arrangement expires.[159]

One requirement, as set out in the Phase I regulations, stipulated that there must exist at least two financial relationships between the physician and the DHS entity. The Phase III regulations change the definition of an indirect compensation arrangement so that physician members and owners of the physician organization are now deemed to have identical (i.e., direct) compensation arrangements as the physician organization itself.[159] A hospital that has a contract for professional services with a physician group (considered indirect under the Phase I regulations because there was a financial relationship between individual physicians and their group practice as well as a relationship between the group practice and the hospital) is considered to have a direct compensation arrangement with the owners and investors of the physician organization.[160] The effect of this change is that a physician organization may not be considered an intervening entity for the purposes of establishing an indirect compensation arrangement, and to avoid Stark liability the physician organization may need to be structured differently.[161]

On August 4, 2008, CMS announced several changes to the Stark law that would be included in the upcoming Inpatient Prospective Payment System for fiscal year 2009.[162] One major provision requires physician owners of or investors in physician organizations to stand in the shoes of that physician organization when examining financial relationships between referring physicians and DHS entities.[163] However, owners who do not receive financial benefits of ownership or investment are not required to stand in the shoes, but may if they choose to do so.[164]

Additionally, the final rule modified the definition of the term "DHS entity" to include not only the entity that bills Medicare but also the entity that performs the service.[165] Therefore, hospitals can no longer refer patients to physician service providers in which they have an ownership interest where the provider sells the service to another entity that bills it.[166] It should be noted that this change only applies to physician organizations, while other arrangements, e.g., an arrangement between a DHS entity, a leasing company, and a physician are analyzed as an indirect compensation arrangement.[167]

SPECIALTY AND SURGICAL HOSPITALS

Specialty and surgical hospitals have experienced a development boom since the early 2000s. Reimbursement levels for these specialties and especially surgeries have been considered to be relatively high in comparison to others, creating the perception that these services are especially profitable.[168] However, the 2010 healthcare reform legislation, comprised of the Patient Protection and Affordable Care Act (H.R. 3590), and the Health Care and Education Reconciliation Act of 2010 (H.R. 4872), place significant restrictions on the growth and development of physician-owned hospitals. Specifically, H.R. 3590 Section 6001 and H.R. 4872 Section 1106 outline new requirements for specialty hospitals, stating that those under development must obtain Medicare certification by December 31, 2010 (amended from H.R. 3590, which set the certification deadline to August 1, 2010).[169] Existing physician-owned hospitals would be eligible for some "grandfathering" benefits; however, they would still be restricted from increasing physician ownership or expanding services.[170]

HOSPITAL INDUSTRY OUTLOOK

The U.S. healthcare delivery system is facing what is perhaps its greatest challenge in the expected demand for increased health services from the aging of the baby-boom generation, the fastest-growing segment of the population. The enactment of healthcare reform in March 2010, requiring increased insurance coverage requirements for individuals and employers, will also increase patient demand for hospital inpatient and outpatient services in the coming years.

As healthcare costs continue to rise faster than inflation in the overall economy, driven by advances in technology and treatment (as well as the growing baby-boomer population), pressures to reduce costs, such as those included in the 2010 healthcare reform legislation, will result in a new paradigm for healthcare delivery. Reimbursement mechanisms are increasingly designed to control costs and access, and hospitals must continually adjust to deal with increasing pressure to contain reimbursement and utilization levels.

The healthcare marketplace continues to experience dramatic change as the business of healthcare becomes increasingly competitive, particularly in the outpatient ancillary services arena. Providers and payers continue to seek to control costs and markets. Legal and regulatory issues also affect change as providers adapt to new opportunities and restrictions. In particular, there are a wide variety of cost, operational, and regulatory pressures impacting the specialty and surgical hospital industry. However, these pressures are offset by the stable and increasing demand for hospital services, particularly for those hospitals already in operation. Hospitals that are operationally efficient will continue to be successful within this environment.

ECONOMIC CONCEPT OF VALUE

Basic Economic Valuation Tenets

Market perceptions of the value of an enterprise are based on investors' knowledge of the historical and current status of the organization and the market and, more importantly, the future trends of the healthcare industry and transactional/capital marketplace within which the subject enterprise operates. The historical performance of a subject enterprise that has operated under the economic and financial structure of the traditional healthcare delivery system may not be a valid indicator of its future performance within the context of a reimbursement and regulatory environment that is driven by cost containment and managed care.

An understanding of the importance of future trends to the healthcare valuation process is illustrated by the following basic valuation tenets:

- All value is the expectation of future benefit; therefore, value is forward looking.
- The best indicator of future performance is usually the performance of the immediate past.
- Historical accounting and other data are useful primarily as a road map to the future.

Traditional healthcare valuation methodologies rely upon the analysis of historical accounting and other data as being predictive of future performance and value. The turbulent status of the healthcare industry since the 1980s has introduced intervening events and circumstances that may have a dramatic effect on the revenue or benefit stream of the subject entity. In such an environment, the "road map of historical performance" becomes less predictive of future performance. An example of how events may change the prediction of future performance is set forth in Figure 11.2.

Value Pyramid

Key value drivers for hospitals may be viewed within the context of the Value Pyramid (Figure 11.3); i.e., the process related to the financial valuation of these enterprises can generally be discussed within the context of two determinants: I, the determination of the appropriate income/earnings/benefit stream for the subject enterprise, and R, the development and selection of the appropriate

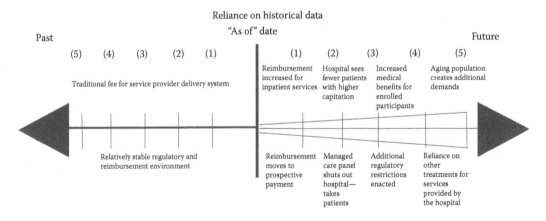

Q: How useful is the past in determining value?

FIGURE 11.2   Value determination.

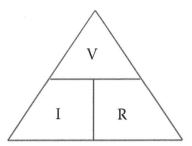

I ➡ Income/earnings/benefit stream as defined by appraiser and appropriate to assignment
R ➡ Risk-adjusted discount rate/cap rate/multiple risk adjusted and applicable to selected
income stream
V ➡ Value

FIGURE 11.3   The value pyramid.

risk-adjusted required rate of return, typically expressed as a discount rate, capitalization rate, or multiple, to apply to the income stream selected.

Aspects of the rapidly changing reimbursement and regulatory environment related to each determinant are key to developing both a forecast of the subject enterprise's future income stream as well as an appropriate risk-adjusted discount rate, capitalization rate, or multiple to apply to the selected benefit stream for the surgical (or specialty) hospital being valued. Keeping these considerations in mind, and within the context of the dynamic healthcare industry milieu, remember also that:

- Because uncertainty breeds the perception of risk, under which circumstances a higher rate of return is demanded by potential purchasers, even high-quality, risk-averse, stable-growth, highly profitable and eminently transferable healthcare entities are often "tar brushed" by the perception of overall market uncertainty, as well as risk related to the subject enterprise's industry sector.
- Other market-motivating factors often drive transactional pricing multiples; e.g., investors' fear of being shut out of their ability to legally maintain or sell their investment represents an undue stimulus or special motivation and synergy that may drive the deal, resulting in prices below or above value.
- The selection of risk-adjusted rates to capitalize an earnings or benefit stream into value requires more than just a cursory analysis of underlying data related to market systematic risk, as a nonsystematic, subject enterprise risk adjustment may also be appropriate.

Given the impact of the reimbursement and regulatory environment on the investor's perception of risk and the resulting impact on the valuation of the subject hospital enterprise, the most important consideration for the healthcare valuator may be to have an in-depth understanding of the current state of those issues in the rapidly changing healthcare industry. The valuation expert must also be aware that the assessment of risk by investors is related to both the actualities and (perhaps more substantially) the perceptions of the market, related to external economic, demographic, and industry conditions, and related to aspects of the specific subject enterprise and the transaction.

BUY OR BUILD? VALUE AS INCREMENTAL BENEFIT

Another important value concept is driven by the economic principle of substitution, which states that the cost of an equally desirable substitute (or one of equivalent utility) tends to set the ceiling of value; i.e., it is the maximum price that a knowledgeable buyer would be willing to pay for a given asset or property. As applied to the healthcare valuation process, this concept is embodied in selecting and applying valuation methods in a manner that recognizes that the fair market value of a healthcare entity is the aggregate present value of the total of all future benefits of ownership to be derived in excess of (incremental to) the level of net economic benefits that may be projected to accrue from an alternative, hypothetical, start-up entity of the same type, setting, format, and location. This benefit of buying rather than building is referred to as the incremental benefit.

The challenge for the healthcare valuator is to arrive at a determination of the present value of forward-looking statements of this incremental benefit, within the context of an industry that is undergoing a massive shift in markets, regulatory and cost structures, care patterns and technology, and investor expectations. The consideration of any value or economic benefit of ownership beyond the point that the hypothetical start-up matches the established business ("merger point") requires a careful analysis of the competitive environment in which a hypothetical start-up would grow (Figure 11.4).

The "equally desirable substitute" that is required by the principle of substitution is more difficult to project at a time when historical trends and assumptions may often have no longer been deemed valid by prospective purchasers or investors. Measuring the depth of the marketplace's perception as to the probability of success for start-ups being diminished by reimbursement and regulatory pressures is subject to similar uncertainties.

THE STANDARD OF VALUE AND PREMISE OF VALUE

At the outset of each valuation engagement, it is important to appropriately define the standard of value, which defines the type of value to be determined (e.g., fair market value, fair value, market value, investment value, book value, etc.), and it is often described as answering the question, "Value to whom?" Each type of value has its own specific meaning to investors.

It is also imperative that the premise of value, an assumption further defining the standard of value to be used under which a valuation is conducted, be determined at the outset of the valuation engagement. The premise of value defines the hypothetical terms of the sale and answers the question, "Value under what further defining circumstances?" (e.g., going concern, orderly disposition, forced liquidation, etc.).

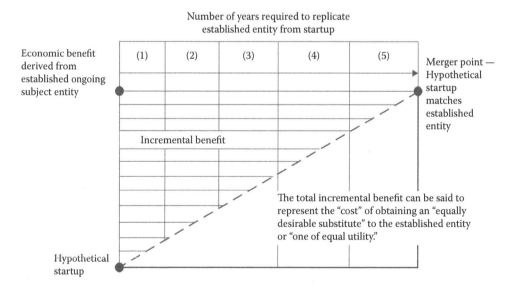

FIGURE 11.4   Merger and acquisition analysis.

The Standard of Value and the Universe of Typical Buyers

This standard of value assumes an anticipated hypothetical transaction, in which the buyer and seller are each acting prudently with a reasonable equivalence of knowledge and that the price is not affected by any undue stimulus or coercion. Implicit in this definition are the following assumptions:

- The hypothetical transaction contemplates a universe of typical potential purchasers for the subject property and not a specific purchaser or specific class of purchaser.
- Buyer and seller are typically motivated.
- Both parties are well informed and acting in their respective rational economic self-interests.
- Both parties are professionally advised, and the hypothetical transaction is assumed to be closed with the typical legal protections in place to safeguard the transfer of ownership of the legal bundle of rights that define and encompass the transacted property or interest.
- A sufficiently reasonable amount of time is allowed for exposure in the open market.
- Payment is made in cash or its equivalent.
- The anticipated hypothetical transaction would be conducted in compliance with Stark I and Stark II legislation prohibiting physicians from making referrals for designated health services reimbursable under Medicare or Medicaid to an entity with which the referring physician has a financial relationship.[171] Stark II defines fair market value as the value in arm's-length transactions, consistent with the general market value.[172] The transaction falls within Stark II's specific exception for isolated financial transactions when:
  - The amount of the remuneration under the employment is consistent with fair market value of the services
  - The amount of the remuneration under the employment is not determined in a manner that takes into account (directly or indirectly) the volume or value of any referrals by the referring physician
  - The amount of the remuneration under the employment is provided pursuant to an agreement that would be commercially reasonable even if no referrals were made to the employer
  - The transaction meets such other requirements as the Secretary of HHS may impose by regulation as needed to protect against program or patient abuse.[173]
- The anticipated hypothetical transaction would be conducted in compliance with the Medicare AKS, which makes it illegal to knowingly pay or receive any remuneration in return for referrals.[174] The Medicare AKS requires the payment of "fair market value in arm's-length transactions . . . and that any compensation is not determined in a manner that takes into account the volume or value of any referrals or business otherwise generated between the parties for which payment may be made in whole or in part under Medicare, Medicaid, or other federal healthcare programs."[175]
- Related to the above, the following definitions of terms apply:
  - "In an excess benefit transaction, the general rule for the valuation of property, including the right to use property, is fair market value."[176]
  - "A disqualified person, regarding any transaction, is any person who was in a position to exercise substantial influence over the affairs of the applicable tax-exempt organization at any time during [a five-year period ending on the date of the transaction]."[177]
  - An excess benefit transaction is a "transaction in which an economic benefit is provided by an applicable tax-exempt organization, directly or indirectly, to or for the use of a disqualified person, and the value of the economic benefit provided by the organization exceeds the value of the consideration received by the organization."[178]

The Premise of Value and the Investment Time Horizon

The premise of value under which a valuation is conducted is an assumption further defining the standard of value to be used. The premise of value defines the hypothetical terms of the sale and answers the question, "Value under what further defining circumstances?" Two general concepts relate to the consideration and selection of the premise of value, i.e., value in use and value in exchange.

Value in Use

Value in use is that premise of value that assumes that the assets will continue to be used as part of an ongoing business enterprise, producing profits as a benefit of ownership. For example, in valuing the assets of a surgical hospital, the valuator must determine whether it is appropriate to value simply the tangible assets, or if it is appropriate to consider the enterprise as a going concern and incorporate the potential value of intangible assets. Orderly liquidation value involves assuming that the equipment is sold, perhaps separately, over a reasonable period of time. Forced liquidation assumes that the equipment is sold as quickly as possible to the first bidder.

Value in Exchange

Value in exchange is often referred to as liquidation value. Liquidation value describes a sale of the assets of a business enterprise under conditions other than its continued operation as a going concern. The liquidation can be on the basis of an orderly disposition of the assets where more extensive marketing efforts are made and sufficient time is permitted to achieve the best price for all assets, or on the basis of forced liquidation where assets are sold immediately and without concern for obtaining the best price. Costs of liquidation should be considered in the value estimate when using this premise of value. Shortening the investment time horizon may have a deleterious effect on the valuation of the subject entity as it presents a restriction on the available pool of buyers and investors and the level of physician ownership, as required under the standard of fair market value.

DEFINING THE ENTITY AND THE INTEREST

It is essential that the valuator clearly and concisely define both the specific business entity and the specific interest or assets within the entity that is being appraised. The valuator must first determine if assets or equity are being valued (e.g., 20 percent of the outstanding shares of stock or 100 percent undivided interest in assets). In addition, a specific written definition and description of the practice as well as the specific interest in that practice, where interest is the subject of the valuation, is important.

The following factors may be encountered during the definition of the entity and the interest and should be carefully considered in the analysis:

- Valuation engagements for a specified minority interest–owned in larger healthcare entities are more complex.
- Larger healthcare entities often include a range of services, requiring a diversity of data for compensation, costs, productivity, performance, etc.
- Larger healthcare entities may be composed of multiple interlocking component entities acting as a consolidated entity while in fact having a significant diversity of ownership of the various legal entities involved with overlapping ownership interests.

CLASSIFICATION OF ASSETS

Table 11.7 illustrates the types of tangible and intangible assets found in various healthcare organizations.

Once the identifiable and separately quantifiable intangible assets are valued, the residual amount of intangible asset value that remains is often referred to as "goodwill." This term may appropriately be considered as the propensity of patients (and the revenue stream thereof) to return to the subject enterprise incremental to that which is quantified as the contribution of the other tangible and intangible assets in the assemblage of assets which comprises the enterprise. Keep in mind that goodwill

TABLE 11.7
Assets Found in Various Healthcare Organizations

I Tangible
  1) Accounts receivable
  2) Cash, investments
  3) Furniture, fixtures, and equipment
  4) Leasehold improvements
  5) Real property
  6) Supplies
  7) Medical library

II Intangible
  1) Payer/customer-related
    a) Managed-care agreements
    b) Provider service agreements/medical directorships
    c) Direct contracting customer lists
    d) Health maintenance organization enrollment lists

  2) Goodwill and patient-related
    a) Custody of medical charts and records
    b) Personal/professional goodwill
    c) Practice/commercial goodwill
    d) Patient lists/recall lists

  3) Human capital–related
    a) Employment/provider contracts
    b) Trained and assembled workforce
    c) Policies and procedures
    d) Depth of management

  4) Intellectual property–related
    a) Practice protocols
    b) Treatment plans/care mapping
    c) Procedural manuals/laboratory notebooks
    d) Technical and specialty research
    e) Patents and patent applications
    f) Copyrights
    g) Trade names
    h) Trade secrets
    i) Royalty agreements

  5) Locations and operations-related
    a) Management information/executive decision systems
    b) Favorable leases, leasehold interests
    c) Going concern value
    d) Asset assemblage factors
    e) Historical documents/charts/relative value unit studies
    f) Supplier contracts, e.g., group purchasing organizations

  6) Governance/legal structure–related
    a) Organizational documents
    b) Non-compete covenants
    c) Income distribution plans

  7) Marketing and business development–related
    a) Print ads, telephone numbers, billboards, etc.
    b) Franchise/license agreements

        c) Joint ventures/alliances, e.g., "call-a-nurse"
        d) Market entrance barriers/factors

   8) **Regulatory/legal-related**
        a) Facility licenses
        b) Medical licenses
        c) Permits – real estate special use
        d) Litigation awards and liquidated damages
        e) Certificates of need
        f) Medicare certification/UPIN
        g) Certifications—e.g., National Committee on Quality Assurance, AAAHC,
           Joint Commission on Accreditation of Healthcare Organizations

   9) **Financial/revenue stream–related**
        a) Office share
        b) Management services contracts
        c) Financing agreements
        d) Underwriting/private placement memoranda
        e) Budgets/forecasts/projections

  10) **Technology-related**
        a) Computer software/network integration
        b) Technical/software documentation
        c) Maintenance/support relationships

is only one of the several intangible assets that may be found to exist in a professional practice, not a catch-all-moniker for all intangible assets in the aggregate.

VALUATION APPROACHES AND METHODOLOGY

There are numerous generally accepted healthcare valuation approaches, methods, procedures, and techniques. The choice of approach(es) and method(s) depends primarily upon the purpose of the valuation report and the specific characteristics of the property to be appraised. The objective and purpose of the valuation engagement, the standard of value, the premise of value, and the availability and reliability of data must all be considered by decision makers in the selection of applicable approaches and methods. The three general classifications of approaches are the income approach, market approach, and the asset/cost-based approach. Within each approach there are several methods, procedures, and techniques available for consideration, as briefly discussed below.

Income Approach

Income approach–based methods measure the present value of anticipated future economic benefits that will accrue to the owner of the entity to be appraised. The economic benefit of ownership has several potential measures, including, but not limited to, net income (before or after tax), net operating income, gross cash flow, net cash flow, and dividend payouts. In addition to estimating the future benefits of ownership of the enterprise to be appraised, an appropriate risk-adjusted required rate of return applicable to the enterprise to be appraised must also be developed, by which the future economic benefits will be discounted.

There are several methods that may be considered under the income approach, including:

1. Discounted net cash flow (DCF) method: Estimates the present value of normalized expected cash flows distributable to the owners of the enterprise to be appraised, with a residual or terminal value ascribed to all periods beyond the discrete forecasted projection.

2. Single period capitalization method: Estimates the present value of the enterprise to be appraised by capitalizing a single year of economic benefit.

Market Approach

Market approach–based methods are premised on the foundation that actual transactions provide guidance to value. There are several methods utilized under the market approach, including:

1. Merged and acquired company method (also referred to as the direct market comparable transactions method): This method analyzes the terms (price, interest, assets included, etc.) of specific transactions involving the acquisition of substantial, control positions (most often the entirety) of similar enterprises.
2. Guideline public company method: This method is based upon the theory that an indication of value of the enterprise to be appraised can be derived through the valuation multiples of the freely traded, minority interest registered shares of publicly traded companies.

Asset/Cost Approach

Asset/cost approach–based methods seek an indication of value by determining the cost of reproducing or replacing an asset. This approach is commonly utilized when the entity has little value beyond the tangible assets or in the event that the entity is not a going concern. There are several methods that may be utilized under the asset approach, including:

1. Asset accumulation method (also referred to as the adjusted net asset value method): This method estimates the value of the total invested capital of an entity by determining the sum of the fair market value of each of its discrete assets.
2. Liquidation value methods: These methods (orderly or forced) estimate the value of an entity by determining the present value of the net proceeds from liquidating the company's assets and paying off liabilities.
3. Excess earnings method: The excess earnings method, also called the Treasury method or the IRS formula method based on Revenue Ruling 68-609, does not neatly fit into any of the three previous approaches. This method is considered by many valuators to be a hybrid method, combining elements of the asset/cost-based approach with elements of income approach methods.

The excess earnings method first values the intangible assets of the entity being appraised utilizing a residual technique, whereby a portion of the benefit stream (e.g., net free cash flow or net income) is attributed to a return on net tangible assets utilizing a market-derived cost of capital for similar tangible assets. Then an appropriate portion of the benefit stream is attributed to the fair market value of the replacement cost of services provided by the owner as owner compensation. Finally, the dollar amount of the benefit that remains after the deduction of these two amounts (the residual) is then presumed to be attributable to the intangible assets. This amount of the benefit stream, which has been determined to be attributable to the intangible assets of the entity being appraised, is then capitalized using a risk-adjusted equity rate of return, and the resulting indicated value of the intangible assets is then added to the value of the tangible assets of the entity being appraised to arrive at an estimate of overall asset value as a going concern.

Methods Typically Not Utilized in the Valuation of Hospitals

The excess earnings method is typically not utilized in hospital valuations. The nature of a hospital as an enterprise providing facilities and technical services is significantly different from that of enterprises where this method may be utilized, e.g., a professional practice, wherein the consideration of the return of an earnings stream incremental to the compensation of a professional provider(s) is often the most significant aspect.

VALUATION ADJUSTMENTS FOR RISK

As noted earlier, the selection of valuation methodologies is based on the purpose of the report and the specific characteristics of the subject property/interest. Once the appropriate valuation methodologies have been selected, certain adjustments may be warranted depending on the various methodologies. When utilizing an income approach–based methodology, an appropriate risk-adjusted required rate of return must be determined. The selection of the appropriate risk adjustment to market-derived required rates of return utilized in the development of selected discount rates, capitalization rates, or market multiples in healthcare valuation requires a thorough understanding of several underlying investment concepts. In developing a discount/capitalization rate to be applied in income approach methods, the following should be considered:

- Investors in hospitals have alternative investments available to them. Therefore, the investment justification for hospitals should be considered in comparison to rates of return available from a broader array of other types of investments.
- High-risk factors are considered to have a greater than average chance of negatively affecting the enterprise's earning power, while low-risk factors are considered less likely to reduce the enterprise's ability to generate profits and cash flow as a future benefit of ownership; accordingly, elements that increase risk will decrease the value of the enterprise, and elements that decrease risk will increase the value.
- Knowledgeable investors in a hospital with a high degree of risk will require a greater return on investment to compensate for the greater risk.
- There will be differences of opinion as to how much risk is represented by any single characteristic of the enterprise, and the risk tolerance of each individual investor is, to a large extent, dependent upon the return on investment required to compensate for their perceived level of risk.

In addition to informed consideration of the effect of volatile market changes on the perception of risk and the resulting adjustment to the required rate of return for investment, the most probable income/earnings/benefit stream for investors should also be carefully analyzed to determine appropriate adjustments to reported results derived from historical performance when utilizing an income approach–based method. This adjustment will reflect the most accurate and appropriate information available on the valuation date of the most probable future performance, often referred to as "normalized earnings." To arrive at an estimate of the normalized earnings for the subject enterprise, the adjustments considered should include, but not necessarily be limited to:

- Actual or expected increase(s)/decrease(s) in fees and reimbursement for services by regulatory edict or competitive market pressures
- Projected increase(s)/decrease(s) in operating expenses based on new operating parameters and market realities, e.g., provider taxes, disclosure requirements
- Expectations of the future stability and growth of the revenue streams and the sustainability of the subject enterprise's earnings within the context of a chaotic healthcare industry and marketplace

In the final analysis, both the valuator's assessment of an appropriate risk-adjusted required rate of return for investment and the forecast of the most probable income/earnings/benefit stream are inextricably related to, should be based upon, and must be carefully correlated to an informed, realistic, and unsparing assessment of a universe of typical buyers' current perceptions of the market as to the future performance of the subject enterprise, as well the market's assessment of risk related to an investment in such an enterprise. Accordingly, the valuation of a hospital is sensitive to government interventions that would have an impact on the liquidity of capital either by disrupting the makeup of the market investor pool or the expected investment holding period time horizon, and the valuation may require a significant additional discount for lack of control or marketability.

With each method utilized, certain adjustments should be considered based upon the specific requirements of each engagement and the inherent indication of value (i.e., the level of value) that results from each method. Valuation engagements involving closely held interests (in contrast to a freely traded or a non-marketable basis) may require a discount for lack of marketability (defined below); those involving minority interests may require a discount for lack of control (defined below); and those involving controlling interests may require a control premium (defined below).

Discount for Lack of Control

A control premium is an increase to the pro rata share of the value of the business that reflects the impact on value inherent in the management and financial power that can be exercised by the holders of a control interest of the business, usually the majority holders.

A discount for lack of control or minority discount is the reduction from the pro rata share of the value of the business as a whole that reflects the impact on value of the absence or diminution of control that can be exercised by the holders of a subject interest.

Discount for Lack of Marketability

There are inherent risks relative to the liquidity of investments in closely held, non-public companies in that investors in closely held companies do not have the ability to dispose of an invested interest quickly if the situation is called for, e.g., forecasted unfavorable industry conditions or the investor's personal immediate need for cash. This relative lack of liquidity of ownership in a closely held company is accompanied by risks and costs associated with the selling of an interest of a closely held company, i.e., locating a buyer, negotiation of terms, advisor/broker fees, risk of exposure to the market, etc. Thus, a discount may be applicable to the value of a closely held company due to the inherent illiquidity of the investment as well as the transactional costs related to its disposition. Such discounts are commonly referred to as discounts for lack of marketability.

CONCLUSION

As one of the fundamental tenets of valuation is that value is the expectation of future economic benefits of ownership, knowledge of regulatory and reimbursement trends in the healthcare industry is a fundamental precondition to the valuation of hospitals. To estimate the future economic benefits of ownership that will be generated by a subject hospital, as well as the future economic risk related to those benefits, investors and healthcare valuators must continuously assess the implications of changing laws and regulations, at both the federal and state levels. Also significant is the ever-changing competitive environment with its increasingly forbidding landscape of new provider and payer configurations, tactics, and strategies.

Finally, economic conditions and events expected to result in a changed paradigm for healthcare delivery, e.g., the rapid acceleration in expected demand for increased health services as a result of the demographic time bomb of the aging baby-boomer generation and pressures to reduce rising healthcare costs, should be examined within the framework of the four pillars of the healthcare industry: regulation, reimbursement, competition, and technology. These four aspects of the healthcare environment set the context from which buyers, sellers, owners, and investors consider the valuation of hospital enterprises.

In evaluating the impact of these economic events on hospital valuation and determining the level of risk related to hospital investment, investors and healthcare valuators may wish to consider the old adage: Love everyone, trust no one, and paddle your own canoe.

- **Love everyone:** A consistent commitment to keeping abreast of industry changes is vital to healthcare valuation. Investors and business valuators should consistently stay in contact with healthcare trade associations, medical and other provider societies, healthcare investment brokers, managed care organizations and intermediaries, and hospital/system players; stay informed by subscribing to healthcare industry newsletters, journals, and health law and policy reporters; and attend conferences, symposiums, workshops, and healthcare industry seminars.

- **Trust no one:** A healthy skepticism of historical data provided by the subject entity, pat solutions for addressing risk analysis and discounts, and conventional valuation wisdom is in order. Professional business valuators are challenged to maintain and demonstrate the requisite skills as well as consistently expend the requisite effort to consider industry economic conditions and events. However, these skills are necessary to determine all of the appropriate adjustments to be made to the subject entity's forecasted earnings/benefit stream, as well as to develop well-reasoned and adequately supported risk adjustments to market-derived discount and capitalization rates within the context of the four pillars of the healthcare industry (i.e., regulatory, reimbursement, competition, and technology).

- **Paddle your own canoe:** Be wary of half-heated research measures and a lack of analytical rigor. Investors and business valuators should not overly rely on outside sources (e.g., management forecasts) for the foundation of their assessment of the impact of economic conditions on financial or capital formation aspects of the healthcare valuation process. Investors and business valuators must stay informed about the almost daily changes in national and regional economic conditions and capital costs impacting the healthcare industry and the subject entity's industry sector; payment and quality initiatives; reimbursement trends affecting the various medical specialties and the subject entity's industry sector; the payer/delivery system mix; healthcare manpower supply; trends in emerging and declining healthcare organizations; regulatory and enforcement initiatives; and other issues related to the healthcare transactional market in general, as well as the particular industry sector and market service area of the subject entity being valued.

CHECKLIST 1: Reimbursement Issues in Healthcare Valuation	YES	NO
Have you considered the contribution of margins from technical component services?	o	o
Have you reviewed the impact of the shift from defined benefits to defined contribution?	o	o
Have you considered the importance of physician supply?	o	o
Have you relied on historic reimbursement data?	o	o
Have you assumed that the federal government reimbursement (Medicare) will always increase?	o	o
Have you looked at state reimbursement (Medicaid) practices?	o	o
Have you considered the payer mix?	o	o
Have you examined incurred but not reported (IBNR) liabilities in capitated contracts?	o	o

CHECKLIST 2: Regulatory Issues in Healthcare Valuation	YES	NO
Have you underestimated the risk of regulatory change (e.g., specialty hospital moratorium)?	o	o
Have you assumed that the regulatory environment of the healthcare industry will remain the same?	o	o

	o	o
Have you fully assessed the implication of regulations on competition?	o	o
Have you reviewed both federal and state regulations?	o	o
Have you assessed the regulations affecting the subject entity and competitors?	o	o
Have you considered regulatory barriers to entry (e.g., certificate of need)?	o	o
Have you assessed the costs of regulatory mandates (e.g., HIPAA, Clinical Laboratory Improvement Act [CLIA] Occupational Safety and Health Administration [OSHA])?	o	o
Have you taken into account the significant costs associated with the movement to electronic medical records systems?	o	o

In addition, see Checklists 3 and 4 for typical steps that must be taken by a valuator in conducting the business valuation process.

CHECKLIST 3: Typical Pre-engagement Steps in the Healthcare Business Valuation Process	YES	NO
Pre-engagement:		
Have you determined whether there is a conflict of interest before signing the agreement?	o	o
Have you provided the appraiser with your detailed description of the appraisal subject, including the specific definition and description of the entity and the specific definition and description of the type and size of the entity?	o	o
Project Parameters:	o	o
Have you worked with the appraiser to determine the amount of time required to complete the assignment?	o	o
Has the appraiser developed and discussed with you a list of assumptions and limited conditions that are expected to be part of the report?	o	o
Engagement Fees and Agreement:	o	o
Has the appraiser developed a budget to estimate the required chargeable hours and fees?	o	o
Has the appraiser submitted a proposal letter and engagement agreement that includes consultant and client responsibilities, a schedule of professional fees, a retainer, and expense requirements?	o	o

CHECKLIST 4: Typical Steps During the Healthcare Business Valuation Process	Yes	No
Has the appraiser given you a detailed work program, including an appraisal staff assignment, and identified the project milestones?	o	o
Does the general industry research collected include information relative to economic, demographic, industry, competition, healthcare industry, and medical specialty trends?	o	o
During the analysis of the data that were gathered, did the appraiser conduct a thorough financial analysis, assessment of risk, and forecasting of future performance?	o	o
Did the appraiser explain the selection of valuation methods depending on factors such as the purpose of the valuation report, the availability of data for each method, and the specific characteristics of the subject entity?	o	o
Did the appraiser communicate the valuation process and provide a discussion draft of the report?	o	o
Did the appraiser complete the engagement within a reasonable time frame once all of the required data were received?	o	o

REFERENCES

1. National Federation of Independent Business v. Sebelius. 2012. Slip Opinion Nos. 11-393, 11-398, and 11-400, 2012 BL 160004, 53 EBC 1513, June 28.

2. Health Resources and Services Administration. 2003. *Changing Demographics: Implications for Physicians, Nurses, and Other Health Workers*, pp. 7–8. http://www.nachc.org/client/documents/clinical/ Clinical_Workforce_Changing_Demographics.pdf.

3. U.S. Administration on Aging, Department of Health and Human Services. June 23, 2010. "Older Population by Age Group: 1990 to 2050," http://www.aoa.gov/AoARoot/Aging_Statistics/future_ growth/future_growth.aspx#age (Accessed 6/25/2012); U.S. Administration on Aging, Department of Health and Human Services. June 23, 2010. "Older Population as a Percentage of the Total Population: 1990 to 2050," http://www.aoa.gov/AoARoot/Aging_Statistics/future_growth/future_growth.aspx#age (accessed June 25, 2012) [Citing U.S. Census Data 2010].

4. U.S. Department of Health and Human Services, National Center for Disease Statistics. 2009. "Health, United States, 2008, with Special Feature on the Health of Young Adults," http://www.cdc.gov/nchs/data/ hus/hus08.pdf#120 (accessed September 9, 2010), p. 3.

5. Health Resources and Services Administration. 2003. "Changing Demographics: Implications for Physicians, Nurses, and Other Health Workers," p. 38. http://www.nachc.org/client/documents/clinical/ Clinical_Workforce_Changing_Demographics.pdf.

6. American Hospital Association (AHA). 2005. "Trends: An Overview of 2003." AHA Hospital Statistics, 2005 Health Forum LLC: p. vii.

7. California Nurses Association. 2007. "Revenue Gains Continue to Outpace Growth in Expenses, Allowing U.S. Hospitals to Enjoy Record Profit and Margin." www.calnurses.org/media-center/in-the-news/2007/october/revenue-gains-continue-to-outpace-growth-in-expenses-allowing-u-s-hospitals-to-enjoy-record-profit-and-margin.html (accessed February 7, 2008).

8. American Hospital Association. 2007. "TrendWatch Chartbook 2007." http://www.aha.org/.

9. Truffer, C.J. et al., 2010. "Health Spending Projections Through 2019: The Recession's Impact Continues." *Health Affairs* 29(3): 1.

10. Centers for Medicare and Medicaid Studies. "National Health Expenditure Projections 2009–2019." http://www.cms.hhs.gov/NationalHealthExpendData/downloads/proj2009.pdf (accessed February 17, 2010).

11. Plunkett, J.W. 2007 *Plunkett's Health Care Industry Trends & Statistics 2008 (Summary)*. Houston, TX: Plunkett Research, Ltd., Ch. 1.

12. Blue Cross and Blue Shield Association. 2002. "What's Behind the Rise: A Comprehensive Analysis of Healthcare Costs." Executive Summary, p. 10.

13. Connecticut Office of Health Care Access. "Hospitals Today." http://www.ohca.state.ct.us/Publications/ Hospital%20Study/HospToday.pdf (accessed October 15, 2002).

14. National Center for Disease Statistics, Centers for Disease Control and Prevention, U.S. Department of Health and Human Services. 2009. "Health, United States, 2008 (with Chartbook)" 1: 3–4; U.S. Department of Health and Human Services. 2008. "National Hospital Ambulatory Medical Care Survey: 2006 Outpatient Department Summary." *National Health Statistics Reports* 4: 2–3; Arlington, S., and Farino, A. "Biomarket Trends: Pharmaceutical Industry Undergoing Transformation," *Genetic Engineering and Biotechnology News* 27(15). http://www.genengnews.com/gen-articles/ biomarket-trends-pharmaceutical-industry-undergoing-transformation/2197/.

15. Stagg Elliott, V. 2010. "More Than Half of Surgeries Are Outpatient," amednews.com, March 24. http:// www.ama-assn.org/amednews/2010/03/22/bisc0324.htm (accessed May 4, 2010).

16. Cullen, K.A., Hall, M.J., and Golosinskiy, A. 2009. "Ambulatory Surgery in the United States, 2006," *National Health Statistics Reports*, No. 11, p. 1.

17. "Advances Allow More Outpatient Orthopaedic Surgeries, Shorter Hospital Stays." 2009. *Vital Signs* 44(Fall): 7.

18. Koenig, L., et al. 2009. "An Analysis of Recent Growth in Ambulatory Surgical Centers: Final Report," KNG Health Consulting, pp. 17–18.

19. U.S. Department of Commerce et al. 1996. "Population Projections of the United States by Age, Sex, Race, and Hispanic Origin: 1995 to 2050." http://www.census.gov/prod/1/pop/p25-1130/p251130.pdf (accessed December 14, 2005).

20. Health Resources and Services Administration. 2003. "Changing Demographics: Implications for Physicians, Nurses, and Other Health Workers" http://www.nachc.org/client/documents/clinical/ Clinical_Workforce_Changing_Demographics.pdf.

21. Fee, D.N. 2002. "Success with APCs." *Healthcare Financial Management* September (2002): 68.
22. American Hospital Association. 1991. *Hospital Statistics.* 1991–92, p. xxxiv. Chicago: Health Forum.
23. American Hospital Association. 1991. *Hospital Statistics.* 1991–92, p. xxxv. Chicago: Health Forum.
24. MedPAC. 2000. *Report to Congress: Selected Medicare Issues,* p. 108. Washington, DC: MedPAC.
25. MedPAC. 2000. *Report to Congress: Selected Medicare Issues,* p. 109. Washington, DC: MedPAC.
26. Solucient, LLC. 2002. *The Comparative Performance of U.S. Hospitals: The Sourcebook.* pp. 1–2. Evanston, IL: Solucient.
27. "Industry Scan." 2002. *Healthcare Financial Management,* September (2002): 22–25.
28. CMS. 2002. "Medicare Hospital Outpatient Payment System," October 30. cms.hhs.gov (accessed April 2, 2003).
29. MedPAC. 2000. *Report to Congress: Selected Medicare Issues,* p. 109. Washington, DC: MedPAC.
30. The Henry J. Kaiser Family Foundation, Focus on Health Reform. 2010. "Summary of New Health Reform Law," March 26. http://www.kff.org/healthreform/upload/8061.pdf http://www.cms.gov/ (accessed September 27, 2010).
31. MedPAC. 2002. *Report to the Congress: Medicare Payment Policy,* pp. 11–15. Washington, DC: MedPAC.
32. CMS. "Acute Inpatient Prospective Payment System." http://www.cms.gov/ (accessed August 16, 2005).
33. "Medicare Program; Hospital Inpatient Prospective Payment Systems for Acute Care Hospitals and the Long-Term Care Hospital Prospective Payment System and Fiscal Year 2013 Rates; Hospitals' Resident Caps for Graduate Medical Education Payment Purposes; Quality Reporting Requirements for Specific Providers and for Ambulatory Surgical Centers; Final Rule." 2012. *Federal Register* 77(170): 53706.
34. Centers for Medicare and Medicaid Services. 2011. "Medicare Program; Hospital Inpatient Prospective Payment Systems for Acute Care Hospitals and the Long-Term Care Hospital Prospective Payment System and FY 2012 Rates; Hospitals' FTE Resident Caps for Graduate Medical Education Payment; Final Rule," *Federal Register* 76(160): 51804.
35. "Medicare Program; Hospital Inpatient Prospective Payment Systems for Acute Care Hospitals and the Long-Term Care Hospital Prospective Payment System Changes and FY2011 Rates." 2010. *Federal Register* 75(157): 50439.
36. "Medicare Program; Hospital Inpatient Prospective Payment Systems for Acute Care Hospitals and Fiscal Year 2010 Rates and to the Long-Term Care Hospital Prospective Payment System and Rate Year 2010 Rates: Final Fiscal Year 2010 Wage Indices and Payment Rates Implementing the Affordable Care Act." 2010. *Federal Register* 75(105): 31127.
37. "Medicare Program; Changes to the Hospital Inpatient Prospective Payment Systems for Acute Care Hospitals and Fiscal Year 2010 Rates; and Changes to the Long-Term Care Hospital Prospective Payment System and Rate Years 2010 and 2009 Rates." 2009. *Federal Register* 74(165): 44020.
38. "Medicare Program; Hospital Inpatient Prospective Payment Systems and Fiscal Year 2009 Rates: Final Fiscal Year 2009 Wage Indices and Payment Rates Including Implementation of Section 124 of the Medicare Improvement for Patients and Providers Act of 2008." 2008. *Federal Register* 73(193): 57892.
39. "Medicare Program; Hospital Inpatient Prospective Payment Systems and Fiscal Year 2007 Rates; Notice." 2006. *Federal Register* 71(196): 59891.
40. "Medicare Program; Changes to the Hospital Inpatient Prospective Payment Systems and Fiscal Year 2006 Rates." 2005. *Federal Register* 70(155): 47503.
41. "Medicare Program; Changes to the Hospital Inpatient Prospective Payment Systems and Fiscal Year 2005 Rates; Final Rule." 2004. *Federal Register* 69(154): 49289.
42. $413.83 is an average of the Capital Standard Federal Payment Rate used for FY 2004 ($414.18 was used from October 2003 through March 2004 and $413.48 was used from April 2004 through September 2004); "Medicare Program; Changes to the Hospital Inpatient Prospective Payment Systems and Fiscal Year 2005 Rates; Final Rule." 2004. *Federal Register* 69(154): 49289.
43. "Medicare Program; Changes to the Hospital Inpatient Prospective Payment Systems and Fiscal Year 2003 Rates." 2002. *Federal Register* 67(148): 50131.
44. "Medicare Program; Changes to the Hospital Inpatient Prospective Payment Systems and Rates and Costs of Graduate Medical Education: Fiscal Year 2002 Rates; Provisions of the Balanced Budget Refinement Act of 1999; and Provisions of the Medicare, Medicaid, and SCHIP Benefits Improvement and Protection Act of 2000." 2001. *Federal Register* 66(148): 39947.
45. "Medicare Program; Changes to the Hospital Inpatient Prospective Payment Systems and Fiscal Year 2001 Rates." 2000. *Federal Register* 65(148): 47117.
46. "Medicare Program; Changes to the Hospital Inpatient Prospective Payment Systems and Fiscal Year 2000 Rates." 1999. *Federal Register* 64(146): 41551.

47. Centers for Medicare and Medicaid Services. 2011. "Medicare Program; Hospital Inpatient Prospective Payment Systems for Acute Care Hospitals and the Long-Term Care Hospital Prospective Payment System and FY 2012 Rates; Hospitals' FTE Resident Caps for Graduate Medical Education Payment; Final Rule," *Federal Register* 76(160): 51813.

48. "Medicare Program; Hospital Inpatient Perspective Payment Systems for Acute Care Hospitals and the Long-Term Care Hospital Prospective Payment System Changes and FY2011 Rates." 2010. *Federal Register* 75(157): 50451.

49. *Federal Register*. 2009. 74(165): 44031.

50. *Federal Register*. 2008. 73(193): 57891.

51. *Federal Register*. 2007. 72(227): 66888.

52. "Medicare Program; Hospital Inpatient Prospective Payment Systems and Fiscal Year 2007 Rates: Final Fiscal Year 2007 Wage Indices and Payment Rates after Application of Revised Occupational Mix Adjustment to Wage Index," Department of Health and Human Services, Centers for Medicare and Medicaid Services, CMS-1488-N, p. 17.

53. MedPAC. 2002. "Report to the Congress: Medicare Payment Policy." March (2002): 18.

54. MedPAC. 2002. "Report to the Congress: Medicare Payment Policy." March (2002): 19.

55. MedPAC. 2002. "Report to the Congress: Medicare Payment Policy." March (2002): 20.

56. Horne-LLP. "Changes to Medicare Market Basket Update." http://www.horne-llp.com/industries/health-care/resources/health-care-reform--advantages--pitfalls/changes-to-medicare-market-basket-updates (accessed November 14, 2012); "Patient Protection and Affordable Care Act," Pub. L.111-148 (March 23, 2010), Section 3401. 124 Stat. 480-488; "Medicare Program; Hospital Inpatient Prospective Payment Systems for Acute Care Hospitals and the Long-Term Care Hospital Prospective Payment System and Fiscal Year 2013 Rates; Hospitals' Resident Caps for Graduate Medical Education Payment Purposes; Quality Reporting Requirements for Specific Providers and for Ambulatory Surgical Centers; Final Rule," 2012. *Federal Register* 77(170): 53480.

57. *APC Desk Reference*. 2004. Ingenix: St. Anthony Publishing/Medicode, p. 4-40.

58. *APC Desk Reference*. 2004. Ingenix: St. Anthony Publishing/Medicode, pp. 4-40–4-41.

59. "Medicare Program: Changes to the Hospital Outpatient Prospective Payment System and CY 2010 Payment Rates; Changes to the Ambulatory Surgical Center Payment System and CY 2010 Payment Rates; Final Rule." 2009. *Federal Register* 74(223): 60419.

60. U.S. Health Care Financing Administration. "Steps in Determining a PPS Payment." www.cms.gov (accessed August 12, 2005).

61. "Patient Protection and Affordable Care Act," Pub. L. 111-148, 124 Stat. 119. March 23, 2010.

62. American Hospital Association Committee on Research. 2010. "Bundled Payment: AHA Research Synthesis Report," May, p. 3.

63. Centers for Medicare and Medicaid Services. 2009. "Press Release to Announce Sites for the CMS ACE Program," January 6, p. 1.

64. "Patient Protection and Affordable Care Act," Pub. L. 111-148, 124 Stat. 399. March 23, 2010.

65. "Patient Protection and Affordable Care Act," Pub. L. 111-148, 124 Stat. 401. March 23, 2010.

66. "Office of Inspector General; Medicare Program; Prospective Payment System for Hospital Outpatient Services." 2000. *Federal Register* 65(68): 18487.

67. "Medicare Program; Announcement of the Calendar Year 2002 Conversion Factor for the Hospital Outpatient Prospective Payment System and a Pro Rata Reduction on Transitional Pass-Through Payments." 2001. *Federal Register* 66(213): 55864; "Medicare Program; Correction of Certain Calendar Year 2002 Payment Rates under the Hospital Outpatient Prospective Payment System and the Pro Rata Reduction on Transitional Pass-Through Payments; Correction of Technical and Typographical Errors." 2002. *Federal Register* 67(41): 9557.

68. "Medicare Program; Announcement of the Calendar Year 2002 Conversion Factor for the Hospital Outpatient Prospective Payment System and a Pro Rata Reduction on Transitional Pass-Through Payments." 2001. *Federal Register* 66(213): 55864; "Medicare Program; Correction of Certain Calendar Year 2002 Payment Rates under the Hospital Outpatient Prospective Payment System and the Pro Rata Reduction on Transitional Pass-Through Payments; Correction of Technical and Typographical Errors." 2002. *Federal Register* 67(41): 9557.

69. "Medicare Program; Changes to the Hospital Outpatient Prospective Payment System and Calendar Year 2003 Payment Rates; and Changes to Payment Suspension for Unfiled Cost Reports." 2002. *Federal Register* 67(212): 66788.

70. "Medicare Program; Changes to the Hospital Outpatient Prospective Payment System and Calendar Year 2004 Rates; Final Rule." 2003. *Federal Register* 68(216): 63459.

71. "Medicare Program; Changes to the Hospital Outpatient Prospective Payment System and Calendar Year 2005 Rates; Final Rule." 2004. *Federal Register* 69(219): 65841–65842.
72. "Medicare Program; Changes to the Hospital Outpatient Prospective Payment System and Calendar Year 2006 Payment Rates; Final Rule." 2005. *Federal Register* 70(217): 68551.
73. *Federal Register.* 2006. 71(226): 68003.
74. *Federal Register.* 2006. 72(227): 66677.
75. "Medicare Program: Changes to the Hospital Outpatient Prospective Payment System and CY 2010 Payment Rates; Changes to the Ambulatory Surgical Center Payment System and CY 2010 Payment Rates." 2008. *Federal Register* 73(223): 68584–68585.
76. "Medicare Program: Hospital Outpatient Prospective Payment System and CY 2011 Payment Rates; Ambulatory Surgical Center Payment System and CY 2011 Payment Rates; Payments to Hospitals for Graduate Medical Education Costs; Physician Self-Referral Rules and Related Changes to Provider Agreement Regulations; Payment for Certified Registered Nurse Anesthetist Services Furnished in Rural Hospitals and Critical Access Hospitals; Final Rule." 2010. *Federal Register* 75(226): 71876
77. "Medicare and Medicaid Programs; Hospital Outpatient Prospective Payment, Ambulatory Surgical Center Payment; Hospital Value-Based Purchasing Program; Physician Self-Referral; and Patient Notification Requirements in Provider Agreements; Final Rule." 2011. *Federal Register* 76(230): 74190.
78. U.S. Department of Health & Human Services. 2011. "Administration Implements Affordable Care Act Provision to Improve Care, Lower Costs," April 29. http://www.hhs.gov/news/press/2011pres/04/20110429a.html (accessed July 28, 2011).
79. Democratic Policy Committee. "Section-by-Section Analysis with Changes Made by Title X and Reconciliation Included within Titles I–IX." http://dpc.senate.gov/healthreformbill/healthbill96.pdf (accessed May 24, 2010).
80. "Medicare Program; Hospital Inpatient Value-Based Purchasing Program." 2011. *Federal Register* 76(88): 26490, 26495; Pollack, R. 2011. "Letter from the AHA to CMS Regarding the Hospital Value-Based Purchasing Program." American Hospital Association. http://www.aha.org/advocacy-issues/letter/2011/110829-cl-1525-p-vbp.pdf (accessed September 9, 2011).
81. *The Health Care M&A Report: Fourth Quarter 1997.* 1997. New Canaan, CT: Irving Levin Associates, Inc., p. 5.
82. *The Health Care M&A Report: Fourth Quarter 1998.* 1998. New Canaan, CT: Irving Levin Associates, Inc., pp. 5–6.
83. *The Health Care M&A Report: Fourth Quarter 1999.* 1999. New Canaan, CT: Irving Levin Associates, Inc., pp. 5–6.
84. *The Health Care M&A Report: Fourth Quarter 2000.* 2000. New Canaan, CT: Irving Levin Associates, Inc., pp. 7–8.
85. *The Health Care M&A Report: Fourth Quarter 2001.* 2001. New Canaan, CT: Irving Levin Associates, Inc., p. 7.
86. *The Health Care M&A Report: Fourth Quarter 2002.* 2002. New Canaan, CT: Irving Levin Associates, Inc., p. xvii.
87. *The Health Care M&A Report: Fourth Quarter 2003.* 2003. New Canaan, CT: Irving Levin Associates, Inc., p. xvi.
88. *The Health Care M&A Report: Fourth Quarter 2004.* 2004. New Canaan, CT: Irving Levin Associates, Inc., p. xvii.
89. *The Health Care M&A Report: Fourth Quarter 2005.* 2005. New Canaan, CT: Irving Levin Associates, Inc., p. xviii.
90. *The Health Care M&A Report: Fourth Quarter 2006.* 2006. New Canaan, CT: Irving Levin Associates, Inc., p. xix.
91. *The Health Care M&A Report: Fourth Quarter 2007.* 2007. New Canaan, CT: Irving Levin Associates, Inc., p. xviii.
92. *The Health Care M&A Report: Fourth Quarter 2008.* 2008. New Canaan, CT: Irving Levin Associates, Inc., p. xxi.
93. *The Health Care M&A Report: Fourth Quarter 2009.* 2009. New Canaan, CT: Irving Levin Associates, Inc., p. xviii.
94. *The Health Care M&A Report: Fourth Quarter 2010.* 2010. New Canaan, CT: Irving Levin Associates, Inc., p. xix.
95. *The Health Care M&A Report: Fourth Quarter 2011.* 2011. New Canaan, CT: Irving Levin Associates, Inc., p. xxv.

96. Lubell, J. 2007. "Hospitals Seen Seeking Closer Doc Partnerships," *Modern Healthcare,* October 4, p. 9

97. Dan Beckham. "New Twist in Employing Physicians." Hospitals and Health Networks, www.hhnmag. com (accessed March 3, 2008).

98. Christian, C.D., and Myre, T.T. 2010. "Integration 2.0: Does Health Care Reform Signal the Twilight of the Private Physician Practice," Valeo Online, July 14. http://www.valeocommunications.com/2010/07/14/integration-20-does-health-care-reform-signal-the-twilight-of-the-private-physician-practice (accessed May 25, 2011).

99. Medical Group Management Association. 2010. "MGMA Physician Placement Report: 65 Percent of Establishing Physicians Placed in Hospital-Owned Practices," June 3. http://www.mgma.com/press/default.aspx?id=33777 (accessed May 25, 2011).

100. Isaacs, S.L. et al. 2009. "The Independent Physician: Going, Going...." *New England Journal of Medicine* 360(7): 656.

101. Iglehart, J.K. 2011. "Doctor-Workers of the World, Unite!" *Health Affairs* 30(4), 556–558.

102 Loxterkamp, D. 2009. "The Dream of Home Ownership," *Annals of Family Medicine* 7(3), 264–266.

103. Isaacs, S.L. et al. 2009. "The Independent Physician: Going, Going...." *New England Journal of Medicine* 360(7): 657.

104. Bazzoli, G.J. 2004. "The Corporatization of American Hospitals," *Journal of Health Politics, Policy & Law* 29(4–5): 888.

105. Informed Healthcare Media. 2006. "Intellimarker: Ambulatory Surgery Centers Financial & Operational Benchmarking Study 2006," August, p. 9.

106. Healthcare Financial Management Association. 2006. "Financing the Future II Report 4: Joint Ventures with Physicians and Other Partners," February, p. 3.

107. Hurley, R.E. et al. 2005. "A Widening Rift in Access and Quality: Growing Evidence of Economic Disparities," *Health Affairs* December 6, p. W5–567.

108. Society for Healthcare Strategy and Market Development. 2011. *Future Scan 2011: Healthcare Trends and Implications 2011–2016.* Chicago: ACHE Managmenet Press.

109. Healthcare Financial Management Association. 2006. "Financing the Future II Report 4: Joint Ventures with Physicians and Other Partners," February, p. 4.

110. Fine, M.N., and Samsa, M.K. 2012. "The 2011 Form 990: More Than Simple Tinkering at the Margins," McDermott, Will & Emery LLP, American Health Lawyers Association, February 10. http://www.healthlawyers.org/News/Health%20Lawyers%20Weekly/Pages/2012/February%202012/February%202010%202012/The2011Form990MoreThanSimpleTinkeringAtTheMargins.aspx (accessed February 28, 2012).

111. Healthcare Financial Management Association. "Achieving Physician Integration with the Co-Management Model." http://www.hfmaconference.org/achieving-physician-integration-with-the-co-management-model/ (accessed July 19, 2010).

112. Evans, M. 2010. "Co-Management Emerges as Alternative to Joint Ventures, Employment by Hospitals," *Modern Physician,* May 10. http://www.modernphysician.com/apps/pbcs.dll/article?AID=/20100510/MODERNPHYSI# (accessed July 21, 2010).

113. Danello, P.F. 2006. "Clinical Co-Management: Hospitals and Oncologists Working Together," *Journal of Oncology Practice* 2(1), 241–247.

114. Devers, K., and Berenson, R. 2009. "Can Accountable Care Organizations Improve the Value of Health Care by Solving the Cost and Quality Quandaries?," Urban Institute, October, p. 1.

115. Center for Medicare and Medicaid Services. 2011. "Pioneer Accountable Care Organization Model: General Fact Sheet," December 19.

116. Health and Human Services. 2009. "HHS Announces 89 New Accountable Care Organizations," July 9. http://www.hhs.gov/news/press/2012pres/07/20120709a.html (accessed October 23, 2012).

117. Muhlestein, D. et al. 2012. *Growth and Dispersion of Accountable Care Organizations: June 2012 Update.* Salt Lake City, UT: Leavitt; Tocknell, M.D. 2012. "Are You Ready for an ACO?," *HealthLeaders Magazine,* May, p. 1.

118. "Medicare Program; Medicare Shared Savings Program: Accountable Care Organizations," 2011. *Federal Register* 76(212): 67916.

119. "Medicare Program; Medicare Shared Savings Program: Accountable Care Organizations," 2011. *Federal Register* 76(212): 67927.

120. Moore, K.D., and Coddington, D.C., 2010. "Accountable Care: The Journey Begins," in *Contemplating the ACO Opportunity,* Healthcare Financial Management Association, p. 5.

121. Gosfield, A.G. 2012. *Medicare and Medicaid Fraud and Abuse,* 2012 edition, Thomson Reuters, p. 31; "Agreements with States," 42 U.S.C. § 1395aa (2010); "Effect of Accreditation," 42 U.S.C. § 1395bb (2010).

122. Miller, R.D., and Hutton, R.C. 2004. *Problems in Health Care Law*, 8th edition. Mississauga, ON: Jones and Bartlett Publishers, p. 61.

123. Miller, R.D. 2006. *Problems in Health Care Law*, 9th edition. Mississauga, ON: Jones and Bartlett, p. 73.

124. "Agreements with States," 42 U.S.C. § 1395aa; Miller, R.D. 2006. *Problems in Health Care Law*, 9th edition. Mississauga, ON: Jones and Bartlett, p. 60; "Medicare and Medicaid Programs; Recognition of the American Osteopathic Association (AOA) for Continued Approval of Deeming Authority for Hospitals." 2005. *Federal Register* March 25, 15333(I)-(II).

125. American Society for Healthcare Engineering of the American Hospital Association. "JCAHO Federal Deemed Status and State Recognition," http://www.ashe.org/ashe/codes/jcaho/deemed_status.html (accessed on June 30, 2009).

126. Kurtz, R. 2008. "Is Accreditation Really Worth It?" *Outpatient Surgery Magazine* 9(3). http://www.outpatientsurgery.net/issues/2008/03/is-accreditation-really-worth-it (accessed May 13, 2010).

127. National Conference of State Legislatures. 2011. "Certificate of Need: State Health Laws and Programs," January. http://www.ncsl.org/issues-research/health/con-certificate-of-need-state-laws.aspx (accessed November 13, 2012).

128. "Definitions," 45 C.F.R. 160.103 (May 31, 2002), p. 701; "Health Insurance Portability and Accountability Act of 1996," Pub. L. No. 104-191 (Aug. 21, 1996).

129. "Definitions," 45 C.F.R. 160.103 (May 31, 2002), p. 701.

130. Centers for Medicare & Medicaid Services. 2010. "New Health Care Electronic Transactions Standards: Versions 5010, D.0, and 3.0," January. http://www.cms.gov/ICD10/Downloads/w5010BasicsFctSht.pdf (accessed November 29, 2011).

131. "Is Your Practice Ready for Version 5010." 2011. *MGMA Connexion,* Supplement, October, p. 9.

132. "Health Insurance Reform; Modifications to the Health Insurance Portability and Accountability Act (HIPAA); Final Rules." 2009. *Federal Register* 74(10): 3297–3299.

133. Centers for Medicare and Medicaid Services. 2011. "Centers for Medicare & Medicaid Services' Office of E-Health Standards and Services Announces 90-Day Period of Enforcement Discretion for Compliance with New HIPAA Transaction Standards," November 17. http://www.cms.gov/ICD10/Downloads/CMSStatement5010EnforcementDiscretion111711.pdf (accessed November 28, 2011); "Health Insurance Reform; Modifications to the Health Insurance Portability and Accountability Act (HIPAA); Final Rules." 2009. *Federal Register* 74(10): 3297–3299.

134. Porter, S. 2009. "Stimulus Package Includes New HIPAA Security Rules: Small Practices Face Greatest Financial Impact," AAFP News Now, March 18. http://www.aafp.org/ (accessed June 17, 2009); "American Recovery and Reinvestment Act of 2009," Pub. L. No. 111-5, 123 Stat. 115 (February 17, 2009).

135. "American Recovery and Reinvestment Act of 2009, Sec. 3001, 13400 et seq," Pub. L. No. 111-5, 123 Stat. 115 (February 17, 2009), pp. 230, 258.

136. "American Recovery and Reinvestment Act of 2009, Sec. 13401-13405," Pub. L. No. 111-5, 123 Stat. 115 (February 17, 2009), pp. 260–268.

137. "American Recovery and Reinvestment Act of 2009, Sec. 13401-13402," Pub. L. No. 111-5, 123 Stat. 115 (February 17, 2009), pp. 260–262.

138. "Breach Notification for Unsecured Protected Health Information." 2009. *Federal Register* 74(162): 42740–42757.

139. Manos, D., and Mosquera, M. 2012. "Final Rules for Stage 2 Meaningful Use Released," Healthcare IT News, August 23. http://www.healthcareitnews.com/news/final-rules-stage-2-meaningful-use-released (accessed September 22, 2012).

140. Greaney, T.L., Johnson, S.H., Jost, T.S., and Schwart, R.L. 1997. *Health Law Cases: Materials & Problems*. Eagan, MN: West Publishing Co., p. 555.

141. Broccolo, B.M. 2005. "Spotlight on Compensation Practices: Where We Have Been and Where Are We Going?." In *Physicians/Hospitals: Recruitment, Compensation, and Contracting Issues*. American Health Lawyers Association, pp. 2, 46.

142. "Employment Tax Audits of Exempt Hospitals Could Turn Up Other Issues, Attorneys Warn." 2009. *Health Law Reporter* 18: 1653.

143. Brauer, L.M., Tyson, T.T., Henzke, L.J., and Kawecki, D.J. 2002. "An Introduction to I.R.C. 4958 (Intermediate Sanctions)." Internal Revenue Service, EO CPE Text, 264. http://apps.irs.gov (accessed December 28, 2009).

144. Sec. 4959: Taxes on Failures by Hospital Organization, Patient Protection and Affordability Act, p. 1967.

145. Revenue Ruling 69-545, 1969-2 C.B. 117, Internal Revenue Service.

146. Quinn, C.L., and Mamorsky, J.D. 2009. "Enforcement Efforts Take Aim at Executive Compensation of Tax-Exempt Health Care Entities," *Health Law Reporter* 18: 1640.

147. "Increase in Medicare, Medicaid Managed Care Plans Has Led to 'More Complex' Health Care Fraud, Wall Street Journal Reports." 2008. Kaiser Daily Health Policy Report, March 19. http://www.kaisernetwork. org/daily_reports/print_report.cfm?DR_ID=51043&dr_cat=3 (accessed November 23, 2009).

148. Drinker Biddle & Reath LLP. 2010. "The Patient Protection and Affordable Care Act," Health Government Relations Group, p. 4. http://www.drinkerbiddle.com/files/Publication/9c21e026-45cf-48de-b7c9-9abcb3f48412/Presentation/PublicationAttachment/f0364126-f959-430c-be4e-9be51aec2f4f/ACA.pdf (accessed February 11, 2011).

149. Centers for Medicare and Medicaid Services. "Fact Sheet: Medicare Fraud Strike Forces." http://www. stopmedicarefraud.gov/strikeforcesfactsheet.pdf (accessed March 8, 2011).

150. Centers for Medicare and Medicaid Services. 2011. "Medicare Fraud & Abuse: Prevention, Detection, and Reporting." https://www.cms.gov/MLNProducts/downloads/Fraud_and_Abuse.pdf (accessed July 2, 2012).

151. American Health Care Association. 2010. "Physician Self-Referral (Stark Law)." http://www.ahcancal. org/facility_operations/ComplianceProgram/Pages/PhysicianSelf-ReferralStarkLaw.aspx (accessed February 7, 2012); Mitchell, J.M. 2007. "The Prevalence of Physician Self-Referral Arrangements after Stark II: Evidence from Advanced Diagnostic Imaging," *Health Affairs* 26(3). http://content.healthaffairs.org/cgi/content/full/26/3/w415 (accessed July 2, 2012).

152. American Health Care Association. 2010. "Physician Self-Referral (Stark Law)." http://www. ahcancal.org/facility_operations/ComplianceProgram/Pages/PhysicianSelf-ReferralStarkLaw.aspx (accessed February 7, 2012); Watnik, R.L. 2000. "Antikickback versus Stark: What's the Difference?" *Healthcare Financial Management* March. http://findarticles.com/p/articles/mi_m3257/is_3_54/ai_60139659/?tag=content;col1 (accessed July 2, 2012).

153. Watnik, R.L. 2000. "Antikickback versus Stark: What's the Difference?" *Healthcare Financial Management* March. http://findarticles.com/p/articles/mi_m3257/is_3_54/ai_60139659/?tag=content;col1 (accessed July 2, 2012).

154. Baumann, L.A., ed. 2002. *Health Care Fraud and Abuse: Practical Perspectives*. Washington, DC: American Bar Association, p. 52.

155. Department of Health and Human Services. 1989. "Financial Arrangements between Physicians and Health Care Businesses: Report to Congress," Office of Inspector General, No. OAI-12-88-01410, p. 18.

156. O'Sullivan, J. 2004. "CRS Report for Congress: Medicare: Physician Self-Referral ('Stark I and II')," Congressional Research Service, The Library of Congress, July 27. http://www.policyarchive.org/handle/10207/bitstreams/2137.pdf (accessed July 2, 2012).

157. Murti, A. 2004. "New Stark Regulations Spell Out Self-Referral Exceptions," *Decisions in Diagnostic Imaging*, May. http://www.imagingeconomics.com/ (accessed June 20, 2008).

158. Barnes, J.K. et al. 2007. "Phase III Regulations Result in Dramatic Changes to Stark Law," *BNA Health Law Reporter* 16(40): 1220; Centers for Medicare and Medicaid Services. 2007. "Medicare Program; Physicians' Referrals to Health Care Entities with Which They Have Financial Relationships (Phase III)," *Federal Register* 72(171): 51012.

159. Barnes, J.K. et al. 2007. "Phase III Regulations Result in Dramatic Changes to Stark Law," *BNA Health Law Reporter* 16(40): 1220; Centers for Medicare and Medicaid Services. 2007. "Medicare Program; Physicians' Referrals to Health Care Entities with Which They Have Financial Relationships (Phase III)," *Federal Register* 72(171): 51087.

160. Barnes, J.K. et al. 2007. "Phase III Regulations Result in Dramatic Changes to Stark Law," *BNA Health Law Reporter* 16(40): 1220; citing "Financial Relationship, Compensation, and Ownership or Investment Interest," 42 CFR §411.354(c)(1)(i).

161. Barnes, J.K. et al. 2007. "Phase III Regulations Result in Dramatic Changes to Stark Law," *BNA Health Law Reporter* 16(40): 1220.

162. Centers for Medicare and Medicaid Services. 2008. "Physician Self-Referral and Hospital Ownership Disclosure Provisions in the IPPS FY 2009 Final Rule," August 4. http://www.cms.hhs.gov/apps/media/press/factsheet.asp?Counter=3226&intNumPerPage=10&checkDate=&checkKey=&srchType=1&numDays=3500&srchOpt=0&srchData=&keywordType=All&chkNewsType=6&intPage=&showAll=&pYear=&year=&desc=&cboOrder=date (accessed August 6, 2008).

163. Centers for Medicare and Medicaid Services. 2008. "Physician Self-Referral and Hospital Ownership Disclosure Provisions in the IPPS FY 2009 Final Rule," August 4. http://www.cms.hhs.gov/apps/media/press/factsheet.asp?Counter=3226&intNumPerPage=10&checkDate=&checkKey=&srchType=1&numDays=3500&srchOpt=0&srchData=&keywordType=All&chkNewsType=6&intPage=&showAll=&pYear=&year=&desc=&cboOrder=date (accessed August 6, 2008); Centers for Medicare and Medicaid Services. 2008. "Medicare Program; Changes to the Hospital Inpatient Prospective Payment Systems and Fiscal Year 2009 Rates; Payments for Graduate Medical Education in Certain Emergency

Situations; Changes to Disclosure of Physician Ownership in Hospitals and Physician Self-Referral Rules; Updates to the Long-Term Care Prospective Payment System; Updates to Certain IPPS-Excluded Hospitals; and Collection of Information Regarding Financial Relationships Between Hospitals," *Federal Register* 73(161): 48699.

164. Centers for Medicare and Medicaid Services. 2008. "Physician Self-Referral and Hospital Ownership Disclosure Provisions in the IPPS FY 2009 Final Rule," August 4. http://www.cms.hhs.gov/apps/media/press/ factsheet.asp?Counter=3226&intNumPerPage=10&checkDate=&checkKey=&srchType=1&numDays=3 500&srchOpt=0&srchData=&keywordType=All&chkNewsType=6&intPage=&showAll=&pYear=& year=&desc=&cboOrder=date (accessed August 6, 2008); Centers for Medicare and Medicaid Services. 2008. "Medicare Program; Changes to the Hospital Inpatient Prospective Payment Systems and Fiscal Year 2009 Rates; Payments for Graduate Medical Education in Certain Emergency Situations; Changes to Disclosure of Physician Ownership in Hospitals and Physician Self-Referral Rules; Updates to the Long-Term Care Prospective Payment System; Updates to Certain IPPS-Excluded Hospitals; and Collection of Information Regarding Financial Relationships Between Hospitals," *Federal Register* 73(161): 48693.

165. Centers for Medicare and Medicaid Services. 2008. "Physician Self-Referral and Hospital Ownership Disclosure Provisions in the IPPS FY 2009 Final Rule," August 4. http://www.cms.hhs.gov/apps/media/ press/factsheet.asp?Counter=3226&intNumPerPage=10&checkDate=&checkKey=&srchType=1 &numDays=3500&srchOpt=0&srchData=&keywordType=All&chkNewsType=6&intPage=&showAll=& pYear=&year=&desc=&cboOrder=date (accessed August 6, 2008); Centers for Medicare and Medicaid Services. 2008. "Medicare Program; Changes to the Hospital Inpatient Prospective Payment Systems and Fiscal Year 2009 Rates; Payments for Graduate Medical Education in Certain Emergency Situations; Changes to Disclosure of Physician Ownership in Hospitals and Physician Self-Referral Rules; Updates to the Long-Term Care Prospective Payment System; Updates to Certain IPPS-Excluded Hospitals; and Collection of Information Regarding Financial Relationships Between Hospitals," *Federal Register* 73(161): 48726.

166. Centers for Medicare and Medicaid Services. 2008. "Physician Self-Referral and Hospital Ownership Disclosure Provisions in the IPPS FY 2009 Final Rule," August 4. http://www.cms.hhs.gov/apps/ media/press/factsheet.asp?Counter=3226&intNumPerPage=10&checkDate=&checkKey=&srchType =1&numDays=3500&srchOpt=0&srchData=&keywordType=All&chkNewsType=6&intPage=&sho wAll=&pYear=&year=&desc=&cboOrder=date (accessed August 6, 2008); Centers for Medicare and Medicaid Services. 2008. "Medicare Program; Changes to the Hospital Inpatient Prospective Payment Systems and Fiscal Year 2009 Rates; Payments for Graduate Medical Education in Certain Emergency Situations; Changes to Disclosure of Physician Ownership in Hospitals and Physician Self-Referral Rules; Updates to the Long-Term Care Prospective Payment System; Updates to Certain IPPS-Excluded Hospitals; and Collection of Information Regarding Financial Relationships Between Hospitals," *Federal Register* 73(161): 48729.

167. Barnes, J.K. et al. 2007. "Phase III Regulations Result in Dramatic Changes to Stark Law," *BNA Health Law Reporter* 16(40): 1220.

168. "Specialty Hospitals: Focused Factories or Cream Skimmers?" 2003. Center for Studying Health System Change, Issue Brief 62 (April).

169. Committees on Ways & Means, Energy & Commerce, and Education & Labor. 2010. "Affordable Health Care for America: Section-by-Section Analysis," March 18. http://www.nachc.com/client/ documents/20091029_HCR_Section_by_Section.pdf (accessed March 23, 2010).

170. Wilkerson, A. 2010. "Bill to Affect Physician-Owned Hospitals" *The Journal Record*, March 23, p. 3.

171. 42 U.S.C.A. § 1395nn(a); Social Security Act § 1877(a).

172. 42 U.S.C.A. § 1395nn(h)(3); Social Security Act § 1877(h)(3).

173. 42 U.S.C.A. § 1395nn(e)(6); Social Security Act § 1877(e)(6).

174. 42 U.S.C.A. § 1320a-7b(b).

175. 42 C.F.R. 1001.952(d)(5).

176. Internal Revenue Service. "Intermediate Sanctions: Excess Benefit Transactions," http://www.irs.gov/ Charities-&-Non-Profits/Charitable-Organizations/Intermediate-Sanctions-Excess-Benefit-Transactions (accessed September 2, 2008).

177. Internal Revenue Service. "Disqualified Person." http://www.irs.gov/Charities-&-Non-Profits/Private-Foundations/Disqualified-Persons (accessed September 2, 2008); Internal Revenue Service. "Lookback Period."   http://www.irs.gov/Charities-&-Non-Profits/Charitable-Organizations/Lookback-Period (accessed September 2, 2008).

178. Internal Revenue Service. "Intermediate Sanctions: Excess Benefit Transactions," http://www.irs. gov/Charities-&-Non-Profits/Charitable-Organizations/Intermediate-Sanctions (accessed September 2, 2008).

12 Research and Financial Benchmarking in the Healthcare Industry

Robert James Cimasi, Todd A. Zigrang, and Anne P. Sharamitaro

CONTENTS

INTRODUCTION

The skills and knowledge of sources required for healthcare financial analysis may differ from those needed for general industry research. This chapter examines the research process as well as various sources of information needed for several types of healthcare financial analysis—related activities, including benchmarking and business valuation, to assist internal analysts and healthcare financial executives in being better informed about the application of research methods.

SOURCES OF HEALTHCARE BUSINESS AND INDUSTRY RESEARCH

TYPES OF RESEARCH AND THEIR ORGANIZATION

Specific and General Research

Two distinct classes of research are required for a valuation engagement: specific research and general research.

- Specific research concerns only the organization of interest and is typically obtained from that organization.
- General research focuses on research not specifically related to the organization, practice, business, or enterprise of interest and may be composed of such elements as industry conditions, demographics, compensation trends, transactions, and industry-specific trends within which it operates. General research is typically gathered to provide a perspective for evaluating the specific data using a number of instruments and methods, which may include benchmarking: "a technique or a tool for performance improvement and good quality practice by striving to be the best."[1]

Organizing Research and Archives Departments

Firms conducting financial analysis as an element of their consulting activities necessarily accumulate research materials to support these types of engagements. The manner in which these materials are organized and stored may represent the beginnings of a research department or library (for general research) and/or an archives department (for specific research). As the volume of materials grows (as it inevitably does), it is important to consider how different types of materials may be organized to facilitate their ongoing use. This organization should support the following functions:

- **Identification:** Before information can be organized, materials must first be identified by the project manager (for client archives) or the researcher (for general research).
- **Classification:** Client archival materials are usually classified by project and subproject, although databases allow for multiple classifications including project type, client contact names, firm contact names, project dates, and so on. Library materials are usually classified by subject as well as author, title, publisher, date, media, publication frequency, etc. More generally, it may be useful when designing a classification system to consider the four major types of classifications:
  1. Subject- or topic-related
  2. Date- or time-related
  3. Location- or geography-related
  4. Form-, media-, or type-related
- **Storage:** Research materials need to be appropriately stored so as to facilitate their timely and efficient retrieval. This requires consideration of both the digital aspects as well as the hard copy versions of the material. Filing or shelving location systems need to be organized in conjunction with electronic databases for searching on the basis of the filing criteria, especially for archives that are not likely to be casually "browsed" by those seeking information. Electronic files also require organization, however, and standards should be created throughout an organization to ensure consistency. At a minimum, directories, subdirectories, and folders should be created within the storage media (e.g., hard drives) for each classification of data, client, and project. Research files and Internet "bookmarks" should also have an organizational system, which may include a subject hierarchy.
- **Retrieval:** Use of an electronic database allows searching by any field, facilitating the identification and location of materials by a variety of search criteria. Other systems use lists or index cards to allow searching by additional information as well as by the shelving

criteria. Document management software packages may be useful for larger collections of documents that require frequent retrieval. Typically, these software applications work by attaching additional information to computer files, much of which must be input manually. However, most micro-computer–based operating systems automatically store information by file creation and modification dates, author, file type, and contents. As long as an effective directory structure and file nomenclature are in place, this level of information may well be sufficient for normal file retrieval requirements.

The acquisition, organization, and maintenance of research materials represent a significant investment in time and expense for most firms. This expense is more readily seen as necessary when it is for the archiving of specific data obtained from a client organization and is considered justified with regard to the time saved when these materials need to be retrieved at some, perhaps distant, date. The justification for the investment in organizing general research and library materials may be more difficult to measure and support. Accordingly, the identification or acquisition, classification, organization, and maintenance of each general research resource should be evaluated individually by comparing the alternative costs of accessing comparable information, with equivalent utility, through either online services, private research firms, or otherwise, only as the occasion arises. For research libraries to justify the cost of their holdings and operation, there needs to be a critical mass of regular use so that costs may be widely amortized. Only then can the cost of procurement, staffing, and retrieval systems be considered an efficient use of capital and operating resources for the benefit of the firm.

SPECIFIC RESEARCH

To successfully develop and complete a financial analysis engagement, the analyst must first make a determination as to both the specific nature and the scope of the information required for each engagement. Knowing which types of source documents will be most likely to contain this information and will also be readily available is central to the successful completion of the consulting engagement. The following is a description of the types of documents and reports specific to the subject entity typically available, with a description of the type of information that normally is required from these documents when conducting financial analysis and consulting projects related to medical practices. Most of this information is analogous to that required for the valuation of other types of healthcare service sector entities.

Documents
- **Historical financial statements:** This information is important for identifying key variables and trends for analysis. Therefore, the consultant should obtain year-end financial statements for a sufficient, relevant period to allow reliable analysis, e.g., the most recent five years. If, however, significant changes such as technological upgrades, product shifts, or environmental changes have occurred, or the five-year period is not long enough to assess the entity's performance during changes in its business cycle or economic conditions, a longer period may be needed. Historical financial statements may be presented in a form that does not allow for meaningful specific and detailed analysis of key assets, liabilities, revenues, and expenses. In such cases, the consultants should request additional schedules that list the components of the line item captions on the financial statements.
- **Tax returns:** Consultants obtain tax returns to understand the entity's tax position and to obtain additional accurate financial data. The returns provide a summary of tax policies and elections that affect tax expense and net income.
- **Forecasts and pro forma statements:** Prospective financial information (e.g., forecasts, pro forma statements, and budgets) should be requested because they can provide an indication of the entity's opinion of its earnings potential as well as its historical ability to meet projections. These data may be especially useful if the consultant must produce a pro forma statement or valuation of future earnings or cash flows.

- **Legal documents:** The consultant should review all significant legal documents to obtain an understanding of the ownership interests and relationships and to determine if contractual arrangements affect the entity's operations and overall value. Some of the documents to be reviewed include:
  - **Articles of incorporation, stockholder, or partnership agreements:** These agreements indicate ownership interests and the owners' rights and obligations. Also, any stock option agreements should be considered. This will help the consultant determine or verify the types of interests involved.
  - **Stock books:** These can help the consultant ascertain the relative size of various ownership interests and identify transactions in the entity's stock.
  - **Existing buy–sell agreements:** These may provide an indication of the value of the entity or an ownership interest in it. Such agreements, however, are often structured based on factors other than the entity's fair market value.
  - **Purchase and sale agreements involving prior transactions of the entity's stock:** These provide indications of the entity's value and any offers or letters of intent to sell or purchase stock should be carefully reviewed under IRS Revenue Ruling 59-60, which includes "sales of the stock and the size of the block of stock to be valued" in a list of factors that, "although not all-inclusive are fundamental and require careful analysis in each case." IRS Ruling 59-60 further requires:

    Sales of stock of a closely held corporation should be carefully investigated to determine whether they represent transactions at arm's length. Forced or distress sales do not ordinarily reflect fair market value nor do isolated sales in small amounts necessarily control as the measure of value. This is especially true in the valuation of a controlling interest in a corporation. Since, in the case of closely-held stocks, no prevailing market prices are available, there is no basis for making an adjustment for blockage. It follows, therefore, that such stocks should be valued upon a consideration of all the evidence affecting the fair market value. The size of the block of stock itself is a relevant factor to be considered. Although it is true that a minority interest in an unlisted corporation's stock is more difficult to sell than a similar block of listed stock, it is equally true that control of a corporation, either actual or in effect, representing as it does an added element of value, may justify a higher value for a specific block of stock.[2]

  - **Managed care and other service contracts:** Types and numbers of managed care contracts should be reviewed, including whether they are with healthcare maintenance organizations (HMOs), preferred provider organizations (PPOs), or point-of-service (POS) contracts; whether they are on a discounted fee-for-service basis and, if so, the size of the discount; whether they include a withhold percentage to only be paid based on quality criteria; or whether they are a flat fee per enrollee ("capitated"). Special terms such as the non-transferability of the contract to a new owner must be noted, e.g., managed care contracts often require that the provider be included on a panel of credentialed providers in order to contract to provide services.
  - **Key managers' employment contracts:** Such agreements can reveal excess compensation above fair market value or "golden parachute" provisions in the event the business is sold.
  - **Loan and lease agreements:** These agreements may contain restrictive covenants, special demand clauses, or working capital requirements that affect the value of the entity. The length and terms of lease agreements is also important.
  - **Documents relating to current, pending, or threatened litigation:** These may indicate major contingent liabilities that may affect an entity's value.
  - **Patent/trademark documents.** These documents may indicate the existence of valuable intangible assets. The absence of these documents could indicate the absence of a value consideration claimed by the client.
- **Operations and staff:** Consultants should also gain an understanding of the entity's operations and key personnel. This can be accomplished by touring the facilities, interviewing

key managers, and obtaining additional operational data. Obtaining enough information to thoroughly understand the entity, its operations, and its environment is the objective. The consultant becomes aware of operational data or contracts that may affect value by reviewing the following types of documents:

- **Corporate documents,** including stockholder and director lists, compensation schedules for officers and directors, schedule of key man life insurance policies and organizational charts.
- **Operational documents,** including business plans, brochures, price lists, catalogs and other product information, sales forecasts, data on customers and suppliers, and capital budgets.
- **Reports of other professionals,** including appraisals on specific assets and reports by other consultants.
- **Other internal information,** including documents or details relating to potential public offerings for debt or equity, venture capital prospectus or similar information, and tracking of incurred but not reported (IBNR) expenses.
- **Loan agreements:** The entity may have loaned or borrowed funds from affiliates. Such loan arrangements may require adjustments to be made to the economic value of the subject entity.
  - **Uncollectible loans receivable** should have been written off.
  - **Collectible loans receivable** may still be considered non-operating assets and should be evaluated separately.
  - **Loans payable to related parties** may be structured as demand notes, but there may be little chance that such loans will be repaid. Such loans may be considered either long-term debt or a form of owners' equity.

Site Visit/Interview Information

The following types of information specific to the healthcare enterprise should be gathered by the financial executive or healthcare consultant. This information may be obtained through an interview, questionnaire, or preferably a site visit.

- **Background information:** Include such information as the number of years the entity has operated at its current location and in the community, as well as the office hours.
- **Building description:** Include the location (urban/suburban), proximity to hospitals and other medical facilities, and its size, construction, electrical and computer wiring, age, access to parking, and so on.
- **Office description:** Approximate acquisition details and price, as well as ownership or lease details, should be included. The square footage and number of rooms, and a description of different office areas should be outlined, including, where applicable, medical equipment, including all diagnostic imaging and major medical equipment; pharmacy; laboratory; examination rooms; waiting rooms; and other areas.
- **Management information systems:** Document types of hardware and software and the cost, age, and suitability of all components, including their management functions, reporting capabilities, and integration among programs.
- **History of the entity:** Give the date founded and by whom; the number of full-time equivalent (FTE) physicians in the enterprise by year; the physicians who have joined and left the enterprise; the dates they practiced at the enterprise; and their relationship and practice arrangement with the entity.
- **Staff description:** Include the numbers and types of non-physician positions, as well as the tenure and salary of all current employees.
- **Competitive analysis:** Include details of hospital programs impacting the enterprise, growth or decline in the volume of business and the reasons, association with other

physicians, competitive strengths and threats, the number and volume of procedures performed, and any change in the number and volume and the corresponding fees.

- **Patient base information:** Encompass income distribution and percentages from different payers, the number of new patients and total patients seen per week, the age mix of patients, the number of hours spent in patient care per week, and the number of surgeries performed.
- **Managed care environment:** Detail the terms and conditions of all managed care contracts including discounts and withholds, the impact on referral patterns and revenues, willingness to participate in risk sharing contracts and capitation, and the entity's managed care reporting capabilities.
- **Hospital privileges and facilities:** List all hospital privileges held by physician members of the healthcare enterprise and the requirements for acquiring privileges at the different local hospitals.
- **Credit policy and collections:** Include policies for billing and payment, use of collection agencies, acceptance of assignments, other sources of revenues, and an aged breakdown of accounts receivable.
- **Financial management:** Include cash management procedures and protections, credit lines and interest, controls to improve payment of accounts payable, late payment frequency, formal or informal financial planning methods, and budgeting processes.
- **Operational assessment:** Include governance structure for the entity, detailing responsibilities and procedures for performance, conflicts, recruitment; outcomes measures; case management; reimbursement; income; continuing medical education (CME); credentialing; and utilization review.
- **Summary:** Allow for discussion of overall relationships with physicians in the community, practice concerns, and needs.

GENERAL RESEARCH

General research data in the healthcare arena encompasses general industry research and information relative to the economics and demographics of the industry, competition, healthcare industry and medical specialty trends, and the managed care environment surrounding the subject entities, as well as transactional data, investment risk/return information, and market environment reports. The assessment of the current and future economic conditions and regulatory and reimbursement trends is critical for determining the financial risk of the hypothetical investment related to the subject entity. Market perceptions of value of an enterprise are based on investors' knowledge of the historical and current status, and, more importantly, of the future trends of the healthcare industry and transactional/capital marketplace within which the subject enterprise operates.

Given the impact of the reimbursement and regulatory environment on the investor's perception of risk and the resulting impact on the valuation of the subject healthcare enterprise, the most important consideration for the healthcare analyst may be to have an in-depth understanding of the current state of those issues in the rapidly changing healthcare industry. The analyst must be further aware that the assessment of risk by investors is related to both the actualities and (perhaps more substantially) the perceptions of the market, related to external economic, demographic, and industry conditions, as well as aspects of the specific subject enterprise and the transaction.

Among the types of pertinent information are the local economy; industry and specialty trends including competition (which may be evaluated using any of the standard theoretical frameworks, including Michael Porter's Five Forces Model[3]); compensation; demographics; technological developments impacting the practice of specialty medicine; managed care; provider networks, plan types, and enrollment levels; supply and demand; alternative treatments and drugs; and the regulatory and reimbursement trends in healthcare.

RESEARCH CHALLENGES

1. Determining survey definitions, questions, sample sizes, survey methods, and other criteria to allow for evaluation of the quality and applicability of the data.

2. Obtaining sufficient data to provide representative sample sizes.

3. Researching survey data for medical subspecialties and some healthcare industry sub-sectors that are comparable when data are divided by Standard Industrial Classification (SIC) Codes. For example, SIC Code 8011 represents both ambulatory surgery centers as well as the myriad medical specialties and subspecialties.

4. Locating robust research support on time and within budget for medical subspecialties and small healthcare industry sub-sectors.

Physician Compensation Data

A growing number of surveys measure physician compensation, encompassing a varying depth of analysis. Physician compensation data, divided by specialty and subspecialty, is central to a range of consulting activities, including practice assessments and valuations of healthcare enterprises. The American Medical Association (AMA) maintains the most comprehensive database of information on physicians in the United States, with information on more than 940,000 physicians and residents and 77,000 medical students.[3] Started in 1906, the AMA Physician Masterfile, which contains information on physician education, training, and professional certification information, is updated annually through the Physicians' Professional Activities questionnaire and the collection and validation efforts of AMA's Division of Survey and Data Resources (SDR).[4] A selection of other sources of healthcare-related compensation and cost data are set forth below.

Physician Characteristics and Distribution in the United States is an annual survey based on a variety of demographic information from the Physician Masterfile dating back to 1963. It includes detailed information regarding trends, distribution, and professional and individual characteristics of the physician workforce.[5]

Physician Socioeconomic Statistics, published from 2000 to 2003, was a result of the merger between two prior AMA annuals: Socioeconomic Characteristics of Medical Practice and Physician Marketplace Statistics.[6] Data have been compiled from a random sampling of physicians from the Physician Masterfile into what is known as the Socioeconomic Monitoring System, which includes physician age profiles, practice statistics, utilization, physician fees, professional expenses, physician compensation, revenue distribution by payer, and managed care contracts, among other categories.[6]

The American Medical Group Association, formerly known as the American Group Practice Association, has conducted the Medical Group Compensation and Financial Survey (known as the Medical Group Compensation and Productivity Survey until 2004) for 22 years. This annual survey is co-sponsored by RSM McGladrey, Inc., who is responsible for the independent collection and compilation of survey data.[7] Compensation and production data are provided for medical specialties by group size, geographic region, and whether the group is single or multispecialty.[8]

The Medical Group Management Association's (MGMA) Physician Compensation and Production Survey is one of the largest in the United States, with approximately 2,000 group practices responding as of the 2009 edition publication.[9] Data are provided on compensation and production for 125 specialties.[9] The survey data are also published on CD by John Wiley & Sons ValueSource; the additional details available in this media provide better benchmarking capabilities.[9]

The MGMA's Cost Survey is one of the best known surveys of group practice income and expense data, having been published in some form since 1955, and obtaining over 1,600 respondents, combined, for the 2008 surveys: Cost Survey for Single Specialty Practices and Cost Survey for Multispecialty Practices.[10] Data are provided for a detailed listing of expense categories and are also calculated as a percentage of revenue and per FTE physician, FTE provider, patient, square foot, and relative value unit.[10] The survey provides information on multispecialty practices by performance ranking, geographic region, legal organization, size of practice, and percent of capitated revenue.[11] Detailed income and expense data are provided for single-specialty practices in more than fifty different specialties and subspecialties.[11]

The Medical Group Financial Operations Survey was created through a partnership between RSM McGladrey and the American Medical Group Association and provides benchmark data on support staff and physician salaries, physician salaries, staffing profiles and benefits, and other financial indicators.[12] Data are reported as a percent of managed care revenues, per FTE physician, and per square foot, and are subdivided by specialty mix, capitation level, and geographic region with detailed summaries of single specialty practices in several specialties.[12]

Statistics: Medical and Dental Income and Expense Averages is an annual survey produced by the National Society of Certified Healthcare Business Consultants (NSCHBC), formerly known as the National Association of Healthcare Consultants (NAHC), and the Academy of Dental Certified Public Accountants. It has been published annually for a number of years, and the 2008 Report Based on 2007 Data included detailed income and expense data from over 2,200 practices and 4,600 physicians in sixty specialties.[13]

RESEARCH CHALLENGES

1. Finding a sufficient sample size for medical subspecialties.
2. Obtaining data divided by urban versus rural practitioners, which is a much greater differential than the various geographic regions provided in most surveys.
3. Matching the survey's focus populations with the type of physician(s) in the subject entity. Locating a copy of the actual survey questionnaire and study methodologies utilized in compiling the reported compensation benchmarks.
4. Locating a copy of the actual survey questionnaire and study methodologies utilized in compiling the reported compensation benchmarks.

Medical Specialty Trends

The characteristics of both the practice and the profitability of different physician specialties vary greatly. Information on trends affecting specific specialties should further refine the types of industry information gathered, including changes in treatment, technology, competition, reimbursement, and the regulatory environment. For many of the subspecialties, oversupply and undersupply issues and the corresponding demand and compensation trends are central to the analysis of potential future earnings and the value of established medical entities. Information that is available and that may be gathered can range from broad practice overviews to, for example, specific procedural utilization demand and forecasts for a precise local geographic area.*

A large number of national and state medical associations and organizations gather and produce information on these various aspects of the practice of different individual physician specialties and subspecialties. Information may be found in trade press articles, medical specialty associations and their publications, national surveys, specialty accreditation bodies, governmental reports and studies, and elsewhere. The AMA and the MGMA both publish comprehensive physician practice survey information.

---

* Claritas is one source of this level of data.

These types of information can be gathered from a variety of sources including journals devoted to individual medical specialties, often published by associations, as well as the more general health administration literature, which often contains articles concentrating on an individual specialty. Contacting the appropriate associations and publishers can often be useful in identifying pertinent articles and information.

RESEARCH CHALLENGES

1. Researching the business aspects of some medical subspecialty practices.
2. Assessing the impact of developments in clinical technologies on the business prospects of the various specialties.
3. Benchmarking multi-specialty practices and integrated clinics.

Competition

Porter's Five Forces of Competition

Michael Porter[*] is considered by many to be one of the world's leading authorities on competitive strategy and international competitiveness. In 1980, he published *Competitive Strategy: Techniques for Analyzing Industries and Competitors*,[14] in which he argues that all businesses must respond to five competitive forces (Figure 12.1).

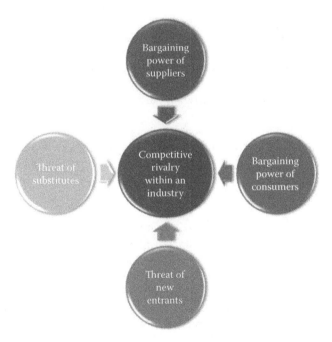

FIGURE 12.1 Five forces of competition. (From Michael Porter, *Competitive Strategy,* New York: The Free Press, 1980, 49–67.)

---

[*] A professor of Business Administration at the Harvard Business School, Michael Porter serves as an advisor to heads of state, governors, mayors, and CEOs throughout the world. The recipient of the Wells Prize in Economics, the Adam Smith Award, three McKinsey Awards, and honorary doctorates from the Stockholm School of Economics and six other universities, Porter is the author of fourteen books, among them *Competitive Advantage, The Competitive Advantage of Nations,* and *Cases in Competitive Strategy.*

1. The threat of new market entrants: This force may be defined as the risk of a similar company entering the marketplace and winning business. There are many barriers to entry for new market entrants in healthcare, such as the high cost of equipment, licensure, the need for physicians and other highly trained technicians, development of physician referral networks and provider contracts, and other significant regulatory requirements. Certificate of Need (CON) laws, which require governmental approval for new healthcare facilities, equipment, and services, have been in place since they were federally mandated in 1974. State CON laws create a regulatory barrier to entry. New medical provider entrants commonly face substantial political opposition by established interests, which is manifested in the CON review process.

2. The bargaining power of suppliers: A supplier can be defined as any business relationship upon which a business relies to deliver a product, service, or outcome. Healthcare equipment is a highly technical product produced by a limited number of manufacturers. This reduces the range of choices for providers and can increase costs.

3. Threats from substitute products or services: Substitute products or services are those that are sufficiently equivalent in function or utility to offer consumers an alternate choice of product or service. An illustration of this in healthcare would be diagnostic imaging as a substitute for surgery, which is often a more costly and risky option for patients. The threat of less invasive or less expensive diagnostic tests other than diagnostic imaging is relatively small for the near-term future.

4. The bargaining power of buyers: This force is the degree of negotiating leverage of an industry's buyers or customers. The buyers of healthcare services are ultimately the patients. However, the competitive force of buyers is manifested through healthcare insurers including the federal and state governments through the Medicare, Medicaid, TRICARE, and other programs; managed care payers (e.g., Blue Cross/Blue Shield affiliates); workers' compensation insurers; and others. In addition to the government, many of these healthcare insurers are large, national companies, often publicly traded, commanding significant bargaining power over healthcare provider reimbursement.

5. Rivalry among existing firms: This is ongoing competition among existing firms without consideration of the other competitive forces that define industries. Healthcare providers face pressure from other existing providers to obtain favorable provider contracts, maintain the latest technology, increase efficiencies, and lower prices.

Demographics

The population demographics of the market service area in which an entity operates and from which it draws its patients are, as with most businesses, linked with its current and potential client base and earnings. High population growth and turnover (immigration and emigration) rates generally lower the value of existing practices with established patient bases, because a new practice could quickly establish itself and become equally profitable. A stable or decreasing population with little turnover would therefore generally increase the value of an existing practice. However, population decline above a certain level may also reduce the profitability and therefore value of existing practices. A growing population can also fuel economic growth, and the cost of services generally, within a market.

Another key demographic factor is the gender and age breakdown and trends for a given population. Demand for certain medical specialties is closely related to gender and age demographics of the group that the specialty typically serves. For example, geriatric practitioners, ophthalmologists, and orthopedists are generally dependent upon an aging population, whereas pediatrics specialists, obstetricians, gynecologists, and neonatologists have higher demand within a younger population. Gender also impacts this last group of specialties.

The U.S. Department of Commerce Bureau of the Census is the largest source of demographic data. State and local information and data on non-census years and trends may need to be collected from other sources. Most states and large metropolitan areas collect and disseminate such data. Local chambers of commerce are another potential source of information for local areas. There are also many organizations that aggregate and analyze these data for reporting and resale. The Centers for Disease Control and Prevention (CDC) have myriad types of information related to the number of people with a certain disease as well as the age distribution of various populations and demographic groups, which can be helpful in determining patient demand for specialty services. Additionally, the CDC often provides projections regarding future prevalence of disease, thereby allowing the analyst to project future demand.

RESEARCH CHALLENGES

1. Locating specific utilization demand data divided by demographic variables such as age and sex.
2. Projecting accurate population growth by demographic criteria within a defined geographic service area.

Economic Trends: Local and National

Generally speaking, economic benchmarking may be used as a substitute for research in market forces, which falls under the umbrella of general research. More specifically, it is understood as a comparison of business operation efficiency based on economic principles or as it affects a particular market.[15] One study hypothesized that economic benchmarking can be used to improve the average performance of a given entity within the marketplace, improve the performance of poorly performing organizations more than others above a certain threshold of performance, or reduce the gaps in performance among organizations.[16]

Economic benchmarking provides a guideline by which consultants can compare the efficiency, needs of, and demands on healthcare organizations, while accounting for market forces. As a segment of what can be considered general research, economic benchmarking is generally utilized to provide basic information with regard to where a given organization stands in terms of its effectiveness and efficiency within the competitive market.[16] This provides a foundation for further organization-specific studies for the purpose of benchmarking an organization's operational and clinical performance and financial status to improve its efficiency and function within the marketplace.

Some common sources of national economic data include the U.S. Bureau of Labor Statistics (http://www.bls.gov); *The National Economic Review*, published quarterly by Mercer; the *Survey of Current Business*, published monthly by the U.S. Department of Commerce; the federal and individual branches of the Federal Reserve Bank; the Bureau of the Census (http://www.census.gov); the Economic and Statistics Administration; and the Bureau of Economic Analysis, along with other governmental, business, and investment company data, journals, and Internet sources. Potential sources of local or smaller-scale economic benchmarking data include local chambers of commerce as well as Claritas (http://www.claritas.com). Information on financial markets and indexes is widely distributed through investment firms, publications, and online services as well as in many business journals and newspapers. Information on financial market returns is also available through many of the types of sources discussed above. A source of historical data on market returns is *Stocks, Bonds, Bills, and Inflation*, published by Ibbotson Associates, which is updated through an annual yearbook and provides data from 1926 to the present.

RESEARCH CHALLENGES

1. Correlating economic income levels with insurance coverage and demand for specific types of health services.
2. Translating national economic trends to the local geographic service area.
3. Translating economic conditions to their impact on the subject entity's healthcare business.

Direct Market Comparable Transactions

This method analyzes the terms (price, terms, interest, assets included, etc.) of specific transactions involving the acquisition of substantial, control positions (most often the entirety) of similar entities. Gathering data on comparable transactions has historically been problematic due to limited reporting of information and an insufficient number of sources from which to assemble information on transactions with characteristics comparable to the subject entity.

However, there is a growing number of resources for transactional data, and many are devoted to various sectors of the healthcare industry. Transactional data can be found in several types of sources: published surveys, Securities and Exchange Commission (SEC) reports, proprietary databases, business brokers, attorneys, and on-line services. It is imperative to exhaust all resources by checking all books published with transactional data in addition to business journals. With a subscription to the Business Journals Network (http://www.bizjournals.com), an individual is able to search thousands of business journals from around the country for transactions dating back many years. Additionally, NewsLibrary (http://www.newslibrary.com) allows a user to search newspapers throughout the United States within a set geographical area and date parameters for information related to transactional announcements. While the number of recent transactions in healthcare is often large enough to allow for the collection of good-quality data for professional practices, there remain other problems associated with the use of the market approach to value. The following outlines the principles and practical details related to the use of market data in market valuation methods.

When there is a relatively efficient and unrestricted secondary market for comparable properties, and that market accurately represents the activities of a representative number of willing buyers and willing sellers, the market is most determinative of the value of the subject property. The principle of substitution states that the cost of an equally desirable substitute, or one of equal utility, tends to set the ceiling of value, i.e., it is the maximum that a knowledgeable buyer would be willing to pay for a property. Substitutes must be used because there are no two companies or practices that are exactly the same. Homogeneous* companies and transactions must be researched to use as substitutes or guidelines to value for the subject company.

When guideline companies are not fully identical to the subject entity, the appraiser can use a technique of abstraction (i.e., adjustments) to make the comparison. This technique involves identifying the chief features, factors, and amenities of similar companies already sold and then determining the amount the differences make in the prices of the guideline transactions. Points of comparison that may be used to make quantitative adjustments to the market transactional data include:

- Date of each transaction
- Tangible or intangible assets that each company owns or utilizes
- Location and market scope of each company
- Age and life cycle (business cycle) of each company
- Financial and management condition of each company at time of sale
- Regulatory environment imposed on each company
- Special financing or other terms regarding each transaction

---

* Homogeneous: the same in structure, quality, etc.; similar; uniform.

Once a set of transactions has been identified and their financial ratios calculated, there may appear to be outliers that have transaction ratios (e.g., price to revenue, price to earnings, and so on) varying significantly from the norm. These outliers are often removed from consideration as potentially misrepresentative transactions. However, transactions should be selected for analysis on the basis of comparability to the subject entity and not on the basis of how close their transaction ratios are to the norm.

Many causes for outliers may warrant exclusion. Characteristics of healthcare enterprises that should be examined for comparability include:

- Payer mix
- Staffing depth and quality
- Service mix (types of services rendered)
- Site of service (hospital, nursing home, office, etc.)
- Geographical location, proximity to hospital
- Relationship of the enterprise with managed care
- Depth of income from managed care and capitation in subject entity
- Competition
- Call coverage
- Development of new treatment protocols
- Covenants not to compete
- Office system and management sophistication
- Years in practice
- Ease of entry
- Growth trend or potential
- Profitability
- Patient age mix
- Collections or accounts receivable
- Doctor to patient ratio for catchment area

Only after a thorough evaluation of the comparability of market transactions should outliers be excluded.

The use of a limited database of transactions may be misleading if it is not statistically representative of the overall market. This may be due to the limited sample size of the transactions reported or available to the researcher. Another potential limitation is that it may be difficult to determine the degree of comparability necessary to assure that the financial ratios derived from the transactions examined are predictive of value for the subject entity. Not all companies and transactions under the same SIC code are truly comparable. For example, general medical practices, which share SIC 8011 with ambulatory surgical centers, primary care practices, and specialty surgery practices, have all historically traded at different transaction ratios.

Furthermore, reported transactional data are often skewed due to the limitations of reported data. The date of the transaction must also be taken into account. Some analyses have found that, for the universe of all transactions in a database, there is no relationship between the ratios for an industry sub-sector and the dates of sales. However, this has been disproved for many specific industry sub-sectors and time periods.

RESEARCH CHALLENGES

1. Researching sufficient details on both transactions and their target companies to ensure that they are at arm's length and truly comparable to the subject entity.
2. Determining the cause of outliers.
3. Finding a sufficient sample size of recent, comparable transactions in the same medical specialty or healthcare industry sub-sector and geographic region.

Guideline Publicly Traded Companies

This method is based upon the theory that an indication of value of the subject entity can be derived through the valuation multiples of the freely traded, minority interest registered shares of publicly traded companies. Investment services' directories and databases that allow searching by an industry code or descriptor may be useful in identifying potentially comparable guideline publicly traded companies. However, as discussed above, the SIC for medical practices (8011) is generally not sufficiently specific to assure comparability among medical specialty practices. The transactional sources described above are another source of guideline companies, which will allow the identification of those public companies acquiring several medical entities within a medical specialty.

If a sufficient number of appropriate guideline companies, in the same medical specialty as the subject practice, can be identified, the consultant will need to collect data on these companies. Often a company's SEC reports are valuable for finding financial operating data and information on the number of outstanding shares of stock. Furthermore, most business libraries should be able to provide historical stock quotes and other data on guideline companies.

RESEARCH CHALLENGES

1. Obtaining data on a sufficient sample size of comparable companies to the subject entity.
2. Assessing the comparability of the service mix provided by the public companies as compared to the subject entity.

The Assessment of Risk

Assessing risk in a healthcare business requires familiarity with the forces that most significantly influence the industry. Accordingly, knowledge of the four pillars of healthcare enterprise value, (i.e., the regulatory environment, reimbursement trends, competition, and impact of technology) is critical. The government, as the largest purchaser of healthcare in the United States, is intimately involved in any potential expectation of future earnings through its virtual control on the industry through tight regulations and provider reimbursement.

Economic conditions and events expected to result in a changed paradigm for healthcare delivery (e.g., the rapid acceleration in expected demand for increased health services as a result of the "demographic time bomb" of the aging baby-boomer generation and pressures to reduce rising healthcare costs) should be examined within the framework of the four pillars of the healthcare industry. These four aspects of the healthcare environment set the context in which buyers, sellers, owners, and investors consider the valuation of various healthcare enterprises.

RESEARCH CHALLENGES

1. Researching and evaluating the different types of competitive threats to the subject entity.
2. Evaluating potential future changes in reimbursement methods and levels.
3. Weighting the risk from current regulations as well as potential regulatory changes.

THE USES OF RESEARCH IN BENCHMARKING

INTRODUCTION

Benchmarking is used to establish an understanding of the operational, clinical, and financial performance of healthcare enterprises. Benchmarking techniques can be utilized to illustrate the degree to which an organization varies from comparable healthcare industry norms, in addition to providing vital information regarding trends in the organization's internal operational performance and financial status. Benchmarking within the healthcare sector serves several purposes:

1. Offering insight into the enterprise and practitioner performance as it relates to the rest of the market (e.g., allowing organizations to find where they rank among competitors, and as a means for continuous quality improvement (CQI))
2. Objectively evaluating performance indicators on the enterprise and practitioner levels
3. Indicating variability, extreme outliers, and prospects
4. Identifying areas that require further attention and possible remediation (e.g., re-distributing resources and staff, and increasing operating room utilization)
5. Promoting improvement (e.g., improving average length of stay and other clinical efficiency measures)
6. Providing enterprises with a value-metric system to determine whether they comply with legal standards for fair market value and commercial reasonableness[17]

Financial analysts, lenders, bond agencies, and valuators regularly utilize benchmarking methods to assist in the assessment of an organization's risk by identifying and quantifying the relative strengths and weaknesses of the organization of interest against competitors within the same industry. The application of benchmarking analysis results to the valuation of a given organization may commonly include such elements as:

1. Adjustment of operating expense, capital items, and capital structure to industry norms (when valuing control position)
2. Adjustment of a discount rate or cost of equity as indicated based on market analysis (business-specific risk premium)
3. Selection of the appropriate financial ratios (e.g., price/earnings, price/revenue, price/earnings before interest, taxes, depreciation, and amortization, etc.) for the purpose of the valuation
4. Selection of the appropriate discounts and premiums, based on the level of value sought (e.g., discount for lack of marketability, control premium, minority discount, etc.)

Healthcare enterprises may utilize both external and internal benchmarking methods, i.e., they may compare key enterprise and practitioner performance indicators against industry standards while evaluating practitioners against their peers within the healthcare enterprise.[18]

Internal benchmarking is considered the first step in a benchmarking process and is often carried out on a smaller scale than the other types of benchmarking, which fall under the umbrella of external benchmarking processes.

The general procedure of external benchmarking, applied across all types, involves:

1. Identifying sources of benchmark data
2. Determining how the data collected by these sources were defined
3. Collecting practice data that are comparable to the benchmark data, as defined by the source
4. Conducting a gap analysis to identify areas for improvement
5. Repeating these steps routinely and frequently[19]

Generally speaking, benchmarking is performed on two levels: one that focuses on organization-wide indicators and another that focuses on the practitioner.[20]

FINANCIAL BENCHMARKING

Financial benchmarking can assist healthcare managers and professional advisors in understanding the operational and financial status of their organization or practice. The general process of financial benchmarking analysis may include three elements: historical subject benchmarking, benchmarking to industry norms, and financial ratio analysis.

Historical subject benchmarking compares a healthcare organization's most recent performance with its reported performance in the past to examine performance over time, identify changes in performance within the organization (e.g., extraordinary and non-recurring events), and to predict future performance. As a form of internal benchmarking, historical subject benchmarking avoids issues such as differences in data collection and use of measurement tools and benchmarking metrics that often cause problems in comparing two different organizations. However, it is necessary to review common-size data to account for company differences over time that may skew results.[21]

Benchmarking to industry norms, analogous to Fong and colleagues' concept of industry benchmarking, involves comparing internal company-specific data to survey data from other organizations within the same industry.[22] This method of benchmarking provides the basis for comparing the subject entity to similar entities, with the purpose of identifying its relative strengths, weaknesses, and related measures of risk.

The process of benchmarking against industry averages or norms will typically involve the following steps:

1. Identification and selection of appropriate surveys to use as a benchmark, i.e., to compare with data from the organization of interest. This involves answering the question, "In which survey would this organization most likely be included?"
2. If appropriate, re-categorization and adjustment of the organization's revenue and expense accounts to optimize data compatibility with the selected survey's structure and definitions (e.g., common sizing)
3. Calculation and articulation of observed differences of organization from the industry averages and norms, expressed either in terms of variance in ratio, dollar unit amounts, or percentages of variation

Financial ratio analysis typically involves the calculation of ratios that are financial and operational measures representative of the financial status of an enterprise. These ratios are evaluated in terms of their relative comparison to generally established industry norms, which may be expressed as positive or negative trends for that industry sector. The ratios selected may function as several different measures of operating performance or financial condition of the subject entity. Common types of financial indicators that are measured by ratio analysis include:

1. Liquidity ratios measure the ability of an organization to meet cash obligations as they become due, i.e., to support operational goals. Ratios above the industry mean generally indicate that the organization is in an advantageous position to better support immediate goals. The current ratio, which quantifies the relationship between assets and liabilities, is an indicator of an organization's ability to meet short-term obligations. Managers use this measure to determine how quickly assets are converted into cash.
2. Activity ratios, also called efficiency ratios, indicate how efficiently the organization utilizes its resources or assets, including cash, accounts receivable, salaries, inventory, property, plant, and equipment. Lower ratios may indicate an inefficient use of those assets.
3. Leverage ratios, measured as the ratio of long-term debt to net fixed assets, are used to illustrate the proportion of funds, or capital, provided by shareholders (owners) and creditors to aid analysts in assessing the appropriateness of an organization's current level of debt. When this ratio falls equal to or below the industry norm, the organization is typically not considered to be at significant risk.

4. Profitability indicates the overall net effect of managerial efficiency of the enterprise. To determine the profitability of the enterprise for benchmarking purposes, the analyst should first review and make adjustments to the owner compensation, if appropriate. Adjustments for the market value of the replacement cost of the professional services provided by the owner are particularly important in the valuation of professional medical practices for the purpose of arriving at an economic level of profit.

The selection of financial ratios for analysis and comparison to the organization's performance requires careful attention to the homogeneity of data. Benchmarking of intra-organizational data (i.e., internal benchmarking) typically proves to be less variable across several different measurement periods. However, the use of data from external facilities for comparison may introduce variation in measurement methodology and procedure. In the latter case, use of a standard chart of accounts for the organization or recasting the organization's data to a standard format can effectively facilitate an appropriate comparison of the organization's operating performance and financial status data to survey results.

OPERATIONAL PERFORMANCE BENCHMARKING

Operational benchmarking is used to target non-central work or business processes for improvement.[23] It is conceptually similar to both process and performance benchmarking, but it is generally classified by the application of the results as opposed to what is being compared.[23] Operational benchmarking studies tend to be smaller in scope than other types of benchmarking but, like many other types of benchmarking, are limited by the degree to which the definitions and performance measures used by comparing entities differ.[23] Common sizing is a technique used to reduce the variations in measures caused by differences (e.g., definition issues) between the organizations or processes being compared.[24]

Common sizing is a technique used to alter financial operating data prior to certain types of benchmarking analyses and may be useful for any type of benchmarking that requires the comparison of entities that differ on some level (e.g., scope of respective benchmarking measurements, definitions, business processes). This is done by expressing the data for differing entities in relative (i.e., comparable) terms.[24] For example, common sizing is often used to compare financial statements of the same company over different periods of time (e.g., historical subject benchmarking) or of several companies of differing sizes (e.g., benchmarking to industry norms). The latter type may be used for benchmarking an organization to another in its industry, to industry averages, or to the best-performing agency in its industry.[24] Some examples of common size measures utilized in healthcare include:

1. Percent of revenue or per unit produced, e.g., relative value unit
2. Per provider, e.g., physician
3. Per capacity measurement, e.g., per square foot
4. Other standard units of comparison

As with any data, differences in how data are collected, stored, and analyzed over time or among different organizations may complicate their use at a later time. Accordingly, appropriate adjustments must be made to account for such differences and provide an accurate and reliable dataset for benchmarking.

SUMMARY

Whether current healthcare reform efforts continue to gain momentum or deteriorate with time, the demand for a uniform standard for benchmarking of healthcare enterprises that includes quality, performance, productivity, utilization, and compensation measures seems to be increasing. Benchmarking will be used progressively more by healthcare organizations to facilitate reductions in healthcare expenditures while simultaneously improving products and service quality. From a management perspective, the use of benchmarking as a performance indicator will become increasingly important in healthcare as quality assurance and effectiveness research becomes more pronounced through pay-for-performance initiatives and increasingly stringent fraud and abuse laws. From a valuation standpoint, as the IRS initiates its 2010 payroll audits, confirming fair market value of compensation for executives, physicians, and other practitioners through benchmarking data will become progressively more important, especially for non-profit hospitals wishing to retain their tax-exempt status.[25] Additionally, if healthcare spending continues to rise, consumers and regulators will continue to view providers with increasing scrutiny, further emphasizing the importance of standardizing comparative measures to benchmark utility and productivity of healthcare provider enterprises.

REFERENCES

1. Fong, S.W., Cheng, E.W.L., and Ho, D.C.K. 1998. Benchmarking: A general reading for management practitioners. *Management Decision* 36(6): 407.
2. IRS Revenue Ruling, 59-60, 1959-1, CB236 IRS Section 2031.
3. Porter, M.E. 1980. *Competitive strategy: Techniques for analyzing industries and competitors*. New York: The Free Press.
4. American Medical Association. AMA Physician Masterfile. http://www.ama-assn.org (accessed August 3, 2009).
5. American Medical Association. 2008. *Physician characteristics and distribution in the United States: 2008 edition*. Chicago: AMA.
6. American Medical Association. 2003. *Physician socioeconomic statistics: 2003 edition*. Chicago: AMA.
7. American Medical Association. 2009. *American Medical Group Association 2009 medical group compensation and financial survey: 2009 report based on 2008 data survey methodology*. AMGA and RSM McGladrey, Inc. http://www.amga.org/Publications/ECommerce/Comp%20Survey/2009Methodology. pdf (accessed September 3, 2009); American Medical Group Association and RSM McGladrey, Inc. 2008. *2008 medical group compensation and financial survey*. http://www.ama-assn.org/ama.
8. American Medical Group Association and RSM McGladrey, Inc. 2008. *2008 medical group compensation and financial survey*. http://www.ama-assn.org/ama
9. Medical Group Management Association. 2009. *Physician compensation and production survey: 2009 report based on 2008 data*. Englewood, CO: MGMA.
10. Medical Group Management Association. 2008. *Cost survey for single-specialty practices: 2008 report based on 2007 data*, p. 14 Englewood, CO: MGMA; Medical Group Management Association. 2008. *Cost survey for multispecialty practices: 2008 report based on 2007 data*, p. 17. Englewood, CO: MGMA.
11. Medical Group Management Association. 2008. *Cost survey for multispecialty practices: 2008 report based on 2007 data*. Englewood, CO: MGMA
12. American Medical Group Association and RSM McGladrey, Inc. 2002. *2002 Medical group financial operations survey*. Englewood, CO: MGMA
13. National Society of Certified Healthcare Business Consultants. *Practice statistics*. http://www.ichbc.org/statistics/index.cfm (accessed September 15, 2009).
14. Porter, M.E. 1980. *Competitive strategy: Techniques for analyzing industries and competitors*. New York: The Free Press.
15. Ajodhia, V., Petrov, K., and Scarsi, G.C. 2004. *Economic benchmarking and its applications*. KEMA Consultants. http://www.infraday.tu-berlin.de/fileadmin/fg280/veranstaltungen/infraday/conference_2004/papers_presentations/paper---ajodhia_petrov_scarsi.pdf.
16. van Helden, G.J., and Tillema, S. 2005. In search of a benchmarking theory for the public sector. *Financial Accountability & Management* 21(3): 341.
17. Schyve, P.M. 1995. The Joint Commission's perspective. In *Measuring clinical care: A guide for physician executives*, S.C. Schoenbaum, ed. American College of Physician Executives; Zismer, D.K. 1999. The physician compensation plan as an instrument of cultural change. In *Physician compensation*

arrangements. Aspen Health Law and Compliance Center; Johnson, B.A., and Keegan, D.W. 2006. Measuring physician work and effort. In *Physician compensation plans: State-of-the-art strategies*. Englewood, CO: Medical Group Management Association; The Healthcare Financial Management Association. 1997. *Financial and clinical benchmarking: The strategic use of data*. Healthcare Financial Management Association.

18. Johnson, B.A., and Keegan, D.W. 2006. Measuring physician work and effort. In *Physician compensation plans: State-of-the-art strategies*. Englewood, CO: Medical Group Management Association.

19. Higgins, M.C., and Raczak, T.M. 2000. Physician compensation for physicians in hospital employment. In *Physician compensation: Models for aligning financial goals and incentives*. Kenneth M. Hekman, ed. Englewood, CO: Medical Group Management Association; Carter, L.R., and Lankford, S.S. 2000. Four basic principles of compensation. In *Physician's compensation: Measurement, benchmarking, and implementation*. New York: John Wiley & Sons, Inc.; Johnson, B.A., and Keegan, D.W. 2006. Measuring physician work and effort. In *Physician compensation plans: State-of-the-art strategies*. Englewood, CO: Medical Group Management Association.

20. Schyve, P.M. 1995. The Joint Commission's perspective. In *Measuring clinical care: A guide for physician executives*, S.C. Schoenbaum, ed. American College of Physician Executives; Carter, L.R., and Lankford, S.S. 2000. The shrinking pie. In *Physician's compensation: Measurement, benchmarking, and implementation*. New York: John Wiley & Sons, Inc.; Johnson, B.A., and Keegan, D.W. 2006. The compensation plan development process. In *Physician compensation plans: State-of-the-art strategies*. Englewood, CO: Medical Group Management Association.

21. NetMBA.com. 2007. *Common size financial statements*. http://www.netmba.com/finance/statements/common-size (accessed August 13, 2009).

22. Fong, S.W., Cheng, E.W.L., and Ho, D.C.K. 1998. Benchmarking: A general reading for management practitioners. *Management Decision* 36(6): 410.

23. Watson, G.H. 1994. A perspective on benchmarking, in conversation with the editor. *Benchmarking for Quality Management & Technology* 1(1): 6.

24. Warren, C.S., and Fess, P.E. 1992. *Principles of financial and managerial accounting*, 3rd edition. Cincinnatti, Ohio: South-Western Publishing Co., 1169.

25. Quinn, C.L., and Mamorsky, J.D. 2009. Enforcement efforts take aim at executive compensation of tax-exempt health care entities. *Health Law Reporter* 1640; Brauer, L.M., Tyson, T.T., Henzke, L.J., and Kawecki, D.J. 2002. An introduction to I.R.C. 4958 (intermediate sanctions). Internal Revenue Service, EO CPE Text. http://apps.irs.gov (accessed December 28, 2009), p. 275–276.

Epilogue

ALL FOR THE PATIENT

The *Merriam-Webster Collegiate Dictionary* (Meriam-Webster Incorporated, Springfield, MA, 2007) defines the word "visionary" as one who is able to see into the future. Unlike some pundits, prescience is not a quality we claim to possess. To the purveyors of healthcare gloom and doom, however, the future for independent hospitals, medical clinics, and healthcare organizations is a bleak fait accompli. If you were of this philosophy prior to reading this book, we hope that you now realize that the bulk of business and management activity for all stakeholders will be management-enabled as healthcare entities and medical providers regain autonomy using hard data, decision-making flow charts, checklists, organizational behavior information, and the healthcare 2.0 enterprise.

For this collaborative patient-centric and institutional migration to occur in the face of the Patient Protection and Affordable Care Act (PP-ACA), healthcare organizations will need to execute the lean managerial principles in this book. Managers will have to blend each chapter with the appropriate traditional business principles outlined, and re-engineer hospitals and medical clinics with the needed connectivity tools and social skills of the modern era.

Hopefully, the *Financial Management Strategies for Hospitals and Healthcare Organizations: Tools, Techniques, Checklists and Case Studies* will prove useful in this regard and serve as a valuable resource for every hospital administrator, CEO, CMO, healthcare professional, nurse-executive, and medical, business, or graduate school student and library in the country.

Do not be complacent, for as onerous as it seems, hospitals may not survive autonomously as business units without utilizing this sort of information. The bar to a new level of organizational financial behavior and economics innovation has been raised in this decade. Although we still need actuarial and accounting data, working capital, marketing techniques, and correct fee-setting, we believe that all administrators and physician-executives will look back on this checklist- and case-model–driven text and recognize it as the turning point in the current healthcare cost delivery imbroglio. Already there are growing signs of this sea change as indicated by the explosion of healthcare technology and new flow-through distribution models that bode well for future health organizations, practitioners, and patients.

Therefore, as medical professionals, executive-level officers, and administrators, please realize that we face the same managed care and political issues as you. In addition, although the multi-degreed experts of this textbook may have a particular business expertise, we should never lose sight of the fact that, *above all else*, medical care should be delivered in a personal and humane manner, with patient interest rather than self-interest, as our guiding standard.

Fraternally,

David Edward Marcinko

Hope Rachel Hetico

Mackenzie Hope Marcinko

Contributing Authors

Index